Paradigms of
Clinical
Social Work
Volume 2

Paradigms of Clinical Social Work Volume 2

Edited by

Rachelle A. Dorfman, Ph.D.

Brunner-Routledge
New York & London

Published by
Brunner-Routledge
29 West 35th Street
New York, NY 10001

Published in Great Britain
Brunner-Routledge
11 New Fetter Lane
London EC4P 4EE

PARADIGMS OF CLINICAL SOCIAL WORK: Volume 2

8   9   0

Printed by Hamilton Printing Company

A CIP catalog record for this book is available from the British Library.
⊗ The paper in this publication meets the requirements of the ANSI Standard Z39.48-1984 (Permanence of Paper).

Library of Congress Cataloging-in-Publication Data
Paradigms of clinical work, Volume 2
Bibliography: p.
Includes index.
1. Social case work. 2. Social case work—United States. I. Dorfman, Rachelle A. II. Title: Clinical social work.
HV43.P35   1988   361.3'2   88–2879

ISBN 0-87630-882-5 (hbk)

To Sandy Orlo Rubin,
who in 1981 charmed us with her free spirit
and in 1998 disarmed us with her courage.

CONTENTS

FOREWORD

The success and usefulness of Rachelle Dorfman's comparative approach to understanding clinical practice in the first volume of *Paradigms of Clinical Social Work* have compelled this second volume. Had any single model or grand theory of clinical practice come to dominate the field, you, *the reader*, would not be holding this second compendium of rival approaches. In fact, as William J. Reid points out in his overview of trends (chapter 13), there has been a virtual explosion of models of clinical intervention in social work and related professions.

What are we *in the social work arena* to make of this expanding diversity? Why have we not experienced an integration of models? Various hypotheses could be advanced. For example, one might speculate that the diversity comes from the exuberance and creativity of clinicians when confronted by the complex array of human problems that clients bring to them, or from the socially constructed nature of human problems that present endless clinical realities. Or an explanation may lie in the structure of knowledge development in our field. There are sharp disagreements about the procedures and standards that should be used to evaluate clinical interventions *and* determine whether or how well an approach "works," and there is no centralized authority to impose preferred models on clinicians and clients. Under these circumstances, old models never die and new theoretical offspring easily survive. Or the diversity may be encouraged in a society that champions free thought and diverse opinions and tolerates those who have different values about how people should live and when, how, and why they should be encouraged to change.

I do not pretend to know the answer, but I am grateful to Rachelle Dorfman for producing a book that provokes such sociological questions about the expanding number of paradigms. But her achievements in this book go beyond stimulating arm-chair speculation. First, she has succeeded in gathering in one handy volume statements from proponents of different models. Conventional textbooks can, of course, review different approaches to practice, but such reviews, authored by the same person with the same voice, lose in texture, tone, and nuance what different advocates convey when they are explaining their own paradigm. Just as clinicians gain insight into clients' lives by hearing their voices, so too do we gain from observing the use of language and metaphor by different contributors.

Second, Dorfman has corralled the efforts of her contributors. A common lament among those who have assembled edited books is that it is like trying to herd cats. Nevertheless, she has managed to keep her contributors within a common structure. Each chapter has roughly the same outline and covers the theoretical material using a similar format of her design. The benefit for the reader is not merely the tidiness of presentation but how the common outline allows the reader to more easily identify and comprehend the differences in assumptions, concepts, and approaches across chapters.

The third achievement of the book is that Dorfman insists on application. Theory—clinical theory included—is wonderfully abstract by itself. We often hear the refrain, "It sounds good, in theory," meaning that theory may be elegant but is unable to bring order and predictability to our chaotic everyday experience. Theory must be tested, and one of these tests is whether it can explain a given, specific case. This is a tough test for any theory because theory by nature is general and abstract, but reality is specific and concrete. In application, we learn about the theory in a different way. We get to see whether what sounds good can actually guide our psychotherapeutic work.

Dorfman's use of the Shore family as a test case for the application of theory is ingenious and revealing. We discover, for example, that some clinical models are more easily applied to this case than others. Some models have therapeutic techniques that are more readily understood. The use of the Shore case, and the wonderfully illuminating 10-year follow-up contained in the Epilogue, helps the reader immensely in connecting theory to application in a way that furthers the comparative purpose of the book.

The emphasis on application, demanded by the Shore case, is unexpectedly humbling because it reveals how difficult it is to capture and understand fully the motivations and nuances of individuals' and families' lives and where they are likely to lead in the years ahead. The continuing story of the Shores, as revealed in the Epilogue, was not and could not have been adequately predicted by any of the contributing theorist-practitioners. This is not criticism of their theories or methods but an observation of the limits of our state of knowledge about the shifting dynamics and unpredictability of human and family development.

The purpose of this book is to enhance clinical social workers' ability to make sense of people's lives so that we may help them in their struggles. The contributing authors who allow us to learn through the comparison of their different clinical models and the architect of this effort—the editor— have clearly succeeded with this task.

Stuart A. Kirk, Professor
Department of Social Work
University of California, Los Angeles

ACKNOWLEDGMENTS

This book's inception was the idea of Carol Meyer. Eight years after the publication of *Paradigms of Clinical Social Work*, I decided to contact the original contributors to see if I could convince them to update their chapters for a second edition. I made the first call to Carol Meyer, professor of social work at Columbia University. Carol, in her inimitable way, said, "No. Nothing needs to be revised. If you *must* do something, put together a new book with more models and new contributors." Later that week, Natalie Gilman, editorial vice president at Brunner/Mazel, echoed my reaction to Carol's idea: "Why didn't we think of that?" Although we never met in person, Carol Meyer influenced my career in innumerable ways. Her death on December 2, 1996, was a great loss to clinical social work. I never thanked her properly, so I am doing it now. Thank you, Carol, for your continuing input and support of my work and for showing me how to stand firm when needed.

Before I commit to another book, I always call my dear friend and editorial assistant, Elsa Efran. I would not embark on the agony of authoring or editing any work without her help. I continue to be amazed with her ability to bring out the best in authors. This book owes its clarity to her. Hugh Rosen, as well, deserves my deepest gratitude. I do not know anyone who is more generous, more modest, or smarter than Hugh. I could not have a better friend or hero. There is a brood of "young 'uns"—big and small, in college and in diapers—who contribute greatly to the joy in my life and thus my ability to stay on task. Thank you, Forest Harrison ("Jay's miracle"), Jeff and Sarri Dorfman, Holly and Howard Kaplan (parents of Shawn and Brett), and Ariana Wang. My own miracle is my husband, Jay Zukerman, who never stops believing in me, putting up with my quest for adventures in foreign lands, and encouraging my creative work.

But most of all, I wish to thank my long-time friend, Sandy Orlo Rubin. When we met, we were unlikely friends. Sandy was a worldly, self-confident, liberated woman, and I was a wide-eyed housewife from the suburbs. I was organized and a mite uptight. She was artistic and a mite chaotic. For the last 20 years we have shared our troubles and triumphs. Sandy, I dedicate this book to you to honor our friendship.

R. A. D.

ABOUT THE EDITOR

Rachelle A. Dorfman, Ph.D., is assistant professor, School of Public Policy and Social Research, University of California at Los Angeles. She is the author of *Aging into the 21st Century: The Exploration of Aspirations and Values* and *Clinical Social Work: Definition, Practice, and Vision* and editor of *Paradigms of Clinical Social Work* (Volume 1). Dr. Dorfman was visiting professor at the University of Hong Kong in 1994. She continues to return to Hong Kong annually to train gerontological social workers for the Hong Kong Social Welfare Department and other social service agencies.

ABOUT THE CONTRIBUTORS

Sonia G. Austrian, D.S.W., is director of the Employee Assistance Program Consortium, an organization serving the employees of five New York City medical institutions. She is on the faculty of the Department of Public Health and Psychiatry at Cornell University Medical College and is an adjunct professor at the Columbia University School of Social Work. She is the author of *Mental Disorders, Medications, and Clinical Social Work*.

Larry E. Beutler, Ph.D., is professor and director of the Counseling, Clinical, School Psychology Program at the University of California in Santa Barbara. He is the immediate past president of the Division of Psychotherapy of the American Psychological Association and a past president (international) of the Society for Psychotherapy Research. He is also a former editor of the Journal of *Consulting and Clinical Psychology* and is presently the coeditor of the *Journal of Clinical Psychology*. He has written extensively in the areas of psychological assessment and psychotherapy, with 11 books and over 300 scholarly articles and chapters. Recent books include *Am I Crazy or Is It My Shrink?* (with Bruce Bongar and Joel Shurkin), *Integrative Assessment of Adult Personality* (with Michael Berren), and *Comprehensive Textbook of Psychotherapy* (edited with Bruce Bongar).

Marshall Bush, Ph.D., is a clinical psychologist and a training and supervising analyst at the San Francisco Psychoanalytic Institute. He teaches courses on control-mastery theory in the Bay Area. He has been in private practice for over 25 years, specializing in psychoanalysis and long-term individual psychotherapy.

John F. Clarkin, Ph.D., is a professor of clinical psychology in psychiatry at the Cornell University Medical College, director of psychology for the

New York Hospital, and co-director of the Personality Disorder Institute. His academic writing has focused on the phenomenology and treatment of personality disorders and the theoretical underpinning for differential treatment planning for psychiatric patients. His research activities have focused on the phenomenology of personality disorders and the treatment of patients with borderline personality disorder and bipolar disorder.

Jonathan Diamond, Ph.D., is a licensed clinical social worker in private practice in Northampton and Greenfield, Massachusetts. His postgraduate training was in marital and family therapy at the Brattleboro Family Institute in Brattleboro, Vermont. He has had experience establishing and coordinating outpatient substance abuse and inpatient dual-diagnosis treatment programs for children, adolescents, adults, and their families. He has lectured and offered trainings and workshops throughout the Northeast on the topics of ethics, family therapy, substance abuse, and adolescent treatment. He is writing a book on the topics of narrative, addictions, and trauma and is co-editing an anthology of poetry and prose entitled *A Less Convenient Fiction: Poets & Writers Revisit the DSM–IV*.

Eda G. Goldstein, D.S.W., is professor and director of the Ph.D. program in clinical social work at the New York University Shirley M. Ehrenkranz School of Social Work. She is consulting editor of *Clinical Social Work Journal* and the *Journal of Analytic Social Work*. She is the author of *Ego Psychology and Social Work Practice* (2nd ed.) and *Borderline Disorders: Clinical Models and Techniques* and has authored more than 30 articles and book chapters. She maintains a private practice with individuals and couples in New York City.

Stuart Kirk, D.S.W., holds the Marjorie Crump Chair in the Department of Social Welfare at the University of California, Los Angeles. He is the former editor-in-chief of the journal *Social Work Research* and coauthor (with Herb Kutchins) of *The Selling of DSM: The Rhetoric of Science in Psychiatry* and *Making Us Crazy: DSM—the Psychiatric Bible and the Creation of Mental Disorder*.

Kevin T. Kuehlwein, Psy.D., is staff psychologist at the Center for Cognitive Therapy, University of Pennsylvania, and adjunct associate professor at Allegheny University of the Health Sciences, School of Health Professions in Philadelphia. He co-edited (with Hugh Rosen) *Cognitive Therapies in Action: Evolving Innovative Practice* and *Constructing Realities: Meaning-Making Perspectives for Psychotherapists*. He has presented on psychotherapy in the United States and abroad. He contributed a chapter to the *Comprehensive Handbook of Cognitive Therapy* on applying cognitive therapy to gay men. Recent works include a chapter on depression for Gregoris Simos's (in press) *Cognitive—Behavior Therapy: A Guide for the Practicing Clinician*.

He also serves on the editorial board of *Cognitive and Behavioral Practice* and has done extensive supervision and training of cognitive therapists. He maintains a private practice in Philadelphia.

Helen Land, Ph.D., is associate professor of social work at the University of Southern California. She has published widely in the area of practice theory and feminist theory and has a particular interest in role strain and its relationship to mental health in women. She also maintains a private practice as a licensed clinical social worker in Los Angeles. She is frequently called upon for AIDS consultation, both regionally and nationally.

Carol H. Lankton, M.A., is a marriage and family therapist in private practice in Pensacola, Florida. She is co-author (with Stephen Lankton) of *The Answer Within: A Clinical Framework of Ericksonian Hypnotherapy, Enchantment and Intervention: An Ericksonian Framework for Family Therapy,* and *Tales of Enchantment: Goal Oriented Metaphors for Adults and Children in Therapy.* She is a clinical member of the American Association for Marriage and Family Therapy and an approved consultant for the American Association of Clinical Hypnosis. She has been an invited faculty member at the International and National Congresses on Ericksonian Approaches to Hypnosis and Psychotherapy and presents training workshops for mental health professionals throughout the world.

Stephen R. Lankton, M.S.W., is a clinical trainer, clinician, corporate consultant, and author. He is a recipient of the Lifetime Achievement Award for Outstanding Contribution to the Field of Psychotherapy from the Milton H. Erickson Foundation. He is the current president of the American Hypnosis Board for Clinical Social Work and holds certification as an approved supervisor in family therapy, is a diplomate in clinical hypnosis and clinical social work, is an approved consultant in clinical hypnosis, and is a fellow in pain management. He co-authored (with Carol Lankton) *Tales of Enchantment, The Answer Within,* and *Enchantment and Intervention* and is the author of *Practical Magic.* He was the founding editor of the *Ericksonian Monographs,* which he edited for 10 years. He has been a keynote speaker, invited faculty, and workshop and seminar leader for hundreds of conferences sponsored by national and state professional organizations and universities. He is a marriage and family therapist practicing in Pensacola, Florida.

John C. Norcross, Ph.D., is professor of psychology at the University of Scranton and a clinical psychologist in part-time private practice. He is the author of 125 articles and editor or author of 10 books, most recently *Psychologist's Desk Reference* (with Gerry Koocher and Sam Hill), *Systems of Psychotherapy: A Transtheoretical Analysis* (4th ed., with James Prochaska), and *Handbook of Psychotherapy Integration* (with Marvin Goldfried). He has served on the editorial boards of a dozen journals and on the boards of directors of several national organizations devoted to psychotherapy.

Jane Peller, M.S.W., is associate professor of social work at Northeastern Illinois University. She is also a co-director of Consultations, a practice and training center in Chicago dedicated to the practice and development of optimistic approaches to working with people. She and John L. Walter are the authors of numerous articles, including the recent "Rethinking Our Assumptions: Assuming Anew in a Postmodern World," which appeared in the *Handbook of Solution-Focused Brief Therapy.* Her national conference presentations include Social Work's World Assembly, the American Association of Marriage and Family Therapy, the *Family Therapy Networker*, and Therapeutic Conversations.

William J. Reid, D.S.W., is professor, School of Social Welfare, Rockefeller College of Public Affairs and Policy, State University of New York at Albany. His authored or co-authored books include *Brief and Extended Casework, Task-Centered Casework, The Task-Centered System, Family Problem Solving, Task Strategies, Task Centered Practice: A Generalist Approach,* and *Research in Social Work.*

Hugh Rosen, D.S.W., is professor and chair, Department of Mental Health Sciences, and associate dean, Graduate Studies, at Allegheny University of the Health Sciences, School of Health Professions, in Philadelphia. He is the author of three books, including *Piagetian Dimensions of Clinical Relevance.* He has also co-edited three books, the two most recent of which are (with Kevin Kuehlwein) *Cognitive Therapies in Action: Evolving Innovative Practice* and *Constructing Realities: Meaning-Making Perspectives for Psychotherapists.* He has contributed several chapters to other edited books and is a member of the editorial board of the *Journal of Constructivist Psychology.*

Arlene Rothschild, M.S.W., is a clinical social worker and an assistant professor of psychiatry at the University of California Medical Center in San Francisco. She has been in private practice for over 25 years, specializing in couples and family therapy. For 9 years she was director of the family therapy and partial care programs at Mount Zion Hospital and Medical Center in San Francisco.

Martha Sweezy, Ph.D., is staff clinician at the Cambridge Hospital Department of Psychiatry. She is a licensed clinical social worker in Massachusetts, where she maintains a private practice. She has worked in the McLean Hospital Department of Psychiatry and taught at Smith College School for Social Work. She is the author of "Why Heroin Should Be Legalized," which appeared in the *Smith College Studies in Social Work.*

John L. Walter, M.S.W., is an international workshop provider and agency trainer in brief therapy. He is also a co-director of Consultations, a practice and training center in Chicago that is dedicated to the development of optimistic approaches to working with people. He is a coauthor (with Jane Peller) of *Becoming Solution-Focused in Brief Therapy*, a skill-building guide to brief therapy. Among numerous other articles, he and Peller recently co-authored "Rethinking Our Assumptions: Assuming Anew in a Postmodern World," which appeared in the *Handbook of Solution-Focused Brief Therapy*. His national conference presentations include Social Work's World Assembly, the American Association of Marriage and Family Therapy, the *Family Therapy Networker*, the American Counseling Association, and Therapeutic Conversations.

Adrienne Wolmark, Ph.D., is an assistant professor and director of the Mental Health Technology Program at Allegheny University of the Health Sciences in Philadelphia. She has also lectured at Smith College School for Social Work. She has taught in the areas of feminist theory and practice, developmental psychology, mental health ethics, and clinical interviewing. In addition to self psychology, her interests include control-mastery theory, gender-identity development, and cross-cultural psychoanalytic practice.

INTRODUCTION

If you were in New York City on the morning of June 21, 1898, and happened to read the *New York Times* while having breakfast, you might have come across the following news article on page 7:

A class in practical philanthropic work was organized by Robert W. DeForest, President of the Charity Organization Society, yesterday morning. The class will work from June 20 until July 30, and is open for graduate students from universities recommended by their instructors, and those who have had experience in philanthropic work.

This brief notice, which could easily have been missed, marked the beginning of the social work profession and of social work education in the United States. The summer course in philanthropic work was extended to a 1-year program and named the New York School of Philanthropy in 1904. In 1910 it was again extended, this time to a 2-year program. In 1919 it was renamed the New York School of Social Welfare, a name that was to change once again in 1963 to the Columbia University School of Social Work.

As I worked on this book, I became aware of the significance of publishing a social work book during the 100th year of the profession. I came to think of the project as another way to pay homage to the centennial anniversary. The text, in my view, epitomizes the social work tradition of being open to new ways of helping clients, incorporating innovative information from other disciplines, and questioning our personal and professional world views and epistemologies.

Part 1 begins with a compelling story of a real family, here called the *Shores* (their case was also used as the example in Volume 1 of *Paradigms of Clinical Social Work*). Each of the practitioners gathered together for this project agreed to elucidate particular theoretical approaches using material from the Shore family case to illustrate concepts in their chapters. The purpose was not to "cure" or "fix" the Shores but to use their family saga as a device to enable us to compare the theories, techniques, and philosophies inherent in each paradigm.

Part 2 consists of seven models. *Ego Psychology and Object Relations Theory* and *Kohut's Self Psychology* are chapters I regretted not including in Volume 1. There is also a chapter that brings social workers up to date on the new directions in *The Cognitive Therapy Model*, and two chapters—*Solution-Focused Brief Therapy* and *Ericksonian Approaches in Social Work*—that present models influenced by Milton Erickson's work. I *also* wanted to go beyond conventional paradigms and include models that have recently captured our interest with their incorporation of postmodern ideas. These include *Postmodern Family Therapy* (in Part 2) and *The Feminist Approach to Clinical Social Work* and *Meaning-Making as a Metaframework for Clinical Practice* (in Part 3). It was also satisfying to include *Control-Mastery Theory*, a little-known model that is well-rooted in psychodynamic theory and appealing in its novel view of the unconscious.

Part 3 consists of four metaparadigms—*The Feminist Approach, Meaning-Making as a Metaframework, Prescriptive Eclectic Psychotherapy*, and *Behavioral Managed Care* (although some may object to labeling this as a paradigm)—that have a higher level of complexity or abstraction than the models in Part 2. The metaparadigms offer fewer specific techniques than the models, but they do provide frameworks from which techniques may be created or, in the case of *Prescriptive Eclectic Psychotherapy*, a systematic guide to selecting techniques from other paradigms. In the final chapter, *The Paradigms and Long-Term Trends in Clinical Social Works*, Reid took on the considerable challenge of reviewing, digesting, and drawing conclusions about the cornucopia of paradigms and metaparadigms presented.

In most instances, each chapter (in Volumes 1 and 2) may stand alone with the Shore family case. Thus, after being introduced to the Shores, the reader may read the chapters in any order and easily compare them in terms of the concept of the person and the human experience, historical perspective, key theoretical constructs, assessment, treatment of choice, the therapeutic process, limitations of the model, and research. There are only two exceptions to the rule. The first is the chapter on behavioral managed care, which presents an overview of clinical social work practice under managed care and alerts us to its major challenges. (This chapter does not refer to the Shores or use the standard format.) The second exception is the chapter on meaning-making as a metaframework. (The standard format is used to facilitate comparisons with the other paradigms, but no reference is made to the Shore family.)

When I decided to edit a second volume, I contacted the Shores for permission to use their story again and to ask them if I could write a 10-year update on their family. They were moved to hear that many readers had expressed curiosity about their fate. All four of the Shores welcomed the opportunity to report on the positive changes in their lives. Although the epilogue should satisfy curiosity, it should also raise provocative questions.

It is clear that the Shores, individually and collectively, are better off than they were 10 years earlier. How did that happen? Nancy has not been a consumer of social work treatment for a decade, Charley says the professionals never helped him, and Michael says that he never took what therapists had to offer. Still, they improved. Would they have had an even better outcome if they were able to make use of the kinds of treatment described in Volume 1 of *Paradigms of Clinical Social Work*? What role did naturally occurring therapeutic experiences play in the family's changes—for example, Rena's witness of the pain of others that put her own concerns into a different light? What role did naturally occurring therapeutic relationships play—for instance, the impact of the stoic and calm Aunt Flo on Nancy? Michael intuited that a relationship would help him. Why couldn't he connect with the counselors he had? Can we scoff at the help Nancy received from repeating comforting clichés to herself or the help that Charley received from "working, relaxing, and watching television?" Do we give enough attention to the impact of financial security on the family's functioning and mental health?

As I mentioned above, I did not initiate the "paradigms project" to "fix" the Shores. The purpose of these works has always been to more fully understand the paradigms of clinical social work and to continue to question our thinking about what we do and why we do it. My hope is that this book raises as many questions as it answers so that on the eve of the next century of social work, social workers can look forward to the thought, debate, and research that will be the foundation for theory building and effective clinical social work.

Happy anniversary, social work!

R. A. D.

PART I
The Case

1

The Case

Rachelle A. Dorfman, Ph.D.

The problems of the Shore family are common ones. Among them are unemployment, illness, and the worrisome behavior of the children. What is uncommon is that the problems never get resolved. Although the family members frequently seek help and are the recipients of various social services, they never seem to function free from symptoms. Individually and collectively, their lives are marked by crisis and emotional distress.

Nancy is 43, and her husband Charley is 51. The children are Rena, 18, who was adopted as a baby, and Michael, 12. Until recently, the entire family lived in the two-unit duplex they own. Nancy, Charley, and Michael still live in the second-floor apartment. Rena, who *had* occupied the first floor apartment by herself since she was 13, has moved out. She lives nearby and is "on her own." Charley has been chronically unemployed for 4 years, and the family survives largely on the disability checks Nancy has received every month for the last 10 years.

Nancy is a large woman. She calls herself "grossly obese" and makes frequent apologies about her appearance. Her hair is graying and her figure is decidedly matronly, but her flawless skin and the gap between her front teeth give her a youthful quality. The only reservation she has about being interviewed is that "after it's done, I will probably run from social worker to social worker trying to do everything suggested."

For most of her 23-year marriage to Charley, her full-time job has been "trying to get everything fixed." She is at her best during family crises. "Then," she says, "I take control. I no longer dread the terrible things that might happen because they have already happened. It is the waiting for the crisis to occur that makes me worry." Her anxiety often turns into panic. She becomes nearly immobilized. Unable to leave the house, she chain-

3

smokes and imagines the worst of all possible outcomes. Anxiety attacks occur daily.

There is no shortage of crises. Recurring flare-ups of a back injury that Nancy suffered as a young nurse incapacitate her without warning, confining her to bed for weeks or months. The flare-ups are not the only crises. Three times, doctors predicted that Michael, who has been asthmatic since early infancy, would not survive until morning. Twice Rena ran away from home and was missing for several days.

The small apartment reverberates with the sounds of their crises. One typical scenario began with an argument. Rena, then 16, lunged forward to hit her mother. Charley, in frustration and fury, pulled Rena away from Nancy and beat her, bruising her face badly. It was on that evening, 2 years ago, that Nancy and Charley told Rena she would have to leave when she turned 18.

A new problem with a potential for crisis is emerging. The downstairs apartment—which is now vacant—has never before been occupied by strangers. (Before Rena, Nancy's elderly grandparents lived there.) Because they need the money, Nancy and Charley have decided to rent it to a young couple. Nancy is anxious about being a landlord. She is trying to train Charley and Michael to keep their voices down and their steps light. She wishes that her family lived downstairs and the tenants lived upstairs and says, "I'd rather they walk on me than we walk on them." Again, she fears the crises that are certain to erupt.

Rena has been in her own apartment a few blocks away for 3 months. Nancy worries about that, too. She feels that as an adopted child, Rena is especially sensitive to having been "put out." Nonetheless, she still argues with Rena about her "laziness" and failure to finish anything, but there is less explosiveness now that she is on her own.

Despite some relief in the tension at home since Rena left, Nancy is still anxious and often depressed. She has gained 15 pounds, sleeps poorly, cannot concentrate, and is forgetful. Most of the time, she stays inside. Outside, she feels that people make disparaging remarks about her; only at home does she feel safe. Her days are filled with baseball games on TV, soap operas, needlepoint, and worrying about what will happen next.

Charley is blond, tall, and broad-shouldered. It is not difficult to imagine that he was once quite an appealing young man. When he was 27, his dreams and schemes interested and excited Nancy. Occasionally, he still talks of outlandish inventions and get-rich-quick schemes. The difference is that his wife no longer believes in him or his dreams. To her, they are annoying at best and embarrassing at worst.

Charley says, "All I ever wanted was to be somebody. I just want to be known for something, to have someone walk by my house and say 'That's Mr. Shore's house.'" He boasts about the time he went to California "to become a movie star" and of all the rich and famous people he knew and still knows. He speaks wistfully of just-missed opportunities for stardom and of inventions that no one took seriously. He likes being interviewed, saying, "It's exciting." Nancy reminds him that the interview is for a clinical book, not a Broadway play.

Five years ago, Charley performed on amateur night at a downtown comedy club. Nearly every Thursday night since then, he has performed for free in front of a live audience, using the name Joe Penn. His pride is unbounded when he is recognized in public as Joe Penn. Occasionally someone will even ask for his autograph.

His wife supports this activity because it makes him happy, but her perspective on his act is somewhat different from Charley's. The show embarrasses her. She says that while it is true that the audience laughs, they laugh at Charley, not at his jokes. "He is not funny," she maintains. Charley's defense is that Nancy's favorite comedian's wife probably doesn't think her husband is funny either.

Over the years, Charley has had scores of jobs. He was a salesman, a janitor, and a self-employed carpet cleaner. Even though he lost jobs regularly, he never had a problem getting a new one until 4 years ago. Several times in the last 3 months, Charley has mentioned suicide, always in response to a suggestion that he, like Nancy, should get on disability because of his "condition." Charley says that he would rather die first. Although he seems serious about this statement, he has no plan or means in mind.

The condition is the bipolar depression that was diagnosed 2 years ago at the time of his first and only psychotic break and consequent 4-week hospitalization. "I always got depressed," he recalls, "but that was different. That time I really went off." Remembering his grandiosity and manic behavior, he says, "I guess you do those things when you are sick." He is maintained on lithium.

A firing precipitated his break. He had completed an expensive cooking course and was determined to prove he could "make it" in his first cooking job. He says he hit the chef when he could no longer tolerate the man calling him names. (His bosses have complained that Charley is too slow and talks too much.)

Since his illness, he has had fewer grand ideas—he just wants a job he can hold. When he does allow himself to dream, mostly he dreams the way he did when he was a child, quietly and by himself. He likes to daydream while he works, which affects his performance. He was fired from his last janitorial job for forgetting to lock all the doors and for not cleaning thoroughly.

Presently, Charley attends a vocational rehabilitation program where he receives minimum wages for training in janitorial services—a job he says he already knows how to do. The program's goals are to develop the work skills and interpersonal skills needed for employment and to place him successfully in a job. Nancy is pessimistic about the outcome. She is angry because no one will tell her the results of his psychological testing. She says that if she knew for certain that Charley wasn't capable of holding a job, perhaps she wouldn't be so angry with him.

About Nancy, Charley says, "She is the best wife in the world, the same as my mother." She even worries like his mother, he says, "but I don't always like that because I don't feel like a man." The duplex they own was given to them by Nancy's Aunt Flo. While Charley appreciates the generosity, he says, "I wanted to do that. I wanted to buy the house."

Nancy agrees that she is parental. She prefers to handle important matters herself, not trusting Charley's competence with dollars, documents, or decisions. She complains that when she sends Charley to the store for two items, he invariably comes home with one of them wrong. But most of all, she complains about not having enough money to pay the bills. "I worry and he doesn't give a damn." Charley says privately, "I worry too, but I act like I don't because there is nothing I can do."

The couple frequently fights about Charley's compulsive lying. He tells Nancy what he believes she wants to hear, claiming he doesn't want to upset her with the truth. He says he would like to stop but he doesn't seem able to.

Charley usually stiffens as soon as he approaches the front door to enter his house. "Will there be a problem? Will Nancy complain about bills? Will Michael come home from school beaten up? They will want me to solve the problems. But I can't."

Being a father has been especially difficult. Charley and his son bicker and fight like small boys. Nancy finds herself storming in, breaking them up, and scolding them both. She says that each one fights for her attention, each trying to outdo the other.

Because father and son tend to relate to each other like siblings, therapists who worked with the family in the past attempted to restructure the relationship by suggesting that Charley teach Michael how to fish and play miniature golf. Charley and Michael always return home from such outings angrily blaming each other for ruining the day. Nancy says, "The whole time they are out, I am in a knot worrying that they are going to come up the steps screaming. I am never disappointed." She wants Charley to act more like a father. Charley wants that too. But, he says, "sometimes you just don't think about what you're doing when you do it."

Twelve-year-old Michael is tall and gangly. When he speaks, one can hear the phlegm rattle in his chest. It seems as though his voice is echoing through the mucus. His habitually knitted brow and his glasses make him appear to be very intense. Michael talks about "feeling funny" and "feeling bad." He feels bad because "asthma has taken away part of my life." His theory is that God gives everyone something he or she is terrific at. He says, "I haven't found mine yet—the asthma keeps me from it. I can't be a great athlete because I can't run fast. I can't have a puppy because I would wheeze. I just want to be good at something." According to his theory, God also puts a scar on everyone. People have to overcome their scars before they can find their special thing. Michael says asthma is his scar and he is waiting to outgrow it so that he can "find himself."

In the meantime, he is unhappy and lonely. Attempts to make friends are unsuccessful. He feels that even when he tries to behave himself, it is useless because his reputation prevents the other kids from relating to him in a new way. They still tease and pick on him. If someone hits him, he neither hits back nor runs away. He just "stays."

When he is not being "silly," he is more successful in relating to adults. Always attuned to the news, he usually knows what is current in world events, politics, and business. He sympathizes with underdogs and victims and talks about becoming a psychologist so that he can help them. He is fiercely patriotic and always truthful. When asked why he tells the truth when a lie would avoid trouble, he says "I am a Boy Scout; I cannot tell a lie."

Scouting is the highlight of his life, but there is trouble there too. Camping trips require a level of coordination, self-control, and social skills that he doesn't have. He gets reprimanded when he puts his tent up wrong or ties his neckerchief incorrectly. When this happens, he says, the other scouts laugh and he feels like a fool.

In junior high, Michael is in a learning disability (LD) class. Although learning disabilities and special classes are part of his history, the current placement was not made because of them—tests show that he has overcome or outgrown any learning disability he had. His poor social judgement is the problem that still lingers and prevents him from being mainstreamed. The same behaviors he calls "silly," his teachers have called "bizarre." These include touching others, making strange noises and motions, and laughing too loud or at the wrong time.

Last summer, Michael went to overnight camp. This spring, his parents received a disturbing letter from the camp. Michael was not invited back. The reason given was more than the typical foul language and mischief of 12-year-old boys. Counselors complained that at mealtimes he played with the utensils and plates, poured things into the pitchers and bowls, and threw food. He did not get along with the other campers and was seen as the instigator of most of the problems that occurred that summer. The staff felt that when he wanted to behave, he could, and that he willfully chose to misbehave.

Michael reports the situation differently. One moment he says that he acts silly because he falls under the influence of others. A moment later he suggests that he acts that way so that others will like him. Still later he says, "I don't really want to act like that. It's really kind of stupid. I don't know why I do it."

Michael is ambivalent about his sister leaving. He agrees that it is more peaceful at home, but now his parents are fussing about him more than ever. Nancy estimates that she spends "80 per cent of her worrying time" agonizing about what will become of Michael.

Rena, who is four blocks away in a basement efficiency apartment, has agonies of another sort. She is attractive, intelligent, and talented. Everyone, including Rena, always expected that she would be successful. But in the last few years, no matter how promising her beginnings, eventually she either quits or fails at everything she starts.

With 31 cents in her purse and no job, she is overdrawn at the bank and can't pay her bills. She has taken loans to pay for college courses she never completed. Rena feels old and tired.

Her parents used to call it laziness when she refused to go to school and stayed in bed until mid-afternoon. They thought she was lazy when she dropped out of high school, and then got a GED. and enrolled in pre-med, only to drop out of that. They believed that if they had allowed her to remain at home, she would have "vegetated" and done nothing at all.

Nancy pressures Rena to go to therapy because she has come to believe that there must be something more seriously wrong with Rena than laziness. Rena has agreed to go for therapy, partly because people usually do what Nancy wants. "Mother," she explains, "has a way of making you feel so bad and guilty, you finally either do what she wants or are mad because she makes you feel so bad." She has also agreed to go because she is lonely and confused. Unfortunately, there is a waiting list for outpatient services at the community mental health clinic, and Rena's name is at the bottom of that list.

Nevertheless, it seems that the therapeutic process has already begun. Rena writes her thoughts in her journal every day, and spends hours wondering about why she is the way she is. She is happy to be interviewed because she says she needs to talk about "this stuff."

She remembers when she didn't want to talk about the stuff or even think about it. At 16, when, at her request, the adoption agency sent some information about her birth mother, she forced herself to not think about it. Now she intends to find out about herself, even if it means thinking about painful things.

Like Michael, Rena has some theories. The first one is that she is so accustomed to living with problems and crises that she must create them when they do not exist. "Just look at my life," she says. "It is the only way I know how to live. When things are going well, I can't stand it."

As proof, she describes her brief college experience. Her attendance was excellent and the work was easy for her. Then she met a boy. Not long after that, she dropped out—blaming it on him. She claims she merely needed an excuse to "mess up," and he was a convenient one.

She calls her second theory "the adoption." Even if her adoption explanation is a "cop-out," she feels that it gives her a starting point from which to consider her life. She notes that she has patterned her life in much the same way as her birth mother did. Her birth mother didn't get along with her parents and was a high school dropout. Like Rena, she picked boyfriends who seemed worse off than herself.

Rejection is another thing Rena thinks about. "I push people so much with my demands that they eventually drop me like a hot potato. Then I can say, 'See what they did to me. They left me out in the cold.'" Sometimes generous to a fault, but more often selfish and demanding, she offers her relationship with her adoptive parents as proof of how she forces her own abandonment.

The most recent project Rena has started is the search for her birth mother. "I want to know her—see what she looks like, talk to her. I would like to sing for my mother." Rena wonders about her birth mother's approval. "She didn't like me before. Will she like me now?"

An attorney is helping Rena through the morass of conflicting state and agency policies that keep her from finding her birth mother. Meanwhile, she attends meetings of adoptees, birth mothers, and adoptive mothers, at which members share information and discuss feelings. Rena is usually found in the hallway asking questions of birth mothers. She asks, "Do you ever think of your kid? How could you do it? Didn't you care?"

FAMILY HISTORY

Nancy

Cute and precocious, Nancy was the cherished only child, only grandchild, and only niece of doting adults. She remembers those early years, the years before age 11, as golden. Although her mother, an exceptionally beautiful and somewhat self-centered woman, was often away socializing with a large circle of friends, there were always Aunt Flo and Gram to shower her with attention, affection, and gifts.

Little Nan was seldom childish, so the adults took her with them to the theater, the ballet, and fancy restaurants. Her manners were beyond reproach. To the delight of the grown-ups, she always cleaned her plate. She remembers, "They thought it was so cute because I ate everything and, at that age, never got fat."

Her earliest memory is of when she was 5: "I remember going to a store and getting a fried egg sandwich. I had to go a different way because I wasn't allowed to cross streets. Nobody was with me. A dog chased me home and tried to take my sandwich. I remember the smell of the sandwich and the dog chasing me. I was worried more about the dog biting my sandwich than biting me! That must have been the first clue to what food was going to be in my life."

Another memory is from the same period: "My father was a waiter. It was a big deal waiting for him to come home at night. He would bring food from the restaurant and we would all be together to eat it."

Her father was a shadowy figure. Between his job and his gambling, he was rarely home. Still, she felt closer to him than to her mother. One night, when she was 11, her parents told her that her father was leaving. It was difficult to understand because her parents never argued. Years later, she learned that the leaving was precipitated by gambling debts to the "mob." Her mother was either unable or unwilling to go.

Although Aunt Flo and Gram still bought her beautiful clothes and knit her angora sweaters, the golden years were over. Mother had to work now, so she was away more than ever, which seemed "just fine" with Mother. Nancy is convinced that her mother never wanted her, a fact that her mother denies. They moved several times in the next few years; Nancy remembers each place in great detail.

The first two summers after the marriage broke up, Nancy's father drove a thousand miles to get her and take her back with him for a visit. Her most vivid memory is from the second visit, when she was 12. She wanted to buy something at the pool, so she went to the hotel room to ask her father for money. "My father was lying in bed undressed and his 'wife-to-be' was ironing, with nothing on from the waist up. That is when I realized he was sleeping with her. Before then, I didn't know anything about that."

After that summer, her father stopped coming for her and stopped calling. He remarried and had more children, but Nancy did not find that out until later. She remembers wondering why he didn't love her. She confided only to Aunt Flo's dog. The poodle would lie by her side as she alternately wept and fantasized about her father's return. Finally, when Nancy was 14, a relative had a chance meeting with her father and reported his whereabouts. She called him immediately.

Nancy feels that if she had not initiated that contact, she would never have heard from him again. Today, when he visits Nancy (about once a year), he talks about his three wonderful children—especially his eldest daughter, Sandy. Nancy cringes every time. Her father has four children, and she is the eldest. She is bitter and resentful.

When Nancy was 15, her family moved into the duplex she still lives in. Gram lived downstairs with Grandfather, and Mother and Nancy lived in the upstairs apartment. The arrangement worked well. Nancy continued to spend a good deal of time with her beloved Gram. She made friends in the new school and began to date.

By high school, Nancy was overweight. Mother, however, was still "movie-star" beautiful. Nancy says, "Boys would come over to see me, but they soon liked my mother better." She felt like an ugly duckling next to her seductive mother clad in tight sweaters.

After high school, Nancy went to nursing school on a full academic scholarship. For the first time, she lived away from home. "All I wanted," she recalls, "was to take care of people." She learned how to do that in the exciting atmosphere of the hospital, where she developed life-long friendships with other nurses and doctors. Some of those doctors are involved now with Michael's treatment.

She calls the nursing years "the best years." "I felt so good about myself, totally in control. I was a damn good nurse. I was capable of handling anything that happened."

The only nursing she has done since injuring her back was part-time, "under-the-table" work in an old-age home. During that 18-month period, she retained none of her old confidence. She feared that at any moment a situation would arise that she could not handle. But, as usual, when emergencies did occur, she handled them quite well. Back pain and the threat of losing her disability payments because she was working illegally forced her to quit.

Following every flare-up of her injury, Nancy repeats the same pattern. Once the pain subsides, she feels a welling of desire to return to school for an advanced degree in nursing and ultimately return to her profession. She calls nursing schools and fills out applications; twice she made appointments with admissions counselors.

Eventually, a pall of gloom comes over her because she again realizes the full extent of her physical limitations. The flare-ups are unpredictable and keep her off her feet for months. Even between acute phases, she is unable to sit for more than short periods without pain. The possibility of completing a graduate degree—much less maintaining a career—appear remote. When Nancy again realizes this, she relinquishes her dream and returns to "earth" and to the family's problems.

Charley

Charley's childhood lacked the comforts of Nancy's. He had few possessions and his clothes were never "right." He felt loved by his mother, but he was hardly the center of anyone's attention. His father, a one-time amateur boxer, was a "tough little guy." He dealt with Charley the same way he dealt with problems on the street—with his fists.

Charley's mother and father fought constantly. Although Father never hit his wife, Mother was known to have taken more than a few swings at Father. Charley remembers one night when he was 5 years old. His father came home drunk, having gambled away his money. "Mom knocked him out cold." The scariest scene from his childhood was the night that his father got out his gun to "kill" his boss, whom he accused of cheating him. Charley doesn't remember the outcome—he only remembers the gray shiny gun.

By contrast, most memories of his mother are pleasant ones. He says, "One day when I was about 6, I was watching Mother scrub the floor. There was an awful smell of ammonia. She stopped working, turned on the radio, and put her feet up. She said her feet were hurting. I rubbed her feet."

Another memory from the same period was from the first grade: "Whenever my friend and I would see each other, we would fall on the floor and wrestle. I remember my first-grade teacher, Miss Brown. She used to stick her long nails in our backs when she grabbed us. We had this cloak room; there were little hooks on the walls. This one time, my friend and I were wrestling in the cloak room. Miss Brown grabbed us both and hung us up on those little hooks."

When Charley was 6, his sister Pat was born. Two years later his sister Louise was born. Charley says he was a lousy brother to his cute kid sisters, always hitting them. He recalls a stunt he pulled on Pat when he was 17 and she was 11. She was with a group of friends and he was with a group of boys. Unexpectedly, they met on the subway. Always playing the clown, Charley took his shoes and socks off, saying that they were on backwards. His companions roared; Pat was red-faced.

Like Michael, Charley was teased daily by the other kids. He got beaten up regularly until he managed to trade a prized toy for protection from a gang of four brothers. At 18, miserable and fed up with the fighting at home and on the streets, he enlisted in the Air Force. He proudly reports that he held that job for 4 years, the longest of any job. He still talks about the Air Force shows he performed in and drops names of the famous people he met during his enlistment.

After his discharge, he went to California. Charley paints the service years and the California period with a flourish. However, when he speaks of his Hollywood adventures and the starlets he dated, the details seem vague and much less compelling than the other details of his life.

Courtship and Marriage

Nancy and Charley's first date was at a picnic in the park arranged by mutual friends. They did not expect to be alone, but before they realized it, their friends had left for another picnic. Nancy will never forget those first few hours together. "He was so funny and handsome," she says. "He was different from anyone I had ever experienced. He told me he had been in the movies in Hollywood. He had ideas, inventions, and plans to have his own business. I believed everything he told me." Although he was only a delivery man for a florist shop, Nancy recalls, "he explained that he was learning the business to open his own shop."

Nancy promised to marry Charley in spite of her mother's and Aunt Flo's prediction that he would never make a decent living. Nancy wanted to prove them wrong. Two years after the picnic, they were married.

Charley's mother was struck and killed by a car shortly before the wedding. His father eventually remarried, and he died of a heart attack several years ago.

The early years of the marriage were relatively free from the problems that currently plague them. Although Charley went from job to job, it didn't worry them. Nancy was more than willing to support the family by working at what she loved most—nursing.

They originally had a rich social life. Over the years, however, they lost many of their friends. Nancy feels that their friends left because, as they matured, they had less and less in common with Charley, who remained a "kid."

The couple's first problem was that Nancy could not become pregnant. Because of Charley's low sperm count and Nancy's irregular ovulation, pregnancy was nearly impossible. After 4 years, doctors suggested adoption. They had been married 5 years when they adopted 6-week-old Rena. Six years later, Michael was conceived.

Rena

Gram called Rena the "the angel from heaven." Once again there was an only child, an only grandchild, and now an only great-grandchild as well. It was easy for the adults to dote on her because she was an exceptionally pleasant baby. At 5 months, Rena was standing. At 11 months, she could name the artist of each painting and print on Gram's walls.

Rena's early memories all include family members. She recalls playing a game with her father when she was just a toddler. She would sit on a special chair while he would go away and come back again. She recalls beckoning him to reappear. She also recalls a family vacation when she collected "teeny tiny" shells of different colors by the water's edge. When the vacation was over, she put them in a jar and took them home with her. She can still hear her mother screaming from the bathroom where Rena kept her "shells" in a jar of water, "Charley, Charley, these shells are moving!" Her father flushed what turned out to be snails down the toilet. Rena says she was very upset for a very long time.

Charley and Nancy knew that Rena was bright, but they did not realize the extent of her giftedness at first. At age 5, Rena bypassed the regular kindergarten program and entered a mentally gifted first grade. At a very young age, Rena began to "belt out" songs like a nightclub performer. Her parents remember other parents asking her for her autograph after an elementary school pageant. Everyone was impressed by her talent and was certain that she would have a future in show business.

She also displayed an unusual artistic talent, wrote poetry and short stories, and had an extraordinary mechanical ability. The latter annoyed Charley, because she was able to "fix anything" and he was not.

Birthdays, a happy time for most children, were unhappy for Rena. She moped about, looking sad and distracted. Eventually, she revealed that she always thought about her birth mother on that day, and wondered if her mother thought about her, too.

In grade school, there was some foreshadowing of her "not finishing anything." Then, however, when she dropped activities before completion, she always replaced them with others that were more challenging. Now she drops them in failure and despair.

The calm of her grade-school years gave way to a turbulent preadolescence and adolescence. Rena says of herself at 12, "I was a different person. I was good in school and never got into trouble. All the elders loved me. I was very intelligent and could talk to anyone about anything. But, like Michael, the kids didn't like me." She spent most of her time downstairs with Gram and Great-grandfather or with Aunt Flo.

Things were not going too well at home, either. Nancy had undergone one back operation and was facing a second. After that second operation, it was clear that she would never be able to stand the rigors of nursing again. Charley had to be the breadwinner. Michael was sick very often at that point, but the most difficult problem of all was Gram's death.

Rena's relationship her great-grandmother had been unusually close. She spent more time in Gram's apartment than in her own family's. When Rena got yelled at, Gram would scream upstairs, "Don't touch that angel from heaven!" Several times, Gram slipped child abuse literature under the door. Rena said Gram was the only one in the whole world who ever loved her.

Shortly after Gram's funeral, Rena—who had been sharing a room with Michael—moved downstairs with her great-grandfather. It seemed a logical and convenient solution to the lack of space and privacy for a developing young girl. A year later, Great-grandfather died, and Rena stayed downstairs alone, sleeping in Gram's bed. Her parents now regret the arrangement. They point to the deterioration in her behavior that followed.

At first things went exceedingly well. Rena, on a whim, auditioned for a role on a proposed TV series, and was one of the six finalists chosen in a national search. All the finalists were invited to New York for a screen test with a major television network. Charley was beside himself with aspirations to manage Rena and make her a star. The entire family was given the "star treatment." Unfortunately, Rena was told that she was "too cute" for the part. Shortly after that experience, Rena won the leading role in the school play. As Dorothy in *The Wizard of Oz,* she sang and danced and won the admiration of the entire school.

When the excitement of those two events passed and life returned to normal, Rena began to cut school. Then the fighting began in earnest. She refused to go to school or to keep the downstairs apartment clean. Charley and Nancy threatened, pleaded, punished, and hit. Twice Rena ran away. When she returned, she always promised to do better.

When she was 15, Rena got a part in a local dinner theater. Charley and Nancy allowed her to do the weekend performances if she attended school. When she was caught cutting again, her parents had her withdrawn from the company. They feel that she has never forgiven them for that.

Eventually Rena quit school. Now a few years older, she speaks of her shame and once more verbalizes her resolve to "do better."

Michael

Michael has been hospitalized 14 times and has spent hundreds of hours in hospital emergency rooms for *asthmatic status,* a type of asthma that gets out of control. (Sufferers are often near death as doctors struggle to bring it under control.) When Michael has an asthma attack, Nancy works closely by phone with the pediatrician monitoring his condition; she injects him with adrenaline and helps him to breathe with a nebulizer. Michael's earliest memory is of not being able to breathe, crying, "Gimme air, gimme air." He says, "Once, an ugly lady came in and gave me a shot instead. I wanted to hit her and tell her I didn't need the shot. I am perfectly fine."

Nancy claims that Michael was born unlucky. When he was only 8 days old, he hemorrhaged from a circumcision wound. Asthma first appeared when he was 6 months old, and he was sickly and prone to high fevers throughout infancy. Nancy worried that he might not grow up at all. Now she worries about what his life will be like. Despite frequent illnesses, he was a happy baby. He walked, talked, and reached all the developmental milestones on schedule.

His worrisome health continued through the toddler stage. At $2^1/_2$, he had his first grand mal seizure and has been on seizure medication ever since. Doctors hold the medication responsible for at least a portion of his behavior problems, specifically the hyperactivity, but no one is quite certain just how much of his problem can be attributed to adverse side effects.

His behavior was first identified as problematic in kindergarten. After 2 months of first grade, he was transferred from the regular classroom to an LD classroom. Teachers said he could not follow instructions and seemed "lost" and confused. The report from the school psychologist stated that he had fine and gross motor coordination problems.

At 12, Michael feels that he is different from the rest of the kids. However, he refuses to accept his very real physical limitations; despite constant failure and rejection, he continues to try out for the track and softball teams. On the other hand, he acknowledges his difference and alienation and says, "Sometimes I feel that I should be in another country or in another time zone. I wish I could start my life over again." He likes the idea of having his story in a book because people "pity the underdog."

PART II
Paradigms

2

Ego Psychology and Object Relations Theory

Eda G. Goldstein, D.S.W.

INTRODUCTION

Ego psychology and *object relations* **theory** are two related and overlapping yet nevertheless distinctive paradigms for understanding human development. Together with *drive theory* and *self psychology*, they constitute the contemporary psychodynamic base of clinical social work. When social workers began to integrate ego psychology into their knowledge base in the 1940s and 1950s, the result was far-reaching changes in the view of the person and the human experience, the nature of human problems, and the treatment process. In embodying changes that expanded and modified Freudian drive-theory's emphasis, ego psychology linked individuals to their social environments: "Here at last was the happy synthesis between the social order and the psychological depths—the ego, which bridged these two worlds" (Briar & Miller, 1971, p. 19).

Originally, ego psychological theory focused attention on (a) the ego as the executive arm of the personality, mediating between inner needs and the external environment; (b) the ego's role in coping and adaptation, and the importance of ego mastery; (c) the ego's many functions; (d) the ego's defenses against anxiety; (e) the interplay of biopsychosocial factors in shaping personality development and successful coping throughout the life cycle; (f) the stages of the life cycle and their contribution to personality and identity development; and (g) the significance of deficits in ego development and maladaptive personality traits and patterns in causing problems in living and more serious types of disorders (Goldstein, 1995).

19

As ego psychological concepts were refined and extended, later theorists and researchers emphasized the importance of the child's earliest attachments and caretaking experiences on personality development and built an object relations perspective into ego psychological theory. According to object relations theory, interpersonal relationships provide the context in which all personality development occurs: The child takes in or internalizes the outside world, thereby acquiring basic attitudes toward the self and others along with other aspects of intrapsychic structure. Object relations theories not only shed light on how both deficiencies and problems in internalized object relations result in later difficulties but also point to new directions in the treatment of personality problems and severe emotional disorders.

Almost 50 years after the emergence of ego psychology, the results of a survey of the 1982 National Association of Social Workers' Register of Clinical Social Workers (Mackey, Urek, & Charkoudian, 1987) showed that 51% of the respondents "identified ego psychology as being the most instrumental to their approach" (p. 368). Although this study was conducted over 10 years ago, ego psychology continues to be popular. It has undergone considerable expansion, most importantly in the addition of object relations concepts; in its application to ameliorating some of the most pressing problems that practitioners encounter; and in the integration of new perspectives on women's development, the adult life cycle, the impact of trauma, and cultural diversity and oppression. The literature on ego psychology, object relations theory, and practice applications is vast and continues to grow. Courses, lectures, conferences, and workshops that deal with ego-psychological and object relations theory attract large numbers of social work practitioners.

THE CONCEPT OF THE PERSON AND THE HUMAN EXPERIENCE

In contrast to Freud's pessimism about human goodness and human growth, ego psychology embodies an optimistic and humanistic view of human functioning and potential. Freudian theory emphasized the unconscious, instinctual, and irrational aspects of the personality. Ego psychology drew attention to the more rational, autonomous, and problem-solving capacities of the ego; the individual's active attempts to adapt to the environment and to gain mastery; and the impact of interpersonal relationships, the environment, society, and culture on personality development. Unlike Freud, who viewed childhood as the major—if not sole—determinant of the personality, ego psychological theorists saw the potential for growth throughout the entire life cycle. Moreover, in highlighting the significance of the interpersonal context in shaping behavior, object relations theorists overcame the more isolated and mechanistic view of the human developmental process that was embodied in drive theory in early ego psychology.

HISTORICAL PERSPECTIVE

Although ego psychology was initiated in the work of Hartmann (1939), it has roots in classical psychoanalytic theory. In "The Ego and the Id" (1923/1961), Freud proposed what became known as *structural theory*. The theory defined the *ego* by its functions: (a) mediating between the drives (id) and external reality; (b) moderating conflict between the drives (id) and the internalized prohibitions against their expression (superego); (c) instituting mechanisms (defenses) to protect the ego from anxiety; and (d) playing a crucial role in development through its capacity for identification with external objects (Goldstein, 1995). Freud saw the ego as deriving its energy from the drives, although weak in relation to them and having no independence from them. In *The Ego and the Mechanisms of Defense* (1936), Freud's daughter, Anna, put forth the first extension of structural theory by identifying the adaptiveness of defensive behavior, describing a greater repertoire of defenses, and linking the origin of defenses to specific developmental phases.

It was Heinz Hartmann, however, in *Ego Psychology and the Problem of Adaptation* (1939), who originated the concept of the *autonomous ego*, proposing that both the ego and the id have their own energy source and originate in an "undifferentiated matrix" at birth. The individual is born "preadapted" to an "average expectable environment" for the species. In contrast to the earlier Freudian view, many ego functions are "conflict-free" and have a "primary autonomy" from the drives.

Later, in *Childhood and Society* (1950) and "Identity and the Life Cycle" (1959), Eric Erikson posited ego development as occurring as a result of the progressive mastery of developmental tasks by delineating eight successive stages of the human life cycle. He emphasized the contribution of biological, psychological, interpersonal, environmental, societal, and cultural influences in the developmental process. Erikson also was among the first theorists to view adulthood as a period for growth and change.

Unlike Erikson, Robert White (1959, 1963) broke away from the Freudian psychoanalytic tradition. He postulated that the individual is born not only with innate and autonomous ego functions that give pleasure in their own right but also with a drive toward mastery and competence. According to White, the ego actively seeks opportunities in the environment in which the individual can be effective. In turn the ego is strengthened by successful transactions with the environment.

While some writers began to study the constitutional and environmental factors that contribute to ego strength, coping capacity, and vulnerability

(Escalona, 1968; Murphy & Moriarity, 1976), others delineated the more specific contributions of the caretaking environment to personality development. For example, attachment theorists such as M. D. S. Ainsworth (1973), John Bowlby (1958), and Rene Spitz (1945, 1965) generated crucial data and theory about the nature and impact of the child's earliest connections to others from their observational studies of children. Further, in close collaboration with one another, Margaret Mahler (1968; Mahler, Pine, & Bergman, 1975) and Edith Jacobson (1964) established the stages by which the child makes the transition from nonrelatedness to attachment to separation–individuation. They further described how the child gradually acquires *self representations* and *object representations* (i.e., basic attitudes toward the self and others) as well as other intrapsychic structures through interactions with significant others. Adhering to both Freud's structural model and the work of Anna Freud and Hartmann, Mahler and Jacobson were considered to be American object relations theorists who bridged their work with ego psychology.

Other object relations theories developed outside the American ego psychological tradition. For example, the British school of object relations—comprising the work of Melanie Klein (1948), W. R. D. Fairbairn (1952), D. W. Winnicott (1965), Harry Guntrip (1969, 1973), and others—has proposed distinctive theories. The work of Otto Kernberg (1984) reflects an attempt to integrate many concepts from the British school into American ego psychology and object relations theory.

Assimilation Into Social Work

Ego psychology had a dramatic impact on social work practice. Beginning in the late 1930s, although more significantly in the post-World War II period, numerous individuals became associated with attempts to assimilate ego psychological concepts into the diagnostic model and later the psychosocial model of social casework. Lucille Austin (1948), Louise Bandler (1963), Eleanor Cockerill & Colleagues (1953), Annette Garrett (1958), Gordon Hamilton (1940, 1958), Florence Hollis (1949, 1964, 1972), Isabell Stamm (1959), and Charlotte Towle (1949) were prominent among these.

As Hamilton (1958) so aptly observed, ego psychology's more optimistic view of human potential at a time when the world was "crumbling to pieces . . . was part of the vision of man's strength and sturdiness under adversity" (p. 22). The use of ego psychology led to a shortening and refocusing of the study and assessment process. It emphasized (a) clients' person–environment transactions in the here and now, particularly the degree to which they cope effectively with major life roles and tasks; (b) clients' adaptive, autonomous, and conflict-free areas of ego functioning as well as their ego deficits and maladaptive defenses and patterns; (c) the key developmental issues affecting clients' current reactions; and (d) the ways in which the stresses of the external environment or a lack of resources and environmental supports create obstacles to successful coping.

Ego psychology provided the rationale for improving or sustaining adaptive ego functioning by means of work with both the individual and the environment. This led to the expansion and systematization of treatment techniques for working with the ego. Ego psychologists recognized the importance of the reality of the client–social worker relationship in contrast with an exclusive focus on its transference or distorted aspects. Ego psychology expanded social workers' understanding of the nature of change, moving beyond an exclusive emphasis on insight.

Ego psychological concepts helped to transform the casework process from a never-ending, unfocused exploration of personality difficulties to a more deliberate and focused use of the phases of the casework process. They underscored the importance of the client's responsibility for directing treatment and his or her own life.

The ego-oriented treatment models developed were supportive and modifying in nature. *Ego-supportive intervention* aimed at restoring, maintaining, and enhancing an individual's adaptive or coping capacities through working on here-and-now issues within a person's environmental context. It relied on a range of supportive techniques such as exploration, ventilation, acceptance, reassurance, direct influence, and person-situation reflection and saw the real helping relationship as a potentially corrective and reparative force in treatment. *Ego-modifying intervention* was designed to change an individual's maladaptive behavior and patterns of relating. It tended to make use of more reflective and interpretive techniques than were suggested for ego-supportive treatment, work with both people's past experiences and their current reality, and deal with the more transferential rather than real aspects of the client–worker relationship.

Efforts to incorporate ego psychology into social work also led to a distinctive problem-solving casework model developed by Helen Perlman (1957). Perlman attempted to bridge the lingering dispute between diagnostic (psychoanalytic) and functional (Rankian) caseworkers and to offer correctives for practices that she viewed as dysfunctional for the client. The problem-solving model also contributed to the generation of crisis-intervention models and more ecologically oriented models (Germain & Gitterman, 1980; Golan, 1978).

Despite ego psychology's potential to be a bridge between person and environment in theory and practice, its critics saw it as focused on a person's inner life at the apparent expense of attention to the role of the environment in shaping personality and effective coping. Followers of ego psychology were sometimes criticized for blaming the victim rather than attending to the effects of oppression, poverty, and trauma. They were also accused of pathologizing the behavior of women, gays and lesbians, and those who are ethnically non-European, rather than respecting their unique characteristics and strengths. Moreover, because the concepts and associated practices stemming from ego psychology were not operationalized and studied, there was insufficient evidence supporting the efficacy of ego-oriented treatment. As clinicians began to turn away from psychodynamic theory and instead embraced alternative theories and interventive models, the dominance of ego psychology waned. Its prominent position in the knowledge base of social work was further eroded in the 1960s, during which the social work profession emphasized social change (*macrosystems intervention*) rather than direct practice (*microsystems intervention*).

Direct practice reasserted its importance during the 1970s and has continued to occupy a prominent role in the social work profession. Along with the resurgence of direct practice, ego psychology has enjoyed a renaissance of interest. Its emphasis on ego functioning and defenses, normal coping strategies, the need for mastery and competence, person–environmental transactions, biopsychosocial factors in development, growth in adulthood, and stress is well-suited to work with a wide range of clients. Refinements and extensions of psychoanalytic ego psychology that address internalized object relations provide a deeper understanding of maladaptive behavior, personality difficulties, and severe types of emotional disorder and have led to new directions in treatment (Applegate & Bonovitz, 1995; Seinfeld, 1990, 1991, 1993, 1996). Integration of knowledge regarding cultural diversity, female development, trauma, and the impact of oppression on certain populations has broadened its applicability (Abarbanel & Richman, 1990; Courtois, 1988; Gilligan, 1982; Ryan, 1985; Weille, 1993; Wilson, 1989). Ego-oriented intervention extends to many diverse populations and provides the conceptual underpinnings to a variety of practice models, including the psychosocial, problem-solving, crisis intervention, and life models. It has important linkages to family and group theories and approaches as well as to the design of service delivery, large-scale social programs, and social policy (Northen, 1988; Slipp, 1988).

KEY THEORETICAL CONSTRUCTS

Ego psychology contains four main sets of concepts: ego functions, defenses, ego mastery and adaptation, and object relations.

Ego Functions

Ego functions are the means by which the individual copes with and adapts to the world. Bellak, Hurvich, and Gediman (1973; see Goldstein, 1995) identified 12 major ego functions:

1. reality testing;
2. judgment;
3. sense of reality of the world and of the self;
4. regulation and control of drives, affects, and impulses;
5. object relations;
6. thought processes;
7. adaptive regression in the service of the ego;
8. defensive functioning;
9. stimulus barrier;
10. autonomous functions;
11. mastery–competence; and
12. synthetic/integrative function.

The assessment of these ego functions gives a measure of an individual's *ego strength*, a composite picture of the internal psychological equipment or capacities that an individual brings to his or her interactions with others and with the social environment.

Within the same individual, certain ego functions may be better developed than others and may show more stability. That is, the ego functions tend to fluctuate less from situation to situation or over time and are less prone to regression or disorganization under stress. Furthermore, even in individuals who manifest ego strength, regression in selected areas of ego functioning may be normal in certain types of situations—for example, illness, social upheavals, crises, and role transitions. Regression in such instances does not necessarily imply ego deficiencies. It is important to note that it is possible for the same individual to have highly variable ego functioning, although in cases of the most severe psychopathology, ego functions may generally be impaired. For instance, a client who is admitted to a psychiatric hospital for treatment as a result of an acute psychotic episode may show problems with reality testing, impulse control, judgment, defenses, regression, and autonomous functioning.

The Concept of Defense

All people use defenses, but the exact type and extent vary from individual to individual. *Defenses* are part of the ego's repertoire of mechanisms for protecting the individual from anxiety by keeping intolerable or unacceptable impulses or threats from conscious awareness. Common defenses (Goldstein, 1995; Laughlin, 1979) include the following:

1. *Altruism,* in which satisfaction is gained through self-sacrificing service to others or through participation in causes as a way of dealing with unacceptable feelings and conflicts.

2. *Asceticism*, in which there is renunciation of certain pleasures in order to avoid the anxiety and conflict associated with impulse gratification.
3. *Denial*, in which there is a lack of acknowledgment or nonacceptance of important aspects of reality or of one's own feelings, impulses, thoughts, or experiences.
4. *Displacement*, in which unacceptable feelings about one person or situation are placed onto another person or situation.
5. *Intellectualization*, in which unacceptable feelings and impulses are warded off by thinking about them rather than experiencing them directly.
6. *Isolation*, in which the feelings associated with particular content or the ideas connected with certain feelings remain out of awareness.
7. *Projection*, in which unacceptable thoughts and feelings are attributed to others.
8. *Rationalization*, in which logical, convincing reasons are used to justify certain ideas, feelings, or actions so as to avoid recognizing their unacceptable underlying motive.
9. *Reaction formation*, in which an unwanted feeling or impulse is replaced by its opposite.
10. *Regression*, in which there is a return to an earlier developmental phase, level of functioning, or type of behavior in order to avoid present anxieties.
11. *Repression*, in which unwanted thoughts, feelings, impulses, and experiences remain out of awareness.
12. *Somatization*, in which unacceptable impulses or conflicts are converted into physical symptoms.
13. *Splitting*, in which two contradictory states such as love and hate are compartmentalized and not integrated.
14. *Sublimation*, in which an unacceptable impulse is expressed in a socially acceptable way.
15. *Undoing*, in which there is an attempt to make reparation for or nullify an unacceptable or guilt-provoking act, thought, or feeling.

Because defenses operate unconsciously, people are not aware that they are using a particular defense. Indeed, all defenses falsify or distort reality to some extent. When a person uses defenses in a flexible rather than rigid fashion with minimal distortion of reality, and if the person is able to function well without undue anxiety, the defenses are said to be effective and adaptive. The same defense, however, can severely limit a person's ability to perceive reality or to cope effectively, and thus may be maladaptive. For example, a certain amount of denial of the possible outcomes of surgery may be helpful in enabling a patient to pursue a risky procedure, whereas the presence of massive denial of the seriousness of a health condition may result in a person's avoidance of necessary medical attention. For example, in the Shore case, Nancy's daughter displays a maladaptive form of denial when she tends to avoid dealing with her educational and occupational problems.

People do not deliberately seek to maintain their defenses, but because such defenses often serve a protective function, efforts directed at modifying them usually are met with resistance. This resistance creates obstacles to achieving the very changes that people would like to occur. Although it may seem desirable to try to lessen or modify certain maladaptive defenses in a given individual because they interfere with effective coping, any effort of this sort will arouse considerable anxiety. In many instances, defenses should be respected, approached with caution, and at times strengthened.

Under acute or unremitting stress, illness, or fatigue, the ego's defenses may fail along with the other ego functions. When there is a massive defensive failure, an individual becomes flooded with anxiety. This can result in a severe and rapid deterioration of ego functioning; in some cases the personality becomes fragmented and chaotic, just as in a psychotic episode. When defenses are rigid, people may appear exceedingly brittle, taut, and driven, and their behavior may seem increasingly mechanical, withdrawn, or peculiar.

Ego Mastery and Adaptation

Some authors (e.g., Hendrick, 1942; White, 1959, 1963) have postulated the existence of a *mastery drive* or *instinct*—an inborn, active striving toward interaction with the environment leading to an individual's experiencing a sense of competence or effectiveness. White described the ego as having independent energies that propelled the individual to gain pleasure through manipulating, exploring, and acting on the environment. He called these energies *effectance* and suggested that feelings of efficacy are the pleasure derived from each interaction with the environment. In White's view, ego identity results from the degree to which one's effectance and feelings of efficacy have been nurtured. Ego identity affects present and future behavior, because it reflects basic attitudes such as one's self-esteem, self-confidence, trust in one's own judgment, and belief in one's decision-making capacities, which shape the way people deal with the environment.

Erik Erikson viewed optimal ego development as a result of the mastery of stage-specific developmental tasks and crises. He argued that the successful resolution of each crisis from birth to death leads to a sense of ego identity and may be said to constitute the core of one's sense of self. Erikson viewed later stages as dependent on earlier ones. The use of the term *crisis* reflects the idea that there is a state of tension or disequilibrium at the beginning of each new stage. The resolution of each stage is described in terms of the achievement of positive and negative solutions. In any individual, however, the resolution of the core developmental crisis posed by each stage may lie anywhere on a continuum from best to worst outcome.

According to Erikson, resolution of each successive life-cycle stage depends as much on those with whom an individual interacts as on his or her own innate capacities. Similarly, crisis resolution is dependent on the impact of culture and environment as it shapes child-rearing practices and provides opportunities or obstacles to optimal adaptation.

Erikson was among the first theorists to suggest that adulthood is a dynamic rather than static period and that ego development continues throughout adulthood. There is mounting interest in, and evidence for, the idea that personality change occurs in adult life. Adulthood is seen to contain both elements of the past and its own dynamic processes that lead to personality changes. Benedek (1970), Butler (1963), Colarusso and Nemiroff (1981), Gould (1978), Levinson (1978), Neugarten (1968; Neugarten & Associates, 1964), and Vaillant (1977) are among those authors who have made seminal contributions to understanding adult developmental processes.

Object Relations

The term *object relations* refers to both the inner structures that the individual develops and the nature of actual interpersonal relationships. Rather than viewing the capacity for object relations as a single ego function, some authors regard the interpersonal world as providing the context in which all ego development occurs. Object relations theorists view the infant as innately object-seeking from birth. Although the interpersonal field exerts influence all through life, the child develops or internalizes basic attitudes toward the self and others as a result of interpersonal experiences early in life. The inner representations of self and others that develop affect all subsequent interpersonal relationships, even to the point of overriding the "objective" attributes of the self and others. For example, it may be difficult to modify a deeply entrenched negative self-concept, despite evidence to the contrary.

The separation–individuation process described by Mahler (1968; Mahler, Pine, & Bergman, 1975) comprises a series of chronologically ordered phases, each of which leads to major achievements in the areas of separation, individuation, and internalized object relations. The phases include the following:

1. The *autistic* phase, in which the child is thought to be in a preattachment phase.

2. The *symbiotic* phase, which marks the beginning of the infant's capacity to invest in another who is perceived as a "need-satisfying object" within the infant's ego boundary and as lacking a separate identity.

3. The *differentiation* subphase (at about 4 or 5 months) in which the infant's attention shifts from being inwardly directed within the symbiosis to being more outwardly directed and the infant begins to separate self-representations from representations of the caretaker (the object).

4. The *practicing* subphase, in which the separation of self and object representations and the individuation process accelerates as the infant's own autonomous ego functions assume more importance.

5. The *rapprochement* subphase, in which there is a back and forth movement between autonomy and dependence, increasing ability to be on one's own alternating with increased fears of separation and loss of the object, and a tendency to see the self and others as all good or all bad.

6. On the road to *object constancy*, in which the child again seems able to be on his or her own without undue concern about the mother's whereabouts as object constancy is achieved, which implies the capacity to maintain a positive mental representation of the object in the absence of the object or in the face of frustration.

Blos (1975) suggested a second separation–individuation phase occurring in adolescence. The healthy adolescent who has an internalized sense of self and others must begin to *disengage* from the more infantile aspects of these inner representations in order to acquire a more realistically based sense of self and others. This disengagement also requires the discovery of new love objects outside the orbit of the family.

Even adults who show optimal functioning may relive separation–individuation themes throughout the life cycle, particularly at life transitional points or during more acute stresses. Those who do not successfully complete this key developmental process will show serious interpersonal difficulties (Blanck & Blanck, 1974).

Numerous object relations theorists, particularly from the British school of object relations, put forth different views of object relations development. For example, Melanie Klein (1948) did not fully emphasize the interpersonal world in shaping the personality because she viewed early instinctual aggression and fantasy as determining the nature of the child's perceptions and experiences of the real world. She did think that real objects could reinforce or challenge the infant's views. In Klein's view, envy, greed, and destructive fantasies about and impulses toward others make the infant anxious, and it fears the objects on which it vents its anger. Rage is projected and results in persecutory fears that are heightened during the paranoid–schizoid position present in the first 6 months of life. This stage also is characterized by the use of early defense mechanisms that help the infant to rid itself of this anxiety. In the last half of the first year of life, infants enter the depressive position, in which their loving feelings temper the aggressive drive and hate. In order to preserve "good" objects, infants make reparation for their aggressive fantasies and impulses and are capable of experiencing gratitude and guilt. Klein believed that both the paranoid–schizoid and depressive positions shape later personality development and psychopathology and always are active in different degrees.

Fairbairn (1952) regarded infants as object-seeking rather than pleasure-seeking. In contrast with Klein, he argued that personality develops as a result of interactions with real rather than fantasized objects. Fairbairn believed that the frustration of not feeling loved or lovable—or that one's love is unwelcome and not valued—results in the development of aggressive impulses. The inability of external objects to provide for the infant's needs leads the infant to acquire a split ego and to build up a world of internal bad objects that also are split into idealized, rejecting, and exciting parts. The internalization of bad objects and the split in the ego that results become closed systems that influence further personality development and psychopathology. They prevent the individual from progressing from infantile dependence to mature dependence and from establishing loving and satisfying bonds with others.

Winnicott (1965) placed considerable emphasis on *good-enough mothering* and the provision of a *maternal holding environment* in children's development. Such environments would be attuned to the child's unique needs and traits and would provide sufficient nurture and structure without being too intrusive, controlling, or suffocating. According to Winnicott, the child's internalization of crucial personality features such as the capacity to be alone results from positive experiences with the mother; ego defects are caused by maternal failures. He also drew attention to the significance of *transitional objects* (concrete objects that are associated with the mother in the child's experience) as a bridge between children and mothers. Winnicott maintained that when good-enough mothering is lacking because of either maternal deprivation or too much *impingement* (i.e., intrusion, control, or suffocation), the infant erects a "false" self, which is a facade that comes into being to please others. As the false self rigidifies, the child becomes alienated from his or her true self. Thus, the false self is a defensive organization that both "hides" and "protects" the true self at the expense of its full expression.

Guntrip (1969, 1973) also stressed the importance of early mothering in shaping the personality. He argued that frustrations caused by external objects, primarily the mother, lead the infant or child to turn away from them and that this withdrawal, the *schizoid problem*, is at the core of all psychopathology. The schizoid problem is characterized by *ego splitting* (a compartmentalization of the ways in which the ego relates to others so that the loving and hating parts remain separated); a withdrawal from interpersonal relationships; attitudes of omnipotence, isolation, and detachment; hopelessness; and a preoccupation with inner reality. The most extreme schizoid mechanisms result in individuals becoming alienated from themselves, without any capacity to love or to experience understanding, warmth, and personal concern for others. Deeply hidden in such individuals is a needy self that is cut off from the outside world.

Kernberg (1984) attempted to link the American ego-psychological–object relations theorists with those of the British school, particularly Klein. He shared Klein's views on instinctual aggression, unconscious fantasy, and primitive defenses, as well as her view of how the child's inborn dispositions and instincts organize perceptions and internalization of the external world. Kernberg argued that what the child takes in psychically usually differs from the actual objects in the environment because drives, affects, fantasies, and defenses shape and distort the child's perceptions and experiences. Like the ego psychologists, Kernberg maintained a reliance on structural theory. He traced the development of an individual's internalized object relations and internal structure through a series of five sequential stages that are similar to those described by Mahler, but he tended to minimize the impact of the child's actual parenting experiences. Kernberg related certain problems in this evolution to the formation of pathological object relations that culminate in borderline and narcissistic disorders.

Newer Theoretical Developments

A number of newer perspectives about women's development can be integrated into ego psychology and object relations theory. These perspectives have major implications for understanding women's strengths and needs throughout the life cycle and for redefining behavior that has been viewed as pathological as being reflective of women's normal development. They also illuminate the causes of certain symptoms and difficulties that women experience when they are deprived of necessary connection or when they experience conflict between a need for affiliation versus a push toward self-enhancement or more autonomous behavior. Further, these views of women's needs have significant ramifications for reshaping the treatment process to be more reciprocal and relational than traditional treatment models.

Some feminist writers (Chodorow, 1978; Gilligan, 1982) have challenged the main thrust of Erikson's views as they pertained to women's development in particular. They argued that he placed too much importance on biological gender differences in contrast with cultural factors and socialization and that he based his views on male experience. Chodorow and

Gilligan also critiqued Mahler's ideas, suggesting that girls have a different individuation process than boys because of girls' primary attachment to a same-sex rather than opposite-sex parent. They saw mothers and daughters as sharing a greater sense of identification and merger with one another, resulting in a more prolonged closeness and a more diffuse individuation process. Furthermore, they viewed female self-development, when compared with male self-development, as involving more permeable rather than rigid boundaries; an emphasis on relationships rather than autonomy; and a greater capacity for empathy, caring, and intuition.

Members of the Stone Center for Developmental Studies, which includes Jean Baker Miller, Judith Jordan, Alexandra Kaplan, Irene Stiver, and Janet Surrey (Jordan, Kaplan, Miller, Stiver, & Surrey, 1991) as well as another prominent feminist writer, Jessica Benjamin (1988), have made similar arguments. For example, the Stone Center group regarded the development of a woman's self as evolving in the context of relatedness, believing that enhanced connection rather than increased self–object differentiation and separateness is women's major goal. Moreover, they contended that women optimally grow and change when they are experiencing an interactive process in which mutual engagement, empathy, and empowerment with significant others occurs. Nonresponsive relationships and disconnection, rather than problems in separation–individuation per se, result in pathology. Benjamin stressed the balance between oneness and separateness, merging and differentiation. In her view, true independence involves both self-assertion and mutuality, separateness and sharing; an individual's inability to reconcile dependence and independence leads to patterns of domination and submission.

These newer theories have been used to put forth a more affirmative view of lesbian development. Traditional conceptions of the early childhood of lesbians saw them as failing to switch their attachment from their mothers to their fathers, remaining fixated on their mothers rather than viewing them as rivals, and then identifying with their fathers. Weille (1993) speculated, however, that because the little girl normally does not give up her attachment to the mother when she turns to her father but instead maintains this bond that provides her with continuity and a core sense of self, it is logical that a normative outcome for women is bisexuality. The daughter maintains her libidinal connection to the mother while developing a triadic relational structure. Reiter (1989) further suggested that the girl's primary and continuing attachment results in her acquisition of a firm gender identity as a woman and that women consequently may have the capacity for greater fluidity in their sexual interests, detracting from their sense of femaleness. This view might help to explain why many lesbians "come out" later in life, after they have had significant relationships with men or have moved back and forth between men and women in their love relationships, thus showing a long-standing bisexual orientation (Burch, 1993).

Recent research supports the view that lesbian object relations and the development of self arise as a variant of positive developmental experiences, in contrast to the traditional belief that they reflect arrested, immature, narcissistic, and undifferentiated object relations. For example, in Spaulding's (1993) study of 24 college-educated lesbians who had positive identities and achieved high scores on measures of psychological stability, the women showed "evidence of highly evolved, differentiated and integrated level of object and reality relatedness" (p. 17). Furthermore, their views of their parents did not correspond to common stereotypes in that these lesbians saw both their mothers and fathers as strong, positive role models who were nurturing, successful, and warm (p. 19).

Finally, greater attention to cultural diversity also has enriched ego psychology and object relations theory. Increasing knowledge of the unique coping capacities and needs of people of color and other ethnic minorities has reshaped the treatment process and led to more respectful and empowering interventive approaches (de la Cancela, 1986; Pinderhughes, 1983; Ryan, 1985; Wilson, 1989).

ASSESSMENT

In ego-oriented treatment, assessment is biopsychosocial in nature and focuses on the client's current and past functioning and life circumstances. It considers the client's needs, problems, gender, ethnicity, race, life stage, social roles, characteristic ego functioning and coping patterns, relationships, environmental stressors, and social supports. The use of clinical or medical diagnoses may provide important information but should be augmented by a broader and individualized biopsychosocial assessment. Thus, concluding that a client has a learning disability, medical problem, emotional disorder, substance abuse problem, and the like has important implications but is not sufficient for the purposes of assessment and the planning of intervention.

The following questions are important guides to the practitioner in the assessment process (Goldstein, 1995):

1. To what extent is the client's problem a function of stresses imposed by current life roles or developmental tasks?
2. To what extent is the client's problem a function of situational stress or of a traumatic event?
3. To what extent is the client's problem a function of impairments in ego capacities or developmental difficulties or dynamics?

4. To what extent is the client's problem a function of the lack of environmental resources or supports or lack of fit between inner capacities and external circumstances?

5. What inner capacities and environmental resources does the client have that can be mobilized to improve coping?

In the case of the Shore family, Nancy, the 43-year-old mother, is facing multiple stresses that impinge on her ability to function effectively in her maternal role, cope with the demands of everyday life, and get any sense of pleasure from being alive. These stressors include the following: (a) an unemployed husband she no longer respects or can count on and who suffers from a bipolar disorder, lies compulsively, and is sometimes physically violent; (b) financial constraints stemming from having to live on her disability income; (c) a chronic back injury that flares up suddenly, causing her extreme pain and discomfort; (d) an asthmatic son who also has had a learning disability in the past and who now does not seem to get along well with peers and displays socially inappropriate and "bizarre" behavior; (e) a financially irresponsible daughter who tends to run away from her problems and who has difficulties pursuing educational and occupational goals; and (f) new responsibilities of being a landlord.

Nancy clearly is overwhelmed at having to cope with these stresses. In terms of ego functioning, she demonstrates intact reality testing and good judgment in most circumstances, seems to be reasonably intelligent and hardworking, and shows some strength in her ability to mobilize herself in the face of the many crises that occur. Furthermore, she tries to be a good wife and mother, and she seems to be the only parent who is able to keep the family functioning. At the same time, she has areas of poor ego functioning, and some of her defenses are not working well while others are maladaptive. For example, she is not able to contain her anxiety and panic, which is unrelenting and leaves her quite uncomfortable, with a sense of imminent danger. It is difficult for her to leave the house. She manifests signs of depression, as evidenced by difficulties in concentrating, forgetfulness, self-referential thinking that others are talking about her, and low self-esteem. She has some problems in impulse control, along with a tendency to engage in regressive behavior—as seen by her withdrawal into watching television, chain smoking, and overeating.

Nancy has few, if any, support systems inside or outside of the home. Her husband and children seem to be more of a drain and an embarrassment than a support, and Nancy does not seem to have any outlets, activities, friends, or other family members who are sustaining. Nancy likely feels quite alone, and in many ways she seems to be running on empty. It is no surprise that she feels depleted and anxious all the time, with little sense of hope for the future. She does not seem to feel either entitled to having or able to set limits on her husband's and children's behavior. Her hopes and plans for the future are elusive. Her occasional efforts to go back to school are met with a recurrence of back pain. Forced to give up her plans, she becomes more depressed and nonfunctional. It is likely that the lack of support for her efforts and the additional stress of school may result in the escalation of her back pain. Thus her wishes to return to school remain at the level of wishful thinking because nothing changes in her life situation that allows her to get the support she needs to work effectively toward a goal.

Although the presence of multiple stressors and the absence of meaningful supports seem crucial to understanding Nancy's problems in coping, there also is evidence that Nancy came to the marriage with a fluctuating sense of mastery/competence, a negative self-concept of herself as "grossly obese," a history of disappointing and nonnurturing interpersonal relationships, a tendency to take responsibility for others rather than take care of herself, and a lack of entitlement to getting her own needs met. There is the suggestion that her mother, despite "cherishing" Nancy, was quite unavailable emotionally and never really wanted her. Her mother saw Nancy as a doll rather than a child with needs. Nancy was encouraged to be more of an adult than a child and was forced to be independent too early. Her true capacities were not validated. This may have resulted in Nancy's inability to nurture herself, to feel entitled to feel good, and to have a secure sense of competence. She quite literally seemed to learn at an early age that she needed to feed herself. Interestingly, her dog seemed more reliable and nurturing than anyone else in her life. Although Nancy seemed to be more connected to her father, he turned out to be an unreliable gambler who also was unavailable and who ultimately abandoned Nancy. This may have set the stage for Nancy to seek a man she could rescue in the hope that he would take care of her. It may also have led to her idealization of Charley and her past denial of his limits. Some of Nancy's problems with her children may stem from her own lack of good parenting.

Thus Nancy shows a complex interplay of multiple current life stressors, an absence of meaningful supports, and long-standing problems in ego functioning and self-concept. She has certain strengths, and it is important to note that she felt a sense of mastery and control when she was in nursing.

TREATMENT OF CHOICE

Ego-oriented treatment approaches can be used with a broad range of clients whose ego functioning is disrupted by current stresses or who show severe and chronic problems in coping, including moderate to severe emotional disorders. Although ego psychology and object relations theory often have been associated with long-term psychotherapy, they also can be used in crisis intervention and short-term intervention. The use of brief treatment requires somewhat different skills than does extended treatment because assessments must be made more rapidly and interventions must be more active and more focused.

THE THERAPEUTIC PROCESS

Goals and Focus of Intervention

The goals of intervention are (a) nurturing, maintaining, enhancing, or modifying coping capacities and (b) mobilizing, improving, or changing environmental conditions or (c) improving the fit between inner capacities and external circumstances.

The focus and nature of intervention follows from the assessment, and the client should be involved in establishing the goals and treatment plan. Although they often are overlapping and not clearly differentiated, ego-oriented approaches can be grouped according to whether their goals are ego-supportive or ego-modifying (Hollis, 1972), as previously noted. Again, ego-supportive intervention aims at restoring, maintaining, or enhancing the individual's adaptive functioning as well as strengthening or building the ego where there are deficits or impairments. In contrast, ego-modifying intervention aims at changing basic personality patterns and deeply rooted concepts of the self and others.

In an ego-modifying approach, a greater understanding of the nature of maladaptive defenses and behavior is required. Also important to the change process are the client's basic attitudes toward the self and others as well as new relationship experiences that help to repair, strengthen, and expand clients' inner capacities.

The Nature and Importance of the Helping Relationship

Social workers convey certain key attitudes and values toward all clients. These include acceptance of the client's worth, a non-judgmental attitude, appreciation of the client's individuality or uniqueness, respect for the client's right to self-determination, and adherence to confidentiality. In contrast with earlier views that stressed the importance of worker neutrality and objectivity, there is currently greater emphasis on the worker's ability to be empathic, to engage in *controlled involvement* (immersion in the client's experience without losing one's own boundaries or sense of self), to convey genuineness, and to encourage mutuality.

Ego-supportive intervention emphasizes the realistic as well as the transferential aspects of the helping relationship. Consequently, the worker in an ego-supportive approach may encourage the client's accurate perception of the worker as a helping agent rather than as a transference figure. The worker provides a human and genuine relationship experience. In many instances, however, the worker uses the positive transference as a tool and becomes a benign authority or parental figure who provides a therapeutic holding environment and fosters the client's phase-appropriate needs and development. In some instances, the worker becomes a "corrective" figure to the client. Even in an ego-supportive approach, a client may develop intense reactions of an unrealistic kind to the worker. Such reactions need to be addressed in most cases. The aim is to restore the positive relationship (Garrett, 1958; Hollis, 1972; Perlman, 1957).

Another important aspect of the use of relationship in an ego-supportive approach is the worker's willingness to function outside of the client-worker relationship in a variety of roles on behalf of the client. It may be important for the worker to be an advocate or systems negotiator for the client or to meet with family members (Grinnell, Kyte, & Bostwick, 1981).

Specific Techniques

Ego-supportive intervention draws on psychological techniques that are more sustaining, directive, educative, and structured, rather than those that are more nondirective, reflective, confronting, and interpretive. Hollis (1972) described six main groups of psychological techniques that are important to ego psychological intervention: (a) sustainment; (b) exploration, description, and ventilation; (c) direct influence; (d) person–situation reflection; (e) pattern-dynamic reflection; and (f) developmental reflection. Education and structuring also are important techniques.

Environmental intervention is critical to intervention efforts within an ego-psychological perspective. For example, it may be important to mobilize resources and opportunities that will enable clients to use their inner capacities or to restructure the environment so that it nurtures or fits better with clients' needs and capacities.

The Nature of Change

In an ego-supportive approach, change results from the following: (a) the exercise of autonomous ego functioning in the service of mastering new developmental, life-transitional, crisis, or other stressful situations; (b) greater understanding of the impact of one's behavior on others; (c) learning and positive reinforcement of new behavior, skills, attitudes, problem-solving capacities, and coping strategies; (d) the use of conflict-free areas of ego functioning to neutralize conflict-laden areas; (e) the use of relationship experiences to correct for previous difficulties and deprivations; and (f) the use of the environment to provide more opportunities and conditions for the use of one's capacities.

In Nancy's case, ego-supportive treatment following many of the principles outlined above seems indicated. Such an approach might be focused on (a) helping to reduce Nancy's sense of aloneness and feelings of being overwhelmed by providing her with an accepting therapeutic relationship in which she can discuss the everyday problems with which she must cope; (b) enhancing her problem-solving capacities with respect to dealing with the stresses in her life; (c) providing validation and support for Nancy's areas of good ego functioning; (d) enhancing Nancy's sense of mastery-competence by helping her practice new behaviors with her family and in the outside world; (e) decreasing her social isolation by connecting to a women's support group or a group for wives of men with manic-depressive illness; (f) helping her to develop a plan by which she could return to school successfully; and (g) encouraging her to take better care of herself. This last could include Nancy taking some control over her compulsive smoking and eating in order to enhance her health, sense of well-being, and self-concept, and possibly connecting her to a 12-step program or other type of self-help group. An evaluation for antidepressant medication that might help her with her depression, anxiety, and panic is also indicated. The use of couple or family treatment should be considered but not used as the primary modality until Nancy feels less overwhelmed and less symptomatic.

LIMITATIONS OF THE MODEL

Changes in society and in the types of clients needing help have focused greater attention on the application of ego-oriented intervention to many client problems and populations (Goldstein, 1995). These include AIDS (Dane & Miller, 1992; Lopez & Getzel, 1984); rape and other forms of violent assault (Abarbanel & Richman, 1990; Lee & Rosenthal, 1983); child abuse (Brekke, 1990); domestic violence (Bowker, 1983); substance abusers (Chernus, 1985; Straussner, 1993); borderline and other types of character pathology (Goldstein, 1990); homelessness and chronic mental illness (Belcher & Ephross, 1989; Harris & Bergman, 1986); and the effects of childhood sexual abuse on adults (Courtois, 1988; Faria & Belohlavek, 1984).

Likewise, ego psychology addresses the special needs of clients from various cultures and from oppressed populations. However, despite its person-in-situation focus, its broad application, and its continuing evolution, it is still criticized for being narrowly focused on the individual; too open-ended, unfocused, and concentrated on the client's early childhood experiences and long-standing problems; and not sufficiently attuned to gender, sexual orientation, class, and ethnic, racial, and cultural diversity.

Many of these criticisms have not taken into account the newer theoretical developments that have enriched ego psychology and object relations theory. Nevertheless, there must be a continuing effort to apply ego psychological principles to the problems of non-White, oppressed, economically disadvantaged, or other special populations in today's practice arena. Furthermore, given the present climate of managed care and cutbacks in service delivery and the resulting emphasis on very brief and often mechanistic interventions, ego-oriented short-term models need to be developed, used, disseminated, and studied to a greater degree than has been done previously. To date, systematic research on the nature and effectiveness of practice based on ego psychological principles has been lacking, and the research findings that do exist often are not integrated by practitioners.

The complex problems that clients present require that practitioners draw on diverse conceptual frameworks and treatment strategies. This is true whether we practice in private or facility-based settings. No theory or interventive model has proven itself to be useful in all—or even most—circumstances. We cannot return to a reliance on those psychodynamic or other theories that conceptually isolate people from their interpersonal relationships or environment. Nor can we disregard clients' difficulties in coping that stem from impairments or deficits in their inner capacities and their need for more supportive and intensive individual, family, and group treatment.

RESEARCH

Over the years, ego psychology as a body of theory has been enriched by research. Greater sophistication in research methodology and design and more willingness on the part of theorists to study their own ideas have led to more systematic study of child and adult development and the ways in which people cope with stress, crisis, and various types of life demands and events. In contrast with these developments, intervention research has lagged considerably.

When social casework and its ego psychological base came under attack in the 1960s, studies of social work intervention were disheartening (Mullen, Dumpson, & Associates, 1972). Upon closer analysis, however, the goals, processes, and outcomes studied were not well selected in the research design (Perlman, 1972). In the years since these studies, outcome studies have yielded more positive results (Rubin, 1985; Thomlison, 1984). Yet the task of operationally defining psychosocial variables, interventions, and outcomes remains difficult.

It is critical that the rich knowledge base for social work practice provided by ego psychology and object relations theory and the interventive models that flow from this body of thought receive more research attention from social work practitioners. Although experimental designs are important, there is a need to use more diverse research strategies. In order to produce clinical research findings that are relevant in today's practice, it will be necessary to encourage more collaborative partnerships between clinicians and researchers and to train social work clinician–researchers.

SUMMARY

This chapter has described the nature of ego psychology and object relations theory, traced their evolution and assimilation into social work, outlined their main concepts, discussed their major assessment and treatment principles, and commented on their limitations and empirical base. Although the most important contributions of these theories have been related to their views of human development, the causes of maladaptive behavior and more severe emotional disorders, and the treatment process, they also have had major implications for service delivery and social policy. For example, the emphasis on the importance of developmental stages, role and life transitions, and stress and crisis to human functioning alerts social workers to the times and conditions during the life cycle that such help is needed. As a result, it can be particularly useful in establishing services aimed at primary prevention rather than just remediation (Roskin, 1980). Concurrently, the awareness of the significance of acute or chronic impairments to the coping capacities that some individuals bring to their life transactions points to the need for a range of remedial, rehabilitative, or sustaining services. Furthermore, because these theories stress the importance of the interpersonal, social, and environmental context in shaping development and in facilitating or obstructing successful coping, the goal of making social policies and institutions more responsive to human life and client needs becomes paramount. Thus, in keeping with the historical commitments of the profession, social workers must actively engage in work with both persons and environments at both micro- and macro-systems levels.

REFERENCES

Abarbanel, G., & Richman, G. (1990). The rape victim. In H. J. Parad & L. G. Parad (Eds.), *Crisis intervention book 2: The practitioner's sourcebook for brief therapy* (pp. 93–118). Milwaukee, WI: Family Service Association of America.

Ainsworth, M. D. S. (1973). The development of mother-infant attachment. In B. Caldwell & H. Ricciuti (Eds.), *Review of child development research* (Vol. 3, pp. 1–94). Chicago: University of Chicago Press.

Applegate, J. S., & Bonovitz, J. M. (1995). *The facilitating partnership.* New York: Aronson.

Austin, L. (1948). Trends in differential treatment in social casework. *Social Casework, 29,* 203–211.

Bandler, L. (1963). Some aspects of ego growth through sublimation. In H. J. Parad & R. Miller (Eds.), *Ego-oriented casework* (pp. 27–44). New York: Family Service Association of America.

Belcher, J. R., & Ephross, P. H. (1989). Toward an effective practice model for the homeless mentally ill. *Social Casework: Journal of Contemporary Social Work, 70,* 421–427.

Bellak, L., Hurvich, M., & Gediman, H. (1973). *Ego functions in schizophrenics, neurotics, and normals.* New York: Wiley.

Benedek, T. (1970). Parenthood during the life cycle. In J. Anthony & T. Benedek (Eds.), *Parenthood: Its psychology and psychopathology* (pp. 185–208). Boston: Little, Brown.

Benjamin, J. (1988). *The bonds of love: Psychoanalysis, feminism, and the problem of domination.* New York: Pantheon.

Blanck, G., & Blanck, R. (1974). *Ego psychology in theory and practice.* New York: Columbia University Press.

Blos, P. (1975). The second individuation process of adolescence. In A. Esman (Ed.), *The psychology of adolescence: Essential readings* (pp. 156–177). New York: International Universities Press.

Bowker, L. H. (1983). Marital rape: A distinct syndrome. *Social Casework: The Journal of Contemporary Social Work, 64,* 347–352.

Bowlby, J. (1958). The nature of the child's tie to the mother. *International Journal of Psychoanalysis, 39,* 350–373.

Brekke, J. (1990). Crisis intervention with victims and perpetrators of spouse abuse. In H. J. Parad & L. G. Parad (Eds.), *Crisis intervention book 2: The practitioner's sourcebook for brief therapy* (pp. 161–178). Milwaukee, WI: Family Service Association of America.

Briar, S., & Miller, H. (1971). *Problems and issues in social casework.* New York: Columbia University Press.

Burch, B. (1993). Heterosexuality, bisexuality, and lesbianism: Rethinking psychoanalytic views of women's sexual object choice. *Psychoanalytic Review, 80,* 83–98.

Butler, R. N. (1963). The life review: An interpretation of reminiscence in the aged. *Psychiatry, 26,* 65–76.

Chernus, L. A. (1985). Clinical issues in alcoholism treatment. *Social Casework: The Journal of Contemporary Social Work, 66,* 67–75.

Chodorow, N. (1978). *The reproduction of mothering.* Berkeley: University of California Press.

Cockerill, E., & Colleagues. (1953). *A conceptual framework of social casework.* Pittsburgh, PA: University of Pittsburgh Press.

Colarusso, C., & Nemiroff, R. A. (1981). *Adult development.* New York: Plenum.

Courtois, C. A. (1988). *Healing the incest wound: Adult survivors in therapy.* New York: W. W. Norton.

Dane, B. O., & Miller, S. O. (1992). *AIDS: Intervening with hidden grievers.* Westport, CT: Auburn House.

de la Cancela, V. (1986). A critical analysis of Puerto Rican machismo: Implications for clinical practice. *Psychotherapy, 23,* 291–296.

Erikson, E. (1950). *Childhood and society.* New York: Norton.

Erikson, E. (1959). Identity and the life cycle. *Psychological Issues, 1,* 50–100.

Escalona, S. K. (1968). *The roots of individuality: Normal patterns of development in infancy.* Chicago: Aldine.

Fairbairn, W. R. D. (1952). *Psychoanalytic studies of the personality.* London: Routledge & Kegan Paul.

Faria, G., & Belohlavek, N. (1984). Treating female adult survivors of childhood incest. *Social Casework: The Journal of Contemporary Social Work, 65,* 465–471.

Freud, A. (1936). *The ego and the mechanisms of defense.* New York: International Universities Press.

Freud, S. (1961). The ego and the id. In J. Strachey (Ed. and Trans.), *The standard edition of the complete psychological works of Sigmund Freud* (Vol. 19, pp. 366). London: Hogarth. (Original work published 1923)

Garrett, A. (1958). Modern casework: The contributions of ego psychology. In H. J. Parad (Ed.), *Ego psychology and dynamic casework* (pp. 38–52). New York: Family Service Association of America.

Germain, C. B., & Gitterman, A. (1980). *The life model of social work practice.* New York: Columbia University Press.

Gilligan, C. (1982). *In a different voice: Psychological theory and women's development.* Cambridge: Harvard University Press.

Golan, N. (1978). *Treatment in crisis situations.* New York: The Free Press.

Goldstein, E. G. (1995). *Ego psychology and social work practice* (2nd ed.). New York: The Free Press.

Goldstein, E. G. (1990). *Borderline disorders: Clinical models and techniques.* New York: Guilford.

Gould, R. L. (1978). *Transformations: Growth and change in adult life.* New York: Simon & Schuster.

Grinnell, R. M., Kyte, N. S., & Bostwick, G. J. (1981). Environmental modification. In A. N. Maluccio (Ed.), *Promoting competence in clients: A new/old approach to social work practice* (pp. 152–184). New York: The Free Press.

Guntrip, H. (1969). *Schizoid phenomena, object relations, and the self.* New York: International Universities Press.

Guntrip, H. (1973). *Psychoanalytic theory, therapy, and the self.* New York: Basic Books/Harper Torchbooks.

Hamilton, G. (1940). *Theory and practice of social casework.* New York: Columbia University Press.

Hamilton, G. (1958). A theory of personality: Freud's contribution to social casework. In H. J. Parad (Ed.), *Ego psychology and dynamic casework* (pp. 11–37). New York: Family Service Association of America.

Harris, M., & Bergman, H. C. (1986). Case management with the chronically mentally ill: A clinical perspective. *American Journal of Orthopsychiatry, 56,* 296–302.

Hartmann, H. (1939). *Ego psychology and the problem of adaptation.* New York: International Universities Press.

Hendrick, I. (1942). Instinct and the ego during infancy. *Psychoanalytic Quarterly, II,* 33–58.

Hollis, F. (1949). The techniques of casework. *Journal of Social Casework, 30,* 235–244.

Hollis, F. (1964). *Casework: A psychosocial therapy.* New York: Random House.

Hollis, F. (1972). *Casework: A psychosocial therapy* (2nd ed.). New York: Random House.

Jacobson, E. (1964). *The self and the object world.* New York International Universities Press.

Jordan, J. V., Kaplan, A. G., Miller, J. B., Stiver, I. P., & Surrey, J. L. (1991). *Women's growth in connection.* New York: Guilford.

Kernberg, O. F. (1984). *Severe personality disorders.* New Haven: Yale University Press.

Klein, M. (1948). *Contributions to psychoanalysis: 1921–1945.* London: Hogarth.

Laughlin, H. P. (1979). *The ego and its defenses* (2nd ed.). New York: Jason Aronson.

Lee, J. A. B., & Rosenthal, S. J. (1983). Working with victims of violent assault. *Social Casework: The Journal of Contemporary Social Work, 64,* 593–601.

Levinson, D. J. (1978). *The seasons of a man's life.* New York: Knopf.

Lopez, D., & Getzel, G. S. (1984). Helping gay AIDS patients in crisis. *Social Casework: The Journal of Contemporary Social Work, 65,* 387–394.

Mackey, R. A., Urek, M. B., & Charkoudian, S. (1987). The relationship of theory to clinical practice. *Clinical Social Work Journal, 15,* 368–83.

Mahler, M. S. (1968). *On human symbiosis and the vicissitudes of individuation.* New York: International Universities Press.

Mahler, M. S., Pine, F., & Bergman, A. (1975). *The psychological birth of the human infant.* New York: Basic Books.

Mullen, E. J., Dumpson, J. R., & Associates (Eds.). (1972). *Evaluation of social intervention.* San Francisco: Jossey-Bass.

Murphy, L. B. & Moriarity, A. E. (1976). *Vulnerability, coping and growth from infancy to adolescence.* New Haven, CT: Yale University Press.

Neugarten, B. L. (1968). Adult personality: Toward a psychology of the life cycle. In W. E. Vinacke (Ed.), *Readings in general psychology* (pp. 332–343). New York: American Book.

Neugarten, B. L., & Associates (Eds.). (1964). *Personality in middle and late life.* New York: Atherton.

Northen, H. (1988). *Social work in groups.* New York: Columbia University Press.

Perlman, H. H. (1957). *Social casework: A problem-solving process*. Chicago: University of Chicago Press.

Perlman, H. H. (1972). Once more with feeling. In E. J. Mullen, J. R. Dumpson, & Associates (Eds.), *Evaluation of social intervention* (pp. 191–209). San Francisco: Jossey-Bass.

Pinderhughes, E. B. (1983). Empowerment for our clients and for ourselves. *Social Casework: The Journal of Contemporary Social Work, 64*, 331–338.

Reiter, L. (1989). Sexual orientation, sexual identity, and the question of choice. *Clinical Social Work Journal, 17*, 138–150.

Roskin, M. (1980). Integration of primary prevention in social work. *Social Work, 25*, 192–197.

Rubin, A. (1985). Practice effectiveness: More grounds for optimism. *Social Work, 30*, 469–476.

Ryan, A. S. (1985). Cultural factors in casework with Chinese Americans. *Social Casework: The Journal of Contemporary Social Work, 66*, 333–340.

Seinfeld, J. (1990). *The bad object*. Northvale, NJ: Jason Aronson.

Seinfeld, J. (1991). *The empty core*. Northvale, NJ: Jason Aronson.

Seinfeld, J. (1993). *Interpreting and holding*. Northvale, NJ: Jason Aronson.

Seinfeld, J. (1996). *Containing rage, terror, and despair*. Northvale, NJ: Jason Aronson.

Slipp, S. (Ed.). (1988). *The technique and practice of object relations family therapy*. Northvale, NJ: Jason Aronson.

Spaulding, E. C. (1993). The inner world of objects and lesbian development. *Journal of Analytic Social Work, 1*, 5–31.

Spitz, R. (1945). Hospitalism: An inquiry into the genesis of psychiatric conditions in early childhood. *Psychoanalytic Study of the Child, 2*, 313–342.

Spitz, R. (1965). *The first year of life: A psychoanalytic study of normal and deviant development of object relations*. New York: International Universities Press.

Stamm. I. (1959). Ego psychology in the emerging theoretical base of social work. In A. J. Kahn (Ed.), *Issues in American social work* (pp. 80–109). New York: Columbia University Press.

Straussner, S. L. A. (1993). Assessment and treatment of clients with alcohol and other drug abuse problems: An overview. In S. L. A. Straussner (Ed.), *Clinical work with substance-abusing clients* (pp. 3–32). New York: Guilford.

Thomlison, R. J. (1984). Something works: Evidence from practice effectiveness studies. *Social Work, 29*, 51–56.

Towle, C. (1949). Helping the client to use his capacities and resources. *Proceedings of the National Conference of Social Work, 1948* (pp. 259–279). New York: Columbia University Press.

Vaillant, G. E. (1977). *Adaptation in life*. Boston: Little, Brown.

Weille, K. L. H. (1993). Reworking developmental theory: The case of lesbian identity formation. *Clinical Social Work Journal, 21*, 151–160.

White, R. F. (1959). Motivation reconsidered: The concept of competence. *Psychological Review, 66*, 297–33.

White, R. F. (1963). Ego and reality in psychoanalytic theory. *Psychological Issues* (Vol. 2). New York: International Universities Press.

Wilson, M. N. (1989). Child development in the context of the Black extended family. *American Psychologist, 44*, 380–385.

Winnicott, D. W. (1965). *Maturational processes and the facilitating environment*. New York: International Universities Press.

3

Kohut's Self Psychology

Adrienne Wolmark, Ph.D., and
Martha Sweezy, Ph.D.

INTRODUCTION

The domain of psychoanalytic thinking has evolved significantly since Freud advanced drive theory as a model for understanding psychic life. Throughout the last several decades, many other frameworks for practice were introduced that built on and diverged from Freud's thinking. Heinz Kohut, a classically trained analyst who for many years subscribed to drive theory, left the fold by articulating important changes in classical metapsychology and by creating a new branch of psychoanalytic practice. As has happened with Freud's propositions, there have been critiques and elaborations of Kohut's original work. The dilemma we faced in writing this chapter was whether to present Kohut's work or to describe the current incarnation of self psychology. We decided to focus on Kohut's ideas as originally presented because, in our experience, the origins of a theory must be grasped in order to understand its evolution.

THE CONCEPT OF THE PERSON AND THE HUMAN EXPERIENCE

Unlike the classical psychoanalytic focus on a person's observed experience, Kohut's concept of self focuses on the client's subjective experience, on "the uniquely personal meanings embedded in an individual's conscious mental life" (Wolfe, 1989, p. 546). When Kohut began to focus on personal meanings, he did not deny the existence of the unconscious, but

45

he did believe that psychoanalysis should not center itself around interpreting the unconscious to the patient. Kohut was more interested in "that
which is knowable 'directly,' through the client's introspection" (Wolfe,
1989, p. 547). In place of the unconscious, Kohut focused on the patient's
conscious experience of self and the patient's experience of others as a dimension of self. This is what he called staying *experience-near* (Kohut, 1984),
or staying with the patient's attribution of meaning to experience. In staying experience-near, the clinician is better able to avoid the culturally laden
danger of fitting the patient to the theory rather than vice versa.

HISTORY

As a classical analyst, Kohut subscribed to Freud's idea that people normally move from self-love to object love. It is important to know that in
psychoanalytic theory other people are referred to as *objects*. Freud viewed
normal narcissistic development as maturation through an increasing investment of libido in the object, whereas pathological narcissism was a
failure to mature through this investment of libido in the object. Because
Freud posited a limited supply of libido, "too much absorption in the self
is . . . at the expense of interest in the other, and . . . too much absorption
in the other is at the expense of the interest of the self" (Eagle & Wolitzky,
1992, p. 137). Kohut (1971) came to distrust this perspective on narcissistic
development and finally decided that treatment based on the idea often
became moralistic and denigrated patients. To avoid placing a moral onus
on self-love, Kohut proposed a separate line of development for narcissism
that can evolve in either a healthy or pathological direction. *Healthy narcissism* involves using one's talents and skills to realize one's goals as well as
developing values and ideals. *Pathological narcissism* involves grandiosity
and exhibitionism and a tendency toward disintegration anxiety as well as
a general failure to achieve one's goals (Eagle & Wolitzky, 1992).

Kohut's change of heart resulted from his clinical experience with
"Miss F" (Kohut, 1968). He found that this patient and others with severe narcissistic disorders did not respond well to classical interpretations.
These patients seemed to need to idealize him and were hungry for admiration. When their needs were interpreted as a regression or retreat from
oedipal conflicts (i.e., conflicts involving sexuality and aggression), their
symptoms were exacerbated. This was the dilemma that catalyzed Kohut's
shift to the viewpoint of the patient. In 1977, Kohut departed from classical
theory altogether, proposing the self as the centerpiece of psychoanalytic
study. Thus, it was through empathic immersion in his patients' subjective
experience that Kohut undertook the revision of psychoanalytic theory and
technique.

KEY THEORETICAL CONSTRUCTS

Deficit Theory

Kohut's theory of development is called a *deficit* theory. Classical psychoanalytic theory is a *conflict* theory. The latter refers to intrapsychic conflict over sexual and aggressive drives, with a particular focus in classical theory on the Oedipal period. In contrast, Kohut's self psychology is a deficit theory because Kohut believed that psychopathology resulted from the absence of certain crucial parental provisions. According to Kohut, those provisions fulfill universal, innate needs. When they are absent, a deficit is created in the child, and development is arrested.

Selfobject Concept

In order to capture his thinking on parental functions and the unique nature of the relationship between a child and a primary caretaker, Kohut (Kohut & Wolf, 1978) coined the term *selfobject.* The selfobject is an object that is experienced as part of the self. To a child, the crucial "archaic" (Kohut, 1984) selfobject(s) is(are) primary caretaker(s) whom the child expects to perform as an extension of the self, fulfilling the needs of the self. According to Kohut,

> [The] nascent self "expects" . . . an empathic environment to be in tune with his psychological need-wishes with the same unquestioning certitude as the respiratory apparatus of the newborn infant may be said to "expect" oxygen to be contained in the surrounding atmosphere. (p. 85)

Kohut (1984) called this the *self–selfobject relationship*. The self–selfobject relationship does not refer to a relationship between two people; rather, it is an intrapsychic phenomenon. It is the self's subjective experience of the object as a part of the self.

Kohut (1971) initially conceived of the selfobject's functions as deriving from two "poles" of human experience: the pole of ambition and the pole of ideals. In optimum development the selfobjects fulfill their functions. The selfobject function deriving from the pole of ambition is *mirroring* (see "Mirroring," below) in which the self's ambitions are accepted and supported. The selfobject function deriving from the pole of ideals is to be idealized (see "Idealization," below), a relationship that provides safety, calmness, and strength. Between the poles of ambition and ideals Kohut proposed a connecting area, or *tension arc*, of talents and skills. Kohut (1984) later elevated this intermediate area to the status of a third pole.

In this third pole, the alter ego, or *twin selfobject*, supports development of the self's talents and skills. These three poles of human experience with their selfobject needs constitute Kohut's human motivational system. As the selfobject accepts the self's needs and also fails to meet those needs in small, nontraumatic ways, the child's grandiosity is gradually transformed into more realistic ambitions, ideals, and abilities.

It is unlikely that the needs for mirroring, idealizing, and twinship describe the full range of possible human selfobject needs. In this, Kohut fails to follow his own admonition to stay experience-near. A theory cannot preordain needs and continue to qualify as experience-near. His theory of self development was an abstraction that did not synchronize with his original goal of "drawing out uniquely personal meanings embedded in an individual's conscious mental life" (Wolfe, 1989, p. 546). This is not to deny the validity and usefulness of Kohut's clinical observations but is to suggest that confining the issue of selfobject needs to those "implicated in the regulation of self-esteem, namely . . . idealization and subject-centered grandiosity" (Gedo, 1989, pp. 418–419) is unduly narrow and limits the clinician's ability to remain experience-near with the patient. (For an expansion on the concept of motivational systems see Lichtenberg, Lachmann, & Fosshage, 1992.)

Pathogenesis and the Nature of Symptoms

The pathogenesis of psychiatric disorders, as understood by self psychology, is disturbances in the relationship of the child and his or her selfobject(s). When the primary caretaker(s) of the child cannot, for a variety of possible reasons, provide the needed selfobject functions, then the self is left in a vulnerable state, stunted in the capacity to achieve empathy for self and others and prone to feelings of crumbling or inner deadness referred to as *fragmentation* by Kohut (1984). The self may then respond to fragmentation feelings with such symptoms as hypochondria, compulsive sexuality, sexual perversions (Lee & Martin, 1991), alcoholism, or drug addiction (Levin, 1991). Kohut (1984) viewed these and other symptoms as defensive, as an attempt to protect and shore up the endangered self. Ornstein (1992) stated that symptomatic behavior, although a source of suffering for the patient and those in his or her environment, is a defense that constitutes "the best possible solution to otherwise disorganizing and painful affects" (p. 19).

Selfobject Transferences

Kohut's theory of treatment is based on the analyst's discerning use of empathy and the patient's establishing a selfobject transference that derives from the mobilization of unfulfilled selfobject needs. There are three selfobject transferences—mirror, twinship, and idealizing—that correspond to the three selfobject needs. In addition, Kohut speaks of a *merger transference*, which is a primitive aspect of all three selfobject transferences rather than a separate selfobject transference in its own right.

Note that *transference* has an altered meaning in self psychology. Freud defined *transference* as a projection of prior conflictual experience with significant objects onto the blank screen of the analyst. In the transference, the patient is viewed by Freud as reexperiencing significant object relationships or as resisting remembering those experiences through acting them out. In contrast, transference in self psychology is a transfer of selfobject needs: "What is 'transferred' is an expectation for the kind of selfobject responsiveness that the patient had been missing in the course of his development" (Ornstein, 1992, p. 19).

The role of the therapist is to become a selfobject for the patient. The function of the selfobject in the pole of ambition is to mirror the self's ambitions. *Mirroring*, in Kohut's words, means to "respond to and confirm the child's innate sense of vigor, greatness and perfection" (Kohut & Wolf, 1978, p. 414). The function of the selfobject in the pole of ideals is to be idealized, or, again in Kohut's words, to be someone "to whom the child can look up and with whom he can merge as an image of calmness, infallibility and omnipotence" (p. 414). The third pole, deriving from the tension arc of talents and skills, Kohut dubbed *twinship* or *alter ego*. Wolfe (1989) explained that the tension-arc was Kohut's

> little-appreciated metaphor ... [for the] incompatibility between an individual's experience of being perfect (the grandiose self) and an experience of being less than perfect, relative to others (the idealized parent-imago). The action of developing talents and skills helps fill in this gap. (p. 550)

In the pole of twinship the function of the selfobject is to be experienced as essentially like the self.

Mirroring

Kohut considered the mirror transference to be "a therapeutic reinstatement of that normal phase of development of the grandiose self in which the gleam in the mother's eye ... mirrors the child's exhibitionistic display ... [and] confirm[s] the child's self-esteem" (1971, p. 116). Kohut thus spoke of mirroring in terms of the proper confirming and admiring response of a parent to a child, but a therapist is not a parent and the appropriate clinical model of mirroring has been a subject of concern for self psychologists following Kohut.

Kohut (1978) writes of two kinds of mirroring responses. The first response is to understand and acknowledge the need of the patient to have her or his grandiosity affirmed. The second type of mirroring response involves praising the patient. Lee and Martin (1991) pointed out that the latter idea, *active mirroring* (p. 134) is controversial and warn that it should be used as a last resort. They state that it is a major concern among therapists "to avoid inflating the grandiose self" (p. 134). They believe that the grandiose state of the self is promoted by some specific behaviors and circumstances, including "mirroring without achievement ... achievement without appropriate effort, and ... excessive mirroring even with appropriate success" (p. 134). In other words, it is vital for therapists to praise only real achievement, no matter how small, and to keep that praise to scale. They suggest that the first phase of mirroring should be to focus on acknowledging the patient's felt needs. If this fails to reduce symptoms, therapists may then (tentatively) introduce active mirroring.

We think that mirroring can be a difficult job with some patients. A population we believe is vulnerable to either overactive intervention in the form of praise or underactive intervention in the form of unconditional acceptance is trauma survivors. We find that trauma survivors often believe they are too powerful (e.g., sexually irresistible or dangerous in some other fashion) and/or have been responsible for their own victimization. Acting-out behaviors based on this belief require empathic limit-setting rather than praise or acceptance. Gedo (1989) warned, "Self psychology seems to expect that infantile attitudes of entitlement have to be validated by the analyst, that the analysand's persisting rage should be understood as the only appropriate response to the frustration of 'selfobject needs'" (p. 421).

Dublin (1992) provides an example of appropriately empathic mirroring with a demanding, out-of-control trauma survivor: "I repeatedly verbalized her desperation and fear. ... I was careful to emphasize that she was not 'bad' for wanting so much (from me). ... what she was crying out for was not unreasonable, even if it was unrealistic" (p. 291). Nevertheless, both therapist and patient needed to understand, "I couldn't provide the kind of nurturing she sought" (p. 291). Dublin was able to empathize with her patient and yet not try to re-parent her, a critical distinction that protects the patient from being infantilized and the therapist from feeling too burdened and abandoning the patient.

Idealization

The idealizing transference, like the mirror transference, develops spontaneously and is in no way created by therapists. In the *idealizing transference*, therapists finds themselves being looked up to and responded to by patients as a source of "perfection," strength, and soothing. This idealization should simply be accepted rather than actively encouraged or interpreted (discouraged). A true idealizing transference is generally not verbalized by patients but is evident in the sense of well-being, calmness, and strength they derive from the therapeutic relationship.

Twinship or Alter Ego

The twinship transference was the last added and conceptually the least developed of Kohut's selfobject transferences. The *twinship selfobject* experience is a companionable experience of being and doing together between the child and the selfobject. In this selfobject experience, the child finds the security of sameness. For example, for the older child, there may be the experience of being "a cook next to a cook or a craftsman next to a craftsman" (Kohut, 1984, p. 200). For the younger child, or even the baby, there is the experience of simply being together and being "a human among humans" (p. 200).

Adolescent friendship is an example of twinship selfobject experiences and their potential curative effect. A mature version of the twinship selfobject experience is evident in mentor and apprenticeship relationships as well as in "inherited" professions, as when a daughter or son chooses the same work as a parent or other influential relative. In a twinship transference, the patient is not seeking an approving and accepting mirroring selfobject but rather is seeking the presence of someone "sufficiently like her to understand her and to be understood by her" (Kohut, 1984, p. 196).

Merger: An Aspect of All Selfobject Transferences

A *merger transference*, referred to often by Kohut (1984), does not represent another separate selfobject transference. Kohut and Wolf (1978) described people with "merger-hungry personalities" as people who

> need selfobjects in lieu of self-structure . . . . The fluidity of boundaries between them and others interferes with their ability to discriminate their own thoughts, wishes and intentions from those of the selfobject. . . . [Experiencing] the other as their own self, they feel intolerant of his independence: they are very sensitive to separations . . . [and] demand—indeed they expect without question—the selfobject's continuous presence. (p. 422)

A merger transference is a mode of relating in which the behaviors described above dominate the clinical picture.

Selfobject Failure

According to Kohut (1984), psychopathology derives from a history of traumatic selfobject failure in which a child's selfobject needs have not been met. There are numerous possible scenarios for selfobject failure. For example, it may have been the consequence of a reverse selfobject relationship (Lee & Martin, 1991) in which the child served to fulfill functions required by a parent with a defective self. Or it may have been the consequence of outright neglect. The lives of the Shore family illustrate these kinds of selfobject failures (discussed under "Assessment" below).

Kohut (1984) considered selfobject failure in the transference to be inevitable and to be part of the process of cure. The difference between past selfobject failures and the selfobject failures that occur in the context of therapy is that the latter should take place in a milieu of adequate selfobject functioning. Selfobject failures in the therapy, therefore, should be "optimally frustrating" (1984) rather than traumatic.

The selfobject failure in the context of the therapy will be followed by an increase in symptoms and needs to be acknowledged and understood in terms of what has just occurred in the therapeutic relationship. According to Kohut (1984), the selfobject failure also eventually needs to be explained to the patient in terms of what occurred in the archaic selfobject relationships of the patient's past. In this process of understanding and explanation, the self-selfobject relationship is repaired, the empathic bond is reinstated, and what Kohut (1984) termed *transmuting internalization* takes place.

Transmuting Internalization

A precondition for transmuting internalization is the milieu of adequate selfobject functioning. In healthy development, multiple nontraumatic selfobject failures within a milieu of adequate selfobjects cause the replacement of the selfobject and its functions with the self and its functions (Kohut & Wolf, 1978, p. 416). The process of achieving transmuting internalization in the context of therapy will include both the inevitable unplanned repetition of selfobject failure and also optimal frustration.

Optimal Frustration

In 1984, Kohut stated that the therapist must not fulfill the patient's need, which is mobilized in the selfobject transference. Rather, the therapist must communicate an understanding of that need. This experience will be optimally frustrating "because, through the analyst's more or less accurate understanding an empathic bond is established ... that substitutes for the de facto fulfillment of the patient's need" (p. 103). According to Kohut, optimal frustration creates structure.

Although agreeing with Kohut regarding transmuting internalization as the action that gives rise to structure, Bacal (1985) took issue with the notion of frustration as the manner in which this structure formation takes place. He believed that this idea is based on drive theory's emphasis on the frustration of impulses and that optimal responsiveness is a more useful way of explaining structure formation and is more consonant with other aspects of self psychology. According to Bacal, the role of the therapist is to understand and communicate this understanding to the patient as effectively as possible. It is the experience of being understood that builds structure and repairs defect.

Structure

Kohut (1984) refers to three kinds of structure—*primary, compensatory, and defensive*. Archaic selfobjects (such as primary caretakers) are precursors of psychic structure; the child does not yet have the ability to perform care-taking functions for the self, such as self-soothing and maintenance of self-esteem. If psychic structure has not been built, then the adult will continue to use selfobjects as archaic selfobjects, in lieu of self structure and mature selfobject relating. According to Shane and Shane (1988), "The main function of ... structure building is to permit a developmental progression from primitive to more mature selfobject need and need fulfillment" (p. 407).

Primary structure is created by the process of transmuting internalization in an adequate selfobject milieu. Compensatory structure is created—in the child or the adult—through the process of transmuting internalization in self-selfobject relationships with other archaic selfobjects (including the therapist) when the primary archaic selfobject(s) have not been adequate. Defensive structure refers to the patient's symptomatic behavior, which is seen as a method of coping with deficits in the self.

Health

Kohut (1984) viewed a healthy person as one who is in possession of a cohesive self with mature selfobject relationships and an ability to empathize with self and others. Kohut did not believe that one outgrows the need for self-selfobject relationships. In his view of human development, separation is neither a desirable goal nor a theoretical endpoint.

ASSESSMENT

Nancy

Nancy appears to be a product of parental neglect by both her mother and her father. She paints her mother as rejecting and abandoning when she was a child and sexually competitive when she was a teenager. Nancy was expected to admire her mother, not vice versa. She describes her father as preoccupied and largely unavailable until he abruptly abandoned her when she was 11 years old. Although he returned briefly, he finally rejected and abandoned her completely. It is clear, then, that Nancy had poor mirroring and little opportunity to develop an idealizing relationship with either one of her parents. Instead, it seems likely that she became the caretaker early on, serving a reverse selfobject function with her mother (being mother's audience) and trying to nurture a fantasy idealization of her father, which he abruptly cut off.

But what of the doting Gram and Aunt Flo? Although Gram and Aunt Flo may appear to have been a source of mirroring for Nancy as a child, there are clues that indicate another reverse selfobject relationship. Nancy reports that her place in the lives of these women was secured by never being childish. In order to have caretakers, she met their need for a "perfect" little girl who could accompany them to adult events and who would please them by eating all the food they served her. Vis-à-vis pathological overeating, Kohut (1977) said,

> The child needs empathically modulated food-giving, not food ....
> If this need remains unfulfilled (to a traumatic degree) then the ...
> joyful experience of being a whole, appropriately responded to self
> ... disintegrates and the child retreats ... to depressive eating. (p. 81)

We find this insight apt for Nancy, who, as we see, became a depressive overeater.

Nancy also reports that her "golden age" was over after her father's departure. This seems curious at first because, except for her mother's greater unavailability, Nancy reports that little had changed. She continued to spend her time with Gram and Aunt Flo. One may wonder, however, if Nancy's relationship with Gram was able to grow as Nancy grew. When Nancy was no longer the cute little girl who could be paraded about for her immaculate manners and who could eat anything and stay thin, she may have been less gratifying to Gram. If a child is to function as a *narcissistic extension*—a reverse selfobject—then an overweight depressed teenager is not equivalent to a perfect little girl. This may account for the thoroughness of Nancy's sense of loss as she began to grow up. When she could no longer serve to delight her grandmother and aunt, she may have felt as emotionally abandoned by them as she was literally abandoned by her parents.

Nursing was in no way a deviation from this childhood job of meeting the needs of others, and Nancy's history of not having her own needs met may have made nursing intolerable. Did Nancy actually have a severe back injury, or did the burden of being a caretaker finally "break her back"? It is unclear whether her illness might, at least in some part, be psychosomatic. Kohut would view psychosomatic symptoms as a form of self-fragmentation, or loss of self-cohesion, in response to a repetition of selfobject failure. The fact that Nancy has had two back operations should not deter the clinician from pondering whether her back pain is psychosomatic. Munchhausen syndrome, in which unnecessary medical intervention is provoked, is more prevalent among people with medical training.

Regardless of the origins of her illness, through it Nancy is likely to have experienced a repetition of selfobject failure and loss. She has lost what she apparently valued most: her friends and colleagues, her income, and her sense of competency and control (or her mature selfobjects). If she did feel as a child that she lost the love of her mother and father, Gram, and Aunt Flo (her archaic selfobjects) because she was not serving their needs, this experience would be repeated when she could no longer serve as a nurse. Self psychology emphasizes first understanding how these losses feel to the patient, and later explaining the way in which the trauma of past losses is being repeated. If the illness is not psychosomatic, the experience of empathy in therapy should help Nancy to be more self-accepting and less self-destructive. As a result, she would to take steps to improve her health as much as she can (e.g., lose weight, stop smoking) and develop realistic goals for her future. If, on the other hand, the illness is psychosomatic, the experience of empathy in the therapy may enable Nancy to become more accepting of her real needs, including the need not to return to nursing. This, in turn, could free Nancy to begin to recover (lose weight, stop smoking) and to develop realistic goals for her future.

Ideally, marriage is an opportunity in adult life to enhance self-esteem through a mature selfobject relationship. In this regard, Nancy's marriage is a lost opportunity. As Nancy and Charley are both acutely aware, Charley's functioning as both a partner and a parent is impaired, enormously increasing Nancy's feelings of being burdened and abandoned—again a repetition of the issues of her childhood. Ideally, parenthood is an opportunity to feel enhanced self-esteem as the provider of self-regulatory functions for a dependent child. However, it is also a time in which issues deriving from one's own experience of childhood will come to the fore. For Nancy, having one non-biological child who effortlessly fulfills all the lost promise of her own childhood, and another biological child who requires enormous attention and medical care and whose social functioning remains seriously impaired, must be an ambivalent experience at best. Parenthood, then, is unlikely to have served an enhancing mature selfobject function for Nancy.

One further observation about Nancy is that she probably suffers from guilt. We believe she is likely to experience guilt when she perceives herself as failing others (not serving their needs); when she feels competitive, jealous, or envious as it is likely she has felt in her relationship with Rena (who replaced her as Gram's adored little girl); or when she feels overburdened and angry, as she feels with Charley and as she likely has felt with Michael. Nancy's career of obsessive worrying at home and her inability to move forward in her life may reflect such guilt. We believe it would be important for the clinician to be aware of Nancy's potential for guilt and to explore it with her. We find the Shore family a clear example of the need for self psychology to encompass a comprehensive theory of guilt (see discussion under "Limitations of the Model").

Charley

Charley's background, rife with abuse and economic hardship, did not provide him with a selfobject milieu sufficient for the formation of a cohesive self. Charley remembers "never being the center of attention." It seems likely that Charley did not receive adequate mirroring and that he never found either his angry father or his overburdened mother to be ideal sources of strength and calm. His feelings of alienation from other children while growing up—whether generated by an identification with his alienated parents or by his grandiosity—indicate a dearth of opportunities for twinship experiences. Moreover, it seems that Charley may have served reverse selfobject functions as a child. In speaking of his history, Charley mentioned a vivid and pleasant memory of helping his tired mother. We wonder about the extent to which he was called on regularly to be a support to his parents.

Charley's "outlandish inventions" and "get-rich-quick schemes" reflect his grandiosity. Kohut would say that Charley's grandiosity, clearly a major contributor to his interpersonal problems at work and at home, is pathological at this point because it was never modified by appropriate (according to Kohut, usually maternal) mirroring; therefore his grandiosity did not mature into realistic ambitions. In contrast, we believe that Charley's grandiosity is reactive in origin and defensive in nature (see "Limitations of the Model" for a discussion of this point). Lack of sufficient maternal availability and mirroring may have made Charley more vulnerable to his father's abuse, but we believe Charley's grandiosity is the product of his feeling chronically humiliated and shamed by his father (and perhaps by teachers and peers in school) as a child. Under the cloak of his grandiosity,

Charley has tried—unsuccessfully—to protect himself from further humiliation and shame.

Charley's violence with Rena illustrates both this narcissistic vulnerability and the archaic nature of his selfobject relationship with Nancy, whom he compares to his mother. When Rena threatens to hit Nancy, Charley responds as if he is the one being threatened, and he attacks Rena. Charley may be a protective "son" to Nancy, but in his role as a husband he clearly experiences himself as a failure—he cannot earn the money to buy his family a house or even support them. Meanwhile, Nancy, who feels betrayed by his grandiosity, humiliates him with public criticism. Although Charley views his compulsive lying to Nancy as telling her "what she wants to hear" in order to avoid upsetting her, it is likely that he lies to protect himself from feeling humiliated in the face of Nancy's disappointment. As a parent, Charley is equally inadequate. Far from being a mirroring or an idealizable figure, he has competed with Michael for Nancy's attention and has been envious of Rena's mechanical ability and probably also of her small but stellar career on the stage.

Apropos of stage careers, we may wonder what meaning Charley ascribes to his career as an amateur comedian. We can surmise that in performing before an audience, Charley seeks mirroring. But does he experience the attention he receives as positive (and therefore as mirroring), or is the experience a repetition of being humiliated in an attempt to get mirroring? The therapist should explore this with Charley, because it is possible that in his desire to be mirrored he traps himself into a repetition of humiliation that reinforces his grandiosity.

Charley's lack of self-cohesion is also reflected in his chronic unemployment. We are told that he was fired in two instances for poor performance (daydreaming and slowness coupled with verbosity). We are not told what caused him to leave numerous other jobs. But Charley's final episode, in which he became psychotic after hitting the chef who had been humiliating him, may have been the outcome of a long history of interpersonal humiliations at work. Kohut (1978) stated that in these kinds of threatening situations "the narcissistically vulnerable individual responds to actual (or anticipated) narcissistic injury either with shamefaced withdrawal (flight) or with narcissistic rage (fight)" (p. 637). In his work career, Charley has evidently both fled and fought.

Charley's failure in work may have been due to overly ambitious work goals—his grandiosity blinding him to realistic expectations—or he may simply have been too prone to narcissistic injury from predictable failure, causing him to collapse in the face of criticism rather than learn from his mistakes. In any case, the experience of being repeatedly criticized and humiliated and repeatedly forced to leave jobs probably occurred in relation to more powerful men—his bosses. These men may have been paternal figures whom Charley longed to experience as idealized sources of strength.

Being rejected by these men, then, would constitute a traumatic repetition selfobject failure similar to the trauma of his earlier relationship with his father. In contrast to this history of work failure, Charley did apparently respond well to the all-male structure of the Air Force. There his work assignments may have been more accurately matched with his capabilities, and his grandiose ambitions may have been held in check by the blunt nature of military hierarchy. Within this setting, Charley may have been able to perform adequately and receive due recognition from a paternal figure. In any case, it would be good to know what Charley believes worked for him in the Air Force because that formula might be worth trying to repeat.

If the keynote of Charley's life has been humiliation and incompetence, insult was certainly added to injury when Charley was diagnosed with bipolar disorder. Charley's low self-esteem made it extremely hard for him to accept this diagnosis without plunging into despair. The relationship with the therapist could be critical in helping Charley to feel more accepting of himself. The therapist should be sure that Charley is receiving good medical care from a psychopharmacologist and should educate him about the disease. In addition, the therapist should explore with Charley the meaning he makes of having a major mental illness and needing to spend the rest of his life on medication.

Rena

One can surmise that Rena has not been adequately mirrored by her father. It is clearly stated that Charley was not able to tolerate Rena's superior mechanical ability. Though no mention is made of it, we may imagine that Charley, the would-be comedian, has also felt ambivalent about Rena's potential success on stage. It is less clear what sort of relationship Rena has had with Nancy. We do not know if Nancy had time alone with Rena as an infant before she handed Rena over to Gram as a replacement for her own younger and more perfect self. Whatever the content of Rena's relationship with Nancy, Rena's genetic endowment of talent and charm makes it likely that she has received ample positive attention—or mirroring—from Gram as well as others outside the family. For Rena, Gram may also have been a source of strength, calm, and security—an idealized selfobject.

In any case, despite Rena's appearance of continual failure, she is actually stronger and more capable than the other members of her family. Rena succeeds at everything she does. Her failures occur only when she undermines herself after being successful. The relevant question is not why Rena fails, but why she cannot allow herself to succeed. In self psychological terms, we view Rena as having acted as a *reverse selfobject* for Nancy. Just as Nancy took care of her elders, Rena takes care of Nancy. First, she tells the interviewer that she always complies with her mother's wishes because "one has to." If Nancy views herself as a caretaker who must sit at home unable to do her job, at least she can worry about her family. Rena gives Nancy reason to worry. We also see that the pain caused by abandonment is a major concern in Rena's life. It becomes clear from Rena's story that she has been careful not to grow up and fulfill her promise because that would mean abandoning Nancy. So on the eve of every success, she fails.

In a *reverse selfobject relationship* as defined by Lee (Lee & Martin, 1991), the child "acts as a selfobject to the mother in the hope that the mother will function as a selfobject for the child" (p. 75). We believe that a child will be motivated to act as a selfobject for an adult not only to retain the self-object bond but also to assuage her guilt. Children usually feel responsible for the suffering of their caretakers. As we will discuss under "Limitations of the Theory," self psychology does not have a comprehensive concept of guilt. We believe that Rena's problem derives largely from guilt—she is a loyal daughter who has proven capable of success in a family where all other family members experience themselves as chronic failures. Therefore, guilt rather than management and maintenance of self-esteem is probably Rena's most entrenched problem. Control-mastery theory addresses the problem of pathological guilt more cogently than does self psychology. In working with Rena, we would target her ability to pursue her goals without believing that she is betraying or abandoning her family. For guidance in this kind of therapeutic process, we refer you to the chapter on control-mastery theory.

Michael

Michael is a portrait of contradictions. On the one hand, he is a boy who views himself, and is viewed by others, as defective. On the other hand, Michael (a) met normal developmental milestones; (b) was a "happy baby;" (c) may be experiencing behavioral problems because of medications for grand mal seizures; (d) is no longer considered to have learning disabilities but remains in a learning disability class due to his behavior; (e) has a normal IQ; (f) stays informed about current events and is often able to relate well to adults; and (g) has given the counselors at his summer camp reason to believe that his misbehavior is willful. It is possible that Michael's behavioral problems are iatrogenic. It is also possible that their genesis is neurological, emotional, or some combination of all these factors. We believe that the first task of working with Michael should be a comprehensive medical, neurological, and psychological evaluation and, if indicated, trials of new medication. But whether Michael's "bizarre" behavior turns out to be iatrogenic (and can be alleviated), neurological, or emotional in origin, the experience of viewing himself and of having been viewed as defective will be central in Michael's treatment.

It is unlikely that Michael has received what Kohut would consider adequate mirroring from his overtaxed mother. Nancy states that her sickly son was "born unlucky." She may, with reason, have experienced Michael as a major drain on her personal resources as well as a source of strain and loneliness in her marriage, given Charley's inability to caretake or parent. Michael has received attention from his mother for being ill, which is presumably not the sort of positive attention Kohut describes as mirroring. Michael has been his mother's patient, and he has apparently had no opportunity to overcome his deficit in mirroring with an idealizing selfobject relationship. Charley, who may be even more competitive with Michael than with Rena, is clearly not available to Michael as an idealized selfobject. It would also appear that Michael has not been able to reach outside the family to find others who could fulfill these selfobject functions for him.

One possible emotional factor in Michael's continued social isolation (an isolation that Rena, with her completely different personality, also suffered) may be that he has experienced guilt in relation to his mother, who spent so much time and energy taking care of him. It is likely that both Michael and Rena feel responsible for their overburdened mother. If crises alleviate Nancy's anxiety and cause her to feel competent once again, her children may unconsciously believe that they are taking care of her when they give her problems to focus on and crises to handle. It is also possible that Michael, despite his overtly conflictual relationship with his father, protects his father by not surpassing him. Thus, Michael may be sacrificing his competency (though clearly not without ambivalence) to try to increase the competency of his parents.

In sum, Michael's health and his school and extracurricular activities have all afforded him continuing experiences of failure and social humiliation. Michael has reason to worry about his overburdened mother and feel responsible for her problems. In addition, Michael's interpersonal difficulties, so much like his father's, may derive from an identification with his father. So, while Michael has deficits in both mirroring and idealizing selfobject experiences, it is also likely that he is subject to conflicts deriving from loyalty to his family.

In conclusion, we see deficits in mirroring and idealizing selfobject relationships as well as conflict engendered by loyalty and guilt passed down through the generations—in one child, a cycle of weak self-development coupled with guilt and in the other child, adequate self-development overshadowed by guilt. In short, we see in the Shore family children caring for parents who have cared for parents.

TREATMENT OF CHOICE

Any one of the Shore family members could walk into a social worker's office. Michael's behavioral problems might bring on a referral for family therapy. Rena might walk in because Nancy is urging her to. Nancy herself could be referred by her medical doctor for her anxiety, eating disorder, chain-smoking, or back pain. Charley clearly requires help with affect regulation and should be referred by his psychopharmacologist for psychotherapy. We view this whole family as entrenched in a cycle of inadequate selfobject relating, but at the same time we believe that Rena's primary issue is guilt rather than self-esteem. Therefore, we view control-mastery theory as appropriate for Rena's treatment, and self psychology (in conjunction with control mastery's comprehensive view of guilt) as a useful lens for guiding the individual treatment of the other members of the Shore family. We are not, however, doctrinaire in our approach to treatment modality. Family therapy could prove extremely useful for the Shores, and it would be appropriate for them to be referred for family treatment due to Michael's school problems. There are family therapists who incorporate ideas from self psychology (see, e.g., Brighton-Cleghorn, 1987; Eldridge & Schmidt, 1990; Solomon, 1988; Ungar & Levene, 1994), but we believe there are many effective modalities of family treatment. Rena, we predict, could improve quite rapidly with either individual or family therapy. Michael might improve dramatically as a result of family therapy. However, we think that Nancy, Charley, and Michael would all benefit from a combination of family therapy and longer term individual treatment.

THE THERAPEUTIC PROCESS

The course of treatment in self psychology is described by Wolf (1983, cited in Baker and Baker, 1987) in five steps. First, defenses (or resistance) against therapy are analyzed with acceptance. In drive theory, *resistance* is viewed as opposition to the pain of the uncovering that takes place in the course of treatment. Kohut preferred the term *defense* and viewed the behavior as self-preservation in patients dreading a repetition of past selfobject failure. Second, there is an unfolding of the selfobject transference. To accomplish this, interpretations must not be judgmental. Third, the selfobject relationship is inevitably disrupted. Ideally, however, this disruption takes place in a milieu of optimal selfobject functioning. Fourth, the disruption is interpreted and mutually understood. And fifth, patients work through their "failures and successes in strengthening the self and [in] attempting to integrate into ... healthy, mature ... self-object and object relationships" (Wolf, 1983; cited in Baker & Baker, 1987, p. 8).

If these are the steps of the therapeutic process, empathy is the linchpin of self psychology's therapeutic technique. For the patient, being heard and understood is an affirming and organizing experience; for the therapist, being empathic is the process of coming to understand the other person's subjective experience. Empathy is not synonymous with caretaking.

Joining with the patient does not imply taking responsibility for the patient; rather, it is the therapist's tool of information gathering. Empathy keeps the therapeutic relationship *experience-near,* or on track with a particular individual's experience and feelings, as opposed to *experience-distant* work, which attempts to fit the individual into the metapsychological grid of a theory.

Empathy allows the therapist to capture the moment-to-moment inner life of the patient. Rowe (1992) wrote that work that focuses on the "why," the motivation of the patient's behavior, may feel unempathic to the patient because it often fails to capture "what" the patient is experiencing. Conversely, when Rowe focused on "what" her patients were experiencing, they felt understood and were themselves able to pursue the "why," or the motivation and explanation for their behavior. According to Kohut, the clinician should first address symptomatic behavior and its connection to current selfobject failure and later move to interpretations. A central tenet of self psychology is that understanding, realized through (perhaps long periods of) empathic immersion, must precede explanation.

The therapist–client relationship is fueled by empathy but centers around the patient's selfobject transference. As the unfulfilled selfobject needs of any one of the Shore family members is mobilized in a therapeutic relationship, it will become clear whether he or she is developing what, in Kohut's terms, would be a mirroring, idealizing, or twinship transference. In any transference, there are complexities that belie the apparent simplicity of Kohut's theory.

First, problems can arise as the transference is mobilized. For example, if Nancy began to openly admire the therapist, this might signal an attempt on her part to mirror the therapist—a repetition of the reverse selfobject relationships of her childhood. This is what Lee and Martin (1991, p. 144) call a *pseudo-idealization.* It is important not to mistake a pseudo-idealization for real idealization. From the self psychological point of view, pseudo-idealization and other defenses are the patients' ways of protecting themselves from retraumatization. On the other hand, in the mobilization of the idealizing transference, therapists may suddenly find that they are the subject of hostile attacks or that they are treated to a subtle depreciation or a rageful withdrawal on the part of the patient. Although this occurs, it is important to rule out traumatic empathic failure on the therapists' part. This behavior may instead signal a resistance to idealization and the wish to merge that is enacted in idealization.

Second, questions often come up while working within the selfobject transferences. In the case of a mirroring transference, it is essential for therapists to develop sound judgment about what they are being asked to mirror. That is, they will not want to find themselves mirroring the patient's false self. An example of this error would be encouraging Nancy to return to nursing (because she says she wants to) before understanding the selfobject functions that nursing served—or failed to serve—for her. Furthermore, in order to mirror appropriately, the therapist must assess the developmental level of the patient, for "to be fully empathic, the mirroring response must be developmentally appropriate and genuine" (Baker & Baker, 1987, p. 3). The therapist would not, for example, want to either underestimate or overestimate Michael's abilities—one reason a thorough assessment of Michael is needed.

Third, countertransference should always be monitored. In a mirror transference, therapists may have difficulty tolerating the boredom of listening to a patient's "self-centered soliloquy" (Wolf, 1980, p. 581). In a twinship transference, therapists may feel compelled to "assert [a] separate identity" (Wolf, 1980, p. 582). In the idealizing transference, therapists may find it hard to tolerate the experience of being idealized. This may trigger their own unanalyzed grandiosity, making them inappropriately encouraging of the idealization, a form of "transference bondage" (Kohut, 1971, p. 164) that reflects therapists' needs, not patients'. Or therapists may be inappropriately discouraging of the idealization, a repetition of selfobject failure. Resistance on the part of therapists to the idealizing transference is, according to Kohut, likely to cause patients to revert protectively to a grandiose self state and halt the progress of treatment.

The therapeutic process is always complex and is formed by the individuals involved. The focus of self psychology is on staying with the patient's experience, recognizing and respecting the patient's need for defenses, surviving the sometimes difficult selfobject experience embodied in the transference without becoming hostile or punitive, understanding—and, to complete the process, explaining—the patient's transferred needs. This, according to Kohut (1984), restarts the patient's arrested development. If the process is concluded successfully, the patient will have achieved the ability to empathize with others and maintain mature selfobject relationships.

LIMITATIONS OF THE MODEL

What follows is our critique of some of Kohut's thinking. These concerns are not uniquely ours. Throughout this section we refer the reader to critics and theoreticians with whom readers can trace the evolution of self psychology and learn about current debates about the theory.

The first concept we consider is grandiosity. The grandiose self and the idealized parent were originally viewed by Kohut as strategies to recapture the lost perfection of early maternal–infant bond understood to exist in a stage of symbiosis. This analytic concept of an infantile stage of symbiosis is refuted by Stern and other infant researchers. Shane and Shane (1988) pointed out the incompatibility between Kohut and infant research on this point:

> Infant research stipulates a self perceived as separate from the other almost from the start, with the achievement of autonomy being but one of the central tasks of the infant, on a par with ... the equally important task of achieving a capacity for interdependence. (pp. 406–407)

That is, the classical psychoanalytic theory positing the infant's subjective perception of itself as omnipotent and as existing in symbiotic union with its mother is not upheld by empirical research. It follows that there is no support for the concept of "normal" infantile grandiosity as an outgrowth of normal infantile symbiosis (for further discussion, see Eagle, 1984, pp. 50–51).

That grandiosity is not a normal developmental state does not, of course, obviate its existence in narcissistic patients. We agree with Miller (1996) who both acknowledged the faultiness of the concept of normal infantile grandiosity and argues that a reactive grandiosity can develop after the child attains the symbolic capacity:

> If the frustrations the child experiences are intolerable, if his needs for exploration and doing are blocked, if he is met only with criticism or neglect, then he will develop reactive grandiose and omnipotent fantasies to compensate for the feelings of dysphoria arising from his frustrations. (p. 43)

Next, we take exception to Kohut's idea that a developmental deficit is somehow incompatible with psychological conflict. We agree with critics (Bacal & Newman, 1990; Eagle, 1984; Miller 1996; Stolorow, Brandchaft, & Atwood, 1987) who argue that the deficit model is overly simplistic and excludes the problem of conflict unnecessarily. Selfobjects do not simply fulfill or fail to fulfill positive functions. A relationship, be it positive or negative, is an engagement that cannot be characterized as a simple lack. A caretaker who fails to fulfill the necessary (positive) selfobject functions often does so—according to Kohut himself—in a negative fashion. The outcome of such faulty selfobject relating will be conflicts as well as deficits. As Eagle (1984) stated, "Someone deprived of adequate love and empathy early in life may have to cope, not only with deprivation of these 'ingredients,' but with such conflict-laden issues as destructive rage, ambivalence, greed, etc." (p. 63).

Third, we are disturbed by Kohut's (1971) choice of analogy in his description of mirroring. He spoke of mirroring as a behavior analogous to the behavior of a parent with a child: "The gleam in the mother's eye ... confirms the child's self-esteem" (p. 116). We find this interpretation of the therapeutic process misleading. Two things are implied—first, that the therapist is a substitute parent, and second, that the patient is entirely regressed to the cognitive and emotional perceptions of a child. We view the therapeutic process differently. The fact that adult patients experience relational–functional deficits and conflicts that derive, in part at least, from troubled primary relationships does not mean, as Kohut stated, that the patient's adult development in therapy will be a continuation of an arrested immature development. We agree with Wolfe (1989), who wrote, "The idea that self development in adulthood is analogous to self development in childhood is highly improbable" (p. 553). The adult, even if regressed, is not cognitively a child. And if the patient is regressed, that regression is unlikely to involve all areas of functioning. As Gedo (1989) noted, "The occurrence of islands of malfunctioning ... is best understood in terms of the frequent coexistence of separate subsets of 'self nuclei' (Gedo & Goldberg, 1973), one of which may undergo regression without involving the other in the process" (p. 425). Whatever transferential issues are being played out in the therapeutic relationship, the therapist is not a parent, the adult patient is not a child, and mirroring is not a direct reinstatement of the parent–child selfobject relationship. In short, adult development in the therapeutic relationship is not isomorphic with child development in the child–parent relationship.

Nevertheless, Wolfe (1989) argued that self psychology already contains the tools for understanding the unique nature of self development in psychotherapy. This could be achieved by clinicians applying Kohut's "more comprehensive ... notion of self as experience" (p. 553) rather than remaining faithful to analytic preconceptions about self development. That is, empathic immersion in the subjective experience of the patient could be used to learn "the particular kinds of self development that occur during psychotherapy" (p. 553).

Our fourth criticism is of Kohut's (1984) view of homosexuality. He continued in the psychoanalytic tradition of referring to homosexuality as a symptom, believing that homosexuality was the defense of a self in some degree of fragmentation resulting from selfobject failure. Although we have no objection to analyzing the selfobject functions of any particular sexual relationship, we do not agree with the categorical classification of homosexuality as pathological and as a symptomatic substitute for the normal developmental goal of heterosexuality.

Contemporary self psychology theorists such as Shelby (1992) agree that sexual orientation often arises as an issue in treatment not because homosexuality is pathological but rather because gay male or lesbian individuals are frequently deprived of necessary selfobject experiences by caregivers who do not adequately mirror or provide twinship for the child's developing gay self. In cases such as these, the meaning of being gay and the narcissistic injuries that the person suffered should be explored with the aim of bolstering a cohesive self, a component of which is a lesbian or gay orientation.

Fifth, we do not agree with Kohut's view of guilt. Kohut never expanded on the classical Freudian understanding of guilt (that it results from a fear of internalized parental authority, or the *superego*). In the beginning, Kohut (1971) differentiated structural conflict (oedipal phase) pathology from deficit (narcissistic) pathology. Ultimately, however, Kohut (1984; cited in Droga & Kaufman, 1995) viewed "all pathology as involving a range of self disorders in response to selfobject failure across development" (p. 262). However, he never amended his limited (classical) view of guilt and hence minimized its importance, along with the importance of conflict. Because it is beyond the scope of this chapter to elaborate a comprehensive theory of guilt, we refer the reader to the control-mastery chapter in this book for such a discussion. Self psychologists and control-mastery theorists have been working together for some years to expand their compatibility. An example can be found in Droga and Kaufman's (1995) "The Guilt of Tragic Man."

One final topic: Kohut did not properly credit the theoreticians whose ideas he borrowed or built on—British object relationists Fairbairn, Balint, Winnicott; American ego psychologists Hartmann and Mahler; humanist Rogers; infant researchers Spitz, Stern, and others. This qualifies as a limitation of the model because all theory is both a product of past theory and a catalyst for future theory. Denying this dialogue is an interruption that interferes with its continuation. Fortunately, Kohut's lacunae have been corrected by subsequent authors (see, e.g., Akhtar, 1989; Kahn, 1989; Lee & Martin, 1991).

RESEARCH

From the classical psychoanalytic perspective, the infant "lives initially in solipsistic isolation and employs hallucinatory wish fulfillment to satisfy needs . . . . Fantasy [is] primary and reality secondary" (Shane & Shane, 1988, p. 405). Current research on infancy (Lichtenberg, 1983; Stern, 1985), however, supports a view of the infant as active and separate from caretakers, yet connected and reality-oriented. Shane and Shane (1988) pointed out that self psychology "because of its comparative freedom to make theoretical change, has more or less adopted the view" (p. 407) of infant observation studies, repudiating the psychoanalytic notion subscribed to by Kohut of "a normal developmental phase characterized by a perception of self merged with other" (p. 407). This atavistic element of Kohut's theorizing has been discussed under "Limitations of the Model."

Although Kohut (1971) based his theory of development of the self on data gathered from the analyses of adults, infant researchers such as Stern (1985) are in agreement with Kohut that the need for affinity persists as development proceeds. Through observational studies of infants, Beebe and Lachmann (1988) have confirmed the importance of *mother–infant attunement*—an equivalent of Kohut's mirroring—for the developing child. Beebe and Lachmann also suggest that—much like Kohut's ideas about the function of selfobject failure and transmuting internalization—the building of psychic structure occurs in the experience of minor failures in attunement. Demos' (1988) observation of infants led her to conclude that empathic responsiveness is crucial in child development. Appropriate caretaker responses—as with Kohut's notion of the function of an idealized selfobject—foster the integration of affects.

Observational studies of caretaker-infant interaction have lent credence to the view that empathy is essential in early development and that perhaps minor lapses of empathy promote growth. Investigators such as Patton, Connor, and Scott (1982) have developed counseling outcome measures for self-psychologically informed treatment. Payne, Robbins, and Dougherty (1991) conducted empirical inquiry with a nonclinical population. These investigators have examined the relationship between adjustment in retirees and the development of goals and ideals from a self psychological perspective. Other research endeavors involving self psychological constructs include the work of Glassman (1988a, 1988b), which compared the models of Kohut and Kernberg with respect to understanding narcissism. Glassman's findings supported the validity of many aspects of self psychology such as viewing aggression as a disintegration product that results from empathic failure. In addition, Robbins and Patton (1985) developed rating scales for career development using the ideas of the grandiose self and idealization, and Lappan and Patton (1986) designed measures to assess the cohesiveness of an adolescent's sense of self. Empirical investigation of self-psychologically informed clinical practice remains to be done.

SUMMARY

To summarize, Kohut introduced "a brilliant and wholly original premise to psychoanalysis" (Wolfe, 1989, p. 548) that the experience of "being one who experiences" (p. 548) could be the focus of psychoanalytic inquiry. Kohut was sometimes successful in his attempt to stay experience-near, and sometimes he was not. Although a Kohutian interpretation is likely to be less blaming or moralistic than a classical oedipal interpretation, it may not be less constraining if the clinician is stretching to fit the patient's problems into the field of self-esteem regulation. We believe that Kohut's formulations on the selfobject transferences are relevant for certain patients—like Nancy, Charley, and Michael Shore—and that the clinician who stays experience-near with these individuals will be able to discern which of Kohut's formulations are relevant. For those patients for whom self-esteem regulation is not the primary concern—like Rena Shore—the clinician who stays experience-near should be able to discern alternate needs and motivations that derive from the patients' cultural context coupled with their unique attribution of meaning to their experience. In our clinical experience, we have found that the therapeutic self-selfobject relationship—in which patients' present needs are understood and accepted, and their past experiences are articulated—generates change.

REFERENCES

Akhtar, S. (1989). Kohut and Kernberg: A critical comparison. In D. W. Detrick & S. P. Detrick (Eds.), *Self psychology: Comparisons and contrasts* (pp. 329–362). Hillsdale, NJ: Analytic Press.

Bacal, H. A. (1985). Optimal responsiveness and the therapeutic process. In A. Goldberg (Ed.), *Progress in self psychology: Vol. 1* (pp. 202–226). New York: Guilford.

Bacal, H. A., & Newman, K. A. (1990). *Theories of object relations: Bridges to self psychology.* New York: Columbia University Press.

Baker, H. S., & Baker, M. N. (1987). Heinz Kohut's self psychology: An overview. *American Journal of Psychiatry 144*(1), 1–9.

Beebe, B., & Lachmann, F. M. (1988). Mother-infant mutual influence and precursors of psychic structure. In A. Goldberg (Ed.), *Progress in self psychology: Vol. 3. Frontiers in self psychology* (pp. 3–25). Hillsdale, NJ: Analytic Press.

Brighton-Cleghorn, J. (1987). Formulations of self and family systems. *Family Process 26,* 185–201.

Demos, V. (1988). Affect and development of the self: A new frontier. In A. Goldberg (Ed.), *Progress in self psychology: Vol. 3. Frontiers in self psychology* (pp. 27–53). Hillsdale, NJ: Analytic Press.

Droga, J. T., & Kaufman, P. J. (1995). The guilt of tragic man. In A. Goldberg (Ed), *Progress in self psychology: Vol. 11. The impact of new ideas* (pp. 259–276). Hillsdale, NJ: Analytic Press.

Dublin, P. (1992). Severe borderlines and self psychology. *Clinical Social Work Journal, 20*(3), 285–293.

Eagle, M. N. (1984). *Recent developments in psychoanalysis: A critical evaluation.* Cambridge, MA: Harvard University Press.

Eagle, M., & Wolitzky, D. L. (1992). Psychoanalytic theories of psychotherapy. In D. K. Freedheim (Ed.), *History of psychotherapy: A century of change* (pp. 109–158). Washington, DC: American Psychological Association.

Eldridge, A., & Schmidt, E. (1990). The capacity to parent: A self psychological approach to parent-child psychotherapy. *Clinical Social Work Journal 18*(4), 339–351.

Gedo, J. (1989). Self psychology: A post-Kohutian view. In D. W. Detrick & S. P. Detrick (Eds.), *Self psychology: Comparisons and contrasts* (pp. 415–428). Hillsdale, NJ: Analytic Press.

Gedo, J., & Goldberg, A. (1973). *Models of the mind.* Chicago: University of Chicago Press.

Glassman, M. (1988a). Intrapsychic conflict versus developmental deficit: A causal modeling approach to examining psychoanalytic theories of narcissism. *Psychoanalytic Process, 5,* 23–46.

Glassman, M. (1988b). Kernberg and Kohut: A test of competing psychoanalytic models of narcissism. *Journal of the American Psychoanalytic Association, 36,* 597–625.

Kahn, E. (1989). Carl Rogers and Heinz Kohut: On the importance of valuing the self. In D. W. Detrick & S. P. Detrick (Eds.), *Self psychology: Comparisons and contrasts* (pp. 213–228). Hillsdale, NJ: Analytic Press.

Kohut, H. (1968). The psychoanalytic treatment of narcissistic personality disorder: Outline of a systematic approach. *Psychoanalytic Study of the Child, 34,* 86–113.

Kohut, H. (1971). *The analysis of the self.* New York: International Universities Press.

Kohut, H. (1977). *The restoration of the self.* New York: International Universities Press.

Kohut, H. (1978). Thoughts on narcissism and narcissistic rage. In P. H. Ornstein (Ed.), *The search for the self: Vol. 2* (pp. 615–658). New York: International Universities Press.

Kohut, H. (1984). *How does analysis cure?* Chicago: University of Chicago Press.

Kohut, H., & Wolf, E. (1978). Disorders of the self and their treatment. *International Journal of Psychoanalysis, 59,* 413–425.

Lappan, R., & Patton, M. J. (1986). Self psychology and the adolescent process: Measures of pseudoautonomy and peer group dependence. *Journal of Counseling Psychology, 33,* 136–142.

Lee, R. R., & Martin, J. C. (1991). *Psychotherapy after Kohut: A textbook of self psychology.* Hillsdale, NJ: Analytic Press.

Levin, J. D. (1991). *The treatment of alcoholism and other addictions: A self psychology approach.* Northvale, NJ: Jason Aronson.

Lichtenberg, J. D. (1983). *Psychoanalysis and infant research.* Hillsdale, NJ: Analytic Press.

Lichtenberg, J. D., Lachmann, F. M., & Fosshage, J. L. (1992). *Self and motivational systems: Toward a theory of psychoanalytic technique.* Hillsdale, NJ: Analytic Press.

Miller, J. (1996). *Using self psychology in child psychotherapy.* Northvale, NJ: Jason Aronson.

Ornstein, A. (1992). The curative fantasy and psychic recovery: Contribution to the theory of psychoanalytic psychotherapy. *Journal of Psychotherapy Practice and Research, 1*(1), 16–28.

Patton, M. J., Connor, G. E., & Scott, K. J. (1982). Kohut's psychology of the self: Theory and measures of counseling outcome. *Journal of Counseling Psychology, 29,* 268–282.

Payne, E. C., Robbins, S. B., & Dougherty, L. (1991). Goal directedness and older adult adjustment. *Journal of Counseling Psychology, 38,* 302–308.

Robbins, S. B., & Patton, M. J. (1985). Self psychology and career development: Construction of the superiority and goal instability scales. *Journal of Counseling Psychology, 32,* 221–231.

Rowe, F. (1992). Reviving the stalemated treatment through a self psychology re-analysis. *Clinical Social Work Journal, 20*(1), 57–66.

Shane, E., & Shane, M. (1988). Mahler, Kohut and infant research: Some comparisons. In D. W. Detrick & S. P. Detrick (Eds.), *Self psychology: Comparisons and contrasts* (pp. 395–413). Hillsdale, NJ: Analytic Press.

Shelby, D. (1992). Homosexuality and the struggle for coherence. In A. Goldberg (Ed), *Progress in self psychology: Vol. 10. A decade of progress* (pp. 55–77). Hillsdale, NJ: Analytic Press.

Solomon, M. F. (1988). Treatment of narcissistic vulnerability in marital therapy. In A. Goldberg (Ed.), *Progress in self psychology: Vol. 4. Learning from Kohut* (pp. 215–230). Hillsdale, NJ: Analytic Press.

Stern, D. N. (1985). *The interpersonal world of the infant: A view from psychoanalysis and developmental psychology.* New York: Basic Books.

Stolorow, R. D., Brandchaft, B., & Atwood, G. E. (1987). *Psychoanalytic treatment: An intersubjective approach.* Hillsdale, NJ: Analytic Press.

Ungar, M. T., & Levene, J. E. (1994). Selfobject functions of the family: Implications for family therapy. *Clinical Social Work Journal 22*(2), 303–316.

Wolf, E. S. (1980). Transferences and countertransferences in the analysis of disorders of the self. *Contemporary Psychoanalysis, 15,* 577–594.

Wolfe, B. (1989). Heinz Kohut's self psychology: A conceptual analysis. *Psychotherapy, 26*(4), 545–554.

4

Solution-Focused Brief Therapy

Jane Peller, M.S.W., and
John Walter, M.S.W.

If you want to be brief, treat each session as the last.—Walter & Peller, 1992
(p. 40)

INTRODUCTION

A solution-focused approach is not just a grouping of techniques or interventions. It is a way of thinking about who people are, what therapy is, and how change occurs. This approach is not merely a model, it is a philosophy—a philosophy that for many clinicians requires an epistemological change. A solution-focused philosophy is deeply rooted in traditional social work values and beliefs such as self-determination and the uniqueness of the individual in fostering her or his own potential, as well as the social work practice belief that the therapy relationship is one of mutuality and purpose. We think these social work beliefs and values naturally direct the worker away from a pathology orientation and toward a way of thinking that draws on clients' strengths and responsibilities. For us, solution-focused therapy is a way to operationalize those most basic social work traditions.

Solution-focused therapy is presently practiced in many different mental health contexts, across ethnic groups, and with people who have been categorized with various types of diagnostic labels. Solution-focused therapy was not designed to be a short-term approach, but because of the as-

71

sumptions a worker makes about people, therapy, and change, the therapy naturally becomes brief in duration. Although there are variations and differences in styles among solution-focused practitioners, they share a basic mind-set about how to think about people and how to approach the therapy process. This chapter presents an overview of that mind-set and the pragmatics of working in this approach.

THE CONCEPT OF THE PERSON AND THE HUMAN EXPERIENCE

The most central concept of the person and the human experience in solution-focused therapy is the belief that people are their own experts regarding what they want and how to change their lives. A solution-focused approach assumes that people know what is right and useful for themselves. It assumes that people can and do have the power to envision what they want to be happening in their lives. Such a mind-set is consistent with the idea that the purpose of therapy is for clients to get what they want. Thus the solution-focused therapist adopts the role of a consultant to clients' change process rather than an expert on how clients should change or should adhere to a predetermined normative standard.

We believe that through this process of conversing about what the client wants, we, the worker and the clients, develop, explore, create, and co-author an evolving story of possibilities and opportunities. Therapy then becomes a consultative process—one of mutual respect, dialogue, inquiry, affirmation, and purpose. Consequently, we prefer to use the term *consultant* or *personal consultation* versus *therapist* or *therapy* when we refer to what two or more people do when they sit down to talk about an issue. Because the word *therapy* brings forth the idea of treatment, disease, cure, and expert position—ideas that do not fit with a solution-focused orientation— we use the words *consultant* and *consultation* throughout the remainder of the chapter in referring to our work.

HISTORICAL PERSPECTIVE

Solution-focused brief therapy developed out of the work of the Brief Family Therapy Center of Milwaukee (BFTC), which formed in the late 1970s. An active group of practitioners at the BFTC during that time collaborated in the early development of the model: Insoo Kim Berg, Steve de Shazer, James Derks, Marilyn LaCourt, Eve Lipchik, and Elam Nunnally. In 1978 they developed a year-long training program that drew on a brief strategic-therapy approach and the work of Milton Erickson. Throughout the years that followed, many people—including Alex Molnar, Wallace Gingerich, Michele Weiner-Davis, Kate Kowalski, Scott Miller, Lawrence

Hopwood, and ourselves—trained, worked as trainers, or participated in research.

The development of the solution-focused approach has been primarily influenced by three areas of thinking. During its early development, the solution-focused model was influenced by the brief problem-focused model of the Mental Research Institute (MRI). In the MRI approach, a brief strategic-therapy approach, therapists looked for the problem-maintaining patterns within a client system and then tried to intervene in order to produce a difference in the pattern (Watzlawick, Weakland, & Fisch, 1974).

The second strand of influence came from the work of Milton Erickson. During the early 1980s, many groups around the country were trying to replicate the impressive results that Milton Erickson achieved. Several practitioners at BFTC who had studied Erickson's work were influenced by the notions of the unconscious, hypnotic commands in therapeutic interventions, and the idea of the client defining the goal of the therapy. The most important idea was that therapists use "what the client brings with him to meet his needs in such a way that the client can make a satisfactory life for himself" (de Shazer, 1985, p. 6).

In the mid-eighties, the development of the solution-focused approach moved from a *problem* orientation, with an emphasis on deconstructing symptoms and intervening in problem patterns, to a solution-construction approach. Some of the early writings from the BFTC group reflect these notions of strategic interventions (de Shazer & Molnar, 1984) and pattern interruption (de Shazer, 1982).

A significant occurrence in the switch from a problem orientation to a solution-construction orientation took place in 1984 when Michele Weiner-Davis, Steve de Shazer and Wallace Gingerich formed a research group to study what was labeled *pre-session change* (Weiner-Davis, de Shazer & Gingerich, 1987). They looked at clients' reports of change since the time when they had set up the therapy appointment. Interestingly, a majority of clients reported change prior to the first session and after setting up the appointment for therapy. The researchers also noted, "It appears that any difference can be developed into a difference that makes a difference as long as the new behavior (or newly perceived behavior) is perceived as an outward and visible sign of change" (Weiner-Davis, de Shazer & Gingerich, 1987, p. 363). From that point, the approach shifted toward searching for what were later labeled *exceptions to the problem*. During the same period, the BFTC group began to think that there does not have to be a connection between the problem or complaint and the intervention (later called the *solution*). This was a revolutionary idea in therapy. Most other therapy models assumed that there was a connection between the problem or cause and the outcome or solution. In his book, *Clues*, de Shazer first stated

For an intervention to successfully fit, it is not necessary to have detailed knowledge of the complaint. It is not necessary even to be able to construct with any rigor how the trouble is maintained in order to prompt solution. Given all of my previous work, this at first seemed counter-intuitive, but it does seem that any really different behavior in a problematic situation can be enough to prompt solution and give the client the satisfaction he seeks from therapy. All that is necessary is that the person involved in a troublesome situation does something different, even if that behavior is seemingly irrational, certainly irrelevant, obviously bizarre, or humorous. (de Shazer, 1988, p. 7)

This shift to assuming that there were positive client changes before beginning therapy and that there was no necessary connection between problems and solutions led to the formulation of the new practice as solution-focused brief therapy (de Shazer et al., 1986).

The third and most recent influence on development of the approach has come from a shift to post-structural and postmodern thinking (de Shazer, 1991, 1994; O'Hanlon, 1994; Walter & Peller, 1996). This is a shift from *systems thinking* to *narrative*. This change altered the proponents' focus from thinking of the client as a system or as part of a system to focusing on *consultation* as a system—a collaborative grouping in which the purpose is defined from within and narratives of possibilities are produced.

Our interpretation of postmodern and post-structural thinking is that proponents of this model have replaced the modernist notions that humans can objectively observe what is apart from them and arrive at conclusions of the basic structure of the object of study. With regard to therapy, the modernist notion is that humans could discover the basic structure, be it normative or abnormal, of an individual psyche or family. On the other hand, post-structural and postmodern thinking assumes that humans can never objectively know what is apart from them. Rather, people all live within and create narratives of our experience. Narratives may be of individual experience, family experience, cultural experience, or scientific experience. Narratives will be different, but all will be stories rather than facts.

The implications that this has for consultation is that we as consultants never have objective facts. Instead, we have stories. We have the clients' stories, we have our stories, we have stories about the others' stories. Consultation then becomes more akin to story creation. Consultant and client become involved in creating new stories, new narratives.

Our interpretation of solution-focused thought also draws from a new movement generally called *social constructionism* and from the philosophies of Ludwig Wittgenstein and Jacques Derrida. From this thinking, proponents of the model believe that narratives are created socially and are never an exclusive individual creation. Rather, meaning-making or narrative creation takes place in conversation either with the individuals themselves or with others. Thus consultation takes place in a conversational domain in which language becomes not just an evolving collection of tools for communication but also a social action.

An example of the way in which language is active and creative can be demonstrated by the use of the word *sublime* rather than *pink* to describe a rose. The adjectives evoke much different experiences of the rose. Likewise, choosing the expression *anxious to change* to reflect a client's affect brings forth a different experience than using the word *desperate*.

Language is also active in the sense that it never exists outside of someone speaking it and using it to communicate. Language is thought of, therefore, as a process rather than an object. We have adopted Humberto Maturana's use of "languaging" in thinking of our work with clients (Maturana & Varela, 1987). Consultants and the clients "language" or create stories together.

The implications of this postmodern paradigm change are that work shifts away from consultants thinking of their roles as experts about the human experience and experts who treat the dysfunctionality in objectively understood structures. We define our expertise not on claims of scientific truth but rather on tentative conclusions of what has worked so far. Rather than treating disorders, we define ourselves as consultants working with clients in creating new narratives around the goals that they determine.

De Shazer's books were the first to describe solution-focused therapy. A subsequent book that had significant impact on the popularity of the model was *In Search of Solutions* (O'Hanlon & Weiner-Davis, 1988), which was more readable by the general mental health practitioner and helped the approach achieve recognition. This was followed by *Becoming Solution-Focused in Brief Therapy*, a manual for learning and practicing the approach (Walter & Peller, 1992). The most recent literature describes the application of the solution-focused approach to different populations and practice situations: domestic violence (Lipchik & Kubicki, 1996), inpatient psychiatric treatment (Vaughn, Young, Webster, & Thomas, 1996), schools (Murphy, 1996), hospital diversion (Booker, 1996), problem drinking (Berg & Miller, 1992), residential treatment (Durrant, 1993), couples work (Hudson & O'Hanlon, 1991), adolescents (Selekman, 1993), and family-based services (Berg, 1994). Other recent work has centered on attempts to integrate postmodernist thought with a solution focus (de Shazer, 1994; O'Hanlon, 1994; Walter & Peller, 1996).

KEY THEORETICAL CONSTRUCTS

The first construct in a solution-focused approach is that consultation is a consumer-driven, consumer-oriented process. In other words, the client defines the goal and purpose of the consultation. Clients (an individual, a family, or a couple or any other individuals) need to define what it is that they want from meeting with the consultant—what they want to be different in their life. In this way, solution-focused consultation is client centered and consumer centered, with the initiation for change directed by clients. The issue of who should attend the consultation sessions is resolved by answering the question, "Who wants something to be different?" The process of forming a goal in the consultation is then determined by client and consultant together. Solution-focused consultants assume that people who seek out a personal consultant are coming for some reason or purpose, even if clients cannot state that purpose very clearly or have not thought through all the reasons for their coming. Solution-focused consultants also assume that a client's purpose in seeking personal consultation may and probably will change over time (Walter & Peller, 1996). This first construct is central to the consultation. If there is not a mutual definition of what the purpose of the consultation is, we do not continue consulting because without a purpose, there is no reason to meet.

Solution-focused consultants generally believe that the process of *goaling* is essential to the outcome of the consultation. Goaling is defined as creating meaning about what clients want to experience or what their lives may be like "beyond the problem" (Walter & Peller, 1996). This idea that there is life beyond the problem leads the consulting to more of a future focus rather than looking at the past or present.

A second key construct is that people have strengths on which they continuously rely as they live their lives. Sometimes people are not aware of their strengths or how they are using them as they cope with their problems. For example, with the Shore family, if one were to ask the family members directly about their strengths, they would probably say that they do not have any strengths—perhaps because they feel so downtrodden and negative about their lives in the present. However, that does not mean that they do not have strengths. We believe that as we converse with clients, their strengths will emerge. Because we believe in a strengths concept, when we listen and converse with our clients, we are respecting their sense of what is right or useful in their construction of the life that they want to happen.

A third key construct is that the consultation is a collaborative process. Solution-focused consultants do not adhere to the notion that therapists have expert knowledge based on scientific research of what is good, normal, and valued. The consultant is not an expert who makes an evaluation of the situation or the person. Instead, the consultant assumes a position of not knowing—of being curious about what has not been developed, what has not yet been invented (Anderson & Goolishian, 1988). The consultant, then, is an expert only in being curious about clients' experiences and the meaning that they ascribe to those experiences. Because solution-focused consultation is a *non-normative approach* (i.e., it does not adhere to set standards in personal growth), clients and consultants mutually collaborate about the meaning of clients' experience. Through this collaboration about meaning—asking questions that invite exploration and presupposing that meetings are purposeful—the purpose of the meeting and the process of goaling evolve.

ASSESSMENT

Psychotherapy approaches seem to be divided into those that are problem-based and those that are competency-based. In the problem-based approaches, it is important to assess, evaluate, and give a diagnosis about what the problem is, how long it has been occurring, and its possible causes and contributing factors, as well as how one might treat or cure the problem, given a set standard of normalcy. Because a solution-focused approach is a consumer-oriented, non-normative approach, it does not concern itself with the etiology of the problem, the diagnostic category of the problem, or how the problem should be altered to fit a standard of mental health. The word *assessment* does not fit into a solution-focused orientation. The definition of *assess* is to determine the importance or value of something (Webster's New Collegiate Dictionary, 1980). In addition, the Latin definition of the word *assesses* is "to sit beside as in the office of a judge," a concept not fitting with an orientation in which we are emphasizing the importance of mutuality, respect for client strengths, and clients' knowledge about what is useful for themselves.

Instead of using assessment as either a concept or as a process to be done to or with clients, the central purpose in the solution-focused approach is creating goals and possibilities. Typically, solution-focused consultants valued goals that were well-defined (Berg & Miller, 1992; O'Hanlon & Weiner-Davis, 1988; Walter & Peller, 1992). Having well-defined goals means that consultants and clients can then evaluate whether the client is on track to achieving the goals and can enable defining when to conclude the consultation. Well-defined goals are stated in the positive, in a process form, and in the here-and-now; are as specific as possible; and are within the client's control (Walter & Peller, 1992).

However, more recent developments in the solution-focused approach have reevaluated the emphasis on well-defined goals and have placed more meaning on the process of goaling, where the word *goal* is used as a verb (Walter & Peller, 1996). The process of goaling moves the consultation away from a problem–solution configuration and into a hypothetical narrative in which clients' lives are free of the problem—into the way in which the clients want their life to be. Goaling then is defined as a mutual process between the consultant and the clients, in which they create a picture or a story about the life that the clients want to happen.

A solution-focused approach differs from a traditional goal-oriented approach in which the therapist thinks of a goal as representing a real event, an end point that must be reached or accomplished in order for therapy to be completed. In a goaling approach, the consultant thinks of goaling as a process for facilitating possibilities and evolving meanings in which the clients are able to experience themselves and their lives in ways that are different and more desirable.

The process of goaling leads the solution-focused consultant to invite conversation in four general areas (Walter & Peller, 1996):

1. What do the clients say that they want from the meeting?
2. How will what the clients want make a difference to them?
3. How will the clients know that they are on track to getting what they want?
4. How might the clients be experiencing some of what they want now?

Assessment is not of the client system but of the consulting system. In other words, consultants are concerned about and focus on how the client and the consultant are developing language that is opening up new possibilities for change.

TREATMENT OF CHOICE

The treatment-of-choice concept has traditionally been based on the assumption that the nature of the problem determined the intervention or treatment. In this approach, we act on the results of research conducted at BFTC (de Shazer, 1988) that showed that change processes and problem resolution are the same across problems areas. We therefore follow the clients' lead in determining what they want and what is working for them.

In the Shore case, the central questions for the consultant to ask of him/herself are "Who wants what?" and "What do they want from us, the consultants?" As defined by the content presented in the case, who wants what is unclear. Mostly, the individual family members are complaining about their lives, wishing that things were different, or wishing someone else were different. The vagueness in their statements is problematic for a solution-focused consultant because the consultants need a commitment by the clients to enter into a goaling process. In other words, we need to be hired by the clients. People who have wishes or complaints are not goaling; they are wishing or complaining. The difference for us is that there is not a statement of action or desire. For example, Charley states that he wants to stop compulsively lying but he doesn't "seem able to." Michael states he wants to "find himself." For us, these are wish statements. Secondly, what they want from the consultant in regard to these wish statements is not clear at this point. For example, Charley wants to buy a house. This is an acceptable goal for a client to have, but Charley does not state what he wants from the social worker in regard to the goal. In addition, we do not know if what he wants from the social worker is within her agency-prescribed role definition. For example, does he want her to find the house, or does he want the consultant to help him get loans?

In some cases, the identified client may not be the person who wants something to be different. In these cases it can be the referral source or a representative from some social service system, court system, child welfare system, or school system that wants the client to be different. In the past, we would have viewed these clients as *involuntary* or *mandated.* Mandated or involuntary clients often turned into "resistant" clients because they did not agree with the goals that had been created for them. Solution-focused consultants do not think in terms of mandated or resistant clients but instead want to converse with clients about what they want from coming to see us. Sometimes the clients actually want something for themselves; sometimes they want only to not to have to come to consultation. In the latter case, we would then work with them on what they would have to do to not have to come to consultation anymore.

THE THERAPEUTIC PROCESS

The Structure of the Consultation Session

Typical solution-focused consultants spend approximately 40 to 45 minutes in conversation with clients. Consultants then take a break in the conversation, so that consultants and clients have time outside of the conversation to reflect on what has transpired. Consultants go into another room to reflect on the conversation and to think about what they might want to share with the clients. After writing down their reflections, they return to the room and share these thoughts with clients, who may also have some reactions that they want to share at that time. Finally, an appointment for the next session is made.

Planning for the next session is also a collaborative process. Solution-focused consultants do not assume that consultation sessions have to occur in any set time frame. Because we believe that clients are the experts of their change processes, we believe that they know best when the next therapy session would be useful for them. Typically, we ask, "Given what we have just mentioned, what do you think about getting together again?" If clients state that they want to meet again, we ask, "And what do you think would be the right time frame? One week, two weeks, a month?" Typically, clients will schedule another appointment in a week and then again in 2 weeks. There will usually be two or three sessions spaced 2 weeks apart and then another one in a month. However, clients are unique and know best about their possibility of change and therefore know when another appointment would be useful for them.

In subsequent sessions, solution-focused consultants build on the changes that occurred in the weeks since the previous sessions. The typical opening question is, "What's different or better since I last saw you?" Opening the conversation with this question leads clients into focusing on the positive and on the differences that are occurring in their life. The question is based on our belief that change is a continual process, one that naturally occurs as people live their lives. If, however, clients report that there has been no change or that the situation has become worse, the consultant would still maintain a position of not knowing and of trying to understand and develop with the clients what they want, how that would make a difference for them, and what they would be doing differently in this problem-solved future.

There is no traditional use of the termination process. Clients are given the option about when to return to the consultant. There is no discussion, as there would be in a traditional approach, about the loss of the relationship or the importance of the therapy. It is also not assumed that a missed session or a no-show is an indication of failure. Instead, it is again assumed that clients know best about their process and that a lack of attendance might mean just that clients are going about their lives and therefore are not thinking of consulting.

The Consultation Conversation

The conversation during the session is a collaborative process centered around four consultant activities: (a) listening and acknowledging, (b) being curious, (c) inviting, and (d) encouraging. These are not sequential activities but are continually revisited during the conversational hour.

Listening and acknowledging

The most basic aspect to all kinds of counseling is to listen and acknowledge what the clients are expressing. Having clients know that they are being heard and acknowledged is the basis for a trusting relationship. We believe that in a solution-focused approach clients feel and sense a respect from the consultant about the clients' strengths and their power to make changes in their life. For example, the consultant does not make lists of what the client is doing wrong or what clients should do to be better or healthier people. Instead, solution-focused consultants listen for clients' strengths and competencies, acknowledge those strengths, and build on how clients can continue to do more of what they want and what works in their life.

In the case of the Shore family, the consultant and clients might identify what seem at first to be insignificant strengths or seemingly minor successes. We wonder what kind of evolving conversation might emerge if a consultant were to say to the Shore family that they have done a great job at coping with so many life difficulties for so long or that they obviously have somehow found ways to manage and keep loving each other in spite of everything. We think it might make a difference to them to know that a professional can hear and acknowledge their desire to keep the family together and the strength that it has taken to keep loving each other.

Being curious

Being curious operationalizes our role as consultants by helping the clients make clear what they want and how to go about getting it. As consultants, we are neither diagnosing nor trying to get the clients to do something. Instead, we are curious with them about what they may create in response to our questions. Being curious means that the consultant is not the expert and is not gathering information to make some evaluation or asking questions as part of a strategy. A position of being curious and of not-yet-understanding (Anderson & Goolishian, 1988) leads consultants to invite conversation about what has not been created yet, mostly about clients' lives, their experiences of themselves, and how they want life to be in the future.

We were very impressed with what we saw as the Shore family's strengths in coping with overwhelming life difficulties and circumstances. As solution-focused consultants, we cannot avoid hearing strengths as people spontaneously mention times that the problem does not happen or ways that they coped with long-standing problems. Because of the belief in people, their resources, and their sense of knowing themselves, a solution-focused consultant verbally and nonverbally focuses and reinforces conversation that amplifies people's strengths. In reading the case description of the Shore family, we naturally underlined and took note not of the problems of the past but of the times that the family members stated something positive in terms of their coping with various situations as well as of their competencies. As consultants, we would be curious about what has not been created yet, about how they might experience life when it is more the way that they want it to be.

As we read about the Shore family, sometimes we were curious about their strengths; sometimes we were curious about how it was different for the client to do, think, or say something different; and sometimes we were curious about how a change might influence and make a difference to someone else. Exploring any or all of the following areas could lead to an evolving story in which the clients might experience themselves and their life differently.

In regard to Nancy:

- How has Nancy coped so far with all the ailments?
- How does Nancy sometimes take control, especially in a crisis?
- What does Nancy do differently during the times that she takes control?
- How does Nancy think differently about herself and others when she takes control?
- If Nancy is "at her best" in a crisis, what does that mean that she does differently?
- Would Nancy like to be more at her best at other times in her life?
- During a panic attack, Nancy becomes "nearly immobilized," but not completely. How is it that she does not become completely immobilized?
- How is Nancy able to do anything at all during those times?
- The anxiety attacks occur daily, but not all day long. What is different during times Nancy does not have an anxiety attack?
- Could Nancy scale the anxiety attacks? Suppose 1 was for *calm* and 10 for a *total anxiety attack*, where would she say she was most of the time? At what point is the anxiety attack "overbearing"? What does she do, think, or say differently right before the anxiety becomes an overbearing time?
- How did Nancy and Charley decide to rent an apartment to someone outside of the family? What was the conversation about this? Was this conversation different from other times?
- What does Nancy want, if anything, about the weight gain, her sleeping patterns, and staying home?
- How does Nancy experience herself differently at home when she feels safe?
- How does Nancy bring herself to support Charley's performing?
- Nancy states that she wants Charley to act more like a father. If he did, what would she be doing differently? How would he perceive her differently?
- Nancy states that she spends 80% of the time worrying. What is different about the other 20% of the time? How does Nancy think differently about herself and about others in the family at those times?
- How do the other members perceive Nancy differently during the 20% of the time?

In regard to Charley:

- When Charley is performing, how does he think differently about himself?
- When Charley has suicidal thoughts, how does he keep going? Why has he not tried to kill himself? What has stopped him?

- What does Charley say differently to himself now that he has fewer grand ideas and wants a job he can hold?
- How has Charley continued to go to the vocational rehabilitation program?
- What, if anything, does he want in regard to buying a house?
- What, if anything, does he want in regard to compulsive lying? How is it a problem for him? How is it a problem for anyone else? How would it make a difference to him, or to anyone else, if he was not compulsively lying? What would he be doing instead of compulsively lying?

In regard to Rena:

- How did Rena recently move out of the house? How has she coped with the change?
- How did Rena think of writing in the journal? How is it helpful to her?
- How is Rena deciding to face the adoption issue?
- What gives Rena the courage to go to the adoption groups?

In regard to Michael:

- What does Michael mean when he says that he wants to "find himself"?
- Suppose Michael had found himself, what would he notice that was different?
- How is Michael different when he is not being "silly"? How does he do that? How is he then more successful in relating to adults?
- What is it that the teacher wants to see different in Michael?
- What makes the staff at the camp think that Michael can behave when he wants to? How are they different at those times?
- Michael stated, "I don't really want to act like that. It's really kind of stupid." How does he want to act instead? What does he want to do instead?
- How is it that Michael continues to challenge himself despite the limitations in track and softball teams, especially when he gets rejected too often?

Inviting

Solution-focused consultants invite clients into a conversation about what it is that they want from consulting and what would be signs to them that their goals were achieved, their problems were solved, or that they were making progress.

Future-based constructions. Future-based constructions are conversations about a hypothetical future in which the clients are experiencing their life in the way that they want. The kinds of questions that are asked to facilitate this conversation invite the clients into envisioning and talking about the future—a future without their problem, a future in which they are succeeding with what they want. Many clients will respond by describing the problems they are experiencing, or they describe what they do not want in their life. Consultants acknowledge these statements and then invite clients to tell us what they do want. Asking clients what they do want comes from our assumption that a positively stated goal gives clients a direction to go toward something, rather than just trying to get away from the problem. The idea is to ask questions that invite a conversation of success in the future, where clients experience their power to define their life as on track for themselves. These future-based questions once again are based on the inherent belief of solution-focused consultants that the clients are the experts in the change process, that they know what it is that they want and what is right for themselves. This process also removes the consultant from a diagnostic position and from a position of projecting the solution to the stated problem onto the client.

The most well-known future-based question is the *miracle question.* This question, first developed at BFTC (de Shazer, 1988), originated from de Shazer's early work in hypnosis with a crystal-ball technique. It has gone through several stages of development since the original form and now is generally asked in this manner:

> Suppose tonight while you are sleeping a miracle occurs, and the problem you came here to deal with was no longer a problem. But because the miracle happened while you were sleeping, you didn't know it happened. What would be signs to you that would tell you the miracle happened?

When asking future-based questions, it is important that the consultant word the questions so that they parallel the clients' presentation of self, or how the clients make meaning of their world, or their learning style. With this in mind, sometimes we might ask a miracle question like this:

> Suppose tonight while you are sleeping a miracle occurs, and *life is the way you want it to be.* But because the miracle happened while you were sleeping, you didn't know it happened. What would be the signs to you that this miracle had occurred?

By asking the miracle question with the phrase *life is the way you want it to be*, we avoid reference to a problem–solution configuration, and instead consultant and client move into a goaling talk.

On the other hand, sometimes we ask the miracle question like this:

> Suppose tonight while you are sleeping a miracle occurs, and *you were on track to having life the way you want it to be*. But because the miracle happened while you were sleeping, you didn't know it happened. What would be the signs to you that the miracle happened?

By asking the miracle question with *on track*, we enable clients to think about small signs of progress that indicate to them that they are achieving their goal that is in the distant future.

However, the miracle question is only one way to ask about the future. There are other ways, especially for people who represent themselves as very practical and logical and do not think in terms of miracles. Sometimes it is more productive to ask about the future with a more practical orientation, such as, for example:

> Suppose when you leave here tonight after this appointment life is the way you want or you are on track to putting your life together in the way that you want, what signs would you notice that would let you know?

No matter in what form the consultant asks the future-based questions, typically clients react in a surprised manner when asked to envision the future. They often have to think about their response, construct a vision of their life the way they want it to be, and then answer. Clients often report that as they begin to envision the future there is a sense of relief and a sense of hope, and that they feel encouraged. Most important, clients report that they feel empowered.

In regard to the Shore family, we wonder what kind of conversation would develop between the consultant and some or all of the family members when talking about a problem-solved future. We wonder how each member would respond to an invitation to talk about a miraculous future. We also wonder how each member might experience each other differently when listening to each other's construction of life the way she or he would like it be after this miracle. Our fantasy is that the conversation might go something like this:

Consultant: (addressing all the family members) Suppose tonight while you are sleeping a miracle occurred, and *you were on track to having life the way you want it to be*. But because the miracle happened while you were sleeping, you didn't know it happened. What would be a sign to you that would tell you the miracle had happened?"

Nancy: I'm not sure; I have never thought about the future. In fact, every time that I do I just get disappointed.

Consultant: I know, but let's assume or imagine for a moment that this miracle occurred and life was the way you want, you were not getting disappointed, what kinds of things would you notice *instead* of being disappointed?

Nancy: Well, I would not worry all the time about Charley and the children.

Consultant: Right, so you would *not* worry, what would you be doing *instead* of worrying?

Nancy: Well, I would be feeling proud of my kids instead of worried and disappointed.

Consultant: Okay, and as you awoke tomorrow morning, after this miracle, and you were feeling proud of your kids, what would be some signs to you?

Nancy: I would think about them more positively.

Consultant: And as you think about them more positively, what else would be signs? For example, what would you be saying differently to them?

Nancy: Well, I wouldn't be yelling at Michael to get ready for school. And I wouldn't be angry at Charley for being such a poor role model.

Consultant: Right, so what would you be doing instead of that?

Nancy: Well, I might be thinking more about myself.

Consultant: And thinking more about yourself, is that something that you might want to do?

Nancy: Yes.

Consultant: Would that be different for you to do?

Nancy: Yes and no.

Consultant: (To Michael) I am wondering, as you have been listening to your mother talk about this miracle, what might you notice that is different after the miracle night?

Michael: It would be really nice if my mother would stop yelling at me.

Consultant: Really, how would that make a difference for you?

Michael: Well, I would feel better about myself.

Consultant: And how would that make a difference for you if you felt better about yourself?

Michael: If I felt better about myself I might not blame myself.

Consultant: And how might you then act differently to others?

Michael: Well, maybe I wouldn't get so mad at other people—I might be nicer.

As one can note in this fictitious yet typical conversation with the Shore family, there is a slowly evolving story of a different experience of their life.

Present-based constructions.   Present-based constructions are evolving conversations about two areas: (a) times when the goal is already happening in the present and (b) what is different about the times when life

is going more the way clients want. Developing present-based constructions is built on the belief that people, and their lives in general, are constantly changing. From minute to minute, people are experiencing, sens-
ing, and feeling different things. However, clients who come in with a
problem have set a stage for their experiences and use that stage to understand all that happens to them. If clients who come in with problems, even
overwhelming problems, have already decided that this problem stage is
"truth," then the "real" reality, the other events or experiences that occur
which do not fit into this stage, are flukes or are not real events or feelings.
However, as consultants and clients converse about these events, experiences, and feelings, differences can be created that allow for clients to view
the events, experiences, and feelings in a new light. Questions from consultants that are present-based constructions might be ones like "Tell me
about times where what you want is happening now," or "Tell me about
what is different about you when your life is going more the way you like
it to go."

Encouraging 4

Solution-focused consultants believe in the power of encouraging the
client to do more of what works and less of what does not work. When in
doubt, solution-focused consultants believe that life is trial and error, and
therefore that one learns from doing something different and seeing if it
works. Solution-focused consultants use the consultation break in the session to reflect on what is working. During the break, the consultant thinks
about three aspects: encouragement, reflections, and suggestions. The *encouragement* section consists of reinforcing aspects that clients have mentioned that are good, useful, or on track for them. The *reflection* section
consists of imparting anything that consultants may want to share with
clients. This could be an educational component, research study, or a personal reaction that consultants might have had. The *suggestion* section often
includes advice for clients to think about.

There seems to be some variance among solution-focused consultants
as to what constitutes suggestions. To consultants who lean toward a brief
strategic approach, suggestions are tasks such as asking the client to do
more of what works, to observe or pretend successes, or to do something
different like experimenting with some aspect of the miracle. Solution-
focused consultants who lean more toward a collaborative approach tend
to ask clients to reflect on what was important, different, or outstanding
for them in the sessions and then to focus on that in between the therapy
sessions.

It would be very tempting for us as consultants to tell the Shore family
what they should do to make their life better. However, because the Shores
have not clearly stated what they want and there has not been a conversation about their life in the way that they want, there is no goal for us to

relate to a suggestion. Instead, we might want to reflect on the love they have for each other and their commitment to keep the family together. We might want to reflect on how each member has found ways to cope with overwhelming life difficulties and how impressive it is that they continue to dream of the future for themselves and for the family. We might want to share with them that for us to be of help, we need to know what they would like from the counseling and mention that perhaps during the time in between sessions they should think more about how the meetings could be of use to them individually or collectively. We would not give them any additional suggestions because we are not sure from the material presented in the case that they have hired us as consultants.

LIMITATIONS OF THE MODEL

The solution-focused approach appears to be as successful with a broad base of clients and a variety of problem areas as other models. However, several issues have emerged as concerns for practitioners.

First, there has been a tendency among practitioners to view the solution-focused approach as a grouping of techniques rather than as a philosophical approach to conversing with clients. When practitioners use a technique or a group of techniques without understanding or changing their thinking about people, therapy, and the process of change, they tend not to pace clients correctly or foster the consulting alliance with such aspects as empathy, warmth, and genuine concern. Without these factors, solution-focused techniques tend to force the client into solutions and become what some have labeled *solution-focused forced* (Nylund & Corsiglia, 1994).

Second, some practitioners also mistakenly think that being solution-focused means giving solutions to clients (Booker, 1996) and view the solution as a Band-Aid to the "real" or underlying issues important to the cause of the problem. They erroneously think of solution-focused consultation as a problem-solving approach rather than as a solution-construction approach.

Third, even though managed care companies have appreciated this orientation because it fits with the company's framework of cost-effective treatment and the belief in emphasizing prevention and wellness, some companies can have unreal expectations of this model. For example, companies have mistakenly expected all clients and practitioners to fit into working with eight or fewer sessions. Time and training is needed for clinicians to adapt a brief model, be it solution-focused or another kind of brief personal consultation. Again, this approach requires an epistemological change, which takes time and training. Also, some companies have at times inadvertently sabotaged a solution-focused perspective. For example when authorizing the number of sessions, some companies think of the traditional spacing of sessions and therefore give only 2 or 3 months for consulting. In a solution-focused approach, it might take 6 to 9 months to use six sessions.

Fourth, although managed care companies want practitioners to be time sensitive, some managed care companies are still requiring practitioners to assess and give a diagnosis on the clients. Diagnosis of pathology arises from a paradigm of problem formation or maintenance. Having to both diagnose and work in a solution-focused manner produces risks of mixing paradigms, which often leads to muddled thinking and muddled results.

Fifth, a competency-based approach, be it solution-focused or some other, uses a different vocabulary to describe and talk about clients and change. This language does not mesh with a pathology-oriented language. Thus, collaborating with other professionals who are using terms like *resistance, pathology, enmeshment,* and *countertransference* becomes difficult because these are problem-based concepts, not competency-based concepts.

Sixth, sometimes the standard of care for a case as interpreted from a problem-based model is not how a solution-focused consultant might interpret the standard, given that the client defines the goal of therapy. For example, a client comes in complaining of depression. The current standard of care would be to suggest that clients take antidepressant medication. The solution-focused consultant would probably inform the client that one approach is the use of medication and that there also are other approaches. Then the consultant would let the client choose.

Seventh—perhaps a minor point to the theory construction, but a practical point to the consultants—is that using a solution-focused approach can wreak havoc on one's appointment schedule. Determining how many clients to add to one's caseload when consultants do not know the spacing of the clients' sessions is difficult. Because one client might return in a week, another in 2 weeks, and yet another in a month, determining if there are enough openings to take on a new client is difficult. This can be problematic in a clinic in which a consultant is required to typically bill 28 client hours a week.

RESEARCH

Research on solution-focused consultation and brief forms of psychotherapy in general has produced some interesting findings. For example, several outcome studies suggest that brief, time-limited therapies are at least as effective as long-term approaches (Gurman & Kniskern, 1981; Koss & Shiang, 1994). In addition, the gains made in psychotherapy tend to be made in the first several sessions, with a diminishing rate of change as time progresses (Howard, Kopta, Krause, & Orlinsky, 1986). Recent research also indicates that 70% of the clients expect 10 or fewer sessions in order to reach their treatment goals, regardless of the treatment model (Garfield, 1986; Orlinsky, Grawe, & Parks, 1994; Pekarik, 1991). Yet only 10% of the clients use more than 10 sessions. In addition, the average number of sessions, regardless of model or whether the therapy was designed to be brief or long-term, was between 5 and 8 sessions (Garfield, 1986). The average number of sessions was 4.7 at BFTC (de Shazer, 1991), a slight decrease over other models. Lastly, research is finding that well-formed goals in therapy are related directly to client expectancies and successful outcome. In other words:

> The more clearly goals are defined, the greater the probability that the subjects [clients] will commit themselves to them .... Those clients who established clear goals are those with higher success expectancies with respect to the problem and with established beliefs that the solution to the problem depends on their own behavior. (Beyebach, Morejön, Palenzuela, & Rodriguez-Arias, 1996, p. 324)

These research findings and several recent studies on the effectiveness of solution-focused brief therapy (De Jong & Hopwood, 1996; Metcalf, Thomas, Duncan, Miller, & Hubble, 1996) suggest several practice implications. First, no matter what model is used, whether long-term or brief, the probability is that most clients are going to want to be in consultation for as short a time as possible. Therefore, it seems logical to work in an approach that respects the clients' wishes and helps them make the changes they want in the time that they are going to give to meeting with a consultant. Second, clients' goals seem to be a keystone in establishing client satisfaction and success in treatment, and therefore clinicians need to practice a model that respects and fosters a process of mutual goaling with the client. Third, because there are hundreds of psychotherapy approaches, obviously there is no one right or best one. If there were a best approach, therapists–consultants would all be working within that approach. Therefore, it behooves us to stay in tune with what our clients are asking for and to do what works in helping them to get what they want and to get on with their lives.

SUMMARY

Solution-focused consultation is a way of thinking, a philosophy rather than just a grouping of techniques or questions to be asked during a consultation hour. The goal of solution-focused consultation is to enter into a process of goaling with clients, to have them envision a world and life beyond their problem and then facilitate creating that world. As one enters into this process with clients, into a mutual construction of a story of their life beyond the problems—a life the way they want it to be—most people naturally realize that they are already doing what they want but have not noticed it before. Other people will naturally do what they want after they have identified it. Still others will do what it is they want when they first experience their strengths or some smaller sign of success.

When pushed to respond to practitioners about which psychotherapy approach is best, we often reflect with them on what we believe to be important. We believe that consistency of approach with one's own personal values leads not only to effective work but also to a sense of integrity and genuineness with one's clients.

Solution-focused consultation reflects the basic beliefs that we hold dear to our hearts about people, personal consulting—and the possibilities of change. A solution-focused approach guides our way of interacting with clients consistently with our beliefs of respect for people as unique individuals, respect for their self-determination, and respect for our relationship as consultants to their change process. Solution-focused consultation is an approach that allows us to foster the traditional values of the social work profession even more strongly.

REFERENCES

Anderson, H., & Goolishian, H. (1988). Human systems as linguistic systems: Preliminary and evolving ideas about the implications of clinical theory. *Family Process, 27,* 371–398.

Berg, I. (1994). *Family based services.* New York: Norton.

Berg, I., & Miller, S. (1992). *Working with the problem drinker.* New York: Norton.

Beyebach, M., Morejön, A. R., Palenzuela, D. L., & Rodriguez-Arias, J. L. (1996). Research on the process of solution-focused therapy. In S. Miller, M. Hubble, & B. Duncan (Eds.), *Handbook of solution-focused brief therapy* (pp. 299–334). New York: Norton.

Booker, J. (1996). Solution-focused hospital diversion: Treatment of first choice. In S. Miller, M. Hubble, & B. Duncan, (Eds.), *Handbook of solution-focused brief therapy* (pp. 205–227). New York: Norton.

De Jong, P., & Hopwood, L. (1996). Outcome research on treatment conducted at the Brief Family Therapy Center, 1992–1993. In S. Miller, M. Hubble, & B. Duncan, (Eds.), *Handbook of solution-focused brief therapy* (pp. 272–298). New York: Norton.

de Shazer, S. (1982). *Patterns of brief family therapy.* New York: Guilford.

de Shazer, S. (1985). *Keys to solution in brief therapy.* New York: Norton.

de Shazer, S. (1988). *Clues: Investigating solutions in brief therapy.* New York: Norton.

de Shazer, S. (1991). *Putting difference to work.* New York: Norton.

de Shazer, S. (1994). *Words were originally magic.* New York: Norton.

de Shazer, S., Berg, I. K., Lipchik, E., Nunnally, E., Molnar, A., Gingerich, W. C., & Weiner-Davis, M. (1986). Brief therapy: Focused solution development. *Family Process, 25,* 207–221.

de Shazer, S., & Molnar, A. (1984). Four useful interventions in brief family therapy. *Journal of Marital and Family Therapy, 10,* 297–304.

Durrant, M. (1993). *Residential treatment: A cooperative competency-based approach to therapy and program design.* New York: Norton.

Garfield, S. L. (1986) Research on client variables in psychotherapy. In S. L. Garfield & A. E. Bergin (Eds.), *Handbook of psychotherapy and behavior change* (3rd ed., pp. 213–256). New York: Wiley.

Gurman, A. S., & Kniskern, D. P. (1981). *Handbook of family therapy.* New York: Brunner/Mazel.

Howard, K. I., Kopta, S. M., Krause, M. S., & Orlinsky, D. E. (1986). The dose-effect relationship in psychotherapy. *American Psychologist, 41,* 159–164.

Hudson, P., & O'Hanlon, W. (1991). *Rewriting love stories.* New York: Norton.

Koss, M. P., & Shiang, J. (1994). Research on brief psychotherapy. In A. E. Bergin & S. L. Garfield (Eds.),. *Handbook of psychotherapy and behavior change* (4th ed., pp. 664–700). New York: Wiley.

Lipchik, E., & Kubicki, A. (1996). Solution- focused forced domestic violence views: Bridges towards a new reality in couples therapy. In S. Miller, M. Hubble, & B. Duncan (Eds.), *Handbook of solution-focused brief therapy* (pp. 65–98). New York: Norton.

Maturana, H., & Varela, F. (1987). *The tree of knowledge.* Boston: New Science Library.

Metcalf, L., Thomas, F., Duncan, B., Miller, S., & Hubble, M. (1996). What works in solution-focused brief therapy: A qualitative analysis of client and therapist perceptions. In S. Miller, M. Hubble, & B. Duncan (Eds.), *Handbook of solution- focused brief therapy* (pp. 335–350). New York: Norton.

Murphy, J. (1996). Solution-focused brief therapy in the school. In S. Miller, M. Hubble, & B. Duncan (Eds.), *Handbook of solution-focused brief therapy* (pp. 184–204). New York: Norton.

Nylund, D., & Corsiglia, V. (1994). Becoming solution-focused forced in brief therapy: Remembering something important we already knew. *Journal of Systemic Therapies, 13,* 5–12.

O'Hanlon, W. (1994, November/December). The third wave. *The Family Therapy Networker, 18,* 19–29.

O'Hanlon, W., & Weiner-Davis, M. (1988). *In search of solutions.* New York: Norton.

Orlinsky, D., Grawe, K., & Parks, B. (1994). Process and outcome in psychotherapy. In A. E. Bergin & S. E. Garfield (Eds.), *Handbook of psychotherapy and behavior change* (4th ed., pp. 270–375). New York: Wiley.

Pekarik, G. (1991). Relationship of expected and actual treatment duration for adult and child clients. *Journal of Clinical Child Psychology, 20,* 121–125.

Selekman, M. (1993). *Pathways to change: Brief therapy solutions to difficult adolescents.* New York: Guilford.

Vaughn, K., Young, B., Webster, D., & Thomas, M. (1996). Solution-focused work in the hospital: A continuum-of-care model for inpatient psychiatric treatment. In S. Miller, M. Hubble, & B. Duncan (Eds.), *Handbook of solution-focused brief therapy* (pp. 99–127). New York: Norton

Walter, J., & Peller, J. (1992). *Becoming solution-focused in brief therapy.* New York: Brunner/Mazel.

Walter, J., & Peller, J. (1996). Rethinking our assumptions: Assuming anew in a postmodern world. In S. Miller, M. Hubble, & B. Duncan (Eds.), *Handbook of solution-focused brief therapy* (pp. 9–26). New York: Norton.

Watzlawick, P., Weakland, J., & Fisch, R. (1974). *Change: Principles of problem formation and problem resolution.* New York: Norton.

Webster's New Collegiate Dictionary (1980). Springfield, MA: Merriam.

Weiner-Davis, M., de Shazer, S., & Gingerich, W. (1987). Using pretreatment change to construct a therapeutic solution: An exploratory study. *Journal of Marital and Family Therapy, 13,* 359–363.

5

Control-Mastery Theory

Marshall Bush, Ph.D., and
Arlene Rothschild, M.S.W.

INTRODUCTION

Control-mastery theory (CMT or CM) is a comprehensive, integrated psychoanalytic theory of mind, pathogenesis, and treatment. It is based on a model of mental functioning that has a high degree of explanatory and predictive power. It is consistent with and open to findings from related scientific disciplines such as cognitive, developmental, and evolutionary psychology. It was formulated by Joseph Weiss (1971, 1989, 1990a, 1990b, 1992, 1993b, 1994a, 1995b, 1997b, in press; Weiss, Sampson, & The Mount Zion Psychotherapy Group, 1986) and has been extensively researched by the San Francisco Psychotherapy Research Group (SFPRG), which is headed by Joseph Weiss and Harold Sampson.

Weiss's theory is "user friendly." The basic concepts are readily understandable and testable by informal clinical study as well as rigorous empirical research methods (Sampson, 1992a; Sampson & Weiss, 1986; Weiss, 1988, 1993a; Weiss & Sampson, 1986). The clinician working within this paradigm is encouraged to think like a research scientist, formulating working hypotheses about the patient's unconscious mental functioning and evaluating the correctness of those hypotheses by the patient's responses to therapeutic interventions. In this way, therapists continually verify their intuitions, correct mistakes, and adjust their technique so as to be maximally helpful to their patients.

THE CONCEPT OF THE PERSON AND THE HUMAN EXPERIENCE

From a philosophical perspective, CMT embraces both constructivism and empiricism. It focuses on the impact of traumatic events on human development and the personal meanings people assign to those events. CMT advances hypotheses about the therapeutic process that can be scientifically tested using both "subjective" and "objective" clinical data.

CMT has a strongly evolutionary, cognitive, interpersonal, and optimistic view of human nature. It postulates a "smart" unconscious that is continuously engaged in complex, adaptive, problem-solving efforts, despite the fact that such efforts are not always successful. It assumes that human beings, as social animals, are innately attuned to the moods and needs of others. Thus, people's sense of well-being is readily affected by the well-being of those they are closest to. Weiss (1993b) considers CMT to be an object relations theory because "it assumes ... that the patient develops his problems in relation to his first objects, his parents and siblings, and that he may resolve his problems in relation to another object, the therapist" (p. 203).

CMT emphasizes prosocial motives in human development and psychopathology. The theory assumes that children are highly motivated by altruism, as well as by self-interest to adapt to their interpersonal environment and help their parents. Because their physical survival and psychological sense of well-being depends on their emotional ties to their parents, they will sacrifice any aspect of their development to preserve those ties. Moreover, children typically feel responsible for other family members. They tend to blame themselves for any misfortunes that they or other family members experience, which makes them vulnerable to developing powerful forms of unconscious guilt. Children express loyalty by complying with parental wishes (as perceived by the child) and identifying with parental needs, feelings, ideas, and behavior.

Psychopathology is rooted in children's efforts to adapt to the traumatic aspects and peculiarities of their family relationships (Sampson, 1990, 1992b; Weiss, 1990a). Those relationships become internalized in the course of development and tend to be repeated in the ways that people treat themselves, their children, and their love objects. Likewise, neurotic symptoms, inhibitions, and character traits arise from unconscious compliances and identifications with unconsciously perceived parental demands and psychopathology.

Among psychoanalytic theories, CMT is unusual in the degree to which it views the unconscious mind as heavily engaged (even during dreams) in adaptive problem-solving efforts that involve complex unconscious planning, information processing, and decision making. People may solve problems unconsciously that they cannot solve consciously. The unconscious ego, guided by considerations of safety and danger (Freud's reality principle), screens environmental stimuli, regulates defensive activity, and controls the flow of mental contents to consciousness. Unconscious assessments of safety and danger are typically registered in conscious awareness as affect signals that elicit caution or provide reassurance that it is safe to proceed. Patients learn about their unconscious mental activities through their intuitions, affective reactions, dreams, and fantasies and by making inferences.

The patient's activity in therapy is understood in terms of the foregoing assumptions about unconscious mental functioning. CMT assumes that patients unconsciously develop plans to enlist the therapist's help in achieving their therapeutic goals. Because patients seek adaptive solutions to their problems, and because adaptive solutions usually necessitate seeing oneself and others realistically, patients are strongly motivated to discover the truth about themselves, their life history, their significant others, and the therapist. Patients work throughout therapy to overcome their internal obstacles to seeing things as they really are.

HISTORICAL PERSPECTIVE

Weiss's ideas about unconscious mental functioning and psychopathology have their historical roots in Freud's ego psychology (1923/1961a) and signal theory of anxiety (1926/1955). According to the signal theory, the ego's defensive activities are regulated by the reality principle—that is, by unconscious appraisals of safety and danger. The ego forms its expectations of danger on the basis of unconscious memories of childhood trauma and danger situations. Neurotic people are characterized by their adherence to maladaptive beliefs in danger situations that have long since passed. Similarly, symptoms are formed as a way to remove oneself from feared danger situations. In his later writings, Freud increasingly emphasized the role of childhood trauma (and the ego's strivings towards mastery of trauma) in the etiology of neurosis (1937/1964a, 1939/1964b, 1940/1964c) and the importance of the superego and unconscious guilt in neurotic suffering (1923/1961a, 1930/1961b).

Weiss's ideas about the adaptive nature of unconscious mental functioning first appeared in "Crying at the Happy Ending" (1952). In that article, he proposed that people unconsciously have a certain degree of adaptive control over their defenses. Therefore, when it is safe to experience a previously warded-off content, they may lift their defenses and allow that content to be expressed. The example he cited was of a moviegoer who does not feel sadness when two lovers are separated but weeps when they are reunited.

Many years of careful study of analytic-process notes and collaborative clinical research on the fate of defenses in psychoanalysis (Sampson, Weiss, Mlodnosky, & Hause, 1972; Weiss, 1967) led Weiss to further develop the hypothesis that the ego unconsciously regulates its defenses according to considerations of safety and danger. In a 1971 article, "The Emergence of New Themes: A Contribution to the Psychoanalytic Theory of Therapy," Weiss described three ways in which the *spontaneous* emergence of formerly repressed material may occur: (a) a change in life circumstances may make it safe for the patient to experience something that previously would have been too threatening; (b) an increase in the ego's control over one of its defenses (through the successful analysis of the defense) may make it safe to experience mental contents that were previously warded off by that defense; and (c) a change in the patient's relationship to the therapist may make it safe for the patient to bring forth formerly repressed material.

Weiss (1971) also presented two fundamental hypotheses about the patient's unconscious motives in therapy. First, he wrote

> The ego, it would seem, is always ready to exploit an opportunity to master a content that it once had failed to master, so that it brings forth such a content whenever it judges that it is safe to do so. (p. 460)

Secondly, Weiss postulated that patients not only make use of conditions of safety (for purposes of mastery) when they arise in the therapeutic relationship, they actively try to create them by unconsciously "testing" the therapist. Unconscious testing of the therapist to disconfirm maladaptive beliefs about situations of danger is considered to be the patient's most essential activity in the therapeutic process, and the therapist's response to the patient's testing is considered to be the most crucial determinant of therapeutic outcome.

Weiss believes that the most debilitating forms of guilt stem not from repressed sexual and aggressive wishes but from children's sense of responsibility for and loyalty to other family members. In *The Psychoanalytic Process: Theory, Clinical Observation and Empirical Research* (Weiss et al., 1986), he described how separation and survivor guilt develop and detrimentally impact development:

> A child may come to condemn himself for what is generally thought of as a normal acceptable wish or developmental goal if he infers, whether or not correctly, that by attempting to satisfy this wish or reach this goal he may threaten his all-important ties to his parents. (p. 49)

Weiss's theory of the therapeutic process, which was originally derived from detailed study of analytic process notes, has found considerable support in years of formal research:

> The present theory has been tested by the Mount Zion Psychotherapy Research Group for over 20 years, using formal quantitative research methods ... In these studies we have found strong support for the idea that the patient exerts control over his unconscious mental life. He keeps mental contents repressed as long as he unconsciously assumes that they are dangerous, and permits them to come forth when he unconsciously decides that he may safely do so. We have also found strong support for the ideas that the patient suffers from pathogenic beliefs; that in therapy he develops plans for disproving these beliefs; and that he works throughout therapy by testing these beliefs with the therapist in order to disprove them. (Weiss, 1993b, p. 20)

KEY THEORETICAL CONSTRUCTS

Pathogenic Beliefs

According to CMT, psychopathology is rooted in unconscious pathogenic beliefs that are primarily derived from the traumatic aspects of an individual's childhood. These maladaptive ideas are usually formed early in life as part of the child's efforts at adaptation and are held in place by the dangers they predict, by unconscious loyalty to parents, and by superego demands for self-punishment. Core pathogenic beliefs are very compelling and cause the child—and later the adult—to experience painful affects of fear, anxiety, guilt, or shame if they are not adhered to. The more severe the traumas underlying a pathogenic belief, the stronger the hold that the pathogenic belief has on the individual.

Pathogenic beliefs give rise to symptoms and inhibitions that serve the function of protecting the child's ties to the real parents and the adult's ties to the internalized parents. These beliefs may warn a person of potentially disastrous consequences connected to pursuing such socially desirable goals as feeling relaxed and happy, forming intimate friendships, enjoying sex, becoming professionally successful, getting married, having children, getting out of a bad relationship, and so on. They may also compel a person to engage in compulsive, self-destructive, or antisocial behavior. Thus they play an important role in maladaptive identifications with pathological parental behavior, submission to unreasonable parental demands, and compliance with unjustified parental blame and criticism.

Although pathogenic beliefs develop from a variety of sources, the most deeply entrenched and crippling ones arise from the *strain* and *shock* traumas of childhood—that is, from the ongoing traumatic aspects of one's primary relationships and unexpected traumatic events. Because of their limited understanding of true causal relationships, their egocentrism, and their magical thinking, children readily draw false conclusions about their responsibility for any mistreatment they receive at the hands of their parents and for any calamities suffered by other family members. The conclusions they reach about how their behavior affects their parents and siblings will later be generalized to all important object relationships. Because young children endow their parents with absolute authority, they may also develop pathogenic beliefs by accepting what their parents tell them, by complying with how their parents treat them, and by identifying with their parents' own pathogenic beliefs.

Patients' Plans, Purposes, and Goals

All purposive human behavior is based on plans and goals. This is no less true of unconsciously motivated behavior than of consciously intended actions. CMT assumes that patients unconsciously know what is best for them. Their unconscious goals are reasonable and adaptive. Patients are highly motivated to pursue those goals, even though they may not appear to be. Their goals include wanting to disprove their pathogenic beliefs, obtain relief from neurotic symptoms and inhibitions, overcome self-destructive behavior patterns, and achieve some measure of happiness and success in their personal relationships and their work.

Patients work to overcome their problems in an orderly fashion. They unconsciously prioritize which goals they may safely tackle first and which they may need to defer until they have developed more internal strength, external support, or confidence in the therapist. Everything they say in therapy is unconsciously intended to elicit information about the therapist's attitude toward their goals and his or her willingness (and capacity) to help them. They try to elicit corrective emotional experiences and valuable insights that will assist them in their struggle to overcome pathogenic beliefs and master their childhood traumas.

In devising their unconscious plans, patients take into account the length of time they expect to be in therapy, the personality of the therapist, the exigencies of pressing life problems, and the strength of their pathogenic beliefs. Patients entering a time-limited therapy will have more limited goals than patients embarking on a long-term treatment. Even patients who appear to have no direction or who claim to be coming to therapy at someone else's insistence will work in accordance with an unconscious plan. These unconscious plans are flexible within limits. They always involve testing the therapist in an effort to disconfirm their pathogenic beliefs. Some patients may spend an entire analysis attempting to disconfirm a few debilitating beliefs. Patients will attempt to coach the therapist about how to pass their tests and make helpful interventions. Their plans are guided by considerations of safety and danger and by an assessment of the therapist's strengths and weaknesses, as well as their own.

The concept of a plan provides a coherent and unifying explanation of the patient's behavior over the entire course of therapy as well as a guide for how the therapist can be most helpful to the patient. Patients are likely to make progress in therapy as long as the therapist makes interpretations that they can use in their struggle to carry out their plans. If the therapist continues to make interpretations that go against the patient's plan, the therapy will stall and the patient may get worse and eventually quit. Weiss (Weiss et al., 1986) drew the following analogy between working with or against a patient's plan and pushing a boulder:

> When the analyst helps the patient to go where he unconsciously wants to go, the analyst feels as though he is pushing a large round rock down a gentle but perhaps bumpy slope. The rock may have its jolts, its stops, and its starts, but it moves forward. When the analyst hinders the patient from going where he unconsciously wants to go, the analyst feels as though he is pushing the rock uphill. It is hard work, and once the pressure on the rock is removed, it may roll backwards; the ground that had been won with such difficulty may be quickly lost. (p. 93)

Testing

Testing is a fundamental human activity, one of the primary means by which we probe our interpersonal world to discover its dangers and opportunities. People may be consciously aware of their testing behavior in everyday life situations (as when a young man puts out "feelers" to see if an attractive female is going to reciprocate his interest). However, in a therapy situation people are generally not aware that they are engaging in such behavior. *Testing* is the primary means through which patients attempt to disconfirm their pathogenic beliefs, correct their transference distortions, borrow strengths from the therapist, and discover how safe it is to lift their repressions (and confront their warded-off wishes, affects, and childhood traumas). Testing also serves to tell patients how much help they will receive in facing the guilt, shame, and anxiety connected to moving toward their goals. The testing is unconscious because it is connected to traumas, pathogenic beliefs, affects, and wishes that the patient cannot yet face. Because patients take some degree of emotional risk in testing the therapist, testing produces strain in the patient. Patients test throughout therapy, usually progressing from more cautious to more high-risk tests. However, in some cases, the dangers predicted by certain pathogenic beliefs may be so great that the patient will never risk testing them.

At the same time that therapists are seeking to gain an increasingly accurate understanding of their patients' unconscious plans, the patients, through their testing, are unconsciously and consciously trying to accurately assess the therapist's strengths, weaknesses, attitudes, and intentions. In one sense, patients are always testing because they draw inferences from any response (or lack of response) the therapist has to their behavior. Patients test their pathogenic beliefs in a variety of ways, and therapists can pass or fail tests in a variety of ways. In preparing tests, patients unconsciously make decisions about the risks of being retraumatized in posing certain tests and about how best to pose tests that the therapist can pass. The patient will work to find ways of testing that fit the therapist's personality, and the therapist will try to find ways of responding that fit the patient's style of testing. Patients usually try to "coach" the therapist after a failed test and typically give the therapist further opportunities to pass their tests before abandoning an important goal or the therapy.

Although most things patients say and do have some testing function, certain behaviors stand out as conspicuous examples of tests, such as actions that call for a response from the therapist or contrast sharply with the patient's usual behavior. The patient's transferences and repetitions almost always serve important testing functions and are enacted for the purpose of mastering important childhood traumas. Patients typically use a variety of testing strategies (including their transferences and resistances) to disconfirm a single prominent pathogenic belief.

Weiss (Weiss et al., 1986) has identified two primary forms of testing in which patients repeat the past in order to disconfirm pathogenic beliefs and give themselves corrective emotional experiences. The form he calls "transferring" is similar to what Freud meant by transference in that patients relate to the therapist as they did to a parent. They hope that the therapist will not traumatize them as the parent did. This is usually done through a series of successive approximations as patients feel increasingly safe to directly revisit their original traumatic situations.

A patient whose parent could tolerate no expression of criticism (or pride, playfulness, sadness, etc.), might, for example, gradually test a pathogenic belief that criticism destroys relationships by becoming increasingly critical of the therapist. If the therapist remains unharmed and friendly despite the patient's criticism, the patient might begin to remember how enraged and rejecting a parent became in reaction to the patient's saying something critical. The patient might then begin to better comprehend the parent's narcissistic fragility and realize that one need not react that way. Transferring is the most direct way to test a pathogenic belief because it symbolically recreates the original traumatic situation that gave rise to the belief.

The second form of repeating the past in the service of testing is referred to as *turning passive into active*. In this type of testing, the patient takes the role of the traumatizing parent and puts the therapist in the role of the traumatized child. Passive-into-active testing is more indirect and may be less stressful for patients (but more stressful the therapist) who use the defense of identification with the aggressor. Highly traumatized patients may work primarily through passive-into-active testing, especially if they have formed strong unconscious identifications with a traumatizing parent. Patients who counter-identify with traumatizing parents may try to avoid this type of testing.

It should be noted that the mechanism of identification with the aggressor may serve other functions than testing. For example, it may be used primarily for defense or self-punishment. In its most primitive form, it represents an effort to master the helplessness of a traumatic situation by taking the role of the aggressor and inflicting a similar trauma on someone else. When employed for testing purposes, it represents an attempt to use the therapist as a role model for dealing with past traumas as well as upcoming stressful situations. For example, someone preparing for a visit from very rejecting parents might temporarily act rejecting toward the therapist in the hope of being able to identify with the therapist's ability to be undaunted by rejection.

How the therapist feels in the session is an important indicator of the type of testing the patient is doing. If the therapist is being made to feel angry, confused, inadequate, guilty, or overly responsible for the patient, it is usually an indication that the patient is testing primarily by turning passive-into-active. If the therapist is feeling relatively comfortable, the patient is probably testing primarily by transferring. Most patients use both testing strategies at different times and sometimes pose tests that involve both transferring and turning passive-into-active at the same time.

The patient's testing behavior is always guided by considerations of safety and danger. Patients who find it safer to test by turning passive-into-active may do so for the first several years of treatment before they feel secure enough with the therapist to test by transferring. Other patients may do the reverse because they feel it is too risky to test by turning passive-into-active until they have gained confidence in the therapist's ability to handle the stress that such testing induces.

ASSESSMENT

During the first few sessions the therapist should try to infer the patient's unconscious plan from the patient's verbal communication, from how the patient makes the therapist feel, and from how the patient responds to what the therapist says. In making provisional plan formulations, it is useful to learn as much as possible about how patients view their childhood traumas; describe their goals for therapy; and see their psychological problems, current life circumstances, and future life opportunities. A plan formulation is specific to each patient because every person's childhood traumas, pathogenic beliefs, life story, and current life situation are unique.

The therapist's formulation should attempt to account for everything the therapist knows about the patient, and it should be revised as needed to accommodate new information and observations. It should contain inferences about what goals the patient will want to pursue, what pathogenic beliefs the patient will work to disconfirm, what traumas the patient will try to master, what insights the patient will need to acquire, and what testing strategies the patient is likely to use. A correct plan formulation enables the therapist to understand the patient's problems, transferences, and resistances, to pass the patient's tests, to make helpful interventions, and to see the continuity and coherence of the patient's behavior over the entire course of the therapy. It also enables therapists to understand their own subjective reactions to the patient.

At the outset of treatment, patients usually try to provide the therapist with the necessary information and clues for understanding their unconscious plan because they urgently want the therapist to pass their tests and make "pro-plan" interpretations. For example, they may indirectly coach the therapist by commenting on what they liked or did not like about a previous therapist, or they may directly tell the therapist what they feel they need. Some patients are so vulnerable to feeling humiliated that they have to conceal their most troubling problems until they feel sufficiently reassured that the therapist will not shame them.

Patients vary considerably in the degree to which they can accept help and allow themselves to be aware of their therapeutic goals, childhood traumas, and pathogenic beliefs. Patients who suffer from severe unconscious guilt may not feel deserving of help and may therefore present themselves as much more disturbed, unlikable, and untreatable than they actually are. Most patients want and need help in combating the superego pressures that make them feel undeserving and bad about themselves.

Knowing about a patient's childhood traumas may provide important clues to the nature of the patient's problems and pathogenic beliefs. For example, Weiss (1993b) discussed how "shock traumas" may create severe problems with unconscious guilt, worry, and a belief in one's own omnipotence:

> The patient who suffers a sudden catastrophe in childhood tends to experience it as a punishment for something bad he had done. Since he considers it a punishment, he may become unduly guilty, and since he believes himself responsible for it, he may develop a belief in his omnipotence. The more severe the catastrophe, the more guilty and

omnipotent he may believe himself to be. In addition, he may infer from the sudden unfortunate turn in his fortunes that catastrophe may strike at any time. He must therefore keep himself vigilant and thus prepared for another blow by fate. (p. 74)

Weiss (1993b) stressed the importance of distinguishing between the patient's adaptive plans for mastery and the kind of self-destructive acting out that represents an unconscious capitulation to one's pathogenic beliefs:

The patient's adaptive plans for working to disprove his pathogenic beliefs should be distinguished from the maladaptive, self-destructive plans a patient makes in obedience to these beliefs. Such plans express patients' poor self-esteem or the unconscious shame, guilt, or remorse that stem from pathogenic beliefs. The patient behaves differently when the therapist challenges a maladaptive plan than when the therapist challenges an adaptive plan. When the therapist challenges a patient's maladaptive plan, such as a plan to relinquish a cherished ambition or to make a bad marriage, the patient is relieved. When the therapist challenges an adaptive plan the patient becomes depressed. (p. 10)

An accurate plan formulation is an invaluable guide for understanding the therapeutic process with a given patient. Therapists new to CMT will benefit greatly from receiving consultation early in the treatment that is aimed at inferring the patient's plan (Gassner, 1990; Rosbrow, 1997).

TREATMENT OF CHOICE

CMT is a general model of mental functioning that is applicable to all forms of therapeutic intervention. It has particular relevance to social work because it enables clinicians to make early assessments of complex individual and family problems and to intervene in pragmatically helpful ways. It has been successfully used by social workers, psychologists, and psychiatrists to treat a wide range of patients—adults (Bader, 1994; Browne, 1993, 1995; Canestro, 1996; Fretter, 1995; Friedman, 1985a; Gootnick, 1982; Kale, 1995; Lowenstein, 1995; Moon, 1995; O'Connor, 1993; O'Connor & Weiss, 1993; Rappoport, 1986; Redmond, 1995; Silberschatz & Curtis, 1991, in press; Sohn, 1995; Suffridge, 1991; Weiss, 1993b; Weiss et al., 1986; Wood, 1997; Zaslav, 1994), children (Foreman, 1993; Foreman, Gibbins, & Berry, 1992; Gibbins & Foreman, 1989; Graf, 1995; Grienenberger & Foreman, 1993), and adolescents (Badger, 1997; Badger & Riley, 1995; Palley, 1997). It has also been used in a variety of formats: long (Fretter, 1995; Sampson, 1989, 1991; Weiss, 1989, 1993a, 1994a, in press, Weiss et al.,

1986) and short-term individual therapy (Coleman, 1989; Curtis & Silberschatz, 1986; Fretter, 1984; Grebel, 1992; Kale, 1986; Kelly, 1989; Linsner, 1987; Meyers, 1993; Norville, Sampson, & Weiss, 1996; O'Connor, Edelstein, Berry, & Weiss, 1994; Silberschatz & Curtis, 1986, 1991); couples therapy (Foreman, 1996; Vogel, 1994; Zeitlin, 1991); family therapy (Edmund, Folsom, Foreman, Gibbins, & Jenney, 1994; Folsom, 1993; Kanofsky, 1996); group therapy (Cooper, 1996; Cristofalo, 1995; Hausman & Maslow, 1995; Maslow, 1994; Maslow & Hausman, 1994); career counseling (Goodfriend & Kramer, 1996); crisis intervention (Nichols, 1989); addiction treatment (O'Connor & Weiss, 1993; Schumacher, 1995); and child-custody mediation (Chase, 1996). It has also been applied to the study of psychobiography (Conrad, 1995; Goldberg, 1997), parenting styles (Shilkret & Vecchiotti, 1997), and students' plans for college (Shilkret & Nigrosh, 1997). Clinicians interested in learning how to apply CMT attend week-long training workshops sponsored by the SFPRG.

THE THERAPEUTIC PROCESS

The CMT view of the therapeutic process follows directly from the theory of psychopathology and mental functioning presented above. It is not based on any particular set of techniques because no set of techniques (divorced from a comprehensive understanding of a particular patient's goals, pathogenic beliefs, and traumas) is correct in the abstract. The therapist's essential task is to use the techniques that will assist patients in carrying out their unconscious plans. Interventions must always be guided by an anticipation of how those interventions will be experienced by the patient.

> The therapist's task is to help the client to carry out his plan for disproving his pathogenic beliefs and pursuing the goals that the beliefs warn him against. The accomplishment of this task is so central that the therapist may judge a particular technique by the criterion "Does it help the client to disprove his pathogenic belief and to pursue the forbidden goal?"
>
> The therapist's approach is case-specific. He attempts to help each client to disprove his particular pathogenic beliefs and to pursue his particular goals. He does this by passing the client's tests, by offering him pro-plan interpretations and by his overall approach and attitude. (Weiss, 1994b, pp. 6–7)

According to CMT, a therapeutic process exists whenever a therapist is working collaboratively with a patient to disprove the patient's pathogenic beliefs and help the patient advance toward his or her therapeutic goals.

Weiss (Weiss et al., 1986) makes the following distinction between a therapeutic process and a neurotic process:

> The concept of therapy as a process in which a patient gradually disconfirms his pathogenic beliefs permits us to make a distinction between therapeutic and neurotic processes. A therapeutic process is one in which the patient disconfirms certain pathogenic beliefs, becomes more conscious of them, and so gains control over the affects, impulses, ideas, and developmental goals he was warding off in obedience to these beliefs. It is a process in which the patient becomes more insightful and less anxious, guilty, and defensive. A neurotic process is the opposite of a therapeutic process. In a neurotic process a patient finds his pathogenic beliefs confirmed by his experiences so that he becomes more frightened, anxious, guilty, or ashamed. He intensifies his repressions and therefore becomes less conscious of his pathogenic beliefs and of the various motives, affects, and ideas that he was warding off in obedience to them. He becomes less insightful and more defensive. (pp. 114–115)

Structural change may be understood in terms of the progress patients make in altering their pathogenic beliefs, overcoming their pathological identifications and compliances, and acquiring new psychological capacities.

The therapist's task, most importantly, is to help patients disconfirm their pathogenic beliefs by passing their tests. Therapists usually have considerable latitude in the range of responses that will pass a patient's tests. Therapists may pass (or fail) tests by their interventions, their manner, their attitude, and their emotional reactions. It is often helpful to give patients insight into their testing behavior as long as such interpretations are compatible with passing the patient's test.

Patients differ widely in how they test, depending on the nature of their childhood traumas, their personality structure, their therapeutic goals, and their strategies for mastery. People with severe trust problems may give the therapist a thin margin of error before jumping to the conclusion that they are in a dangerous situation and terminating the treatment. Severely traumatized patients may pose passive-into-active tests that are enormously difficult to pass and that severely tax the emotional resources of the therapist. Patients who feel omnipotently responsible for the therapist may present only very mild or disguised tests.

Sometimes, after an unsuccessful course of treatment, patients change their testing strategies. For example, after a failed therapy, a patient may switch from having an intensely erotic transference with the first therapist to having a conspicuously nonerotic transference with the second therapist. Certain patients may chose to see two different therapists simultaneously so that they can test one by transferring and the other by turning passive into active. Treatability depends on whether a patient is able to pose passable tests, tolerate therapist errors (failed tests and anti-plan interventions), and provide sufficient coaching (or other forms of feedback) to get the therapist back on track.

In addition to passing specific tests, therapists use interpretation to expand patients' insight into their self-destructive behaviors, maladaptive defenses, pathological compliances and identifications, and unconscious pathogenic beliefs, goals, and testing. They increase the patient's feelings of safety in the therapeutic relationship by interpreting transference dangers, providing superego protection, challenging the patient's false self-blame, and adopting a stance that counteracts the patient's pathogenic beliefs.

Having the authority of the therapist behind the patient's goals may help the patient feel more entitled to pursue those goals. The therapist may also enable the patient to feel more normal and less ashamed by placing the patient's problems in a broad explanatory perspective that includes the adaptive functions the patient's symptoms were originally intended to serve. Therapists should attempt to demystify patients' psychopathology and help patients feel good about themselves.

Therapists may make it safer for patients to undertake new challenges by helping them develop new capacities and increase their control of defenses they were formerly unable to regulate. For example, a woman who cannot control her submissiveness may need to avoid intimate relationships (for fear of being dominated) until she develops the capacity to be noncompliant. A man who suffers from intense shame may need to increase his ability to experience pride before he can begin to face a problem he feels ashamed of. Numerous examples of such therapeutic principles may be found in *How Psychotherapy Works* (Weiss, 1993b).

The CM approach to treating patients requires that the therapist be empathically in the moment with the patient while simultaneously maintaining the intellectual distance to make inferences about the patient's unconscious testing and about whether the therapist is passing those tests. In order to accomplish this, therapists should try to keep in mind everything they know about the patient. Understanding a person's childhood traumas, pathogenic beliefs, and life story gives the therapist empathy for the patient's unconscious fears and wishes and helps the therapist anticipate how different kinds of interpretations will be heard by the patient.

CM therapists use patients' reactions (both inside and outside of the therapy) to gauge the effectiveness of their approach. When the therapist makes interventions that pass the patient's tests or support the patient's plan, the patient feels reassured and may become momentarily less anxious, bolder, and more insightful. The patient's increased sense of confidence in the therapist may lead to the posing of more high-risk tests or to the emergence of formerly warded-off contents. When the therapist's interventions fail a test or oppose the patient's plan, the patient may "coach" the therapist, attempt to make the test more obvious, or return to a test the therapist had previously passed. Repeated failures of the patient's tests or consistent anti-plan interpretations may retraumatize the patient by validating the patient's pathogenic beliefs. The patient may subsequently become depressed, give up important life goals, comply with the therapist's anti-plan interpretations, and engage in self-destructive behavior.

Therapist interventions that mildly fail tests or slightly impede the patient's progress can generally be easily corrected, especially with healthier patients. All therapists fail tests and make anti-plan interpretations at times. Once a therapist recognizes that a test has been failed, a variety of things can be done. The failure can be discussed with the patient, who usually finds it reassuring that the therapist can recognize, admit to, and correct mistakes. In some instances it may be best to simply wait for the next opportunity to pass a similar test. Weiss (1993b) described how therapists can recognize failed tests:

> Often the therapist may infer from the patient's response that he has failed a test. The patient usually reacts differently when the therapist fails a test than when he passes it. If the therapist fails a test by giving a poor intervention, the patient may respond less enthusiastically than usual, or he may become slightly depressed or silent. Also, he may fail to bring forth new material, or he may ignore the interpretation or change the topic. If the patient responds in one of these ways, the therapist may ask him, "How do you feel about what I just said?" or "Have I missed the point of what you were saying?"
>
> Once the therapist begins to understand how he has failed a particular test, he may explain his failure to the patient. For example, he may tell a patient, "When you were complaining, you wanted me to help you realize you had a right to complain. Therefore, you were disappointed when I tried to encourage you. You took this to mean that I didn't want to hear your complaints." (p. 118)

Sometimes a failed test may be inferred from the fact that the therapy becomes stalemated (although real stalemates need to be differentiated from prolonged passive-into-active tests in which the patient claims to be making no progress as part of a test). The failure of an important test is especially damaging if the patient reacts by giving up a major goal without giving any indication of it or makes a self-destructive decision that cannot be reversed.

Therapists sometimes realize they are being tested without being sure what the test is until after the patient responds by advancing or retreating. At other times, therapists may not realize that the patient has been posing an important test until there is an unexpected new development in the therapy. At that point, the therapist may be able to retrospectively recognize the nature of the testing in which the patient has been engaged.

Patients usually test the same pathogenic beliefs in a variety of ways over a long period of time. The length of time a treatment takes is largely determined by the strength of the patient's pathogenic beliefs and the nature of testing required to disconfirm those beliefs. An important pathogenic belief is never tested only once unless the therapist badly fails the test. Pathogenic beliefs stemming from highly traumatic experiences can only be disconfirmed gradually (if at all) because the danger of being retraumatized if the therapist fails the test is too great.

Complex sets of pathogenic beliefs often need to be tested sequentially. For example, a patient who is afraid of both being rejected and being possessed may alternate between giving the therapist rejection and possessiveness tests. If the therapist passes a possessiveness test, the patient may suspect it is because the therapist does not care about the patient, and vice versa. Some pathogenic beliefs, such as a belief in eventual betrayal, inherently take a very long time to disconfirm.

Weiss (1993b) recommended that when patients test their pathogenic beliefs through displaying a persistent attitude, the therapist in turn adopt a consistent attitude that will counter the patient's pathogenic beliefs. He wrote, "For example, in treating a patient who displays a persistently friendly attitude in order to test the belief that he should be rejected, the therapist should return the patient's friendliness" (pp. 102–103). Sampson (1994) developed the importance of this principle in an article entitled "Treatment by Attitudes."

An understanding of passive-into-active testing may help a therapist more effectively treat and sympathize with patients who might otherwise seem untreatable or unbearable, such as highly resistant, obnoxious, or acting-out patients. Severely traumatized patients who test primarily by turning passive-into-active usually induce very disturbing affects (worry, shame, confusion, anger, guilt, etc.) in the therapist. Weiss (1993b) offered the following advice for dealing with such patients:

> In order to pass the patient's passive-into-active tests, the therapist tries to demonstrate a better way of dealing with the patient's disturbing behavior than the patient used in childhood to deal with his parents' disturbing behavior. The therapist's approach and attitude are as important as his interpretations, if not more so. In general, the therapist should not interpret the patient's disturbing behavior as soon as he displays it. Before he interprets it, he should attempt to demonstrate that he is able to deal effectively with it. (p. 114)

Because patients often feel guilty and confused about why they are revisiting their childhood traumas upon their therapist, interpreting the mastery and testing function of such behavior can be quite helpful and relieving. Moreover, the patient may borrow the therapist's capacity to see his or her disturbing behavior in a sympathetic light. The therapist should always try to make the patient feel safe in the therapeutic relationship and should attempt to reduce the patient's irrational feelings of guilt, shame, and anxiety.

THE SHORES

The Shore family sounds likable and poignant. They suffer from severe internal conflicts and reality problems but resist succumbing to despair. If they were to be treated as part of a CMT research project, an individualized case formulation would be prepared for each family member. The formulation would contain hypotheses about each person's unconscious plan for therapy, information about pertinent childhood traumas, and conjectures about potentially helpful insights. In the short space available for comment on the Shores, we present a CMT approach to understanding them in terms of their childhood traumas, pathogenic beliefs, unconscious compliances and identifications, and problems with unconscious guilt and shame.

Michael

Michael is inspiring because of his refusal to give up his goals despite repeated failures. He attempts to learn as much as he can about the adult world and has developed a philosophical perspective that makes his suffering bearable and understandable. He displays a strong drive toward mastery in the face of daunting problems. His earliest memory of struggling for air may reflect an unconscious pathogenic belief that life is supposed to be hard and that everything should be as much of a struggle for him as it is for his parents. Because Nancy intensely worries about his medical and emotional problems, Michael may believe that he is an incredible burden who robs other people of their happiness. He not only keeps his mother constantly worried, he also makes his father feel helpless and inadequate by presenting problems his father can't solve. On the other hand, in a crisis Nancy is at her best and can obtain momentary relief from her chronic worry, so Michael may also hold the contradictory belief that his mother needs him to be handicapped. He may therefore have problems partly to energize and mobilize her.

The memory of wanting to hit an ugly nurse who gave him a shot (instead of giving him air) and wanting to tell her he was perfectly fine suggests that he feels misunderstood, is angry at his mother for placing him in the patient role, and has identified with his father's use of denial both to combat feeling defective and to offer reassurance to his mother. Michael identifies with his father in wanting to be great at something, but he may also need to fail in order to protect (in the sense of not outdoing) his father, who suffers from low self-esteem and intense feelings of inadequacy.

Michael's feelings of inadequacy may stem from several sources—real physical handicaps, an inability to make his parents happy or proud (an intergenerational family dynamic), an identification with his parents' sense of shame about themselves, and ostracization by his peer group. To the extent that his problems are not organic, his bizarre and inappropriate behaviors may reflect an identification (motivated by unconscious loyalty and survivor guilt) with his father's clowning and inappropriate behavior. Michael may hold the pathogenic belief that he does not deserve to be accepted and respected by his peers because his father is not accepted and respected. His interest in becoming a psychologist may express a wish to understand and cure his parents, as well as an identification with Nancy's desire to take care of others. Michael's constant squabbling with his father may stem more from Charley's need to avoid taking a parental role than from Michael's problems with authority.

Michael's goals for therapy might be to feel like a normal boy, to feel like less of a burden to other people, to feel less responsible for his parents' unhappiness, to make friends, to have accomplishments he can feel proud of, and to be able to protect and defend himself when he is mistreated. He might find ways of testing the therapist to disprove his pathogenic beliefs that he is very burdensome, worrisome, and unlikable. He would probably want the therapist to show confidence in him, to not be easily provoked by his challenging and provocative behavior, to enjoy working with him, and to not feel overly burdened by his problems. He may also want to use the therapist as a mentor and role model for how to relate to other people in constructive ways.

Rena

Rena exhibits the tragic consequences of survivor guilt and feeling unloved by a mother she could never make happy despite her extraordinary gifts and accomplishments. Under the weight of her mother becoming a near-invalid and losing all hope of returning to nursing, her father's chronic unemployment and psychotic break, and her brother's life-threatening illness and daily humiliations in school, she became overwhelmed by her guilt about being better off than her parents and brother. She unconsciously feels terribly sorry for the rest of her family because life is such a struggle for them. Because of her pathogenic belief that her success came at her family's expense, she gave up being successful and began acting like an invalid herself. She replaced her pride in her accomplishments with shame about her failures. She dropped out of high school, got a GED, and tried to prepare for medical school, but couldn't. She also could not allow herself to be liked by other children, probably because her brother was unable to make friends. The fact that she is now thinking of pursuing nursing suggests that Rena has both identified with Nancy and does not feel she the right to surpass her mother by becoming a doctor. She has shifted from trying to make her father happy by being a performer to trying to make her mother happy by becoming a nurse. Choosing boyfriends who are worse off than she is further suggests that she feels compelled to identify with Nancy.

Rena accepted her parents' blame and criticism and has come to believe that she looks for excuses to "mess up," creates problems when none exist, forces people (most notably her parents) to reject her so that she can feel like a victim, and chooses to be lazy. Saying that "Gram was the only one in the whole world who ever loved her" suggests that Rena felt unloved by Nancy and may have started singing in an attempt to cheer up her depressed mother and to disprove the pathogenic belief that she was unlovable.

Why Rena felt so unloved by Nancy and so preoccupied with thoughts of her birth mother is unclear. Nancy may have unconsciously felt compelled to repeat her own childhood rejections with Rena out of guilt toward her mother (i.e., so as not to enjoy her daughter more than her mother enjoyed her). Nancy's preoccupations with Michael's asthma and lack of attention to Rena's giftedness may have contributed to Rena's feeling that she didn't matter. Having been given up for adoption only strengthened the idea that she was unlovable. At the time of the initial interview, Rena felt compelled to find out why her birth mother gave her up. Being allowed to live alone in the downstairs apartment reinforced Rena's belief that she was unwanted and impossible to deal with. Her irresponsible behavior sounds like a plea for limits and a manifestation of depression that went unnoticed by her parents, who were themselves very depressed and unable to exercise reasonable parental authority with their daughter.

Rena's goals for therapy would probably involve wanting to overcome her survivor guilt towards her family so that she can pursue her ambitions and enjoy being successful. She will probably test the therapist to disprove the ideas that she is impossible, unlovable, and deserving of rejection, and she may act rejecting herself in the hope of being able to identify with the therapist's capacity to not comply with rejection. She will want her therapist to support her ambitions, enjoy her talents, and not be hurt by her accomplishments.

Charley

Charley constantly struggles to disconfirm the pathogenic belief that he is a worthless failure who deserves to be neglected, shunned, and ridiculed. He desperately seeks attention and admiration through brag-ging, clowning, and composing grandiose schemes, which only makes him appear more needy and pathetic in Nancy's eyes. His deep sense of shame and inadequacy probably has several origins—feeling he could never make his long-suffering mother happy, complying with his father's rejection and mistreatment of him; identifying with his father's deficiencies and narcis-sistic vulnerabilities, and feeling ashamed of his parents' constant fighting and neglect of him (his clothes were never "right"). Feeling alone, unpro-tected, and despairing as a child, he escaped into a world of denial in fan-tasy. His manic–depressive break speaks to the possibility of some organic underpinnings to his problems.

The lack of parental nurturing and guidance in Charley's childhood, combined with his unconscious identifications with an abusive, immature and irresponsible father, make it difficult for him to relate to his children as an adult authority. He lies to his wife in an attempt to cheer her up and assuage her anxieties. He wants to make her happy but feels unable to re-alistically obviate her worries about money. He may unconsciously believe that he deserves to be poor (because his parents were poor) and be treated by Nancy in the same way his father was treated by his mother (with con-tempt).

Charley's goals for therapy will include wanting to feel proud of him-self and to become a better parent and provider. He may test to see whether he can make his therapist happy (in the mother transference) and whether his therapist will need to put him down (in the father transference). He may also belittle the therapist in the hope of being able to identify with the therapist's capacity to withstand being shamed. A pro-plan stance might involve being responsive to Charley's humor, acknowledging his accom-plishments, being protective of his self-esteem, empathizing with his feel-ings, protecting him from behaving self-destructively, and helping him feel less responsible for his wife's anxiety and depression.

Nancy

Nancy suffers from an intense sense of omnipotent responsibility for her family. She lives in a state of heightened arousal and vigilance, constantly anticipates catastrophes, and believes that she alone can fix family prob-lems. She tortures herself with worry, feelings of shame about being obese, and thoughts about other people making disparaging remarks about her weight should she leave the house. She unconsciously believes that she does not deserve to enjoy herself or her family (because she had an un-happy mother who lost her husband and could not take pleasure in her daughter). She fights with her daughter, worries about her son, and feels embarrassed by her husband.

The two biggest traumas of her childhood seem to have been feeling unwanted by her mother and feeling abandoned by her father when he unexpectedly left the family. Nancy developed the pathogenic beliefs that she is unlovable and that terrible things can happen when you least expect them to. Like Charley, she felt very alone with her sadness and consoled herself with fantasies about her father's return.

Nancy tried to overcome her feelings of unlovability, unimportance, and helplessness by becoming a proficient nurse and marrying a handsome man, but her disabling back injury and Michael's near-death asthmatic crises reconfirmed her childhood pathogenic beliefs. She took these traumatic events as punishments for enjoying her life and forgetting to worry about all the bad things that can happen at any time. Having learned her lesson, she now takes pleasure in nothing and worries to the point of having daily anxiety attacks.

Nancy's goals for therapy might include worrying less, feeling less responsible for her children's problems, developing a more loving relationship with her daughter, getting closer to Charley, enjoying her life more, and rebuilding her self-confidence and self-esteem. She will benefit from having a therapist who does not feel overly responsible for her, who can appreciate her wit and perceptiveness, and who can enable her to not use worry as a magical protection against and preparation for impending disaster. She will probably pose both worry and rejection tests in her efforts to overcome her pathogenic beliefs. If she gains sufficient confidence in her therapist's skill and good intentions, she may feel safe enough to tackle her weight problem.

If the resources were available, the Shore family might benefit from a combination of long-term individual and family therapy. Each person has well-established pathogenic beliefs that could potentially be disconfirmed by the kind of testing and interpretive work that occurs in individual therapy. There is also a significant degree of mutual misunderstanding that might be corrected through family therapy. Each person seems to want to make positive changes on both an individual and familial level.

LIMITATIONS OF THE MODEL

CMT has been least applied in severely disturbed psychotic populations. It remains to be determined whether patients with grossly impaired reality testing or horrific life traumas have the capacity to pose passable tests and to benefit from pro-plan interpretations. There are also special populations (such as drug addicted patients) that may require placement in a structured, pro-plan treatment setting before they can feel sufficiently safe and hopeful to test their pathogenic beliefs. Patients who are too discouraged, distrustful, or impaired to initiate testing on their own may require a therapist who can, at least initially, provide the experiences needed to counter the pathogenic beliefs that limit their ability to test.

RESEARCH

Over the past 25 years, the SFPRG has carried out numerous quantitative research studies to test the basic tenets of CMT. These studies use an innovative repeated-measures single-case design. The findings to date provide strong support for the following hypotheses:

1. Patients unconsciously decide when to lift their repressions and inhibitions according to considerations of safety and danger.
2. Patients are powerfully motivated to master their problems in therapy, and they develop adaptive unconscious plans for how to do so.
3. A patient's unconscious plan can reliably be inferred from a few initial sessions.
4. Patients' plans include strategies for testing the therapist in order to disconfirm their pathogenic beliefs.
5. Plan formulations have predictive power in that they enable judges to reliably identify tests, to determine whether the therapist is passing or failing the patient's tests, and to assess how helpful or detrimental particular interventions are likely to be.
6. Passed tests and pro-plan interventions are associated with therapeutic progress, whereas failed tests and anti-plan interventions are associated with a lack of progress or therapeutic retreats.
7. Survivor guilt plays an important role in many types of psychopathology.

The first quantitative research studies (Weiss et al., 1986) used the transcripts and process notes of a successfully completed analysis. The therapist was a traditional psychoanalyst who was unfamiliar with CMT. The patient, Mrs. C, was a young married woman who agreed to be recorded for research purposes. Four of the initial studies (Curtis, Ransohoff, Sampson, Brumer, & Bronstein, 1986; Gassner, Sampson, Weiss, & Brumer, 1982; Shilkret, Isaacs, Drucker, & Curtis, 1986; Silberschatz, Sampson, & Weiss, 1986) were designed to test hypotheses based on the CMT higher mental functioning model of the unconscious against contradictory hypotheses based on the automatic functioning model of the unconscious contained in traditional psychoanalytic theory. These studies tested the assumptions that patients are highly motivated to gain insight into the unconscious sources of their problems and will test the therapist to disconfirm their pathogenic beliefs. Moreover, patients will begin to lift their repressions, overcome their inhibitions, and become aware of their pathogenic beliefs when they unconsciously decide that it is safe to do so.

Gassner et al. (1982) used an ingenious methodology to test predictions about how previously uninterpreted, repressed mental contents would be experienced by the patient when they first emerged in consciousness. All of the findings strongly supported the predictions based on CMT, indicating that Mrs. C was bringing repressed contents to consciousness because she wanted to master them and felt safe to do so. In a related study, Curtis et al. (Curtis, Ransohoff, Sampson, Brumer, & Bronstein, 1986) tracked changes in Mrs. C's inhibitions about being assertive as well as intimate. As Mrs. C's expressions of self-assertion and intimacy became more direct, she simultaneously became more relaxed, more spontaneous, and less driven. These results support the CMT view of how inhibitions are overcome rather than the automatic functioning hypothesis that such changes result from a shift in the dynamic balance between psychic forces that operate beyond the control of the ego. A third study, by Shilkret et al. (1986), successfully tested the CMT hypothesis that Mrs. C would strive to overcome her problems with feeling guilty, weak, and overly responsible for others by developing insight into her irrational unconscious beliefs in other people's fragility and her power to hurt others. In the first quantitative study of testing, Silberschatz (1986; Silberschatz, Sampson, & Weiss, 1986) showed that Mrs. C attempted to master her problems with feeling overly responsible for others not only through acquiring insight but also through unconsciously testing the analyst to disconfirm the pathogenic beliefs responsible for this problem. Silberschatz also demonstrated that Mrs. C's transference demands represented unconscious tests rather than wishes for drive gratification.

Two other studies used a plan formulation to predict Mrs. C's immediate reactions to the analyst's interventions. Caston (1986; Caston, Goldman, & McClure, 1986) found that although pro-plan interventions significantly correlated with increases in insightfulness and boldness, anti-plan interventions did not correlate with negative changes in the patient's behavior. Bush and Gassner (1986) prepared a plan formulation specific to the termination phase of Mrs. C's analysis which they used to successfully predict Mrs. C's immediate reaction to the analyst's termination interventions. The correlation (.44) between the planfulness rating of the analyst's interventions and the shift score in the patient's attitude towards termination was highly significant ($p < .0001$) in the predicted direction.

The methods used in the empirical studies of Mrs. C have since been refined and applied to the study of other analyses, short-term therapy with a wide variety of adult patients, and child therapy. A protocol for reliably formulating a patient's plan for therapy has been developed (Curtis & Silberschatz, 1997; Curtis, Silberschatz, Sampson, & Weiss, 1994; Curtis, Silberschatz, Sampson, Weiss, & Rosenberg, 1988; Fretter, Bucci, Broitman, Silberschatz, & Curtis, 1994; Rosbrow, 1993) and used successfully to predict patient reactions to therapist behaviors in a number of studies. Pro-plan interpretations and passed tests have consistently been found to be significantly associated with immediate signs of therapeutic progress (Broitman, 1985; Bugas, 1986; Davilla, 1992; Foreman et al., 1992; Fretter, 1984; Graf, 1995; Grienenberger & Foreman, 1993; Kelly, 1989; Linsner, 1987; Silberschatz & Curtis, 1986, 1993; Silberschatz, Curtis, Fretter, & Kelley, 1988; Silberschatz, Fretter, & Curtis, 1986; Silberschatz, Sampson, & Weiss, 1986). Studies by Fretter (1984) and Norville (1989; Norville, Sampson, & Weiss, 1996) showed that pro-plan interpretations have long-term as well as immediate positive effects.

O'Connor, Edelstein, Berry, and Weiss (1994) sought to obtain indirect evidence for the concepts of unconscious planning and testing by studying global changes in a patient's level of pro-plan insight over the course of short-term therapy. Although prior research demonstrated that patients become more insightful immediately after passed tests and pro-plan interpretations, it has also been clinically observed that on a macro-level there seems to be an overall drop in level of insight after the initial few sessions, which reverses as patients approach termination. Weiss (1993a) explained this phenomenon in the following way: At the outset of treatment, patients display pro-plan insight because they unconsciously want to clue the therapist in to their therapeutic goals and pathogenic beliefs and provide coaching on how the therapist should respond to their tests. Once they begin testing, however, they appear to lose insight because their testing often involves making false statements about themselves that they want the therapist to challenge. As they approach termination, they regain their insight in preparation for leaving.

O'Connor et al. (1994) and Edelstein (1992) first tested these hypotheses by tracking level of insight across four brief (16-session) therapies that were preceded by an initial intake evaluation and followed by two post-therapy evaluations held 6 months apart. For all four patients, the level of pro-plan insight across the 19 sessions followed a similar pattern: high insight at the beginning, which progressively dropped towards the middle and began to rise as termination approached. In each case the data fit a parabolic curve. The findings supported the hypothesis that patients have an unconscious plan for therapy that involves orienting the therapist at the outset and then testing their pathogenic beliefs by making false statements about themselves. In another phase of this research, each therapist's interpretations were rated for plan-compatibility. The two patients who received the most pro-plan interpretations were found to have high levels of insight in their 6-month follow-up interviews. The patient who received moderately pro-plan interpretations was found to have a moderate degree of insight in the 6-month follow-up interview. The patient who received mostly anti-plan interpretations had a low level of insight in the 6-month follow-up. The latter finding led Weiss (1993a) to conclude that a drop in insight toward the middle of an unsatisfactory therapy may represent patient compliance with anti-plan interpretations rather than testing. Hence, the postulated relationship between level of insight and testing should hold for patients who receive predominantly pro-plan interpretations.

Direct support for the hypothesis that patients lose insight in the service of testing was found in a pilot study of the relationship between testing and level of insight in a 16-session therapy characterized by a high degree of pro-plan interpretations (Weiss, 1995a). When the frequency of testing behaviors in each session (as determined by an experienced CMT rater) was correlated with the level of pro-plan insight in each session, they were found to be inversely related. In a series of ongoing research studies on longer therapies and recorded analyses, the SFPRG is examining the interrelationships between the plan-compatibility of the therapist's interventions, the patient's level of pro-plan insight, and the patient's testing behavior (Weiss, 1996).

Another line of ongoing research by O'Connor and her colleagues (O'Connor, Berry, Weiss, Bush, & Sampson, 1997) is attempting to test Weiss's ideas about the role of interpersonal guilt in psychopathology (Bush, 1989; Engel & Ferguson, 1990; Friedman, 1985a, 1985b; Mulherin, 1997; Weatherford, 1989). O'Connor et al. (1997) developed a questionnaire measure of maladaptive interpersonal guilt (the IGQ) that contains scales for Survivor Guilt, Separation Guilt, Omnipotent Responsibility Guilt, and Self-Hate Guilt. Thus far the IGQ has been administered to 6 samples of college students, a group of therapists, a group of white- and blue-collar workers, and a large sample of recovering drug-addicted individuals (Herbold, 1996; Meehan et al., 1996; Menaker, 1995; O'Connor, 1995; O'Connor, Berry, & Weiss, in press; Webster, 1996; Weiss, 1995a, 1997a). The recovering addicts scored significantly higher on all types of guilt than the nonclinical samples. Within each sample, the different forms of interpersonal guilt significantly correlated with psychological problems. Survivor guilt correlated with measures of shame (supporting Weiss's view that people develop proneness to shame out of survivor guilt), pessimism, submissiveness, maladaptive perfectionism, chronic maladaptive jealousy, excessive worry, introversion, unhappiness, and a sense of fraudulence. Elevated survivor guilt was found to be detrimental to all aspects of emotional well-being, whereas omnipotent-responsibility guilt was specifically related to depression. Survivor and self-hate guilt also correlated with a self-report measure of childhood neglect. A number of other studies using the IGQ are currently being carried out.

There are several good summaries of the research carried out by members of the SFPRG (Foreman, 1995; Sampson, 1992a; Sampson & Weiss, 1986; Silberschatz & Curtis, 1986; Silberschatz, et al., 1988; Silberschatz,

Curtis, Sampson, & Weiss, 1991; Weiss, 1993a, 1995b; Weiss et al., 1986) for readers who would like to further pursue this topic.

SUMMARY

CMT is a new cognitive-adaptational psychoanalytic model of mind, personality, psychopathology, and therapy. It focuses on the decision-making and problem-solving activities of unconscious mental life. It assumes that patients are strongly motivated to resolve their conflicts, and that they unconsciously devise adaptive plans for enlisting the therapist's help in pursuing their goals. Psychopathology is assumed to result from unconscious pathogenic beliefs that develop out of childhood trauma. In the therapeutic process, patients unconsciously test the therapist in order to disconfirm their pathogenic beliefs and acquire strengths that they lack. The theory leads to testable predictions about how patients will respond to particular types of interventions. It enables therapists to infer a patient's plan for therapy and to devise a stance that will be maximally helpful for the patient. The theory has been successfully applied to a wide range of patients and therapeutic modalities and has strong empirical support.

REFERENCES

Bader, M. J. (1994). Helping the patient get better. *Tikkun, 9*(3), 11–14.

Badger, S. (1997, January). *Control-mastery theory with adolescents: The therapist's attitude and ability to promote collaboration between client, family, school, and community resources.* Presentation to the San Francisco Psychotherapy Research Group Friday Lecture Series, San Francisco.

Badger, S., & Riley, S. (1995, January). *Working with adolescents from a control-mastery perspective.* Presentation to the San Francisco Psychotherapy Research Group Friday Lecture Series, San Francisco.

Broitman, J. (1985). Insight, the mind's eye. An exploration of three patients' processes of becoming insightful. *Dissertation Abstracts International 48*(8). (University Microfilms No. 85-20425).

Browne, D. (1993). *Treatment of multiple personality disorder using control-mastery theory.* Unpublished manuscript.

Browne, D. (1995). Control-mastery theory and treatment of DID patients. *Process Notes (A publication of the San Francisco Psychotherapy Research Group)., 2*(1), 4–7.

Bugas, J. S. (1986), *Adaptive regression and the therapeutic change process.* Unpublished doctoral dissertation, Pacific Graduate School of Psychology, Menlo Park, CA.

Bush, M. (1989). The role of unconscious guilt in psychopathology and psychotherapy. *Bulletin of the Menninger Clinic, 53*(2), 97–107.

Bush, M., & Gassner, S. (1986). The immediate effect of the analyst's termination interventions on the patient's resistance to termination. In J. Weiss, H. Sampson, & The Mount Zion Psychotherapy Research Group (Eds.), *The psychoanalytic process: Theory, clinical observation, & empirical research* (pp. 299–322). New York: Guilford.

Canestro, P. (1996, June). *Working with federal prisoners from a control-mastery perspective.* Presentation to the San Francisco Psychotherapy Research Group Friday Lecture Series, San Francisco.

Caston, J. (1986). The reliability of the diagnosis of the patient's unconscious plan. In J. Weiss, H. Sampson, & The Mount Zion Psychotherapy Research Group (Eds.), *The psychoanalytic process: Theory, clinical observation, & empirical research* (pp. 241–255). New York: Guilford.

Caston, J., Goldman, R. K., & McClure, M. M. (1986). The immediate effects of psychoanalytic interventions. In J. Weiss, H. Sampson, & The Mount Zion Psychotherapy Research Group (Eds.), *The psychoanalytic process: Theory, clinical observation, & empirical research* (pp. 277–298). New York: Guilford.

Chase, D. (1996, April 5). *Control-mastery theory and child custody mediation.* Presentation to the San Francisco Psychotherapy Research Group Friday Lecture Series, San Francisco.

Coleman, J. (1989). *The role of plan-compatible insight in the outcome of seven brief psychotherapies.* Unpublished doctoral dissertation, Wright Institute Graduate School of Psychology, Berkeley, CA.

Conrad, B. (1995). *Personality and psychopathology reconsidered: A quantitative/qualitative control-mastery psychobiography on Henri de Toulouse-Lautrec.* Unpublished doctoral dissertation, Wright Institute Graduate School of Psychology, Berkeley, CA.

Cooper, L. (1996, May). *Control-mastery theory and Tavistock Group Relations Conferences: Is there a fit?* Presentation to the San Francisco Psychotherapy Research Group Friday Lecture Series, San Francisco.

Cristofalo, J. (1995, May). *Using control-mastery theory in a therapy group for single men and women that focuses on relationship issues.* Presentation to the San Francisco Psychotherapy Research Group Friday Lecture Series, San Francisco.

Curtis, J. T., & Silberschatz, G. (1986). Clinical implications of research on brief psychodynamic psychotherapy I. Formulating the patient's problems and goals. *Psychoanalytic Psychology, 3*(1), 13–25.

Curtis, J. T., & Silberschatz, G. (1997). Plan formulation method. In T. D. Ellis (Ed.), *Handbook of psychotherapy case formulation* (pp. 116–136). New York: Guilford.

Curtis, J. T., Ransohoff, P., Sampson, F., Brumer, S., & Bronstein, A. A. (1986). Expressing warded-off contents in behavior. In J. Weiss, H. Sampson, & The Mount Zion Psychotherapy Research Group (Eds.), *The psychoanalytic process: Theory, clinical observation, & empirical research* (pp. 187–205). New York: Guilford.

Curtis, J. T., Silberschatz, G., Sampson, H., & Weiss, J. (1994). The plan formulation method. *Psychotherapy Research, 4,* 197–207.

Curtis, J. T., Silberschatz, G., Sampson, H., Weiss, J., & Rosenberg, S. (1988). Developing reliable psychodynamic case formulations: An illustration of the plan diagnosis method. *Psychotherapy, 25,* 256–265.

Davilla, L. (1992). *The immediate effects of therapist's interpretations on patient's plan progressiveness.* Unpublished doctoral dissertation, California School of Professional Psychology, Alameda, CA.

Edelstein, S. (1992). *Insight and psychotherapy outcome.* Unpublished doctoral dissertation, Wright Institute Graduate School of Psychology, Berkeley, CA.

Edmund, J., Folsom, H., Foreman, S., Gibbins, J., & Jenny, S. (1994). *The center of the storm: A control-mastery approach to child and family therapy* [Film]. (Available from San Francisco Psychotherapy Research Group, 2420 Sutter St., San Francisco, CA 94115)

Engel, L., & Ferguson, T. (1990). *Imaginary crimes: Why you punish yourself and how to stop.* Boston: Houghton-Mifflin.

Folsom, H. (1993). *Family therapy.* Unpublished manuscript.

Foreman, S. A. (1993). Control mastery theory and child psychotherapy. *The California Psychologist, 26*(4), 14–23.

Foreman, S. A. (1995). The theory, research and clinical application of the work of the San Francisco Psychotherapy Research Group. In B. Boothe, R. Hirsig, A. Hilminger, B. Meier, & R. Volkart (Eds.), *Perception, evaluation, interpretation: Swiss monographs in psychology* (Vol. 3, pp. 58–65). Lewiston, NY: Hogrefe & Huber.

Foreman, S. A. (1996). The difficult couple. In H. Kessler (Ed.), *Treating couples* (pp. 165–188). San Francisco: Jossey-Bass.

Foreman, S. A., Gibbins, J. D., & Berry, J. (1992, June). *Assessing the efficacy of therapist interventions in child psychotherapy*. Presented at the 23rd Annual Meeting of the Society for Psychotherapy Research, Berkeley, CA.

Fretter, P. (1984). The immediate effects of transference interpretations on patients' progress in brief, psychodynamic psychotherapy. *Dissertation Abstracts International, 46*(6). (University Microfilms No. 85-12112)

Fretter, P. (1995). A control-mastery case formulation of a successful treatment for major depression. *In Session: Psychotherapy in Practice, 1*(2), 317.

Fretter, P., Bucci, W., Broitman, J., Silberschatz, G., & Curtis, J. (1994). How the patient's plan relates to the concept of transference. *Psychotherapy Research, 4*(1), 58–72.

Freud, S. (1955). Inhibitions, symptoms and anxiety. In J. Strachey (Ed. & Trans.), *The standard edition of the complete psychological works of Sigmund Freud* (Vol. 20, pp. 75–175). London: Hogarth. (Original work published 1926)

Freud, S. (1961a). The ego and the id. In J. Strachey (Ed. & Trans.), *The standard edition of the complete psychological works of Sigmund Freud* (Vol. 19, pp. 1–66). London: Hogarth. (Original work published 1923)

Freud, S. (1961b). Civilization and its discontents. In J. Strachey (Ed. & Trans.), *The standard edition of the complete psychological works of Sigmund Freud* (Vol. 21, pp. 57–145). London: Hogarth. (Original work published 1930)

Freud, S. (1964a). Analysis terminable and interminable. In J. Strachey (Ed. & Trans.), *The standard edition of the complete psychological works of Sigmund Freud* (Vol. 23, pp. 209–253). London: Hogarth. (Original work published 1937)

Freud, S. (1964b). Moses and monotheism. In J. Strachey (Ed. & Trans.), *The standard edition of the complete psychological works of Sigmund Freud* (Vol. 23, pp. 1–137). London: Hogarth. (Original work published 1939)

Freud, S. (1964c). Splitting of the ego in the process of defense. In J. Strachey (Ed. & Trans.), *The standard edition of the complete psychological works of Sigmund Freud* (Vol. 23, pp. 271–278). London: Hogarth. (Original work published 1940)

Friedman, M. (1985a). Survivor guilt in the pathogenesis of anorexia nervosa. *Psychiatry, 48,* 25–39.

Friedman, M. (1985b). Toward a reconceptualization of guilt. *Contemporary Psychoanalysis, 21*(4), 501–547.

Gassner, S. (1990). The implications of "control-mastery" theory for supervision. In R. Lane (Ed.), *Psychoanalytic approaches to supervision: Current issues in psychoanalytic practice* (pp. 138–140). New York: Brunner/Mazel.

Gassner, S., Sampson, H., Weiss, J., & Brumer, S. (1982). The emergence of warded-off contents. *Psychoanalysis and Contemporary Thought, 5*(1), 55–75.

Gibbins, J. D., & Foreman, S. A. (1989, June). *The plan formation of a child psychotherapy case*. Presented at the 20th annual meeting, Society for Psychotherapy Research, Toronto, Canada.

Goldberg, H. (1997, April). *Bruno Bettleheim, Jerzy Kosinski and Job: Survival without guilt*. Presentation to the San Francisco Psychotherapy Research Group Friday Lecture Series, San Francisco.

Goodfriend, R., & Kramer, P. (1996, May). *Control-mastery theory and career consulting: How they unite to meet patients' needs*. Presentation to the San Francisco Psychotherapy Research Group Friday Lecture Series, San Francisco.

Gootnick, I. (1982). The problem of treating an intensely suffering patient: To gratify or frustrate. *Psychoanalytic Review, 69*(4), 487–496.

Graf, T. (1995). *Effects of therapist interventions in the context of child testing of pathogenic beliefs during child psychotherapy*. Unpublished doctoral dissertation, Wright Institute Graduate School of Psychology, Berkeley, CA.

Grebel, J. (1992). *Manifestations of insight in brief psychotherapy*. Unpublished doctoral dissertation, Pacific Graduate School of Psychology, Menlo Park, CA.

Grienenberger, J. F., & Foreman, S. A. (1993, June). *The effect of therapist interventions on the therapeutic alliance in child psychotherapy*. Paper presented at the 24th Annual Meeting of the Society for Psychotherapy Research, Pittsburgh, PA.

Hausman, S., & Maslow, J. (1995, May). *The application of control-mastery theory to group treatment with severely socially dysfunctional adults*. Presentation to the San Francisco Psychotherapy Research Group Friday Lecture Series, San Francisco.

Herbold, J. (1996, April). *Perfectionism, shame and guilt in adult children of alcoholics*. Poster session presented at the annual meeting of the Western Psychological Association, San Jose, CA.

Kale, C. (1986). The therapist's effect on patient progress in brief psychodynamic psychotherapy. (Doctoral dissertation, Pacific Graduate School, 1986). *Dissertation Abstracts International, 47*(9). (University Microfilms N. 86-23649)

Kale, C. (1995, October). *The development of pathogenic beliefs in adults with chronic illnesses*. Presentation to the San Francisco Psychotherapy Research Group Friday Lecture Series, San Francisco.

Kanofsky, S. A. (1996, April). *Control-mastery approach to family therapy*. Presentation to the San Francisco Psychotherapy Research Group Friday Lecture Series, San Francisco.

Kelly, T. (1989). *Do therapist's interventions matter?* Unpublished doctoral dissertation, New York University.

Linsner, J. P. (1987). *Therapeutically effective and ineffective insight: The immediate effects of therapist behavior on a patient's insight during short-term dynamic therapy*. Unpublished doctoral dissertation, City University of New York.

Lowenstein, M. (1995, June). *The emergence of "true" and "false" memories in a control mastery therapy*. Presentation to the San Francisco Psychotherapy Research Group Friday Lecture Series, San Francisco.

Maslow, J. (1994, May). *Group therapy with men who struggle with achievement: A control-mastery approach*. Presented to the Marin Chapter of the National Association of Social Workers, Corte Madera, CA.

Maslow, J., & Hausman, S. (1994, November). *The application of control-mastery theory to two distinct psychotherapy group populations*. Presented at the annual conference of the California Society for Clinical Social Work, Monterey, CA.

Meehan, W., O'Connor, L. E., Berry, J. W., Weiss, J., Morrison, A., & Acampora, A. (1996). Guilt, shame and depression in clients in recovery from addiction. *Journal of Psychoactive Drugs, 28*(5), 125–134.

Menaker, A. (1995). *The relationship between attributional style and interpersonal guilt*. Unpublished doctoral dissertation, California School of Professional Psychology, Alameda, CA.

Meyers, T. E. (1993). *The immediate effects of accurate interpretations on patient affects in brief psychodynamic psychotherapy*. Unpublished doctoral dissertation, The Professional School of Psychology, San Francisco.

Moon, T. (1995, March). *Survivor guilt, politics and HIV prevention in the gay community*. Presentation to the San Francisco Psychotherapy Research Group Friday Lecture Series, San Francisco.

Mulherin, K. (1997, March). *Prosocial behavior in children: From egocentrism to altruism*. Presentation to the San Francisco Psychotherapy Research Group Friday Lecture Series, San Francisco.

Nichols, N. (1989). Crisis intervention through early interpretation of unconscious guilt. *Bulletin of the Menninger Clinic, 53*(2), 115–122.

Norville, R. (1989). Plan compatibility of interpretations and brief psychotherapy outcome. *Dissertation Abstracts International, 50*(12B), 5888. (University Microfilms No. 90-12770)

Norville, R., Sampson, H., & Weiss, J. (1996). Accurate interpretations and brief psychotherapy outcome. *Psychotherapy Research, 6*(1), 16–29.

O'Connor, L. E. (1993). Control mastery theory: Treating the addict. *California Psychologist, 25*(6), 24, 29–30.

O'Connor, L. E. (1995, April). *Survivor guilt and depression*. Presented as part of a workshop at the annual meeting of the American Psychological Association, Division 39, Santa Monica, CA.

O'Connor, L. E., Berry, J. W., & Weiss, J. (in press). Interpersonal guilt, shame, and psychological problems. *Journal of Social Clinical Psychology*.

O'Connor, L. E., Berry, J. W., Weiss, J., Bush, M., & Sampson, H. (1997). Interpersonal guilt: The development of a new measure. *Journal of Clinical Psychology, 53*(1), 73–89.

O'Connor, L., & Weiss, J. (1993). Individual psychotherapy for addicted clients: An application of control mastery theory. *Journal of Psychoactive Drugs, 25*(4), 283–291.

O'Connor, L., Edelstein, S., Berry, J., & Weiss, J. (1994). The pattern of insight in brief psychotherapy: A series of pilot studies. *Psychotherapy, 31*(3), 533–544.

Palley, R., (1997, January). *Adolescent development and the role of unconscious guilt in the treatment of teenagers.* Presentation to the San Francisco Psychotherapy Research Group Friday Lecture Series, San Francisco.

Rappoport, A. (1986). *Psychodynamic psychotherapy for agoraphobia.* Unpublished manuscript.

Redmond, H. (1995, June). *Latin American women and control-mastery theory.* Presentation to the San Francisco Psychotherapy Research Group Friday Lecture Series, San Francisco.

Rosbrow, T. (1993). Significance of the unconscious plan for psychoanalytic theory. *Psychoanalytic Psychology, 10*(4), 515–532.

Rosbrow, T. (1997). From parallel process to developmental process: A developmental/plan formulation approach to supervision. In M. Rock (Ed.), *Psychodynamic Supervision* (pp. 213–236). Northvale, NJ: Jason Aronson.

Sampson, H. (1989). How the patient's sense of danger and safety influence the analytic process. *Psychoanalytic Psychology, 7*(1), 115–124.

Sampson, H. (1990). The problem of adaptation to reality in psychoanalytic theory. *Contemporary Psychoanalysis, 26*(4), 677–691.

Sampson, H. (1991). Experience and insight in the resolution of transferences. *Contemporary Psychoanalysis, 27,* 200–207.

Sampson, H. (1992a). A new psychoanalytic theory and its testing in formal research. In J. W. Barron, M. N. Eagle, & D. L. Wolitzky (Eds.), *Interface of psychoanalysis and psychology* (pp. 586–604). Washington, DC: American Psychological Association.

Sampson, H. (1992b). The role of "real" experience in psychopathology and treatment. *Psychoanalytic Dialogues, 2*(4), 509–528.

Sampson, H. (1994, Fall). Treatment by attitudes. *Process Notes (Publication of San Francisco Psychotherapy Research Group), 1*(1), 8–11.

Sampson, H., & Weiss, J. (1986). Testing hypotheses: The approach of the Mount Zion Psychotherapy Research Group. In L. Greenberg & W. Pinsof (Eds.), *The psychotherapeutic process: A research handbook* (pp. 591–613). New York: Guilford.

Sampson, H., Weiss, J., Mlodnosky, L., & Hause, E. (1972). Defense analysis and the emergence of warded-off mental contents: An empirical study. *Archives of General Psychiatry, 26,* 524–532.

Schumacher, P. (1995, June). *A control-mastery approach with chemically dependent criminal justice patients.* Presentation to the San Francisco Psychotherapy Research Group Friday Lecture Series, San Francisco.

Shilkret, C., Isaacs, M., Drucker, C., & Curtis, J. T. (1986). The acquisition of insight. In J. Weiss, H. Sampson, & The Mount Zion Psychotherapy Research Group (Eds.), *The psychoanalytic process: Theory, clinical observation, & empirical research* (pp. 206–220). New York: Guilford.

Shilkret, R., & Nigrosh, E. (1997). Assessing student plans for college. *Journal of Counseling Psychology, 44,* 222–231.

Shilkret, R., & Vecchiotti, S. (1997, April). *Parenting style, guilt, and college adjustment.* Presentation at the biennial meeting of the Society for Research in Child Development, Washington, DC.

Silberschatz, G. & Curtis, J. (in press). Research on the psychodynamic process in the treatment of older persons. In N. E. Miller (Ed.), *Psychodynamic research perspectives on development, psychopathology, and treatment in later life.* New York: International Universities Press.

Silberschatz, G. (1986). Testing pathogenic beliefs. In J. Weiss, H. Sampson, & The Mount Zion Psychotherapy Research Group (Eds.), *The psychoanalytic process: Theory, clinical observation, & empirical research* (pp. 256–266). New York: Guilford.

Silberschatz, G., & Curtis, J. (1986). Clinical implications of research on brief dynamic psychotherapy II. How the therapist helps or hinders therapeutic progress. *Psychoanalytic Psychology, 3*(1), 27–37.

Silberschatz, G., & Curtis, J. (1991). Time-limited, psychodynamic psychotherapy with older adults. In W. A Myers (Ed.), *New techniques in the psychotherapy of older patients* (pp. 95–108). Washington, DC: American Psychiatric Press.

Silberschatz, G., & Curtis, J. (1993). Measuring the therapist's impact on the patient's therapeutic progress. *Journal of Consulting and Clinical Psychology, 61*(3), 403–411.

Silberschatz, G., Curtis, J., Fretter, P., & Kelly, T. (1988). Testing hypotheses of psychotherapeutic change processes. In H. Dahl, H. Kachele, & H. Thomas (Eds.), *Psychoanalytic process research strategies* (pp. 129–145). Berlin: Springer Verlag.

Silberschatz, G., Curtis, J., Sampson, H., & Weiss, J. (1991). Mount Zion Hospital and Medical Center: Research on the process of change in psychotherapy. In L. Beutler & M. Crago (Eds.), *Psychotherapy research: An international review of programmatic studies* (pp. 56–64). Washington, DC: American Psychological Association.

Silberschatz, G., Fretter, P., & Curtis, J. (1986). How do interpretations influence the process of psychotherapy? *Journal of Consulting and Clinical Psychology, 54*(5), 646–652.

Silberschatz, G., Sampson, H., & Weiss, J. (1986). Testing pathogenic beliefs versus seeking transference gratifications. In J. Weiss, H. Sampson, & The Mount Zion Psychotherapy Research Group (Eds.), *The psychoanalytic process: Theory, clinical observation, & empirical research* (pp. 267–276). New York: Guilford.

Sohn, N. (1995, November). *Spousal suicide: The role of survivor guilt in the surviving patient's suicidality and other challenges in the continuation of therapy.* Presentation to the San Francisco Psychotherapy Research Group Friday Lecture Series, San Francisco.

Suffridge, D. R. (1991). Survivors of child maltreatment: Diagnostic formulation and therapeutic process. *Psychotherapy, 28,* 67–75.

Vogel, R. (1994). The origins and resolution of marital discord from a control mastery perspective. *Journal of Couples Therapy, 4*(3/4), 47–63.

Weatherford, S. (Gassner). (1989). Unconscious guilt as a cause of sexualized relationships. *Bulletin of the Menninger Clinic, 53*(2), 108–114.

Webster, R. (1996, April). *Interpersonal guilt and jealousy: Are there two types of jealousy?* Poster session presented at meeting of the Western Psychological Association, San Jose, CA.

Weiss, J. (1952). Crying at the happy ending. *Psychoanalytic Review, 39*(4), 338.

Weiss, J. (1967). The integration of defenses. *International Journal of Psycho-Analysis, 48,* 520–524.

Weiss, J. (1971). The emergence of new themes: A contribution to the psychoanalytic theory of therapy. *International Journal of Psycho-Analysis, 52,* 459–467.

Weiss, J. (1988). Testing hypotheses about unconscious mental functioning. *International Journal of Psycho-Analysis, 69,* 87–95.

Weiss, J. (1989). The nature of the patient's problems and how in psychoanalysis the individual works to solve them. *Psychoanalytic Psychology, 7*(1), 105–113.

Weiss, J. (1990a). The centrality of adaptation. *Contemporary Psychoanalysis, 26*(4), 660–676.

Weiss, J. (1990b, March). Unconscious mental functioning. *Scientific American, 103,* 1–9.

Weiss, J. (1992). The role of interpretation. *Psychoanalytic Inquiry, 12*(2), 296–313.

Weiss, J. (1993a). Empirical studies of the psychoanalytic process. *Journal of the American Psychoanalytic Association, 41* [Suppl.], 7–29.

Weiss, J. (1993b). *How psychotherapy works: Process and technique.* New York: Guilford.

Weiss, J. (1994a). The analyst's task: To help the patient carry out his plan. *Contemporary Psychoanalysis, 30*(2), 236–254.

Weiss, J. (1994b). The therapist's task. *Process Notes (Publication of San Francisco Psychotherapy Research Group), 1*(1), 4–7.

Weiss, J. (1995a, December). *Annual report to the board of directors from the chairman of the board of the San Francisco Psychotherapy Research Group.* (Available from San Francisco Psychotherapy Research Group, 2420 Sutter St., San Francisco, CA 94115)

Weiss, J. (1995b). Bernfeld's The facts of observation in analysis: A response from research. *Psychoanalytic Quarterly, 64,* 699–708.

Weiss, J. (1997a, May). *Progress report and grant request to the Broitman Foundation.* (Available from San Francisco Psychotherapy Research Group, 2420 Sutter St., San Francisco, CA 94115)

Weiss, J. (1997). The role of pathogenic beliefs in psychic reality. *Psychoanalytic Psychology, 14,* 427–434.

Weiss, J. (in press). The patient's unconscious plans for solving his problems. *Psychoanalytic Dialogue.*

Weiss, J., & Sampson, H. (1986). Testing alternative psychoanalytic explanations of the therapeutic process. In J. M. Masling (Ed.), *Empirical studies of psychoanalytic theories* (Vol. 11, pp. 1–26). Hillsdale, NJ: Analytic Press.

Weiss, J., Sampson, H., & The Mount Zion Psychotherapy Research Group (Eds.), (1986). *The psychoanalytic process: Theory, clinical observation, & empirical research* (pp. 3–138). New York: Guilford.

Wood, P. (1997, March). *The treatment of eating disorders from a control-mastery perspective.* Presentation to the San Francisco Psychotherapy Research Group Friday Lecture Series, San Francisco, CA.

Zaslav, M. (1994). Psychology of comorbid PTSD and substance abuse: Lessons from combat veterans. *Journal of Psychoactive Drugs, 26*(4), 393–400.

Zeitlin, D. (1991). Control-mastery theory in couples therapy. *Family Therapy, 18*(3), 201–230.

6

The Cognitive Therapy Model

Kevin T. Kuehlwein, Psy.D.

INTRODUCTION

Cognitive therapy has been defined in many different ways. In this chapter, I speak primarily in terms of Aaron Beck's model because his is the most fully developed system, although there are other models of varying similarity in the cognitive or cognitive–behavioral therapy field. *Cognitive therapy* is an active–directive type of psychotherapy that involves ongoing collaboration between therapist and client focused largely on the investigation, evaluation, and modification of those cognitive patterns that may be dysfunctional for the client. The cognitive model posits that psychological distress is determined largely by the interpretations that people make of the situations they encounter, rather than coming directly from those situations themselves. Furthermore, these interpretations are just a subset of those that are possible or adaptive in any situation. By changing one's beliefs, one can significantly alter one's emotion, behavior, and physiological response to situations.

Rather than being defined primarily by the specific types of interventions most commonly used by the therapist, cognitive therapy is best viewed as an approach in which therapists use the cognitive model to understand clients and their problems and develop interventions (Beck, 1991a). So, although the dominant theme in cognitive therapy is *collaborative empiricism*—therapist and client as a team identifying and testing various important beliefs the client has—the methods for this process are only as limited as a therapist's and client's imaginations. Fur-

125

thermore, although primary attention is given to modification of cognitions of various levels, behavioral methods are also often used as a means of reducing symptomatology, teaching or refining certain skills, and furthering cognitive change by experientially testing the validity and adaptiveness of certain beliefs. Targeted cognitive changes produce marked positive changes in the behavioral, emotional, and physiological spheres also.

Levels of Cognitions

Three basic levels of cognitions are examined in cognitive therapy. The most surface-level cognitions—*automatic thoughts* (ATs)—are often most accessible to clients because they are most situation-specific. Therapist and client usually investigate these first because of their accessibility. For example, Michael Shore, the young son who suffers from asthma, views his asthma thus: "This is a scar God gave me to overcome."

The next, deeper level consists of *conditional assumptions* or rules. These typically clarify what conditions are necessary (in the client's eyes) for such key human constructs as success–failure, lovability–unlovability, control–helplessness, connection–rejection, adequacy–inadequacy, and the like. These types of assumptions are an attempt by clients to impose a sense of order or predictability on their world. For example, "If I get everybody to laugh, people will like me," may be a belief that Mr. Shore has that drives him to perform at the comedy club. Many times these are less directly verbalized and may indeed often need to be inferred from a client's patterns and later confirmed (or rejected) via the therapist's questioning. For example, Rena, the adopted daughter in the Shore family, seems to believe, "If somebody puts her baby up for adoption, it means she doesn't care about the child" or "If I try something, I'll eventually fail."

The deepest level of cognitions involves *schemas* or *core beliefs*. These are core organizing principles that largely determine a person's world-view, self-image, and sense of relatedness to others. Beck postulates that such deep beliefs are latent until activated by certain relevant environmental stimuli—for example, a rejection core belief may be triggered by an experience suggesting possible rejection. The problematic aspect of schemas is that they tend to emerge full-force when they are triggered, bringing a cascade of dysfunctional emotional, physiological, behavioral, and other cognitive responses with them. It is no surprise that many clients have difficulty understanding how to better control their emotional and behavioral responses to many schema-triggering situations when this rapid, destabilizing process occurs.

Compensatory Strategies

Closely linked with these deeper level beliefs are some of the client's more dysfunctional behavioral patterns, called *compensatory strategies.* These (e.g., attention-getting in both the father and the son of the Shore family) represent attempts to achieve the positive poles of the conditional assumptions and to avoid feeling the negative effects of the negative core beliefs. Examining the adaptiveness of these strategies and linking them to the deeper beliefs and assumptions from which they derive can help clients avoid performing these behaviors mindlessly and thereby set the stage for considering and practicing new behaviors. These new and therefore often anxiety-producing behaviors help undermine old, maladaptive beliefs by providing experiential proof that the client can change in various ways.

THE CONCEPT OF THE PERSON AND THE HUMAN EXPERIENCE

Information-Processing and Phenomenological Perspectives

Beck looks at human behavior from two simultaneous perspectives: a phenomenological one and an information-processing one. He uses the phenomenological perspective to explore with clients their idiosyncratic, privately constructed experience. In this way he avoids both the exclusive focus on external behavior that was characteristic of the early behaviorists and the heavily interpreted, non-empirical focus of the psychoanalysts' assumptions of the internal experience of clients. Beck does not assume to know exactly how clients are constructing their world, but rather he inductively draws out the complex web of beliefs surrounding dysfunctional patterns to better understand their various components. For more information on related constructivist approaches, the interested reader may see Rosen (Rosen & Kuehlwein, 1996; and chapter 10 in this volume).

The information-processing aspect derives from cognitive science research on how humans are constantly appraising (accurately or not) their world and then feeling and behaving (often maladaptively) in accordance with these judgments. People do this in ways designed to promote our survival (Weishaar, 1993) and actively structure their meaning-making in hierarchical ways. Therefore, some ways of understanding their experience are judged deeper or more central to their existence than others (Safran, Vallis, Segal, & Shaw, 1986). These typically are related to people's self-definition or sense of survival. Cognitive mechanisms within us also automatically and selectively highlight certain types of information and fail to attend to other types judged less significant at the moment. Other cognitive mechanisms affect the types of data people see and understand. Data deemed irrelevant to us are therefore not consciously attended to (Weishaar, 1993).

Evolutionary Hypothesis

Beck maintains that this automatic but often dysfunctional cognitive shift occurs because of built-in automatic biases fostered by eons of evolutionary selection (Weishaar, 1993). For example, when people are anxious, a whole evolutionary program consisting of various fairly predictable cognitive–affective–behavioral–physiological responses is rapidly activated. Cognitively, they are especially alert to signs of threat or potential threat, and they tend to overinterpret ambiguous stimuli in the direction of harm and exaggerate the perceived threat from other sources. Physiologically, their bodies shift toward a fight-or-flight response, with changes in respiratory patterns and blood flow to vital organs significantly altered as a means of facilitating possible escape from an identified threat. Behaviorally, their eyes and other sense organs scan for signs of potential danger. Emotionally, they experience a sense of unease and anxiety. All of this occurs rapidly and automatically—without any need for people to reflect on it or calculate. Evolution favors genes that lead to anxious responses, Beck hypothesizes, because organisms many centuries ago had a far greater chance of detecting and escaping danger by overestimating threat than by underestimating it and thereby experiencing serious attack or death. So too, he theorizes, depression and other disorders may have evolutionary roots of greater benefit. In depression, for example, the person experiences a sense of loss or failure. This then leads to an automatic behavioral program of disinvesting in social relationships so as to avoid further potential hurt (Beck, 1987). Unfortunately, what these evolutionary holdovers also mean is that certain programs are automatically triggered at certain times, even if they are inappropriate. Therefore, what may have been evolutionarily beneficial to our ancestors many millions of years ago may not be ideal in today's conditions. Indeed, it can even be quite dysfunctional in a number of ways. By using the lens of evolution to understand otherwise puzzling current dysfunctional patterns, Beck has been able to help both therapist and client avoid stigmatizing clients' rationally dysfunctional—but evolutionarily appropriate—choices.

Continuity Hypothesis

Beck's view of all human behavior as existing on a continuum contributes to the nonstigmatizing nature of his approach. There are no sharp distinctions between the characteristics of those who are suffering psychiatric disturbance and those who are not (Beck, 1991a). People who are distressed exhibit patterns of cognition and behavior that are common to nondistressed people, but they do this in extreme, rigid ways. When people suffer psychiatric distress, they show exaggerated signs of bias in how they interpret their world. This occurs through the activation of a particular mode (e.g., anxiety or depression) of information processing that actively structures the data that they perceive. These modes, furthermore, actually predispose the client to search for data that confirm certain dysfunctional beliefs (Giesler, Josephs, & Swann, 1997). For example, "normal" people will at times sense "voices" inside their heads (e.g., "Oops, now look what you did!" when they note themselves making a mistake). However, they are able to discern that these are not real external voices but rather represent their own natural narration of their ongoing experience. Because of this (especially when they are not distressed), they can fairly easily stop and examine these thoughts as though someone else had verbalized them and they were reflecting on them. For example, it appears that Rena Shore, the adopted daughter, is currently unable to externalize and then examine the negative messages in her head telling her that her birth mother could not possibly have loved her. As a result, she remains trapped in this dysfunctional belief. It is her difficulty in reconsidering this automatic thought (AT)—not the fact that she has the AT to begin with—that is so dysfunctional.

HISTORICAL PERSPECTIVE

Beck developed cognitive therapy in the early 1960s while working as a psychoanalyst (Beck, 1963). Unsatisfied with the relevance to the client's symptoms of the reported material produced in session, he began to suspect that there was another level of cognition in his clients that existed just below their free associations. This second level—perhaps analogous to the Freudian preconscious in its relatively easily accessibility—typically went unreported because clients were only dimly aware of it. By noting visible shifts toward negative emotion in his clients' faces, however, Beck began to suspect this second level of negatively tinged cognition going through the minds of his clients. He therefore stopped clients when he noted this shift and asked them about it: "What's going through your mind right now?" His depressed clients reported a raft of self-critical thoughts (e.g., of personal failure, defeat, and loss) that represented unspoken but critical commentaries on themselves. They also demonstrated negative views of themselves, the world around them, and the future—the *depressive cognitive triad*. Beck quickly realized that these unspoken assumptions (and not deeply repressed childhood fantasies or experiences) were responsible for much of the distress of his clients. Soon he began to detect patterns of failure, defeat, deprivation, and loss in his other depressed clients. These themes greatly conflicted with the predicted ones offered by the prevailing psychoanalytic theories for depression, which held that depressed clients primarily experienced anger directed toward themselves. This discrepancy between the theorized and real thought content intrigued him.

As a result, Beck began to doubt the prior, less empirically based theories about psychopathology and appropriate treatment derived from psychoanalysis. Instead, he shifted his attention to systematic study of the actual thought content of depressed clients. He believed that clients' inaccurate ATs were persuasive to his clients not because of their veracity—indeed, they were often highly distorted views of reality—but because they occurred so automatically that clients did not even seem to be aware of them as constructions. For this reason, they did not stop to examine them for accuracy or adaptiveness. Beck noticed several classes of misconceptions among their ATs (e.g., clients making negative prediction about the future or viewing most things in terms of polar extremes instead of seeing gradations in constructs). He therefore began to draw his clients' attention to their possible cognitive errors or distortions and to question clients in ways that helped them think more about their thinking (i.e., *metacognition*). This skill of decentering, gradually developed and refined over the course of therapy (and discussed more fully later), enabled clients increasingly to disembed themselves from the maladaptive constructions of their phenomenological world and to experiment with and reinforce new, more adaptive ways of understanding. With this disembeddedness from prior constructions of the world came more rapid improvement in their depressive symptoms on all fronts: affective, behavioral, and physiological. Rosen (1985, 1989) has elucidated that these *cognitive distortions*—more dysfunctional ways of construing experience—have their historical analogs in the early, more egocentric cognitive developmental stages of young children that Piaget investigated. These maladaptive cognitive patterns, then, represent domains of our experience in which we as adults are not functioning intellectually in as sophisticated or adaptive a fashion as we might be.

KEY THEORETICAL CONSTRUCTS

Cognitive Specificity

Cognitive therapy holds that clients with certain types of psychological distress have relatively distinct profiles or themes in their cognitive content that distinguish them from people who do not suffer from this distress. For example, themes of defeat, loss, deprivation, and failure characterize major depressive disorder. In similar fashion, the perception of imminent collapse of an important bodily system (brain, heart, etc.) characterizes panic disorder. This idea of disorder differentiation is called *cognitive specificity*. In personality disorders, clients show an imbalance in their behavioral strategies that flow from their maladaptive cognitive profiles. A narcissistic personality-disordered man, for example, is overdeveloped in the interpersonal strategy of self-aggrandizement (itself an acceptable behavior if not taken to extremes) and underdeveloped in the area of empathy. In the Shore family, the problems of the mother—apparently suffering from depression and agoraphobia or panic—are relatively distinct from the problems of the apparently bipolar father.

Cognitive Primacy

According to the cognitive model, problems arise from a multitude of processes but result in an entire coherent syndrome of cognitive, affective, behavioral, and physiological symptoms. Once this syndrome is activated, however, it is primarily the cognitive aspects of this syndrome that drive the other parts. This theory is referred to as *cognitive primacy*, although one should note that Beck does not argue *causal* primacy for cognition. Beck differentiates these concepts, stating that once the depressive syndrome is already activated (by whatever means), dysfunctional depressive cognitions and processes mold the associated behavioral, motivational, and emotional reactions of the person (Weishaar, 1993). For example, depressed clients show deficits in all of the above spheres, but it is their cognitive symptoms that largely account for those deficits. The depressed and hopeless feelings derive from beliefs such as, "I am a failure," "I deserve to suffer," "Nobody loves me," and "Nothing will help me get better." Depressed individuals show the negative biases in the cognitive triad—negative view of self, future, and world around themselves. Likewise, these negative beliefs actively demotivate the individuals, causing them to pull back from many of their previously common behaviors that led to either pleasure or satisfaction. The withdrawal of energy toward these goals often helps to perpetuate the cycle by providing "evidence" (e.g., fewer interactions with friends) that seems to support the dysfunctional beliefs ("See, no one cares about me"). This dysfunctional behavioral pattern thus reinforces the clients' original beliefs and thereby deepens and prolongs depression. It is for this reason that cognitive therapy focuses so strongly on cognitive change. Indeed, theorists and researchers have contended that cognitive change must occur in order for long-term change to happen. Therefore Beck suggests that we as therapists intervene especially at the level of changing the cognitive aspects of dysfunctional patterns. Because these seem to drive the rest of the program, change in a client's cognitive processes must occur in order to effect durable change in other spheres.

Cognitive Vulnerability

As suggested above, cognitive therapy claims that people have certain cognitive vulnerabilities. Certain types of situations are more likely to trigger dysfunctional responses in us because of how they are thematically connected to specific personal meanings we carry around with us, frequently without conscious awareness. An example from the Shore family is how the father "would rather die" than go on disability. Clearly such a bald statement indicates a strong vulnerability around the issue of the admission of weakness. Once therapists have a good idea of what a client's vulnerabilities are, they can better predict the types of future stressors that will evoke a dysfunctional response in the client. They can then help the client develop better ways of interpreting and then responding to these stressors. Beck has formulated two broad categories for cognitive vulnerability, which he has labeled *sociotropy* and *autonomy* (Beck, 1983). The first category indicates that people's self-esteem and idea of who they are revolves primarily around the quality and number of their interpersonal relationships. The second category (although not exclusive of the first) implies that people's self-esteem and idea of who they are largely depends on their sense of achievement and personal freedom. People in the first category would likely react with depression if they experienced the loss—or threat of loss—of an important relationship. People in the second category would likely become depressed if they were demoted or laid off from work. These two categories are not exhaustive of cognitive vulnerability but only represent some common tendencies encountered in therapy.

Maintenance of Disorders

Another tenet of the cognitive model is the idea that these various *DSM–IV* (American Psychiatric Association, 1994) syndromes—although not caused by their associated maladaptive cognitive patterns—are largely maintained and often exacerbated by negative cognitive patterns as well as their emotional, behavioral, and physiological sequelae. Therefore, when clients are depressed, they will tend to understand a great deal of their internal and external experience from a deep set of cognitive structures (*schemas* or *core beliefs*) that predispose them to focus on the more negative aspects of situations and see the world and themselves in quite absolute terms. This often occurs even to the exclusion of seeing or recalling more relevant context around such circumstances that could help them see things in a more positive light. It is this *disruption* of normal, more functional cognitive processing, rather than any "irrationality" of these beliefs, that Beck emphasizes (Beck & Weishaar, 1989). Unlike Ellis (1989), Beck is more concerned with the adaptiveness of a client's cognitions and cognitive processes than their discrepancy from any consensual reality per se. This approach meshes with Beck's earlier mentioned hypotheses about the evolutionary significance of cognitive processes (i.e., certain cognitive–affective–behavioral–physiological response patterns exist in us currently because there was some evolutionary advantage to them in our distant ancestors). For other differences between Ellis and Beck, the interested reader is directed to Kuehlwein (1993).

Automatic Processing

The disruptive cognitive shift described above is rarely a self-aware process but rather occurs as a result of the almost automatic activation of certain cognitive–affective–behavioral modes. These cause people both to process incoming information along certain dysfunctional lines and to preferentially seek out certain types of data that support their negatively biased views (Giesler et al., 1997). This is done automatically—not through conscious effort—but it does not require the complex concept of repression invoked by psychoanalysts. Rather it is a natural function of the activation of certain deep, personal meaning-making structures (schemas) that are evoked by situations in the world that are thematically related to them. These schemas, Beck postulates, are often formed from early experiences of the individual. For example, if a client has had significant experiences of people leaving him when he was younger—foster care, perhaps—then he may later carry around a tacit core belief, "People will abandon me." Certain experiences in the present that are suggestive of discord, conflict, or separation are therefore likely to evoke in the client a whole system of reactions—cognitive, affective, behavioral, and physiological—that create a heightened concern with people leaving him. This can become so strong that he may interpret relatively minor (to outsiders) incidents as signs that others will leave him. As a result, he will act internally and externally as though this dreaded event is imminent or has even already taken place. Clearly, this type of automatic reaction can be very problematic for a person and his or her associates, especially if that person is prone to interpret almost any sign of discord as indicating abandonment. The therapist and client then must identify these types of problematic situations, look at them more closely to see whether the client's current interpretation of them is the most adaptive, and help the client decenter from these dysfunctional beliefs if it is not. Then the therapist and client can consider other options for the client to explore that might represent more adaptive ways for the client to understand the situation. In the Shore family, this phenomenon is perhaps best exemplified by Rena, the adopted daughter who now seems to lack follow-through in her actions. As she has focused more on the fact of her adoption, she has seemed to falter more and more in areas that had been strengths of hers, as if the perception of her birth-mother having not loved her leads her to doubt her own worth and therefore her abilities in the present.

Decentering

It must be noted that deeper levels of beliefs are often less obvious to clients and yet are more central to clients' understanding of and personal identity in the world. For this reason, clients usually have increased difficulty identifying these *as* beliefs (since they often *seem* so obviously true). Clients also have a greater problem in decentering or stepping back from these beliefs to examine how well they are working for them in various situations. Therapists therefore help clients to gain increased distance from their dysfunctional beliefs in a variety of ways. First, a therapist must help the client understand the part of the cognitive model that posits a strong connection between how the client interprets a situation and the resulting feelings and behaviors. The therapist can best do this by using examples from the client's currently experienced life. It appears that clients more readily decenter from their dysfunctional beliefs if they can externalize them. For this reason, therapists often specifically write down (or get clients to write down) cognitions to be examined or say them aloud so that clients can see or hear them in a different, often less compelling context. For certain clients, simply the act of viewing their ATs in black and white can sometimes produce such comments as "That sounds really stupid now," indicating that they have made an important shift in perspective toward a more positive belief. Therapists have at their disposal a large number of decentering techniques, only a few of which can be mentioned below. The interested reader is directed to McMullin (1986) and Kuehlwein (in press) for more ideas of how to assist clients to decenter.

Behavioral Change

Although cognitive therapy primarily focuses on helping clients restructure their dysfunctional cognitions, it acknowledges that clients can also have behavioral skills problems (in addition to the compensatory strategies mentioned above) that need to be addressed. To this end, cognitive therapy often helps clients focus on learning and applying certain skills. In the Shore family, for example, it appears that the members need to better understand each other and practice new ways of interacting. In the following example, note how the questions chosen to be addressed to the oddly behaving son are primarily designed to promote behavioral change but nevertheless also have a strong cognitive component. Questions the therapist could ask Michael to influence him to reflect on and change his behavior include the following:

- What do you think it means to others when you _____ [give example of dysfunctional behavior]?

- What behaviors of yours do you think are hardest for others to understand?
- How is your behavior with other people similar to theirs?
- How is it different?
- What impression do you *want* to give to others?
- What possible behaviors of yours would lead them to this impression?
- What behaviors of people around you would you like to do more often?

It is, of course, important to prompt the child with corrective feedback if he truly has no idea what negative effects are likely to flow from his behaviors. In this way, the therapist could gradually improve the child's social understanding and thereby increase the potential for more adaptive behaviors.

Techniques

I have purposely kept this section rather lean because of my prior comment that cognitive therapy is not defined by its techniques. Instead, the guiding principle should be one of helping clients to decenter, which can be done in a multitude of collaboratively creative ways. That said, one of the key decentering techniques used in cognitive therapy is, of course, *directed questioning* (also called *guided discovery*). Here therapists explore the phenomenology of their clients' thought processes and the interconnections between these and other patterns, both dysfunctional (to examine and modify) and functional (to bridge from these to less functional patterns). Questioning is by no means random, however. Rather, therapists use the Socratic process (Overholser, 1993a, 1993b) as they actively seek to help clients see things in a more balanced fashion and make new connections in their experience. Therapists thereby enable their clients to increasingly see how they actively construct reality and how other possibilities are not only possible but often better, more adaptive explanations of the same phenomena. Key questions to stimulate new thinking include these:

- What is the evidence for and against that thought?
- What is the quality of that evidence? How likely are others to see it the exact same way?
- What are other possible interpretations of that situation?
- What might be the advantages and disadvantages of seeing things this other way?
- If things aren't ideal, what's the worst that would happen? Could you survive that?
- What's the best that would happen? What's the most likely thing to happen?

In many cases, Socratic questioning is designed to associate for clients two disparate, conflicting parts of their experience to produce a motivating sense of disequilibrium. The resulting unease of logical inconsistency typically results in clients' reflecting more on their thinking and eventually choosing to restructure dysfunctional cognitions.

Thematically related to the questioning process are such techniques as the *Dysfunctional Thought Record* (DTR), a written listing and weighting of advantages and disadvantages of a particular belief or behavior, and role-plays.

The DTR is a common tool for cognitive therapists whereby therapists first help clients break down and investigate in written form the various components of a distressing event. These components include the objective situation, interpretations of the situation, and emotional reactions to their interpretation. Clients write these in a column format ideally as soon as they can, while the cognitions are still "hot." By externalizing this all on paper (or, less commonly, aloud), clients can better decenter from the interpretations and then explore other more adaptive interpretations of what happened. They then write alternative interpretations in the last column, which directly addresses the belief and possible cognitive distortions (see Appendix A) in the automatic thought column. Clients typically experience a great sense of relief when they complete such a sheet, and their belief in their dysfunctional thoughts is also reduced.

In a sense, a rational–emotional role play is a shortened, enacted, and therefore more emotionally evocative version of a DTR. Here therapists help the clients to distill the two sides of an issue that exist within the individual—the rational side, which knows what belief is more accurate or adaptive, and the emotional side, which typically clings to a more dysfunctional belief in spite of evidence to the contrary. By cleaving these and having clients argue each point of view to their imaginary other side, therapists and clients can better understand the arguments and depth of feeling of each side. This often helps clients more fully address underappreciated points detracting from full acceptance of the new, more adaptive belief. Simple, forceful, and repeated defense of the more functional belief by declamation can also serve to better anchor it against the tugging of the less functional one.

A therapist can likewise role play being a friend or acquaintance of the client who has a similar problem and thought, and verbalize this to the client to see if it stimulates a shift in perspective. If not, the therapist can then model a more adaptive response so that the client better understands how to construct and emphasize a more functional interpretation even though distressed.

Other common techniques include clients asking clients to gather evidence to explore the accuracy of their ATs outside the session (the *survey method*); developing positive, more adaptive and multisensorial imagery of situations that clients fear, and suggesting that clients behaviorally and prospectively test their dysfunctional thoughts by conducting behavioral experiments. Following such experiments, clients bring back the collected data so that their original beliefs can be evaluated. Frequently this leads to cognitive modification, but sometimes—when the ATs were correct—it leads to exploration of the reasons behind the outcome and to subsequent problem solving as to how to avoid such an outcome in the future. For more complete descriptions of such techniques, see McMullin (1986) and Beck (1995).

Views of Noncompliance

Resistance is a term not often encountered in cognitive therapy because it has most commonly denoted a psychoanalytic view of a client's willful, stubborn blockage of reasonable therapeutic progress. According to the cognitive approach, it is more appropriate for therapists to view any therapeutic noncompliance as arising out of an interaction of the therapist's incomplete case formulation and the client's cognitive variables. With an incomplete case formulation, the therapist may make premature if well-intended attempts to implement an intervention that does not adequately mesh with important aspects of the client's current meaning-making. From this perspective, then, noncompliance could be seen as indicative of an inadequate fit between the therapist's desired intervention and "where the client is" phenomenologically. Note that this conceptualization of therapeutic impasses itself may contribute to the rapider, less rancorous resolution of any noncompliance issues. Rather than leading to anger and entrenchment on both sides, this approach can more profitably elicit a spirit of curiosity and problem solving, leading to better conceptualization of the clients and their problems. In the Shore family, for example, prior well-meaning therapists might have encountered problems because they assigned the father the inappropriate task of teaching the son how to do certain things. Apparently these prior therapists did not take into account the father's own need to be the center of attention and his lack of knowledge of how to appropriately interact with his son in the father role. The interested reader is directed to Rosen (1989) and Newman (1994), who have both written on this topic.

Symptom Persistence

According to cognitive therapy theory, clients persist in dysfunctional patterns not for any deep, repressed desires to suffer but because their cur-

rent ways of making meaning are inadequate to their situations and are simultaneously (and unfortunately) the best they can call on at the moment.
In other words, their current meaning-making structures are sufficiently
able to explain some important aspects of their experience, but not sufficiently developed or differentiated to provide understanding at a deeper,
more adaptive level. An example of this can be seen in panic and agoraphobia, from which Nancy Shore apparently suffers. With panic, the client
notes sensory data like her heart pounding very fast and interprets this (not
without some reason) to mean that she is suffering a terrible bodily catastrophe, such as a heart attack. A cognitive therapist would therefore help
her to explore other reasonable interpretations of these phenomena—for
instance, that the body is responding very appropriately by mobilizing for
what is perceived as an emergency but is unfortunately a false alarm message from the brain. Unfortunately (in some cases) people's brains have
been selected evolutionarily over the millennia to focus on signs of danger
during anxiety rather than to seek more benign explanations of why such
rapid, intense bodily arousal occurs.

ASSESSMENT

Cognitive therapy assessment is of several types. It is recommended, of
course, that before beginning treatment the client have a full *DSM–IV* diagnosis so that the therapist will understand all of the client's current clinical disorders and stressors. In addition, however, the therapist should assess within the first few sessions important historical background variables
with a self-report instrument (e.g., Lazarus & Lazarus, 1991). Certain types
of experiences that may have led to the formation or strengthening of dysfunctional beliefs within the client (e.g., crises, early childhood problems,
and traumas) are especially important. Negative messages the client constructed during these periods are especially pernicious, given that a child's
developing cognitive apparatus is especially unsophisticated in separating
feeling from fact, impression from reality. Family and cultural messages are
also very relevant. In Nancy Shore's case, it is clear from her earliest memory (being pursued by a dog trying to snatch her food) that she valued food
very highly and felt a strong need to protect her access to it. This historical
emphasis on food likely contributes to many of her problems with eating
and weight.

In cognitive therapy the therapist also provides ongoing assessment of
several important domains: cognitive, affective, behavioral, physiological.
Baseline data are noted for later comparison purposes. At the outset of
therapy, many of these patterns are obvious in that the client will actually
describe them as presenting problems. However, this is often less common with physiological and cognitive symptoms. Clients are frequently

not fully aware of these symptoms or at least do not always connect them to their presenting problems. Therapists therefore explore these symptoms by asking questions like the following:

- When you are most upset, what's going through your mind?
- What types of mental images or metaphors come to mind with respect to your problems or situation?
- What's your understanding of the reasons for your difficulties?
- What changes have you noticed in your body (for example, increased fatigue or sleep problems, body tension, sexual difficulties, pains) since these problems began?

With the Shore family, the therapist might like to ask questions like the following:

- What does it mean to you when [family member] does [behavioral action]?
- How much do you think [family member] knows what it means to you?
- How do you think [family member] is likely to interpret your doing [behavioral action]?
- What could you do to make sure that [family member] better understands what effect their [behavioral action] has on you?

As a result of noting patterns in clients' problems over time, the therapist gradually develops a case formulation. This conceptualization is a working framework of how the various pieces of a client's life fit together—what historical experiences led to what current beliefs, and what emotions and behaviors flow from these. Sharing this evolving document with clients to elicit corrective feedback often greatly assists clients in decentering from their various negative patterns. (Just as importantly, it allows therapists to decenter from their inaccurate or incomplete understanding of the clients!) It further allows for the co-construction of a more accurate portrayal of the problems most in need of modification as well as the context around them. In the case of the Shore family it would likely help the family members to better understand themselves and each other. This would in turn decrease much of the interfering and blaming behaviors that are currently occurring, and the family could move to the problem-solving stage. Symptom assessment is also achieved by periodic self-report measures (Beck Depression Inventory, Beck, 1978; Beck Anxiety Inventory, Beck, Epstein, Brown, & Steer, 1988; & Beck Hopelessness Scale, Beck, Weissman, Lester, & Trexler, 1974). These are typically administered on a weekly basis so that the therapist can quickly detect progress or lack of it and revise the therapy accordingly.

TREATMENT OF CHOICE

Cognitive therapy can be applied to a wide variety of problems and disorders. There is good research evidence to support its effectiveness with most of the common Axis I psychiatric disorders (Hollon & Najavits, 1988) and less compelling but significant clinical evidence to suggest its efficacy with Axis II disorders (Beck, Freeman, & Associates, 1990; Young, 1990) and other common therapeutic problems. Therapists have successfully extended the model to couples (Beck, 1988; Dattilio & Padesky, 1990) and groups (Covi & Primakoff, 1988; Freeman, 1983; Hollon & Evans, 1983; Yost, Beutler, Corbishley, & Allender, 1986). However, the model has been much less developed or tested with families. It also appears to be useful with many different types of clients.

THE THERAPEUTIC PROCESS

Structure

The therapeutic process of cognitive therapy involves several aspects. One of the most integral is the provision of structure. Each session is structured so that it strongly focuses on the problems that are judged most important to tackle. Therapist and client therefore begin each session by setting the agenda together. The following are the most common agenda items: (a) check on mood since last session (often accomplished partly via self-report questionnaires like the Beck inventories mentioned above), (b) quick review of any important events since last session, (c) a bridge from the prior session as to what was most important as well as reviewing the prior homework, (d) discussion of topic(s) for this session, (e) assignment of homework for the coming week, and (f) elicitation of feedback about the current session or process of therapy. Structure also exists across sessions. Earlier ones focus primarily on detecting and understanding the context around more surface-level automatic thoughts and illustrating how beliefs strongly influence emotions and behaviors (and how a client's reactions can trigger this same cycle in others). The therapist also looks for opportunities to elicit from the client how different interpretations of the same situation lead to different emotional, physiological, and behavioral reactions. The therapist next teaches the client how to decenter from his or her ATs by seeing them as interpretations or theories emanating from the client's ongoing construction of reality (vs. truth existing externally in the world). Through Socratic questioning and therapeutic exercises the therapist helps the client to consider alternate interpretations of these same data—interpretations that will be more adaptive for the client in the long term. Later sessions involve therapist and client noting larger patterns and deeper beliefs (conditional assumptions and core beliefs) and subjecting these to similar analysis and revision. These later sessions also can involve the client's learning new skills in areas in which such skills are underdeveloped (e.g., problem solving, assertiveness, parenting, communication). The final segment of therapy focuses on the skills of relapse prevention: understanding one's most likely vulnerable patterns and situations in the world that would likely elicit dysfunctional beliefs and behaviors. Then the client is taught how to develop strategies (based on past therapeutic successes) for coping with these possible future situations in order to feel greater confidence and ability to cope when faced with similar situations.

Ongoing Socialization

The therapist reinforces the cognitive model many times during the course of therapy by using examples from the client's own life to illustrate the above aspects of the cognitive model. For example, it would be helpful for Nancy and Charley Shore to appreciate that the dread that Charley feels coming home each night derives from his fear that Nancy will immediately present him with a multitude of problems that he will be unable to solve and that he therefore chooses to avoid this by telling her what he thinks she wants to hear. Exploring this in front of Nancy may lead to a discussion of how people in general (not just Charley) often try to avoid unpleasantness and how this is something that everyone in the family may do from time to time. Socialization does not occur only at the outset of therapy. Rather, it is an ongoing process whereby the therapist looks for good opportunities to illustrate—with the client's own material—the connections between cognition, emotion, behavior, and physiological symptoms. The therapist also seeks to uncover and highlight instances where a shift in beliefs leads to emotional and behavioral change. Educating the client in the cognitive model also includes presenting the various cognitive distortions that are most commonly seen in dysfunctional thinking. Cognitive therapists frequently provide clients with a single-page list of these at the beginning of therapy. Then, in each session therapists gently direct the clients' attention to ones that they are displaying so that clients may more easily either "undo" these once they notice them or actually stop themselves as they are engaging in them. Frequently clients will increasingly use cognitive-therapy terminology for their cognitive distortions as they catch themselves earlier and earlier in the negative cycle.

Importance of the Therapeutic Alliance

Therapists help achieve the therapy goals partly by helping to foster and maintain a strong therapeutic alliance with their clients. This relationship, much like Bowlby's "secure base" (Bowlby, 1988), enables clients to feel more secure as they venture out to experiment with new perspectives and behaviors. Therapists employ empathy, warmth, and unconditional positive regard to build and maintain a good therapeutic relationship. They also elicit ongoing feedback from their clients so as to ascertain how well the clients are understanding the content of the sessions. In addition, they provide the rationale for exercises done inside or outside the session and ask both what the clients are learning from each session or homework assignment and how the clients feel about the therapy process itself. When therapists pay special attention to these variables, their clients' sense of trust in the therapist and the therapy process greatly increases. It also typically increases clients' willingness to explore new options in thinking and acting. Therapists also periodically assess how their clients' most critical beliefs, emotions, and behaviors are shifting in intensity and duration by comparing these with baseline levels.

Homework

Cognitive therapists recognize that deep, lasting change requires the repeated examination and restructuring of often long-held beliefs that are frequently supported by years of habit and are interwoven with a raft of associated maladaptive behaviors. Therefore, clients must continue the decentering process of stepping back from their dysfunctional beliefs and behaviors and looking at them with new eyes outside the therapy room. They also need to practice these new ways of thinking and behaving on a regular basis. Each therapy session, therefore, is only a prelude to the more critical follow-up work in a client's ongoing life in general. For this reason, cognitive therapy puts a large emphasis on these outside-session tasks, called homework or self-help assignments. Every session includes both a careful review of the previous week's tasks and a collaboratively agreed-upon assignment for the coming week. These assignments are derived from the momentum of the session so that the client may further investigate or solidify important issues or meanings that have been explored. For example, clients are frequently asked to read a chapter or article to better understand themselves, someone else, or a phenomenon (e.g., anger). This process, called *bibliotherapy*, need not consist wholly of self-help books, but may include any readings relevant to a client's problem. Homework even more typically includes writing something down to capture it more accurately and increase objectivity about it, or doing something behaviorally (e.g., increasing one's exercise or activity level). Frequently, clients will reinforce nascent, more adaptive beliefs by reading "coping cards" several times per day. A coping card for Rena might read

> "It's not that I'm destined to fail in all circumstances. It's just that when I get doubts about my performance in some activity and then

pull back on my efforts it's harder to succeed. I need to see my doubts as normal fears, but not 'truth.' When I act in spite of my fears I weaken them and increase my chances for success. I actually have a lot going for me!"

At other times, clients will verbalize and then later test out a hypothesis in the real world. This is called a *behavioral experiment*. In Nancy Shore's case, the therapist might suggest that Nancy first write down and then test her hypotheses about what would happen if Nancy were to take a walk around the block.

LIMITATIONS OF THE MODEL

Although its basic tenets are simple, successful cognitive therapy application requires a great deal of hard work and finesse as therapists and clients collaboratively determine goals and therapeutic priorities and then seek appropriate interventions by which to investigate and modify problematic beliefs of all levels. Cognitive therapy clients must be capable of and willing to devote a strong effort and time outside the session to exploring and modifying cognitions, behaviors, and other patterns that may have a certain familiarity or even comfort to them while at the same time still being dysfunctional in many respects. Long-standing problems (e.g., Axis II disorders) often require more time in therapy and greater periods of discomfort than many clients (or third-party insurance companies) prefer. Furthermore, therapists must coordinate a great deal of information and revise their theories about their clients periodically so as to correct misperceptions and better account for the clients' experiences.

Comparatively few controlled studies have been done on the use of cognitive therapy with families or couples. Its use with certain disorders (e.g., bipolar, psychotic, or chemically dependent clients) is still evolving. Conceptualizing the problems of a family or other interpersonal unit is much more difficult than considering those of an individual, for example. It is not clear how successful the average cognitive therapist would be in making this transition from individual to system.

The model has been much better researched on specific syndromes rather than on important problems that may not appear as major psychiatric disorders in the *DSM–IV*. For example, cognitive therapy has been employed for overcoming communication difficulties between people or increasing compliance with medical regimens, but research here is much more limited. Some (see, e.g., Safran & Segal, 1990) have criticized cognitive therapy as being too individualistic and not sufficiently attuned to interpersonal or systemic dynamics, but there is a movement afoot for therapists to work on responsibly integrating the strengths of cognitive therapy principles with those of other strong, more interpersonally attuned models.

As with other therapeutic models, cognitive therapy is also seeking to address issues of cultural and subcultural differences rather than to assume that all client populations would respond in the same way to the model and its application. Cognitive therapists—like other therapists—should be sensitive to culturally diverse beliefs, emotions, and behavior, including responses to aspects of therapy that may impact treatment (e.g., Kuehlwein, 1992; McGoldrick, Pearce, & Giordano, 1982).

RESEARCH

Cognitive therapy has always been closely tied to research. Beck himself has tackled many disorders, including depression (Beck, Rush, Shaw, & Emery, 1979), anxiety disorders (Beck, Emery, & Greenberg, 1985), personality disorders (Beck et al., 1990), and drug abuse (Beck, Wright, Newman, & Liese, 1993). In each instance, Beck and his colleagues strove to understand the disorder's unique features and then devised specific assessment and treatment approaches based on this careful study. The cognitive therapy manual *Cognitive Therapy of Depression* (Beck et al., 1979) is a model of clarity for therapists who wish to successfully treat depressed clients, and it has spawned many research studies. The model was first tested in controlled trials on individuals with unipolar depression. Here cognitive therapy has been found to match or exceed the well-documented effects of antidepressant medications (Murphy, Simons, Wetzel, & Lustman, 1984; Rush, Beck, Kovacs, & Hollon, 1977). In addition, cognitive therapy often appears to have continuing positive effects after treatment is concluded (Blackburn, Eunson, & Bishop, 1986; Shea et al., 1992; Simons, Murphy, Levine, & Wetzel, 1986). Clients therefore experience lower relapse rates in comparison to other therapies (pharmacological or psychotherapeutic) once treatment is withdrawn. Other studies have indicated that the model is highly effective with panic disorder (Clark, Salkovskis, Hackmann, & Gelder, 1991; Salkovskis & Clark, 1990), and effective with generalized anxiety disorder (Butler, Fennell, Robson, & Gelder, 1991), and obsessive–compulsive disorder (Emmelkamp, Visser, & Hoekstra, 1988), just to name a few. Ongoing studies are examining its effects on cocaine-addicted populations and other groups.

SUMMARY

Cognitive therapy is a powerful, modern therapy approach that combines phenomenological and information-processing approaches (including evolutionary perspectives) to understand the problems of clients. Its strong emphasis on the therapeutic relationship and its less pejorative views of client noncompliance help therapists more successfully weather typical therapeutic ruptures and obstacles. By collaboratively using various experiential and empirico-deductive means to help clients decenter from their dysfunctional patterns of cognition, therapists can assist their clients in exploring other, more adaptive ways of constructing their worlds. This translates into important shifts in emotions, behavior, and physiological symptoms. The sessions and course of therapy are structured to provide maximum attention to the most important problems facing the clients. Clients furthermore greatly consolidate and extend their therapeutic gains by continuing to work regularly (cognitively and behaviorally) on key issues outside the therapy session as they increasingly practice being their own therapists. This therapeutic modality has proved effective for a wide variety of common psychiatric disorders and common problems. Research—already strong—continues to amass in new areas as well as to refine questions posed in prior research. Although it is by no means a therapeutic panacea, cognitive therapy offers a great number of clients a technology to better their lives. It may also be seen as a strong candidate for a metamodel by which to understand all therapeutic change (Beck, 1991b), inasmuch as all therapeutic change must include cognitive reorganization to endure.

REFERENCES

American Psychiatric Association. (1994). *Diagnostic and statistical manual of mental disorders* (4th ed.). Washington, DC: Author.

Beck, A. T. (1963). Thinking and depression: Idiosyncratic content and cognitive distortions. *Archives of General Psychiatry, 9*, 324–333.

Beck, A. T. (1978). *Depression inventory.* Philadelphia: Center for Cognitive Therapy.

Beck, A. T. (1983). Cognitive therapy of depression: New perspectives. In P. Clayton (Ed.), *Treatment of depression: Old controversies and new approaches* (pp. 265–290). New York: Raven.

Beck, A. T. (1987). Cognitive models of depression. *Journal of Cognitive Psychotherapy: An International Quarterly, 1*, 5–37.

Beck, A. T. (1988). *Love is never enough.* New York: Harper & Row.

Beck, A. T. (1991a). Cognitive therapy: A 30-year retrospective. *American Psychologist, 46*, 368–375.

Beck, A. T. (1991b). Cognitive therapy as the integrative therapy: A reply to Alford and Norcross. *Journal of Psychotherapy Integration, 1*, 191–198.

Beck, A. T., Emery, G., & Greenberg, R. L. (1985). *Anxiety disorders and phobias.* New York: Basic Books.

Beck, A. T., Epstein, N., Brown, G., & Steer, R. A. (1988). An inventory for measuring clinical anxiety: Psychometric properties. *Journal of Consulting and Clinical Psychology, 56*, 893–897.

Beck, A. T., Freeman, A., & Associates. (1990). *Cognitive therapy of the personality disorders.* New York: Guilford.

Beck, A. T., Rush, A. J., Shaw, B. F., & Emery, G. (1979). *Cognitive therapy of depression.* New York: Guilford.

Beck, A. T., & Weishaar, M. E. (1989). Cognitive therapy. In A. Freeman, K. M. Simon, L. Beutler, & H. Arkowitz (Eds.), *Comprehensive handbook of cognitive therapy* (pp. 21–36). New York: Plenum.

Beck, A. T., Weissman, A., Lester, D., & Trexler, L. (1974). The measurement of pessimism: The Hopelessness Scale. *Journal of Consulting and Clinical Psychology, 42,* 861–865.

Beck, A. T., Wright, F. D., Newman, C. F., & Liese, B. S. (1993). *Cognitive therapy of substance abuse.* New York: Guilford.

Beck, J. S. (1995). *Cognitive therapy: Basics and beyond.* New York: Guilford.

Blackburn, I. M., Eunson, K. M., & Bishop, S. (1986). A two-year naturalistic follow-up of depressed patients treated with cognitive therapy, pharmacotherapy and a combination of both. *Journal of Affective Disorders, 10,* 67–75.

Bowlby, J. (1988). *A secure base: Clinical applications of attachment theory.* London: Routledge.

Butler, G., Fennell, M., Robson, P., & Gelder, M. (1991). Comparison of behavior therapy and cognitive behavior therapy in the treatment of generalized anxiety disorder. *Journal of Consulting and Clinical Psychology, 59,* 167–175.

Clark, D. M., Salkovskis, P. M., Hackmann, A., & Gelder, M. (1991, November). *Longterm outcome of cognitive therapy for panic disorder.* Paper presented at the 25th annual meeting of the Association for Advancement of Behavior Therapy, New York.

Covi, L., & Primakoff, L. (1988). Cognitive group therapy. In A. J. Frances & R. E. Hales (Eds.), *American Psychiatric Press review of psychiatry* (pp. 608–626). Washington, DC: American Psychiatric Press.

Dattilio, F. M., & Padesky, C. A. (1990). *Cognitive therapy with couples.* Sarasota, FL: Professional Resource Exchange.

Ellis, A. (1989). Rational-Emotive therapy. In R. J. Corsini & D. Wedding (Eds.), *Current psychotherapies* (4th ed., pp. 197–234). Itasca, IL: Peacock.

Emmelkamp, P. M. G., Visser, S., & Hoekstra, R. J. (1988). Cognitive therapy vs. exposure in vivo in the treatment of obsessive-compulsives. *Cognitive Therapy and Research, 12,* 103–114.

Freeman, A. (Ed.). (1983). *Cognitive therapy with couples and groups.* New York: Plenum.

Giesler, R. B., Josephs, R. A., & Swann, W. B. (1997). Self-verification in clinical depression: The desire for negative evaluation. *Journal of Abnormal Psychology, 105,* 358–368.

Hollon, S. D., & Evans, M. D. (1983). Cognitive therapy for depression in a group format. In A. Freeman (Ed.), *Cognitive therapy with couples and groups.* New York: Plenum.

Hollon, S. D., & Najavits, L. (1988). Review of empirical studies on cognitive therapy. In R. E. Hales & A. J. Frances (Eds.), *Psychiatric Press review of psychiatry* (vol. 7, pp. 643–666). Washington, DC: American Psychiatric Press.

Kuehlwein, K. T. (1992). Working with gay men. In A. Freeman & F. Dattilio (Eds.), *Comprehensive casebook of cognitive therapy* (pp. 249–255). New York: Plenum.

Kuehlwein, K. T. (1993). A survey and update of cognitive therapy systems. In K. T. Kuehlwein & H. Rosen (Eds.), *Cognitive therapy in action: Evolving innovative practice* (pp. 1–32). San Francisco: Jossey-Bass.

Kuehlwein, K. T. (in press). The cognitive treatment of depression. In G. Simos (Ed.), *Cognitive-behavior therapy: Toward the 21st century.*

Lazarus, A. A., & Lazarus, C. N. (1991). *Multimodal life history inventory* (2nd ed.). Champaign, IL: Research Press.

McGoldrick, M., Pearce, J. K., & Giordano, J. (Eds.). (1982). *Ethnicity and family therapy.* New York: Guilford.

McMullin, R. E. (1986). *Handbook of cognitive therapy techniques.* New York: Norton.

Murphy, G. E., Simons, A. D., Wetzel, R. D., & Lustman, P. J. (1984). Cognitive therapy versus tricyclic antidepressants in major depression. *Archives of General Psychiatry, 41,* 33–41.

Newman, C. F. (1994). Understanding client resistance: Methods for enhancing motivation to change. *Cognitive and Behavioral Practice, 1,* 47–69.

Overholser, J. C. (1993a). Elements of the Socratic method: I. Systematic questioning. *Psychotherapy, 30,* 67–74.

Overholser, J. C. (1993b). Elements of the Socratic method: II. Inductive reasoning. *Psychotherapy, 30,* 75–85.

Rosen, H. (1985). *Piagetian dimensions of clinical relevance.* New York: Columbia University Press.

Rosen, H. (1989). Piagetian theory and cognitive therapy. In A. Freeman, K. M. Simon, L. Beutler, & H. Arkowitz (Eds.), *Comprehensive handbook of cognitive therapy* (pp. 189–212). New York: Plenum.

Rosen, H., & Kuehlwein, K. T. (Eds.). (1996). *Constructing realities: Meaning-making perspectives for psychotherapists.* San Francisco: Jossey-Bass.

Rush, A. J., Beck, A. T., Kovacs, M., & Hollon, S. D. (1977). Comparative efficacy of cognitive therapy and pharmacotherapy in the treatment of depressed outpatients. *Cognitive Therapy and Research, 1,* 17–37.

Safran, J. D., & Segal, Z. V. (1990). *Interpersonal process in cognitive therapy.* New York: Basic Books.

Safran, J. D., Vallis, T. M., Segal, Z. V., & Shaw, B. F. (1986). Assessment of core cognitive processes in cognitive therapy. *Cognitive Therapy and Research, 10,* 509–526.

Salkovskis, P. M., & Clark, D. M. (1990). Affective responses to hyperventilation: A test of the cognitive model of panic. *Behaviour Research and Therapy, 28,* 51–61.

Shea, M. T., Elkin, I., Imber, S. D., Sotsky, S. M., Watkins, J. T., Collins, J. F., Pilkonis, P. A., Beckham, E., Glass, D. R., Dolan, R. T., & Parloff, M. B. (1992). Course of depressive symptoms over follow-up: Findings from the National Institute of Mental Health treatment of depression collaborative research program. *Archives of General Psychiatry, 49,* 782–787.

Simons, A. D., Murphy, G. E., Levine, J. L., & Wetzel, R. D. (1986). Cognitive therapy and pharmacotherapy for depression: Sustained improvement over one year. *Archives of General Psychiatry, 43,* 43–48.

Weishaar, M. E. (1993). *Aaron T. Beck* (Key figures in counselling and psychotherapy series). Thousand Oaks, CA: Sage.

Yost, E. B., Beutler, L. E., Corbishley, M. A., & Allender, J. R. (1986). *Group cognitive therapy: A treatment approach for depressed older adults.* New York: Pergamon Press.

Young, J. E. (1990). *Cognitive therapy for personality disorders: A schema-focused approach.* Sarasota, FL: Professional Resources Exchange.

APPENDIX A. COGNITIVE DISTORTIONS

1. *Labeling:* Defining yourself or others solely or largely in terms of negative events (e.g., "I *am* a failure" vs. "I failed at *this.*"). Seeing someone globally and largely (or entirely) in terms of past faults or imperfections.

2. *Selective attention:* Focusing (like a zoom lens) on a negative detail *out of context,* ignoring more meaningful aspects around this fact and thus "coloring" the whole experience on this basis, like how a tiny drop of food coloring colors an entire glass of water.

3. *Overgeneralization:* Drawing conclusions or general rules on the basis of one or more isolated incidents, then applying this conclusion or rule across the board to even unrelated situations—for example, seeing one failure experience as a *constant pattern* of failure stretching into the future.

4. *Magnification/minimization:* Overestimating or underestimating the significance or magnitude of an event so as to distort it and its meaning for you.

    (a) Magnification: Making mountains out of molehills, making things seem even worse than they are—in other words, "catastrophizing."

    (b) Minimization: Downplaying the importance of something that is usually quite significant.

5. *Personalization:* Assuming that outside events or comments relate to you without evidence backing this up. This includes placing excessive responsibility or blame on yourself while overlooking other factors that could be involved and even more important.

6. *All-or-nothing thinking:* Seeing things at either one extreme or the other, with nothing in between (e.g., anything less than total success = total failure). You often ascribe or give the most negative meaning or category to yourself or others.

7. *Emotional reasoning:* Using emotions *on their own* to determine the truth or falsity of something. Assuming that your negative emotions and conclusions must reflect reality: "I feel it so strongly, it must be true!" or "I feel guilty, therefore I must have done something wrong."

8. *Disqualifying the positive:* Overlooking positive experiences in your life by pretending that they "don't count," or only seeing or believing the negative aspects of a situation. This enables you to continue to believe strongly in a dysfunctional belief that your own experiences run counter to.

9. Should *statements:* Using absolute words [*must, ought, have to, should*] with yourself or others. Using them with yourself makes you feel bad or guilty for not living up to often unrealistic standards (and often makes you *less* likely to meet these standards in the future because you feel less capable). Using them with *others* tends to make you feel angry, frustrated, and resentful toward them for not living up to your expectations.

10. *Jumping to conclusions* (three types):

    (a) Mind-reading: Assuming *without* checking it out that someone is feeling or thinking negatively toward you.

    (b) Fortune-telling: Predicting things will turn out badly and then becoming *persuaded* that your prediction is already true and sometimes even reacting as though the event has already happened.

    (c) Arbitrary inference: Coming to a conclusion without evidence to support it or even when evidence actually *contradicts* your belief.

Notes:

(1) These distortions can often overlap.

(2) With some problems (e.g., drug abuse), unrealistic *positive* versions of these biases often occur.

7

Ericksonian Approaches in Social Work

Stephen R. Lankton, M.S.W., and
Carol H. Lankton, M.A.

INTRODUCTION

The work of Milton Erickson (1901–1980) spanned 50 years, and he hypnotized 30,000 diverse subjects. Erickson did not create theories to explain people. He favored the idea of learning in an open-minded way what each client had to teach. He then responded in novel, creative, flexible, and uncommon ways in an effort to intervene most effectively, solve the problem, and promote developmental creativity. Within this atmosphere—in which novel responses to clients prevail as the ideal in an approach with no theory—we examine several characteristics that pertain to how problems and people are viewed. These include the availability of experiential resources (characteristics and psychological abilities); the importance of action for clients; the utilization of client behavior; indirect interventions; and techniques such as hypnosis, paradoxical prescription, and unusual assignments.

Problems are thought to occur when people do not know (consciously or unconsciously) how to get desired psychological resources into situations and contexts in which they are needed in order to respond to unfolding life-cycle demands in a healthy manner (Haley, 1973, p. 150). Consequently, assessment is an activity that frames the presenting problem in terms of the experiential resources available and needed within a developmental and interpersonal climate experienced by all the individuals in the family. Therapy is directed toward helping clients create a rearrangement in their

149

relationships so that developmental growth—that is, a creative reassociation of experiential resources—is maximized.

The therapist takes an active role and shares responsibility for initiating therapeutic movement and "creating a context in which change can take place" (Dammann, 1982). This is often facilitated by introducing conversational material into the therapy session and using outside assignments. Ericksonian approaches aspire to getting clients active and moving (Zeig, 1980) in their lives. Hypnotherapy, anecdotes, therapeutic metaphors, and indirect suggestions illustrate the development of new behaviors or motivate participation in the homework assignments (C. Lankton & S. Lankton, 1989; S. Lankton & C. Lankton, 1983). It is from the learning brought about by new actions—not as much (if any) as from insight or understanding— that change develops. It may be, in fact, that change results in eventual insight, not the other way around.

Utilization is a term that Erickson used to describe the process of appreciating whatever behavior the client offers and using it in the client's best interest as a means to a desirable end. Utilization features aspects of positive framing and paradoxical prescription. It is applied to here-and-now material presented from the client as well as to potential abilities that may previously have been considered problems or liabilities. No behavior is labeled as *resistance* but rather is accepted and in some manner used to facilitate a context for change. For example, members of the Shore family worry about each other as their favorite method of showing love and concern. Rather than attempting to stop them from worrying and calling their resulting hesitation or anxiety resistance, the therapist may ask them to worry even more diligently or in a prescribed fashion to better demonstrate their love. This utilizes their immediate behavior to increase joining and comfort and reduces the discomfort or anxiety that attempting to take this choice away would create.

Indirection is a method of offering ideas that is a well-known principle of Erickson's work (Rossi, 1980a). Indirect suggestions stimulate clients' own thinking. Although content can be quite clear and specific, there is no authoritarian demand in indirection. Performance pressure is diminished because the therapist is not directing but merely stimulating the clients' thinking about a variety of possible ideas. This results in a bit of ambiguity that can give rise to a pleasant mental excitement or curiosity toward change.

Ericksonian therapy has become closely associated with hypnosis, paradoxical prescription, unusual assignments, and rapid positive outcomes that baffle traditional attempts to solve the same problem. Overall, however, it is known for supporting the power, health, and positive intentions that clients have, both consciously and unconsciously. There are many divergent ways of proceeding under the rubric of Ericksonian approaches, as is evidenced by the unique interpretations of numerous faculty presenting at Ericksonian congresses. Some have favored certain techniques and excluded others, but all have embraced these foundational beliefs.

THE CONCEPT OF THE PERSON AND THE HUMAN EXPERIENCE

A central feature of Ericksonian approaches is respect and positive regard for the client. When Erickson's work first demonstrated this view in the mid-1930s, this was still a radical idea and was inconsistent with mainstream therapy in which many therapists distrusted clients and searched for expected pathology. Erickson insisted that each person operates from a core of health, positive intentions, and almost unlimited unconscious resources.[1] He admired the uniqueness of every person and maintained that all people have great potential despite their varied and often less than ideal learning opportunities. Psychological resources can be developed through demonstration and modeling, but people must also be given permission to use these psychological resources before they can apply them in relevant situations. However, the assumption is that the potential for any resource is available and that people can be expected to make the best choice possible for themselves at any given time. Erickson reasoned that any behavior offered was that client's best attempt to cooperate in accomplishing a desired result, whether that was playing a particular role, solving a problem, or acquiring a skill.

Each developmental stage—and even each new day—presents people with a need to adjust aspects of their lifestyle and effect small changes in behavior. Each of these changes is evidence of problem-solving behavior and can be a resource if used in the proper context. Major problems are solved by acquiring (and making automatic) the skills and resources required for these daily developmental adaptations. People are motivated to solve problems and automatically make better choices once that choice becomes available and organized. Therefore, therapy does not focus on removing old, limiting choices but rather on stimulating clients' awareness and their ability to make better choices now.

The Shores have gained a reputation among social service agencies as a family whose problems never get resolved and whose members never function free from symptoms. Based on this reputation, it would be tempting for a new therapist to see them as difficult, resistant, or hopeless clients who probably cannot be helped. As this impression is subtly conveyed to the family, it becomes a co-created, self-fulfilling prophecy. On the other hand, framing the Shores' various problems as their best available choices for accomplishing developmental demands leads to an appreciation of the family and their health-seeking impulses. They have used

---

[1] *Editor's note:* Similar concepts have been core beliefs of the social work profession for more than 60 years.

their inner strengths and have made courageous efforts to survive and be happy despite many potential setbacks. This view inspires the self-fulfilling prophecy that they are on their way to solving the problems that confront them. They simply need to modify their attempts by including resources not yet applied in a directed fashion for their own betterment.

Each person relies on internal resources (experience, urges, memory, fantasy, ideas, etc.) as he or she attempts to adjust to life's daily demands. Simultaneously, each person is part of the environment that makes demands on the others in the family. Along with the family of origin, the environment includes work, school, neighborhood contacts, bills, and so on. Thus, creative problem-solving comes from maintaining relations that allow for flexibility in stimulating each other's personal resources instead of inadvertently stimulating and reinforcing each other's limiting beliefs and negative attributions.

Growth and change at the unconscious level are accomplished as people stimulate one another to organize still more complex and appropriate ways of adapting or to disorganize and reorganize new constellations of experiences and transactions. This learning may take place at unconscious or conscious levels. For example, children unconsciously learn the expression of aggressive and affectionate behaviors from parents through modeling. Conscious learning includes such behavior as deliberate acts of memorization, imitation, and rehearsal. Both levels of learning are continuous during socialization and may reinforce or inhibit one another depending on circumstances.

HISTORICAL PERSPECTIVE

Milton Erickson was a pioneer in the practice of psychotherapy, family therapy, social work, hypnosis, and psychiatry. He developed methods of working with clients that emphasized common—even unconscious—natural abilities and talents. This was in distinct contrast to traditional approaches, which emphasized dysfunctional aspects of clients and attempted to analyze, interpret, or develop insight for this pathology during therapy sessions. Erickson framed change in ways that used any behavior, reduced dependence on therapy, bypassed the need for insight, and expanded creative adjustment to developmental demands, while removing the presenting problem and allowing clients to take full credit for changes achieved in therapy.

There is no obvious or singular influence on the development of Erickson's thinking except that he came from a farming background in which practical and common-sense approaches to solving problems were highly valued. He also struggled with polio and severe physical challenges, which he approached as merely problems to be solved. He delved into realms of highly focused concentration in his self-guided and strong-willed regimen of relearning movement, balance, walking, and other functions after polio had left him paralyzed as a teen. Subsequently, he studied hypnosis with Clark Hull at the University of Wisconsin, although it may have been Erickson who influenced Hull's further study of that area. During the mid-1930s, Erickson was interested in Freud's notion of the unconscious and its influence on behavior. Erickson's early research focused on tracing a client's symptom or neurosis to its origin in the past. Within a decade, Erickson shifted his focus from historical causes of symptoms to the present functioning and immediate interactions of clients. He favored an eclectic and pragmatic method of using anything that would work to promote change and problem solution.

Erickson's pragmatic contributions were appreciated by biologist and communications expert Gregory Bateson and members of his Palo Alto research project, who in 1952 elected to investigate Erickson's work as it represented elements of communication facilitating change. The group discussed examples of Erickson's work in the important 1956 paper, "Toward a Theory of Schizophrenia" (Jackson, 1968). At the Mental Research Institute in Palo Alto, Paul Watzlawick, John Weakland, and Richard Fisch studied Erickson's models and techniques as they related to change in human systems and brief strategic therapy (Watzlawick, Weakland, & Fisch, 1974). In 1957, Erickson founded the American Society of Clinical Hypnosis and edited its journal for 10 years. In 1963, Jay Haley published an account of Erickson's strategic therapy, further clarifying elements of his novel approach. Bateson continued to wrestle with illusive problems of epistemology and ontology and their relationship to then-conventional therapy, using Erickson's work to illustrate the emerging alternative.

Traditional therapy was based on assumptions traceable through Plato, Aristotle, René Descartes, and Isaac Newton that there is an observable and objective reality that is independent of people's efforts to observe it. There were not many detractors from this approach. In the latter part of the 18th century, David Hume—and soon thereafter Immanuel Kant, in his *Critique of Pure Reason*—suggested that people, by observing, create order in the universe. Kant emphasized that order may not be present until humans observe it. Freud took exception to Kant's premise, "There is nothing in the id that could be compared with negation; and we perceive with surprise an exception to the philosophical theorem that space and time are necessary forms of our mental acts" (Freud, 1966, p. 538). With this emphasis, the entire profession of therapy was influenced with the belief, common to psychoanalysis, that people could know the truth of a separate reality and that acts of observation did not alter this external reality. This posture toward reality was separation from it, studying it by reduction. The simple act of reducing and labeling seems innocent enough on the one hand, but does not credit the "observer" with the action of inventing the label that is applied or with punctuating the strip of ongoing experience said to begin and end according to the limits of the label. Consequently, traditional therapy, in its attempts to search for an objective truth about problems rooted in the past, developed a rich language to describe the intrapsychic domain of single individuals. This description often attributes pathology to the individual and typically excludes his or her present life context.

The therapeutic stance of separateness and searching for problems often results in the taking of an adversarial position. The language of therapy reflects this adversarial posture with metaphors such as *resistance, conflict, defense, hidden motive, suppression, power*, and *attack*. Szasz (1961) and Laing (1967, 1972) have described the individual and social injuries that are byproducts of attempting to help within such a framework. Placed in an adversarial position, purposefully or inadvertently, labeled individuals will easily demonstrate more behavior that will reinforce a therapist's conviction about the independent existence of an internal pathology. It is this very trend that Erickson wished to avoid throughout his career (Erickson, 1985).

Erickson suggested that traditional therapy made clients lie in the proverbial "Procrustean bed" of theory by cutting off their legs to make clients fit. His approach has demanded that therapists rethink their adherence to rigid structural models. Therapies based on traditional paradigms usually rely on generalizations about individuals, and the most successful Ericksonian approaches recognize the uniqueness of individuals.

KEY THEORETICAL CONSTRUCTS

Problem behaviors are often identified as *undesirable* by family members or as *pathological* by mental health personnel, but these are only labels affixed to a strip of behavior in a particular context. Defining and framing the problem needs to set the stage for movement toward desired change. Placing a pejorative label on individuals or families, even in the name of science, does not contribute to the effectiveness of therapy.

Symptom Development

Presenting problems can be specified and isolated, but more often they represent attempts to solve a class of problems of which the attempts at solution are also part of the problem. For example, a client who develops a snake phobia as a result of some unpleasant interaction with a snake presents a specific and isolated problem. On the other hand, when people attempt to solve developmental problems with skills that will not do the job, in an environment that is not helping people most efficiently use the tools and potentials they have, symptoms often develop that become "forms of communication. As such, these symptoms are frequently important signs or cues of developmental problems that are in the process of becoming conscious" (Erickson & Rossi, 1979, p. 143).

Because of her reinforcement history, Nancy Shore may insist that the family organization allow her the luxury of being unquestioned. During courtship this arrangement may have seemed attractive to Charley and became further reinforced as part of the relationship, but after marriage and especially during child-rearing stages of development, such an arrangement in the relationship is now seen to be unacceptable and as part of the problem. However, the rule of family organization may prescribe the continuance of this mode of problem solving by Nancy. If environmental situations require attention to Charley's needs, the family's style of interaction is not sensitive to that requirement. Perhaps Nancy's inability to solve problems in other ways, such as taking a receptive position when asking for help while also stopping her dominating behavior, has resulted in the anxiety symptoms she brings to therapy. A further example of the process of symptom development may be how Michael exaggerates a crying episode or perhaps experiences social rejection as an inefficient communication to Nancy to stop dominating. Charley may develop a presenting problem of blackouts or a bridge phobia for the same reason. Any of these symptoms may serve to indicate that the behaviors that have customarily been used to solve problems are now not working and that people are overusing inappropriate tools for the job. One can determine whether a presenting problem is a symptom or a problem that stands on its own by understanding the history of the problem, the solutions that have been attempted, and the problem's function within the family system.

Communication in the family and the larger ecosystem provides each individual with the necessary clues about how to develop a symptom. The actual selection of a unique symptom is always a complex and somewhat mysterious matter. It would be an extreme oversimplification to say that the symptom is "caused" by a given behavior or sequence of behaviors. Instead, a symptomatic display is determined by a complex interaction of communication, patterns of adaptation, physical health—and, perhaps, serendipitous creativity or random change. It may be primarily triggered by the overuse of a problem-solving behavior or the under-use of other resources. All the while, family members continue to communicate and inadvertently shape experiences that give rise to it.

Psychiatrist Eric Berne has discussed and documented some phenomena of communication that may contribute to the rise of specific symptoms (Berne, 1972). For example, in a family in which "colorful" metaphors for solving problems were centered around the anal sphincter (e.g., "he's tight," "this is a pain in the ass," "kick in the butt"), it might be expected that problems related to the anal sphincter would arise (e.g., encopresis, spastic colon, diverticulosis). Communication in a family is continually framing events, focusing awareness, and evoking experience. In these ways, it parallels the intense aspect of hypnotic communication. Berne stated that "The child is, in effect, hypnotized by his parent into carrying out a certain life pattern" (1972, p. 343), whereas Laing wrote extensively about how parents place limits on the child's problem-solving (1967) by acting as lay hypnotists (1972, p. 80).

Although it seems reasonable that all members of a system share the problem in some way, it is also likely that some people in the system are functioning with fewer limits on their experience than are others. Therefore, some individuals will appear healthier than others, even though all members may be said to share the problem.

The individual who is most symptomatic may have chosen—or may seem to have been chosen—to operate beyond the allowed behavioral and experiential limits (as defined by themselves or others). Some symptoms, such as panic attacks, are beyond the range normally considered voluntary, whereas others such as extramarital affairs involve actions normally thought to be voluntary. However, the issue of free will is not really the point. Instead, Ericksonian approaches want to help clients unlimit problem-solving needed at each developmental stage. Consequently, the "truth" of how symptoms arise is far less important than how creative adaptation can arise.

Interpersonal–Developmental Framework

All problems presented for therapy are examined through a lens that focuses on the big picture or the comprehensive context. Within this framework, individual, dyadic, triadic, family-system, and extended-system units of influence are considered. A family, an individual, or an organization of any size can be viewed as going through continuous cycles of stability and instability as they traverse stages of interpersonal development. For example, at the family level, the birth of a child or relocation of a home are periods of noticeable instability when contrasted with times that are characterized by homogeneous routines and a relative redundancy of daily living patterns. For the individual, graduation from college, a new job, or physical illness are examples of such unstable periods. Even here, however, the larger context of family of origin or extended system influences must be taken into account.

The family cycle of stability–instability is most often initiated by the changes brought on by requirements of particular developmental stages. At each new stage of development, novel experiences or alterations in the usual types of experiences and transactions must be learned. For instance, when the birth of a baby signals a change in the family to the child-raising stage of development, hundreds of new experiences, transactions, and behaviors must be learned: postponing one's gratification for the sake of the child's needs, learning to ask for help with the child, being able to experience joy in the child's growth, acquiring a vast array of care-taking skills, and so forth.

If these experiences are readily available as resources due to previous learning, the disorganization within the family system is relatively short and the transition to new creative organization is relatively easy. Conversely, to the extent that resources are not available, the disorganization becomes more debilitating. Correction of disorganization comes with the implementation of problem-solving mechanisms and techniques used individually and collectively by the members of the family.

Growth and Adaptation

Distinguishing between dynamic adjustments and problems blocking such movement is a key component to therapy. In order to decide if problems exist in the family, therapists may first ask the family what its problems are, but many times the family may perceive necessary and natural adjustments that occur in many families as their personal inadequacy, problem, shame, and the like. Mental health is not the absence of problems but rather a recognition that they can be solved. Clients sometimes say that they believe that if things go wrong, they must have done something bad. However, life is hard, and lots of things outside of individual control go wrong. Mental health involves handling these things without blaming oneself or others. Growth is accomplished by associating conscious and unconscious experiences in ever more complex constellations. These complex associations become "experiential building blocks" that provide the foundation on which people maximize social, biological, and subjective satisfaction and communicate with others. Certain adjustments may seem to provide the building blocks for one phase of life but adversely influence the choices made at another phase. One major reason for this adverse influence is that certain creative adjustments can be difficult or impossible without the earlier experiential building blocks or without the proper environmental stimuli necessary to evoke needed resources. An adjustment that seems most appropriate in childhood may be characterized as depression in adolescence—for example, suppression of the development of age-appropriate perceptions in favor of attending to the sanctions or needs of others (e.g., parents).

Problems can develop from limited use of personal experience or from communication that evokes behavior that was not wanted. There is an ongoing interplay of personal resources and social elicitation, personal response to elicitation, personal response influencing subsequent elicitation, and so on. Ultimately, no particular adjustment ought to be seen as final, since environmental demands for creativity in later years may be far more complex, sophisticated, and subtle than could have ever been anticipated in one's earlier life.

The Shore family's host of unresolved problems are described in the case, but we do not know how the family members themselves view the situation. We do not have information about what problem they would want to change, or in what way they would change it. We know that Nancy has a stated ambition to "get everything fixed" but that she actually feels "best" during a family crisis because then she takes control and her focus is removed from her standard activity of anticipating catastrophic happenings. She is described as having anxiety and becoming immobilized. Details are unavailable about how specifically she notices anxiety or how exactly having everything fixed would look and sound. How, specifically, will having tenants downstairs bring problems? Also, what prevents her taking control of daily problems as they arise? Does she herself experience her weight as a problem? If so, how? Or is she simply anticipating some external disapproval from others who are probably too preoccupied with their own problems to notice her?

The same questions apply to Charley. What prevents him from going ahead and defining his life as a success? What is the source of his arbitrary criteria? How would he know? What would have to happen? Would there be any problem if he were to suddenly become a "success"? How does he know he isn't a very good father? What would a good one look, and feel, and sound like? What prevents him from becoming one?

The consciously defined purpose or goals for each person's behavior may be narrow compared to the potential and creative adaptation that is possible. This family presents the children as problematic while narrowly defining the appropriate and available roles for each child according to arbitrary standards of success—for instance, the idea that there is a correct timetable for career decisions and that people must move in accordance with those or be labeled *lazy*, or the boy's idea that asthma must be "outgrown" before life can proceed.

In the couple dyad, Nancy may seek therapy, complaining that Charley will not share the worry and is incompetent. She, in turn, withholds support about his importance as a person from him. What if Nancy were to reveal her fears about asking for help and her desire to have Charley share the load with her? Charley might possibly respond with empathy for her, tears, and a pledge to be close and to show his emotional self to her as she desired. But this would be so uncharacteristic for either of them that they probably would have difficulty either saying these new lines or believing the other if they did say so. Each of their perceptions and thoughts about the other forms a negative self-fulfilling prophecy. And, too, it is easier for them to view and deliver the negative than the positive; they each need to build the complex experiences that lead to this problem-solving gestalt of feelings, perceptions, and behaviors.

If he wishes to be close to her for the various pleasures and rewards of intimacy (smiles, supportive statements, empathy, eye contact, joy, sexual contact, etc.), Charley can see that his efforts will probably not pay off. Nancy essentially rebuffs and punishes his overtures. Although it is possible that he might continually attempt to convince her of his importance and worth and desire to share the load, it is more likely that he will simply stop trying. A punishing atmosphere is not a fertile soil in which to grow the seeds of emotional expression and intimacy. This is even more true when the behaviors and experiences are in need of being learned, strengthened, or conditioned.

As an interrelated part of this vicious cycle, Nancy has learned to not reach out to another person, especially when she feels sad or scared. Charley has settled for the feelings of importance he can get with his comedy act and has learned to handle his general anxieties by lying to Nancy in an attempt to tell her what she wants to hear and thus delay or avoid her criticism. When Nancy senses that he has anxieties that he covers up with lies, she concludes that she has to do everything without any support and with the extra hardship of dealing with Charley. In turn, she attempts to solve that problem by self-soothing (through food, cigarettes, and withdrawing), and this conflict leads to panic attacks.

All of these choices allow her to avoid reaching out to him. She is like a frightened child waiting for her parents to notice her and make amends. But Charley does not notice such behavior as a plea for support, help, and attention. He does not recognize that in this way he could finally do something important and "be somebody" for her. He takes her angry criticism as valid feedback of his ineptitude and her worry as the proof of her love. He may secretly appreciate her apparent ability to take care of everything, even while he laments that in so doing she keeps him from feeling "like a man." Ironically, this may even be how his parents educated him about the roles of husband and wife—and in compliance he actually demonstrates his competence at learning what he was taught! He does not like the lack of support that comes as a result, but he cannot understand or respond to Nancy's worry and helpful criticism as she would like. Of course, as long as he complains about the lack of trust and continues to lie to her when she blames him, she gathers further evidence that she is the only one who cares, and she feels "put upon," pressured, angry, and overwhelmed.

The enormous range of problem-solving resources the Shores use is being reduced by conscious mind limitations of perceptual "filters," beliefs, and the redundancy that comes from using the same behavioral expressions, mannerisms, and words. There are so many ways that each of them could change the scenario. Charley could risk releasing his tensions as tears. He could learn a new criterion for feeling, such as feeling important just by virtue of being alive and being capable of courage to show vulner-ability and imperfection. Nancy could find a more effective way to show her love for Charley than worrying about him; she could go ahead and support the notion that he is important and worthwhile "just for being." Instead of using her energy for worry, she could apply it to moving toward solutions. She and Charley could commiserate and empathize with each other, instead of Nancy blaming, attacking, and feeling solely responsible for solving problems as Charley defends, lies, and feels inadequate. In so doing, he could give her attention for her buried sadness, and she could reach out and hug him when she feels isolated and overwhelmed with all the responsibility. She could verbally reassure Charley that she honestly can tolerate knowing his truth so that he can risk telling it to her. He could "smother" her with nurturing when he sees her getting anxious and wor-ried. Some of these solutions may be better than others, in the sense that they open up doorways for future growth. Others only solve the immedi-ate problem but do nothing to change the frame in which the problem oc-curs. Each of these would require learning from their available experiences and behaviors. The result of this scenario would leave them far better pre-pared to combine their efforts for effectively solving continual problems they encounter in living—and would do so without dragging in social ser-vice workers.

The complexity of unconscious resources that could come together to create one of the above solutions is more diverse still. Consider the choice of Nancy choosing to ask for attention and help when she is anxious, sad, and feeling isolated. This could be motivated by memories of herself being left by her father (she could tell her husband how sad she was as a child and elicit his sympathy and support in this metaphoric solution), or she could motivate herself with encouraging self-talk (stating something about how she deserved to reach out, she was worth it, and she would give it a try). She could conclude that Charley really wants her to contribute when he is withdrawn and feeling inadequate (it is his way of telling her that he wants her to approach him), or she could nurture Charley and reinforce the notion that he is important to her, which would shape his behavior into a more expressive mode—and which, in turn, would bring reinforcement for the effort.

Relevant Resources

Solutions to problems take different sets of visceral, cognitive, behav-ioral, and perceptual resources. Nancy's previous learning most likely con-tains the bits and pieces of unconscious experience that would allow her to use the above possibilities for solving problems. Likewise, Charley could regroup any number of unconscious tools for improved functioning. Better still, they might each reorganize their experience so as to make mutually reinforcing changes at levels of unconscious urge, perception, cognition, behavior, expectation, role, and—finally—family organization.

Resources include any previous experiences, behaviors, feelings, beliefs, and perceptions that have contributed to the client's adaptation, some of which may be known to the client and some of which may not be immediately obvious. Erickson used whatever the client presented as a potential resource for change. For example, with a "crude" woman who perceived the space between her front teeth as a horrible disfigurement, Erickson had her learn to spit water between her teeth. Later, he used this skill as the basis for an important social interaction when he instructed her to spit water on the male coworker who visited the water cooler at the same time she did each day. She did this and ran away. He chased her, kissed her, and eventually dated and probably married her (Haley, 1973). Her initially perceived disfigurement became a resource.

Clients have bits and pieces of experiences (resources) needed to solve any current problems. Although many clients may not have—or may not perceive that they have—all the resources to resolve an immediate issue, such as accepting and nurturing (in the case of the Shores), they typically have subsets of related resources (such as friendly behavior to colleagues, tenderness toward a sibling or friend, feeling comforted by a parent, etc.) that create these resources. With these existing experiences as a positive foundation, therapists seek to develop the specific and sometimes larger resources needed for problem resolution in the marital or family system.

Problems develop when people do not know how to draw on desired psychological resources in the contexts in which they need them. There are four interrelated processes that occur at all times:

1. People have various unique resources to use in all situations.
2. Resources form the behaviors by which we communicate.
3. As people communicate, they evoke various resources and behaviors in others, who simultaneously evoke various resources and behaviors in them.
4. This interactive process continues on a moment-by-moment basis and changes the resources and communication as it does.

ASSESSMENT

How family members punctuate ongoing experience, how it is labeled, and how it is altered by each person's view of reality provides an immediate illustration of the flexibility or limits used by each person to solve the situation he or she perceives to be "a situation."

Assessing Levels of Functioning

Assessment facilitates an understanding of any system on at least four essential levels of functioning. These are family organization, social roles, communication and behavior, and beliefs and perceptions that define and limit the use of unconscious resources. Each of these interactive dynamics influences the others.

The *family organization* delineates the degree of role diversity that is possible for its members. What are the various roles being played, and what type of role-defining transactions have occurred countless times and in a multitude of ways prior to these roles' becoming typical? These transactions can occur as verbally stated beliefs, perceptual predisposition, behavioral modeling, physical abuse, and so on.

The *social roles* that have been defined for each member hold together complex groupings of experience. They limit and influence sets of communications that individuals within the system will make. *Communication* refers to verbal, nonverbal, emotional, and behavioral aspects of transacting. If family structure does not allow or encourage a particular member to develop a role for being assertive, aggressive, or angry, for example, that member will not be able to generate communications congruent with solving problems in that manner. To the extent that not playing this role is a firmly engraved expectation and learning, even an occasional transaction of demanding anything from anyone—even in response to blatant wrongdoing—will not be an acceptable option. Members learn to play particular roles, and their communications can be seen to be congruent only in these roles.

Such communications are assessed as the interface between roles allowed by the family and the level of beliefs and unconscious resources. The kinds of communications that family members are allowed (the ones they rehearse to themselves and are reinforced for delivering) determine the kinds of *belief systems and perceptions* they then formulate. Self-images are consolidated, often rigidly depicting family members in terms of the selected roles ("I can't handle things going right"). Once this belief system has been formulated, unconscious resources that could mediate contrary experiences will not impinge on the normal waking state of the individuals and are not a part of the system of perception. Or, if they do, they are considered a conflict or indication by the individual that therapy is needed to get rid of these "unnatural" perceptions. For example, if a person who believes she is not the kind of person who can have aggressive impulses or can "handle" things becomes aware of her impulses or capability, she will deny those urges. In the same way, a person who believes he cannot be confident in front of a group will spend all of his time noticing his lack of confidence when he is in front of groups. A belief is a way of saying, in effect, "This range of experience is the only range of stimuli I can notice."

If family complexity is conceptualized in this way, specific problems presented for therapy are usually described in terms of conflicts taking place between these coexisting elements of these interactive dynamics. For example, conflicts between family organization and role limits in the Shore family might be worded as "Rena is not fitting into the family; her potential for success is threatening." Problems between role limits and available communications are expressed when Charley says, "I try to be more of a father but fail" and when he says, "I worry too but can't do anything so I pretend not to notice." Problems of incongruence between allowed communication or behavior and held beliefs are evident when Nancy says, "I'm only okay in a crisis" and "I'm anxious all the time." Conflict at this level also includes the absence or presence of communication and behaviors that are not in keeping with the conscious belief system. An example is someone who believes he should fit in better, like Michael does, but who does not have the appropriate behaviors for doing so. Another way of expressing such a conflict is, "I don't cry—I can't cry." In these statements, we see the recurrence or absence of a behavior that in turn reinforces a belief and shapes a perceptual disposition.

Interpersonal Impact of Communications

One of the most important aspects of assessment is what people learn about the interpersonal impact of communications. Because each person's selection of communications is largely outside of awareness, careful attention to these behaviors is most informative. For instance, compare what one learns about a person who greets others with a warm smile but is capable of stopping the smile with what one learns about a person who cannot release the smile and just smiles constantly. In this example, the second person will most certainly have difficulties with problem-solving well beyond the strict interpersonal dimension of "making a first impression" in which the smiling was first detected. However, assessment of these problems begins by ascertaining the person's interpersonal postures with the therapist and others present in the session. Assessment may include establishing sufficient rapport, determining how to best communicate with a client, reducing a crisis, and recognizing clients' motivation for therapy, but the manner in which each of these actions progresses—the manner itself—provides invaluable assessment data.

Initial Contact Parameters

The presenting problem and preliminary goals are determined during the assessment, which includes the intake procedure and the initial interview. During that period, family organization is assessed, including a conceptualization of the current stage of development (and related demands) as well as the demands of the next logical stage of development the family will be entering. An understanding is developed of the family's way of explaining typical time structuring, involvement with extended career and social networks, and each person's involvement with the symptom(s). We are particularly interested in how engaging in the symptom represents an adaptive response or "best choice" (S. Lankton & C. Lankton, 1983) to the interpersonal and developmental demands currently being encountered.

Background information about the development of the problem will facilitate answering this question. Who knows about the problem, how does each person in the family respond to the problem, what is being accomplished by having the problem (and by talking about it or not talking about it, etc.), and what might be accomplished if the problem were not present? What is the history of the problem, and has there been previous treatment for it? General background information, including family-of-origin descriptions from each spouse, is also helpful, even if it might initially seem unrelated to the specific presenting problem.

Analysis of interactive dynamics yields information about the interpersonal orientation and perceptual, cognitive, behavioral, and emotional flexibility of each client. The therapist continues to be attentive to these factors throughout the course of treatment because they provide ongoing information about clients' experiential resources and flexibility. We are interested in both the available and avoided behaviors and always consider how the ability to engage in avoided behaviors might contribute to a more satisfactory response to developmental demands and a reduction of the symptoms or complaints.

Calibrating Communication

Tentative hypotheses quickly emerge about what it is like to live in a particular family structure, with its available roles, behaviors, emotional resources, communication skills, and beliefs. To fill in the initial sense of being in this family, we encourage a structured form of communication between family members to create a context for experiencing family dynamics in action. Typically, we ask the two people in the greatest conflict, at the most distance, or experiencing the most misunderstanding in the system to engage in a carefully directed sequence of sharing a single short statement and feeling (about their desire, goal, problem, or so on) with the other family member. The second member is asked to accurately repeat both the thought and the feeling just stated by the partner before sharing any additional data or responses. Then the second person responds with his or her thought and feeling, which the first member must then repeat accurately. It is usually possible to "track" the typical way in which each member uses communication tools to solve (or not solve) a problem. Members will display how, in this context, they make available communications and behaviors, supporting attitudes, or limit themselves and others with inflexibility, whether perceptual, cognitive, or emotional. In the context of exercises like this, one can see how family members usually communicate with and behave toward each other and whether they exhibit supportive attitudes or limit themselves and others by being inflexible (perceptually, cognitively, or emotionally).

Assessment Merges With Treatment

Assessment and treatment are inseparable to a large degree, although the initial phase of assessment occurs before the end of the first interview. The calibration procedure just described often creates a segue into treatment, which makes the former indistinguishable from the latter. Because it clarifies the existence of agreed-upon goals and frames the situation so that it attributes motivation to clients, the assessment phase is also treatment. With some families, of course, accomplishing these assessment goals continues over several sessions. Typically, however, conversation about these tentative hypotheses results in several specific goals being clarified and other goals being communicated but not verbally clarified within the first session, and the phase of treatment devoted to those goals begins immediately.

Assessment is an ongoing process in Ericksonian therapy. It continues throughout therapy as an integrated participation with clients. Use of or reaction to each intervention yields new and valuable information that influences the setting of additional goals. These reactions help guide therapy. A therapist with an ongoing assessment orientation will discover new information in constantly changing ways, including simple observation, structured interaction, clients' responses to metaphor and ambiguous function assignments (described below) or skill-building assignments, home visits, and the conventional verbal interview.

TREATMENT OF CHOICE

Assessment as just described results in a treatment plan with specific goals. It does not result in categorizing individuals with diagnoses or giving dysfunctional labels to the family. Goal setting does not focus on the absence of an undesirable state but rather on the presence of a desirable state. Furthermore, goals should be behavioral and phenomenological, as opposed to global and abstract.

Similar treatment goals are likely to apply in many cases, modified somewhat with regard to presenting problems and between-family differences, gender, ethnicity, and stage of development. For example, basic affective experiences such as the ability to feel angry, sad, tender, loving, afraid, and confident are routinely relevant as treatment goals, with the determination of which specific ones to retrieve dependent on the roles being taken in a particular family. Similarly, certain problem-solving behaviors, such as the ability to express feelings; delegate authority; cooperate; set limits on calls from a parent; be friendly to peers; nurture others in the family; ask for help; and even rebel, compete, or otherwise disaffiliate can be routinely applied when these skills have previously been unavailable or avoided for whatever reason. Goals related to attitude or change in cognitive beliefs are subject to the greatest variety because there may be many beliefs about why it is unacceptable to feel or behave in particular ways. It is in this area, especially, that therapists must understand the uniqueness of clients and the variety of challenges they face. Thus, interventions focusing on larger goals of attitude changes and belief changes (e.g., metaphors with themes that challenge particular beliefs or attitudes) will typically be offered over the course of treatment while clients have the ongoing experiences of changes in smaller, more defined behaviors and concomitant feelings that will challenge and erode those limiting attitudes and beliefs and help solidify new roles.

Setting Specific and Dynamic Goals

Negotiating goals involves a moment-to-moment process in which the therapist is stimulated by the client's behavior and reactions. At the same time, the therapist's behavior stimulates clients' subsequent behavior. Within this recursive process, goals for each family member can be shared or identified and addressed in a logical or pragmatic sequence taking into account which members are most receptive, rigid, flexible, and distressed. Like assessment, and inextricably linked to it, the process of setting goals is ongoing throughout the treatment until the decisive goal of symptom or problem resolution is accomplished and new relational patterns are established.

We always ask each member what he or she would like to have changed in the family and how that change should be accomplished. Even if members contradict each other, each input becomes the basis of a goal. However, as Erickson pointed out, rarely are families in the pain of seeking therapy able to formulate solid, "go-to" or future-oriented goals and congruently express them (Rossi, 1980d, p. 171). As a result, each member expresses wishes in accordance with his or her own flexibility of communication, understanding of the problem, belief of what is possible, and so on.

Typically, clients underrate their current resources and what they would be capable of achieving in their family. Rather, they focus on their limitations and the difficulty of the symptom or problem and only aspire to gaining the merest relief from the intensity of pain. In other words, they do not usually think to set as a goal the possibility of their fondest dreams coming true in terms of relating ideally within their family and social network.

Therapists, too, participate in the setting of goals by assessing everything said by all members, both verbally and nonverbally. They also discuss the symptom and possible achievements and then ask themselves, "What experiences and transactions does it seem that this family really needs in order to not only resolve this symptom but move creatively into and through the current stage of development in such a way as to lay the groundwork for comfortably entering the next logical stage and its inherent demands and creative opportunities?" The answer to this question may not come all at once. Occasionally the "answers" that come to mind prove to be wrong—that is, the goals that might appear to be relevant to the clients are eventually discovered to be irrelevant after all, in which case they are abandoned as new understanding comes and new goals set.

It is not unusual for different family members to have different or contradictory goals. For example, the father who wants his 18-year-old daughter to obey the same family rules as her younger siblings, stay at home more, and participate in the same family events that she did as a younger child may be in direct opposition to the adolescent, who is striving for independence and separation from her family. This difference becomes part of the therapeutic conversation and is discussed by all the participants. The therapist may offer interventions such as developmental reframing of the issue, possibly by means of tasks marking differences between siblings of different ages or tasks that may allow the father and daughter to connect in a new way.

Therapists cannot separate themselves from personal values in the process of assessing and setting goals, although every effort is made to be as neutral as possible. However, it is reassuring to realize that clients will only follow suggestions or benefit from interventions that are relevant to accomplishing goals consistent with their values. The therapist will have the opportunity to discover how a goal that had appeared to be relevant did not pan out to be relevant for that client after all, and it can then be abandoned or modified. Therapists may waste clients' time when we fail to be relevant, but it is not possible to force values or install them in a passive client, although frequently a "value clash" challenges attitudes and stimulates thinking in such a way that new values come to be held by both clients and therapist.

Presupposing Success

As therapy continues, it is important for therapists to show support and belief in the family's ability to accomplish goals by implying that they will develop through the life cycle in desirable ways, usually far beyond the scope of simply correcting the immediate symptoms of their imbalance or distress. By implying the eventual achievement of the family's desired goals sometime in the future, a contract has been created for the development of specific goals leading to this desired future.

For example, the Shores have hinted that they want more intimacy, connection, and trust in their relationship but have been somewhat vague about what this would entail. Therapists can ask them to picture themselves several months in the future at a time when they will have resolved certain difficulties and will be able to see things they may not have previously seen clearly. By presupposing that they will succeed, therapists provide emotional support and an opportunity to speculate about what they might be seeing in this future time when they will be interacting differently. Therapists can speculate abstractly at first, watching for nonverbal indicators in the form of ideomotor communication back to them confirming or disagreeing with their views. All the while, therapists then speculate more specifically in areas that have been confirmed as relevant by their reaction. For example, the therapist might say, "What I think you're going to see are people who have grown and matured. There will be pride in what you've done yourself. You will have accomplished being comfortable asking about and hearing the feelings of the partner and you won't feel frightened to respond with kindness and love. I see more laughter and a future where you will be sharing responsibilities, relaxing, parenting, and increasing affection. Maybe you see something more or maybe you need to think about it longer." In response to a speculation like this from the therapist, both members have the option to nod their agreement or disagreement or to "search" inwardly for how this possibility has personal meaning and relevance. As each partner, with eyes closed, nods or otherwise signals nonverbal or vocal identification or confirmation, an unconscious contract emerges that exists with as much significance as the conscious treatment contract.

The therapist then transforms these somewhat specific *goals* into specific *terms* as much as possible—specific changes in affect, behavior, belief, self-image, and family structure for each member. Then clients are aided in the process of reaching the goals by interventions that the therapist suggests and selects. When we use therapeutic metaphor as an intervention, as therapists working in this framework often do, we design the metaphor around the specific goal and then tell the story to the clients. Because it is in a metaphoric package, we do not explicitly state ideas about the goal itself. In this way, we only stimulate thinking and experiencing related to the goal. But clients are simultaneously free to respond in ways that are relevant for them, even if that means "tuning out" the therapist or modifying the story to mean something uniquely different and more personally relevant than the therapist originally intended. In this way, we proceed indirectly—that is, by not giving directives, orders, or expectations that clients change as we would select but rather by prompting them to change in unique ways that fit for them.

THE THERAPEUTIC PROCESS

A consistent hallmark of Ericksonian approaches to therapy is that there is little consistency with regard to a standard way of structuring therapy! For instance, therapy may involve all family members, sometimes only the identified patient, or sometimes everyone except the identified patient. At times, this decision is based on a strategic rationale; at other times, it is made out of necessity. Although therapy might proceed most ideally when all involved members can be present and motivated, we are willing and able to operate with less than these ideal conditions. Nonetheless, therapy is conceived with utmost regard for the larger context. Even when we are only working directly with one member of a family, we work within the interpersonal/developmental framework. In these cases, that member's changes are considered in light of the indirect influence they will exert on all absentees with whom the one member is involved.

Duration of Therapy

Psychological healing and change is sometimes an intangible thing to measure or predict. Clients and insurance providers alike frequently want to know how long therapy for a particular problem is going to take—as though every problem requires identical treatment and duration. The uniqueness of every client that practitioners of Ericksonian approaches honor is never more apparent than in this issue. Duration of therapy is necessarily varied, depending on motivation of the family, amount of pain, severity of symptoms, rigidity of family, amount of resources available, how clients define the goals, and the therapist's ability to communicate with the family and understand how the family is stuck or what the symptom accomplishes. Although a comprehensive or holistic approach is valued, Ericksonian therapists are pragmatic and seek to help families accomplish as much as possible in the shortest possible time period. Ideally, a therapist will seek to intervene at all relevant levels in a significant way in one session so that the symptom and its supporting family organization begins to be reorganized, new relational patterns can develop, and further therapy becomes unnecessary. This actually does happen, from time to time. More often, however, in the first session we come to understand what else will need to be accomplished in the second session, and then the same with the third and fourth, and so on.

Therapy is a discontinuous process that can be carried on intermittently for years with different therapists in response to changing circumstances, or weekly for years with the same therapist hammering away at one continuing problem. Ericksonian therapists attempt to communicate that clients have the resources they need and are in control of their lives. This message may continue over four to eight sessions—and very occasionally for up to 1 or 2 years. Some clients are not amenable to any therapy contact beyond the first few sessions. In a family in which roles are rigidly upheld by redundant communication, symptoms seem to be a highly symbolic manner of expression. With such families, therapists must put aside any idea of negotiating a broader treatment contract in favor of doing whatever small amounts of therapy the family will tolerate and accept in a short time. This may be the merest disruptive intervention, such as a paradoxical prescription (S. Lankton & C. Lankton, 1986), an ordeal assignment (Haley, 1984), or a strategic reframing of an existing communication that helps the family nudge past a developmental snag they are encountering and change the way they currently come together around the symptom or actually inhibit a dangerous behavior pattern.

Medication Management

Many families who come to therapy have one or more members on medication for depression, anxiety, psychosis, or bipolar conditions. In such cases, it is often a goal of therapy to facilitate a member's learning to respond to interpersonal and developmental challenges in creative ways so that medication will no longer be required as a means for containing depressive, anxious, or psychotic feelings, behaviors, and beliefs. Instead of masking feelings and subduing impulses that form symptoms, we would rather understand the positive intention or the function of the symptom and help members co-create a better option for accomplishing that function that involves neither symptoms nor drugs. Therapists need to work in harmony with a psychiatrist or a physician toward that end when it is a possible choice. The exceptions tend to be clients being maintained for psychotic or bipolar imbalance who usually are expected to take lithium or antipsychotic medication on an ongoing basis. This would be true in the Shore family for Charley, who has been taking lithium since his psychotic break and the onset of his bipolar depression. The goal here would probably not be to discontinue medication but rather to become effective in ways he can't expect the medication to "fix." Michael is taking asthma and anti-seizure medications on a continuous basis, and these are said to contribute to several unpleasant side effects, particularly an increased hyperactivity. Thus, therapy goals would involve his learning skills to counter the unwanted effects of his medication, much the way in which a chemotherapy patient focuses attention on the healing benefits of the potent chemicals and less on the predicted drawbacks. Certainly, the therapy should be open to the possibility that Michael might learn to breath normally without asthma or medications, but the viability of that goal would have to become clear gradually over time.

Therapists must be aware about medications and their various effects in their work with families in which one member is hospitalized or with outpatient populations who seem to be dependent on their medication in order to maintain their outpatient or minimally functional status. Erickson, although a psychiatrist himself, preferred to avoid prescribing medications for even his psychotic clients in many cases, and he worked to teach alternative choices and methods of functioning to these individuals as well as others who would normally have been maintained with medication. As chief psychiatrist at inpatient units, Erickson demonstrated how effectively communication and strategic interventions could be used with clients who had long since been abandoned as "hopeless" by others (Rossi, 1980d). He was able to be effective with these people due to an abundance of patience, persistence, and creativity on his part. Unfortunately, these characteristics are rare and seem expensive in today's world of managed care. Mental health workers who see themselves short of time (and sometimes energy) often see medicating the symptom as an easier choice.

Helping clients adopt the proper attitude toward the medication issue is a goal at some point in most therapy. Some clients come with the culturally induced myth that there are pills for anything that hurts, and they have great expectations for finding a drug to relieve them of any suffering, solve problems, remove weight, stop smoking, and so on. The other extreme is the attitude that the necessity to take any drug constitutes a weakness to be ashamed about because it is a personal failure. There are frequent adjustment reactions in the lives of all healthy people who pass through developmental stages and encounter loss, trauma, anxiety, and times of not knowing what is wanted or important. Although the resulting suffering is awkward, uncomfortable, frightening, and sad, at most times it is helpful to encourage people to go ahead and have their natural feelings that are part of their ability and health. They can be reminded that it is a process from which they will emerge, usually all the sooner if they refrain from taking steps or drugs to inhibit, deny, mask, block, or avoid the unpleasant but natural feeling. With other clients, however, it is appropriate to encourage them to use the time-limited support that medication can offer without feeling undue shame, just as they would allow themselves to use a support bandage for a stressed joint so that healing could occur more rapidly.

Unobtrusive Joining

The utilization approach entails acceptance of the client and produces rapid rapport. We speak the experiential language of each client system "to include the patient's own style of speech, whether abrupt, impolite, or even outrageously profane"—although such profanity is soon discarded (Rossi, 1980a, p. 301). One observable feature of this process is taking on the actual language, sentence structure, phrasing, and body posture of clients as we speak to each of them. Making a strategic and therapeutic difference without exerting or imposing control is a balance the therapist maintains throughout therapy. The Ericksonian therapist emphasizes that power and credit for change goes to the family. Therapists stimulate memories, ideas, and understandings according to the client's desires, which have been communicated by the family members.

Clinical Skills

Observational skills are one of the most basic requirements for a therapist. The goal of the observation should not be to derive the "truth" about a client or family but rather to receive as much communication from clients as possible. Erickson's contention that all behavior is ideomotor communication (Erickson & Rossi, 1981) suggested that the more the therapist is able to observe, the more communication will be received, and the more relevant responses will develop. An Ericksonian therapist will carefully observe family members and focus his or her awareness on discovering the dynamics or characteristics of the family system. Ericksonian therapists work to notice and respect all messages family members send, both verbal and nonverbal.

Essential therapist skills include the conventional qualities of intelligence, courage, patience, perceptiveness, caring, warmth, genuineness, and honesty. There is sometimes an ethical concern about the honesty of strategic approaches, in that interventions may not always appear to be straightforward or may be better understood and articulated by therapists than by clients. For instance, although it largely recommends continuing a symptom or interpersonal pattern, a paradoxical prescription has the ultimate purpose of helping clients reach their goal (of not having the symptom at all) by having the symptom in a different manner under their control or by at first making only minor changes in the pattern of the symptom. Indirect communications are sometimes intended to overload, confuse, or bypass the conscious mind but are not designed to be manipulative or dishonest. The goal of such communication is to stimulate thinking about a variety of ways a goal can be understood or accomplished.

Positive framing must be entirely honest and congruent in order for it to have any desired effect. All positive labeling is founded on the congruent belief that people are making the best choices available to them at all times, and it is always possible to frame the problem as having some positive, adaptive purpose for which the family can be complimented. Perhaps the therapist, in addition to honest optimism, must have the inclination to look for the good in people, to believe in their innate worth and the availability of resources and potentials, and to look for how their "stuckness" is their best effort at satisfying developmental demands.

These basic qualities are manifested in a variety of interventions, depending on therapists' personal style and preferences of working. Some practitioners tend to emphasize homework assignments, others emphasize paradoxical directives, still others emphasize metaphor, or hypnosis, and so on. Utilization as a guiding principle facilitates creating a treatment alliance. With regard to joining a family to create a treatment alliance, we strive to utilize anything and everything offered by clients because people are making the best choices they are currently able to make. Even "undesirable" behaviors are valuable communications that can be used to understand clients and propel them toward desired changes.

Interpersonal flexibility is perhaps the greatest therapeutic "technique" an Ericksonian therapist can have. For example, in some families, appropriate empathy that meets them at their model of the world will include conventional elements such as reflective and active listening, positive regard, and self-disclosure. However, for other families, meeting them at their model of the world may instead require the temporary use of challenge, admonition, confrontation, or apparent alliance with one family member against another. Flexibility also allows therapists to use ambiguity, humor, confusion, metaphor, or other types of fascination. But all of these different techniques are used with the belief that symptomatic or destructive behaviors were learned for some adaptive purpose and offer valuable information about the demands on and resources within the family system.

Empathy, positive framing, utilization, and paradoxical prescription are related to such an extent that it is appropriate to consider them as a single, four-part intervention. Empathy and resulting rapport are prerequisite to trust and therapeutic alliance. For a behavior to be utilized or therapeutically prescribed, it must first be framed positively with the belief that it exists for some reason. There is some positive intention even though the behavior itself may accomplish little except to increase problems within the family. A therapist working with the Shore family would find ample problems to address in this way. Simply holding the attitude of expectation that each problem exists for some positive purpose will be beneficial, and formulating the actual "prescription" will automatically evolve. For example, we could select the problem of Nancy's weight and empathize about what a burden this has become for her. We could positively frame her eating as a best choice to get deserved gratification. Paradoxically, she might be urged to eat even more in such a way that she can gain 5 more pounds before she loses the desired amount because it is still too soon to expect the dependable gratification of tenderness and joy in her marital relationship. In this way, we will have focused her awareness simultaneously on finding joy, her relationship with her husband, and her ability to control her weight.

Even when no obvious "symptom" is presented, there are always interpersonal orientations or typical roles or characteristics that can be positively framed and prescribed to be continued because they provide a means to accomplishing the positive intention. Similarly, it is possible to frame positively the intention behind destructive behaviors and to recommend that the clients continue to work toward accomplishing that intention using nondestructive alternatives to reach their goal.

Intervention Techniques

Techniques used within an Erickson approach vary depending on the case. These include but are not limited to paradoxical assignments, ambiguous function assignments, skill-building assignments, therapeutic ordeals, therapeutic metaphors, conscious–unconscious dissociation, hypnotic induction, therapeutic binds, indirect suggestion, and reframing. Ideally, therapy will help clients stimulate or guide comprehensive changes in a coordinated manner.

When interventions are designed and delivered but new relational patterns do not develop and symptoms fail to be resolved, then treatment plans must be subject to constant revision. In these instances, there are several possibilities to consider. Were the goals relevant, or are there additional goals that had not been recognized? If no new goals emerge and the existing ones continue to appear relevant, then therapists have a choice of applying the same interventions again more effectively (perhaps shaped by learning from client feedback) or selecting different interventions targeted at the same goal. Each problem is a unique occurrence, and it is ineffective to create a routine set of interventions that are rigidly applied to apparently similar problem categories.

Concentrating attention with hypnosis

A variety of possible reasons for introducing trance come from the motives and difficulties of clients. These reasons are presented in a positive, goal-directed, choice-enhancing framework. They may vary from obvious suggestions that the reason for hypnosis is to assist them in reducing pain or to accomplish something that may at first seem unrelated to concerns they originally wished to address.

It is possible to simply notice naturally occurring altered states of inwardly focused attention and suggest that this absorption experience be intensified. This is not very different from the often routine suggestion to someone experiencing a particular emotion to "go with" that feeling. Although this directive is not usually associated with hypnosis per se, formal hypnotic induction need not sound any more unusual than this. However, it may include additional "focusing inward" suggestions such as "You can close your eyes as you allow yourself to become more absorbed with that feeling and perhaps notice that things outside you can seem irrelevant for the moment, the more you just go with that feeling and focus all of your attention on discovering where it might lead you." The words *trance* or *hypnosis* need never be used, especially when they would unduly arouse fearful reactions because of the false meanings they often carry. In other instances, however, trance can be suggested by using its formal label. Doing so is no more menacing or mysterious than simply asking a husband to "turn to your spouse and say that to her." After all, it is just another intervention. In and of itself, it causes and cures nothing. It is simply a modality for exchanging ideas, as are other more commonly accepted interventions.

In Ericksonian therapy, clients are oriented to trance with operational definitions that demystify it. Trance is described as a common ability under their control; the therapist simply participates peripherally in order to stimulate the clients' thinking and focus. Clients often begin by attending to some external object to assist them in becoming more absorbed in the process of concentration. As clients become absorbed, therapists proceed with induction suggestions, usually including conscious–unconscious dissociation (S. Lankton & C. Lankton, 1983). Framing the trance experience occurs before, during, and after formal or informal induction. Resources retrieved during trance are associated to relevant concerns so that problem solving will be enhanced. Even if no immediate solutions are forthcoming from the time spent concentrating in trance, the comfortable dissociation and increased understanding, objectivity, and closeness and rapport that develop are likely to be beneficial in the general process of working on solutions together.

Illustrating via metaphor

A therapeutic *metaphor* is a story with dramatic devices that captures attention and provides an altered framework through which clients can entertain novel experience. Metaphor is a form of two-level communication that uses words with multiple connotations and associations so that a client's conscious mind receives communication at one level while his or her unconscious mind processes other patterns of meaning from the words at another level (Erickson & Rossi, 1979; S. Lankton & C. Lankton, 1983, 1986). The therapeutic intention is to motivate, occupy, fixate, or interest the client's conscious frame of reference while generating an unconscious search for new or previously blocked experiences, meanings, or solutions.

In using metaphor, the therapist can organize relevant experiences, make or illustrate a novel point for the client, suggest solutions not previously considered by the client, seed ideas to which the therapist can later return, and help reframe or redefine a problem so that the client can come to appreciate it placed in a different context with a different meaning (Zeig, 1980).

Telling clients anecdotes, case stories, examples, and so on—all of a metaphoric nature—is frequently used in hypnotic trance but is also an intervention that can be used in waking-state communication. Absorption is deepened when several stories are told to clients who are in trance and therefore free to have associations uninterrupted by verbal interaction with the therapist. The construction strategy for designing goal-oriented metaphors is the same, whether the story will be told in trance or in more casual therapeutic conversation. Essentially, relevant stories are selected in response to the therapist's having a particular goal in mind and probing his or her own experiences to identify what the goal is like, in which life contexts the goal is likely to occur, any personal understanding or experience with it, and so on. Metaphors can be directed at changes in family structure, self-image, affect, behavior, and attitude, depending upon the unique protocols for sequencing information used for each of these goals (C. Lankton & S. Lankton, 1989; S. Lankton & C. Lankton, 1986). In this way, therapeutic metaphor is simply a means of focusing awareness on achieving a particular goal. It describes a logical context and process for the goal such that suggestions can be given, tangential to the story line, to invite clients to personally identify and apply the learning from within themselves to their goals.

Homework assignments

Skill building, paradoxical prescription, and ambiguous function assignments are three types of assignments (C. Lankton, 1988) and are all useful—although, of course, not with every client. Skill-building assignments tend to be reserved for those clients who are particularly impoverished with regard to a specific set of skills, with whom therapists cannot communicate as efficiently, and with whom there can be an extended therapy relationship. Clients who have been diagnosed "psychotic" or "borderline" may fit this category, having somewhat limited skills and communication abilities but unrestricted availability. For example, the Shores might benefit from a variety of skill-building assignments for several members. Nancy could be assigned the task of doing volunteer work or taking group exercise classes—learning, without being told, to be more other-centered. Charley might learn parenting skills by being an assistant scoutmaster or teaching a class for young comics. The focus of the learning is usually not made explicit because the resulting self-consciousness often sabotages the effort.

Paradoxical prescriptions involve continuing to do the majority of something that perhaps had been considered to be a symptom or part of the problem, but doing so with a slight modification, with positive labeling for the intention behind it, and with encouragement to do the behavior voluntarily (as opposed to involuntarily). Acting in this manner alters or disrupts the usual routine of the behavior. The particular version of alteration is also usually further elaborated upon in great detail within the course of hypnotic induction and therapeutic metaphor in the session so the client fully understands what is to be done and gained. Typical family structure is disrupted as it relates to the symptom or problem dynamic (S. Lankton & C. Lankton, 1986).

Ambiguous function assignments are extremely specific with regard to the activity to be performed, but no explanation is given as to why it should be done, except that the therapist recommends it with an air of compelling expectancy based on the conviction that something valuable will ensue. Otherwise-unknown assessment information will certainly result, and there is an increased involvement in therapy for the client who experiences altered thinking, feeling, and understanding as well as disruption of rigid consciousness sets. These assignments often become catalysts that promote an active and personal integration of concepts that might have been elicited or emphasized within the session in a more conceptual, abstract, or rational manner. Family organization that has already been somewhat disrupted with paradoxical prescriptions is further challenged to reorganize with this process. Family members carrying out an ambiguous assignment can no longer apply the usual power hierarchy to solve the ambiguity. Indeed, no one knows what the purpose of the assignment is until after the assignment is successfully completed.

Creating ambiguous function assignments is a process that is limited only by the therapist's creativity. Of course, the assignments must be legal, safe, possible, and ethical. These assignments do not involve the acquisition of a particular skill or the continuation or alteration of an existing behavior. We design a very specific activity in which clients actively do something they would not normally do; the activity usually involves an object of some sort that may or may not have symbolic significance at the outset. After completing the assignment, clients are usually asked to speculate about what the purpose might have been or why the therapist asked them to do such a thing. Although initial answers are valued and reinforced as meaningful, they are not usually accepted as complete. We can proceed in such a way as to look at progressively deeper levels of interpretation by the client in response to questions such as, "Yes, and what else did you learn?" Eventually, clients will reach a point of maximum therapeutic receptivity after they have exhausted easy answers and are searching within themselves for deeper meaning.

Ambiguous function assignments can be used with individuals, family dyads, or entire families. For example, the Shores might be instructed to rearrange five pictures on the walls of their home at a prescribed time each day, coming to an agreement about placement without using words. Rena could be told to select three of Nancy's old purses or bags and to fill one with stones, one with books, and one with coins and old keys. She would then carry all three bags as she walked back and forth three times from her new apartment to the old apartment. Charley and Michael might be sent out together to build a fire and feed it several specific items that would either melt, sparkle, or burn. In each case, they would be asked to describe the process, success, difficulties, and particularly what value they discovered and what they learned.

LIMITATIONS OF THE MODEL

Clients, therapists, and insurance providers must all deal somehow with times when change does not happen. The temptation is to blame the model or the resistance of the client. However, we propose a no-fault arrangement that avoids assigning blame and acknowledges the limitations of any model, namely that therapists are not experts who can "fix" clients; that some problems are very difficult to unravel; and that clients have different success retrieving, organizing, associating, and using desired resources. In fact, our definition of *resistance* is that it is an upside-down and backward way of cooperating. We recognize that it has long been part of the official language of therapy, but the practice of therapy is evolving and slowly abandoning its adversarial metaphors. We note that people only use suggestions that are relevant for them to follow. When clients do not respond in the manner the therapist has anticipated, there is some good reason why this is so, and additional understanding can be gained by examining the responses that did occur. We do not find our clients resisting us because we do not attempt to impose anything on them. What is too often casually labeled as client resistance is actually an indication that clients are attempting personal growth into areas where they have doubt, lack experiential and transactional tools, or are fearful to proceed. For instance, standing up for one's own needs in the face of an intrusive parent, while necessary, might seem easy to the therapist to carry out but might be met by much anxiety due to the client's conditioned visceral reaction or inexperience using selective memories to create a feeling of confidence. Yet this, by some, might be termed *resistance*. Instead, therapists need to rethink such situations, reassess resources, facilitate a strengthening of the experience of the desired resources as well as the association to the specific context, engage in additional and different interventions designed to help the client reach the same goal or goals from a different angle, and so on. We label neither ourselves nor clients as *failing* or *resisting*.

Common Mistakes

Therapists often confuse techniques with approach. It is easier to discuss Erickson's techniques than to find appropriate words to convey the subtle but important difference embodied in his approach because it has frequently been associated with his distinctive techniques. Therefore, novices will often attempt to apply a technique without an adequate sense of how to let the techniques develop out of a natural interaction with clients. The utilization approach (Rossi, 1980d) and the cooperation principles (Gilligan, 1986) should guide interventions. However, lacking such understanding, flexibility, and security, a therapist can arbitrarily choose an intervention that may satisfy his or her need to be active or "uncommon" but does not come from a grasp of the situation, context, and client.

Therapists learning to incorporate the approach often have difficulty taking a stance outside the traditional approach in which they were trained. In short, a therapist can try to treat a label. This common mistake surfaces in training and supervision and reflects a total misunderstanding of the importance of Erickson's overall contribution. A revealing question such as "What metaphor could I use with a borderline client?" speaks to this problem. The questioner has revealed the typical problem of attempting to salvage a therapeutic relationship built on the epistemological "errors" of a traditional approach by the use of new and "flashy" techniques from an entirely different approach.

Therapists may attempt to intervene when they merely hear about complaints or problems that are presented. They will apply techniques such as hypnosis to dig up further historical material in an attempt to better reveal the problem. In this error, therapists fail to realize that historical memories, especially with hypnosis, are very malleable—not "true." They fail to engage clients in conversations regarding goals and solutions that are being sought. The Ericksonian approach and techniques developed out of it are designed to get clients moving toward goals. Beginning with that purpose in mind, and keeping it in the foreground, is often hard for therapists who wish to have the security that comes from talking about problems, unpleasant feelings, and early childhood traumas. Although there may be a place for these things in any session, they are not the major focus. Therapists who are not goal directed and future directed will misdirect clients with the techniques that arise from Erickson approaches.

Ethics of the Approach

Results are often achieved for goals broader than the original presenting problem, and much learning will take place without being strained through the conscious-mind filters of each family member. Although this is true in all therapies, Ericksonian approaches are perhaps more sensitive to the psychological level or unconscious influences occurring in therapy. This sensitivity leads to awareness of a last limitation of the approach. Moment-by-moment pragmatics of therapy must be effective and accountable. However, the openness to new ideas, essential to effective intervention, occurs when the limitations of conscious-mind biases and beliefs are bypassed by means of indirect interventions.

Effective intervention with a choking person does not—indeed, cannot—require informed consent. In therapy, similarly, requiring prior conscious consent may effectively stop therapy and block progress toward a more specific presenting problem (e.g., stopping nightmares). In these situations, the Ericksonian approach frequently works from the knowledge that clients follow suggestions that are most relevant for them and that prove to be in their best interest. Hence, an unconscious contract based on tacit or implicit approval can be obtained from a client. But once again, this may raise the question of ethics and informed consent as it has been viewed historically (Edgette, 1989; Zeig, 1985).

RESEARCH

Just as good training and supervision for therapists is important, so too is the need for developing a research methodology that measures the effectiveness of training and therapist performance. Therapists in training must learn to be comfortable and confident, often with less feedback than in other approaches. They must learn to rely to a greater extent on highly trained and developed observational skills. And, although no two interventions are alike, accountability is accomplished by its emphasis on pragmatic and reality-based goals with clients. Furthermore, despite the uniqueness of each intervention, well-specified protocols or intervention patterns do exist, are becoming more widely known, and may provide the basis for further refinements for effectiveness and therapy outcome.

Excellent quantitative research on the effects of Ericksonian techniques is being conducted and published (see, e.g., Godin, 1988; Hollander, Holland, & Atthowe, 1988; Matthews, Bennett, Bean, & Gallagher, 1985; Matthews, Kirsch, & Allen, 1984; Matthews & Langdell, 1989; Matthews & Mosher, 1988; Murphy, 1988; Nugent, 1989a, 1989b; Omer, Darnel, Silberman, Shuval, & Palti, 1988; Otani, 1989; Sherman & Lynn, 1990; Woolson, 1986). Others have researched the role in therapy of expectation (Kirsch, 1990; Kirsch & Lynn, 1995; Kirsch, Moayed, Council, & Kenny, 1992;), hypnosis as an adjunct (Kirsch, Montgomery, & Sapirstein, 1995), hypnosis as a working tool (Green et al., 1990; Lynn, 1992; Lynn et al., 1990; Lynn, Nash, Rhue, Frauman, & Stanley, 1983; Rodolfa, Kraft, & Reilley, 1985), and indirection techniques as an effective tool (Lynn, Neufeld, & Mare, 1993; Matthews, Bennett, Bean, & Gallagher, 1985; Matthews & Mosher, 1988; Woolson, 1986).

Although these studies are important contributions to the understanding of Ericksonian techniques and the use of indirection and hypnosis, they tend to be laboratory studies rather than treatment studies, and they are based on small samples. More outcome research comparing the effectiveness of Ericksonian techniques (e.g., metaphor, ambiguous function assignments, and paradoxical prescriptions) with other techniques is called for. Finally, as the profession continues to grow through the current trends created by the changing therapeutic paradigm, it is expected that the influence of the Ericksonian strategic approach will continue to grow and flourish among researchers as well as clinicians.

SUMMARY

The applied techniques of an Ericksonian approach require a shift in the paradigm of therapy. The shift is founded on principles of active intervention with a set of presuppositions about people's basic resourcefulness and good intentions. It relies on a brief therapy model that is (a) goal oriented, (b) based upon a developmental model of human growth, (c) participatory, and (d) flexible enough to create unique understandings and even unique interventions for each case. Lip service is often paid to making such a shift, but a comprehensive theory of change or technique is seldom presented to accomplish it. These values were abundantly presented in Milton Erickson's work and profoundly influenced many people. This group includes theoreticians such as Bateson, Weakland, and Jackson and therapists such as Satir, Haley, Zeig, and ourselves. The further dissemination of Erickson's approach into other areas of psychiatry, family therapy, hypnosis, psychotherapy, and social work is a job that is not fully complete. Success depends on realizing that this approach is not a set of interventions or a bag of clever therapeutic tactics but rather a fundamentally different manner of viewing clients and problems. It is opposed to the historical trends that turn therapists' energies toward causation from the past, and it is a departure from the theory and practice of the helping professions that have turned our attention toward illness. Instead, it looks for the health in clients and families and directs attention toward the creative achievement of immediate and future goals.

REFERENCES

Berne, E. (1972). *What do you say after you say hello?: The psychology of human destiny.* New York: Grove.

Dammann, C. (1982). Family therapy: Erickson's contribution. In J. Zeig (Ed.), *Ericksonian approaches to hypnosis and psychotherapy* (pp. 193–200). New York: Brunner/Mazel.

Edgette, J. (1989). Tempest in a teapot: Ethics and Ericksonian approaches. In S. Lankton (Ed.), *The Ericksonian monographs, Number 5. Ericksonian hypnosis: Application, preparation and research* (pp. 105–116). New York: Brunner/Mazel.

Erickson, M. (1985). *Life reframing in hypnosis: The seminars, workshops, and lectures of Milton H. Erickson* (Vol. 2; E. L Rossi, M. O. Ryan, & F. A. Sharp, Eds.). New York: Irvington.

Erickson, M., & Rossi, E. (1979). *Hypnotherapy: An exploratory casebook.* New York: Irvington.

Erickson, M., & Rossi, E. (1981). *Experiencing hypnosis: Therapeutic approaches to altered state.* New York: Irvington.

Freud, S. (1966). *The complete introductory lectures on psychoanalysis* (J. Strachey, Trans.). New York: Norton.

Gilligan, S. (1986). *Therapeutic trances: The cooperation principle in Ericksonian hypnotherapy.* New York: Brunner/Mazel.

Godin, J. (1988). Evocation and indirect suggestion in the communication patterns of Milton H. Erickson. In S. Lankton & J. Zeig (Eds.), *The Ericksonian monographs, Number 4. Research, comparisons and medical applications of Ericksonian techniques* (pp. 5–11). New York: Brunner/Mazel.

Green, J. P., Lynn, S. J., Weekes, J. R., Carlson, B. W., Brentar, J., Latham, L., & Kurzhals, R. (1990). Literalism as a marker of hypnotic "trance": Disconfirming evidence. *Journal of Abnormal Behavior, 99,* 16–20.

Haley, J. (1963). *Strategies of psychotherapy.* New York: Grune & Stratton.

Haley, J. (1973). *Uncommon therapy: The psychiatric techniques of Milton H. Erickson, M.D.* New York: Norton.

Haley, J. (1984). *Ordeal therapy.* San Francisco: Jossey-Bass.

Hollander, H., Holland, L., & Atthowe, J. (1988). Hypnosis: Innate ability of learned skills? In S. Lankton & J. Zeig (Eds.), *The Ericksonian monographs, Number 4. Research, comparisons and medical implications of Ericksonian techniques* (pp. 37–56). New York: Brunner/Mazel.

Jackson, D. (Ed.). (1968). *Communication, family, and marriage: 1.* Palo Alto, CA: Science & Behavior Books.

Kirsch, I. (1990). *Changing expectations: A key to effective psychotherapy.* Pacific Grove, CA: Brooks/Cole.

Kirsch, I., & Lynn, S. J. (1995). The altered state of hypnosis: Changes in the theoretical landscape. *American Psychologist, 50,* 846–858.

Kirsch, I., Moayed, C., Council, J., & Kenny, D. (1992). Expert judgments of hypnosis from subjective state reports. *Journal of Abnormal Psychology, 101,* 657–662.

Kirsch, I., Montgomery, G., & Sapirstein, G. (1995). Hypnosis as an adjunct to cognitive-behavioral psychotherapy: A meta analysis. *Journal of Counseling and Clinical Psychology, 63,* 214–220.

Laing, R. D. (1967). *The politics of experience.* New York: Ballantine Books.

Laing, R. D. (1972). *The politics of the family.* New York: Ballantine Books.

Lankton, C. (1988). Task assignments: Logical and otherwise. In J. Zeig & S. Lankton (Eds.), *Developing Ericksonian psychotherapy: State of the arts. The proceedings of the Third International Congress on Ericksonian Psychotherapy* (pp. 257–279). New York: Brunner/Mazel.

Lankton, C., & Lankton, S. (1989). *Tales of enchantment: Goal-oriented metaphors for adults and children in therapy.* New York: Brunner/Mazel.

Lankton, S., & Lankton, C. (1983). *The answer within: A clinical framework of Ericksonian hypnotherapy.* New York: Brunner/Mazel.

Lankton, S., & Lankton, C. (1986). *Enchantment and intervention in family therapy: Training in Ericksonian approaches.* New York: Brunner/Mazel.

Lynn, S. J. (1992). A non-state view of hypnotic involuntariness. *Contemporary Hypnosis, 9,* 21–27.

Lynn, S. J., Green, J. P., Weekes, J. R., Carlson, J. B., Brentar, J., Latham, L., & Kurzhals, R. (1990). Literalism and hypnosis: Hypnotic versus task-motivated subjects. *American Journal of Clinical Hypnosis, 33,* 113–119.

Lynn, S. J., Nash, M. R., Rhue, J. W., Frauman, D., & Stanley, S. (1983). Hypnosis and the experience of nonvolition. *International Journal of Clinical and Experimental Hypnosis, XXXI*(4), 293–308.

Lynn, S. J., Neufeld, V., & Mare, C. (1993). Direct versus indirect suggestions: A conceptual and methodological review. *International Journal of Clinical and Experimental Hypnosis, XLI*(1), 124–152.

Matthews, W., Bennett, H., Bean, W., & Gallagher, M. (1985). Indirect versus direct hypnotic suggestions—An initial investigation: A brief communication. *International Journal of Clinical and Experimental Hypnosis, XXXIII*(3), 219–223.

Matthews, W., Kirsch, I., & Allen, G. (1984). Posthypnotic conflict and psychopathology— Controlling for the effects of posthypnotic suggestion: A brief communication. *International Journal of Clinical and Experimental Hypnosis, XXXII,* 362–365.

Matthews, W. J., & Langdell, S. (1989). What do clients think about the metaphors they receive? *American Journal of Clinical Hypnosis, 31*(1), 242–251.

Matthews, W. J., & Mosher, D. L. (1988). Direct and indirect hypnotic suggestion in a laboratory setting. *British Journal of Experimental and Clinical Hypnosis, 5,* 63–71.

Murphy, M. (1988). A linguistic-structural model for the investigation of indirect suggestion. In S. Lankton & J. Zeig (Eds.), *The Ericksonian monographs, Number 4. Research, comparisons and medical implications of Ericksonian techniques* (pp. 12–27). New York: Brunner/Mazel.

Nugent, W. (1989a). Evidence concerning the causal effect of an Ericksonian hypnotic intervention. In S. Lankton (Ed.), *The Ericksonian monographs, Number 5: Ericksonian hypnosis: Application, preparation and research* (pp. 23–34). New York: Brunner/Mazel.

Nugent, W. (1989b). A multiple baseline investigation of an Ericksonian hypnotic approach. In S. Lankton (Ed.), *The Ericksonian monographs, Number 5: Ericksonian hypnosis: Application, preparation and research* (pp. 69–84). New York: Brunner/Mazel.

Omer, H., Darnel, A., Silberman, N., Shuval, D., & Palti, T. (1988). The use of hypnotic relaxation cassettes in a gynocologic-obstetric ward. In S. Lankton & J. Zeig (Eds.), *Research, comparisons, and medical applications of Ericksonian techniques* (pp. 28–36). New York: Brunner/Mazel.

Otani, A. (1989). An empirical investigation of Milton H. Erickson's approach to trance induction: A Markov chain analysis of two published cases. In S. Lankton (Ed.), *The Ericksonian monographs, Number 5: Ericksonian hypnosis: Application, preparation and research* (pp. 35–54). New York: Brunner/Mazel.

Rodolfa, E. R., Kraft, W. A., & Reilley, R. R. (1985). Current trends in hypnosis and hypnotherapy: An interdisciplinary assessment. *American Journal of Clinical Hypnosis, 28,* 21–26.

Rossi, E. L. (Ed.). (1980a). *The collected papers of Milton H. Erickson on hypnosis: Vol. 1. The nature of hypnosis and suggestion.* New York: Irvington.

Rossi, E. L. (Ed.). (1980b). *The collected papers of Milton H. Erickson on hypnosis: Vol. 2. Hypnotic alteration of sensory, perceptual and psychophysical processes.* New York: Irvington.

Rossi, E. L. (Ed.). (1980c). *The collected papers of Milton H. Erickson on hypnosis: Vol. 3. Hypnotic investigation of psychodynamic processes.* New York: Irvington.

Rossi, E. L. (Ed.). (1980d). *The collected papers of Milton H. Erickson on hypnosis: Vol. 4. Innovative hypnotherapy.* New York: Irvington.

Sherman, S. J., & Lynn, S. J. (1990). Social-psychological principles in Milton Erickson's psychotherapy. *British Journal of Experimental and Clinical Hypnosis, 7,* 37–46.

Szasz, T. (1961). *The myth of mental illness: Foundations of a theory of personal conduct.* New York: Hoeber-Harper.

Watzlawick, P., Weakland, J., & Fisch, R. (1974). *Change.* New York: Norton.

Woolson, D. A. (1986). An experimental comparison of direct and Ericksonian hypnotic induction procedures and the relationship to secondary suggestibility. *American Journal of Clinical Hypnosis, 29,* 23–29.

Zeig, J. (Ed.). (1980). *A teaching seminar with Milton H. Erickson*. New York: Brunner/Mazel.

Zeig, J. (1985). Ethical issues in Ericksonian hypnosis: Informed consent and training standards. In J. Zeig (Ed.), *Ericksonian psychotherapy, Volume 1. Structures* (pp. 459–474). New York: Brunner/Mazel.

8

Postmodern Family Therapy: New Voices in Clinical Social Work

Jonathan Diamond, Ph.D.

INTRODUCTION

This chapter explores the application of postmodern ideas and practices in clinical social work and family therapy and proposes a narrative metaphor for recovery and healing. As Roberts (1994) wrote, these therapies, linked to the postmodern tradition in other disciplines, "emphasize construction of reality through language and consensus; a collaborative view of treatment; and an awareness of the different political, social, and cultural realities of and constraints on each of the participants" (p. 24). A more egalitarian attitude towards professional relationships and a commitment to combating oppression are trademarks of both narrative therapy and social work. Narrative therapy, especially as practiced by two of its most recognized authors, Michael White and David Epston (see, e.g., White & Epston, 1990), has distinguished itself through the creative use and deployment of therapeutic letters.

Narrative therapy is only one of many new voices on the postmodern family therapy landscape. My reasons for choosing it to represent the postmodern perspective were simple: It is currently the approach enjoying the most popularity and professional interest, and as a result, it is generating the most conflict and debate. In addition, it is one of the lenses that I find most compatible with my own outlook on therapy.

A note of caution to the reader who, like myself, has become a bit of a "paradigm junkie," foraging through the professional literature in search of a daily fix of cybernetics, chaos theory, metaframeworks, or the latest postmodern discourse: this chapter is not an attempt to grab hold of the rising star of narrative and postmodernism. Rather, it is a critical reading of these ideas and their usefulness in therapy—the things themselves, not the myth. This particular telling emphasizes aspects of the story that have been forgotten or omitted. It looks at how thinking about therapy and much of therapists' understanding of people and events (and their theories about both) are embedded in the stories therapists tell about them.

Consequently, this chapter does not present a comprehensive theory of therapy or a new model of treatment. I share Hoffman's (1993) opinion that the field already has more than it needs or knows what to do with. This chapter merely attempts to locate a set of ideas about the use of narrative as well as deconstructive and other postmodern practices that help people address some of the problems they face in their lives—ideas that readers can easily apply to their own lives and experiences.

There are two things I feel it necessary to do prior to describing some of the innovative contributions narrative and other postmodern forms of practice have to offer social workers. First, I locate myself in this work in a way that will help the reader better understand the choices I made when deciding what to include and what to leave out of this particular account of postmodern family therapy. Second, I take time out to honor some of the thinkers and therapists whose ideas, although not customarily identified with postmodern practices, anticipated these developments and in many ways paved the way for the wider acceptance and acknowledgment of those ideas in the field.

Situating Myself

I first began using letter writing and other narrative practices in my work in 1986 in groups I ran for substance-abusing teens and children from alcoholic and drug-addicted families. When working with problems of addiction, I often ask clients to write "good-bye" letters to alcohol or their drug of choice. A 14-year-old client named Miranda wrote the following letter:

~~Dear~~ Narcotics, Pot (acid, alcohol) etc.

thanks for all You've done for me. You've helped me forget my problems, You've made me feel good, You've made me see the world in a whole new perspective, You've made me fail out of my freshman year, You've made me Ruin the lining of my esophagus and stomach.

You've made the Relationship with my Parents go down hill, You've given me a who gives a shit attitude—i've gotten fucked up Emotionally and Physically. (Relationship wise also) I've gotten used by abusing you: even after all those complaints I don't want to give you up Because i'll be alone.

Rena Shore's story reminds me of my therapy with Miranda. Thus both of these young women's experiences, along with other clinical illustrations, are explored in more depth later in the chapter. I include Miranda's letter here as an example of this type of work and to create a relationship with you, the reader, that honors the humanness and the sacredness of the therapeutic relationship.

In addition to being a very soulful communication, Miranda's letter harnesses the spirit of collaboration, the construction of reality through language (i.e., the power of naming and putting our experience into words), and the intersection (in the form of her addiction) of personal and cultural oppressions that have become the cornerstones of narrative and other postmodern therapies. Such an exercise creates a ritual that helps clients and therapists honor the primacy of the clients' relationship with drugs and alcohol and explore the specific roles that chemicals (and other problems or habits) play in clients' lives. In Miranda's case, the letter also helped assess her ability to let go of her addiction.

At the time of my therapy sessions with Miranda, I drew my ideas from therapeutic approaches to addictions that, along with Alcoholics Anonymous and other 12-step programs, have a rich history of using writing as a tool for recovery. In 1989 I participated in a postgraduate externship in marriage and family therapy with Lynn Hoffman and Bill Lax at the Brattleboro Family Institute. Hearing about my work with these adolescents, Hoffman suggested I explore the ideas of family therapist Michael White. He and co-author David Epston developed an entire clinical approach organized around letter writing and correspondence, aptly called *narrative* or *re-authoring therapy*. The match was a good one.

White and Epston contrast their literary approach with the dominant biological and disease metaphors for human suffering inherited from science and medicine. They use *therapeutic letters* to help fashion their own and their clients' experience of therapy according to less "problem-saturated" descriptions of their lives. White and Epston invite clients to "externalize" in their correspondence the problems they are up against, a process that "encourages persons to objectify and, at times, to personify the problems that they experience as oppressive" (White & Epston, 1990, p. 147).

Letter writing seems to create distance between clients and their dilemmas. Encouraging people to define their values and sense of self, separate from their problems, oftentimes leads to a shift in perspective from "I am the problem" to "I am up against a problem." The act of writing itself is an important and powerful tool for people in therapy. Writing helps clients like Miranda and Rena, who described her journal as an intimate part of her healing, to recover from abuse, addiction, and abandonment struggles and to reclaim their bodies and their histories by gradually fitting images and then names to their traumatic experiences.

David Epston (1994) offered the following story of why writing a letter seemed so natural an extension of therapy for him—a mystery, he said, he had been trying to solve for some time. Upon visiting the town in Canada where he grew up, he met with his mother's best friend, Dorothy, who said she had kept every letter his mother ever wrote to her.

> I was confused by this revelation as, for the life of me, I could not recall my mother ever writing Dorothy a letter. After all, they spent hours on the phone every day and were neighbors. "Didn't you know?" she asked me. "She wrote me a letter after every phone call! She said she wanted to get it down. She said that talk wasn't enough." (p. 63)

Letters, says Epston, ought to be moving experiences, doorways through which everyone can enter the family's story and be touched by the bravery, the pain, and even the humor of the narrative. Miranda's letter created an entrance for me into her life; it closed the gap she experienced between herself and others, bridging her world and ours. Writing and externalizing problems in this fashion helps people connect with the larger culture. It brings them from silent isolation into language and community restoring—and re-*storying*—their faith in themselves and their future. I also find, in my own and my clients' therapy, that writing inspires another kind of hope more introspective in nature. Journal and letter writing allows people to occupy the parts of themselves that feel uninhabitable, the interior spaces in their lives they never knew were there or had long since abandoned.

This last point suggests another guiding principle that social work and narrative therapy (as well as other postmodern forms of practice) have in common. Therapy is never just a collection of stories about our clients. It is stories about ourselves as well. Ours is always both a professional and a personal journey. The Shores' experiences, painful as they are, are stories of clinical reflection and spiritual growth. They present as many potential roads to healing and courses of treatment as there are theories of therapy. For example, the ideas I have chosen to focus on in this chapter are colored by the path I have traveled to cope with growing up in a violent and alcoholic family. My decision to become a therapist and the way I practice my profession is intimately connected to my own recovery.

Honoring Our Forebears

A frequent concern expressed about narrative and postmodern thera-pies—one I share—is that their contents represent, as the saying goes, "old wine in new bottles." In an effort to avoid having a similar complaint raised about this chapter, I honor some of the thinkers whose ideas I consider the precursors of many of the brightest and most sparkling concepts of narrative and postmodern family therapy.

Harry Aponte (1976) championed the needs of the poor and people of color long before such a position was recognized as a "paradigm shift" in thinking about therapy. He made his therapeutic choices not because the family therapy theories of his time advocated for clients' rights to self-determination (they did not) but because he believed it was the right thing to do. Gregory Bateson, Donald Jackson, and Jay Haley (Bateson, Jackson, Haley, & Weakland, 1956) were challenging thinking about language and traditional mental health constructs long before what sociologists call the *interpretive turn* took place in philosophy, psychology, anthropology, and other disciplines. The challenges that feminist family therapists, who came of age in the women's and gay liberation movements, posed to established and entrenched relations of power are strikingly evident. Their efforts con-tinue to bring issues of sexism, gender, identity, sexual orientation, and homophobia to the forefront of family therapy concerns.

Although I realize that thinking about these issues has changed signif-icantly since these pioneers first began formulating their ideas, I find it more important to pay homage to their contributions than to critique their shortcomings. This is in keeping with the overall tenor of the chapter, in which I have tried to embrace an analytic attitude of curiosity and inquis-itiveness. Where there are controversies, I point them out and share with the reader my own interpretation and understanding of them. However, in the process of fleshing out differences and conflicts, I avoid the tendency to demonize or villainize one participant or another in the conversation or argument because, to paraphrase a well-known rabbi, it is not by a per-son's sins that you get to know someone but by what the person celebrates (Metzger, 1992).

THE CONCEPT OF THE PERSON AND THE HUMAN EXPERIENCE

In a narrative or postmodern framework, *interpretation* is not meant in the strictly analytic sense. As White and Epston (1990) observed,

> Social scientists refer to the interpretive method when they are study-ing the process by which we make sense out of the world. Since we can not know objective reality, all knowing requires an act of interpre-tation . . .

In regard to family therapy—which has been our area of special interest—the interpretive method, rather than proposing that under-lying structure or dysfunction in the family determines the behavior of family members, would propose that it is the meaning that mem-bers attribute to events that determines their behavior. (pp. 2–3)

Jerome Bruner (1986) claims that narrative (i.e., human) experience is not modeled on formal logic but poetics. He separates understanding and knowledge into two different modes of thought—the *paradigmatic*, which is scientific and based on logic (he calls it *logo scientific*), and *narrative*, which is poetic–hermeneutic. Bruner's perspective has become a popular one for therapists looking for a "theory and praxis" for understanding the narra-tives and stories "that they and the people they seek to help bring to the therapeutic context" (Laird, 1989, p. 433). White and Epston's narrative ap-proach uses Bruner's notion of "stories of literary merit" to support their ideas.

Bruner proposed that "Stories . . . are about events in the real world . . . but they render the world strange, rescue it from obviousness, fill it with gaps" that call on the reader to become a writer and a composer at the same time (Bruner, 1986, p. 25). As a result of the reader's personal relationship to them, stories have a *relative indeterminacy*, an ambiguity and uncertainty about them that offers each one of us—drawing on our own imagination and lived experience—the opportunity to have our own unique experi-ences and interpretation of them. This is what Bruner meant when he said that stories and literary texts "initiate performances of meaning rather than actually formulating meaning themselves" (p. 25). The text analogy in psy-chology and social work advances the idea that the stories and narratives people live by help them organize their experience and determine their in-teractions with others. This is in contrast to analogies and models of prac-tice that are pathologizing of people's lives and relationships—"analogies that would propose an underlying structure or pathology in families and persons that is constitutive or shaping of their lives and relationships" (White & Epston, 1990, p. 12).

HISTORICAL PERSPECTIVE

If postmodern theories discussed in this chapter teach us anything, it is that our theories about therapy and the stories we tell about them, like history, do not proceed according to some grand narrative or master plan. Like our conversations with clients, they are messy processes, each one with its own unique rhythms and patterns. My purpose in undertaking the writing of this story is to create a safe space in which all its characters and readers—social workers, psychologists, psychiatrists, psychoanalysts, nurses, addiction counselors, teachers, and students—interested in the application of narrative and postmodern concepts to psychotherapy and recovery might raise questions and concerns and begin a dialogue.

Narrative Therapy in a Postmodern Framework: Hermeneutics, Story, and Voice

A great deal of postmodern family therapy literature is dedicated to exploring the differences and interplay of the concepts of hermeneutics, story, and voice as they apply to the process of psychotherapy. In actuality, the lines between them are blurry, and there is considerable overlap and cross-pollination among the three. However, as I understand them and use them in this chapter, hermeneutics, more than story and voice is concerned with matters of *epistemology* (how we know what we know). Clinicians whose work is informed by this tradition—for example, the conversational approach of family therapists Harlene Anderson and Harold Goolishian (Anderson, 1991, 1993, 1994; Anderson & Goolishian, 1988, 1992) or the work of analyst Roy Schafer (1976, 1992)—locate therapy in the domain of language and meaning.

Hermeneutics is descended from the study and interpretation of the Bible and religious texts. As applied by the authors and therapists whose work is presented in this chapter, hermeneutics is based on the premise "that human beings, both individually and in concert with one another, actively construct and co-construct meaning out of their life experiences as opposed to receiving knowledge in pure form directly from the external world" (Hugh Rosen, personal communication, 1996).

On the other hand, *story*, which is also a meaning-making approach, emphasizes the roles that myth, ritual, tradition, creativity, and imagination play in people's lives. However, the use of story as a metaphor for psychotherapy and human development has political implications. Stories and rituals can help us make connections between oppressive cultural narratives (e.g., racism, sexism, homophobia) generated by the dominant political ideologies of our times and the intimately personal ways these negative messages shape our experience of our spiritual practices, sexual relations, parenting, work, and other human relationships. Examples of this perspective in the family therapy community include the "narritual" approach of Roberts and Imber-Black (Black, 1993; Black, Roberts, & Whiting, 1988; Roberts, 1988, 1994) and "the letters to ourselves" that Peggy Penn and Marcia Schienberg (Penn, 1992; Penn & Schienberg, 1991) encourage us to write, as well as the narrative work of White and Epston (White, 1989g; White & Epston, 1990).

Finally, *voice* is about agency, identity, and self-determination. Its domain includes relations of power; people's resistance to domination, exploitation, and abuse; and other acts of courage. In the face of increasing attacks on people's personal and cultural identities, breaking silence and speaking out sustains us and offers hope. Many therapists (e.g., Hoffman, 1993; Levin, 1992; Olson, 1995) are adding the metaphor of *voice* to those associated with hermeneutics and other literary forms (such as story and narrative) being adopted by psychotherapy and the other human sciences. Drawing on Ong's (1982) work, they look at how women historically have been excluded from male preserves of knowledge, which, since Plato, have been based on literacy, oratory, and speech. These authors see women's identity as having closer ties to an oral tradition that is less rhetorical and more conversational in nature—practices that contributed to the rise of the novel and the growing presence of women's voices in literature and the humanities. They join Gilligan (1982), Belenky (Belenky, Clinchy, Goldberger, & Tarule, 1987), and Miller's (1976) call for research and therapy "in a different voice," based on an "ethic of care," empathy, and concern.

This story is, like all intellectual chronicles, a complex one with many different versions and accounts. Out of the vast network of possibilities, I present a drama with a limited cast of characters. In addition to the clinicians whose work is mentioned above, the list includes

1. The stories of race, gender, and justice of Charles Waldegrave (1990) and his colleagues at the Family Centre in Wellington, New Zealand. Performer and activist Gil Scott-Heron talks about how, in the eyes of the oppressed, when a society discusses issues of justice it usually means "just-*us*," and these privileges often come to a dominant group at the expense of a marginalized and excluded other. Waldegrave and his co-workers have developed a model they call *just therapy* that takes into account the gender, cultural, social, and economic context of people seeking help.

2. The reflecting process of Norwegian family therapist Tom Andersen (1987, 1991, 1992, 1993). Unfortunately, as Salman Rushdie observed in another context, every conversation in therapy is an act of censorship, as it prevents the telling of other stories. Anderson's innovative use of the two-way mirror in his consultations with people (and its adaptation by his associates at the Brattleboro Family Institute) provide clients and therapists with opportunities to tend to both the said and unsaid aspects of therapy. The use of letters and other types of writing in therapy also allows for the exploration of these kinds of dialogues, offering therapists another way to attend to the unspoken aspects of a person's experience. Both innovations, to be discussed further in the chapter, challenge the binary logic and all-or-nothing thinking we all—clients and therapists alike—can succumb to when trying to resolve painful problems in our lives.

3. Social constructionists thinkers Kenneth Gergen (1985, 1988, 1989, 1991), Mary Gergen (1988), and Philip Cushman (1991, 1995), who

explore how values are culturally and politically shaped. These theorists see knowledge as a "cooperative enterprise of persons in relationship," only understandable within its own unique culture and history (Gergen, 1985, p. 275). Their writings have strongly influenced the collaborative styles of Lynn Hoffman (1993), Harlene Anderson and Harold Goolishian (Anderson, 1991, 1993, 1994; Anderson & Goolishian, 1988, 1992), and many other narrative and postmodern therapists (McNamee & Gergen, 1992).

4. The family scripts and community dialogues of Sally Ann Roth (Roth, Chasin, Chasin, Becker, & Herzig, 1992) and Kathy Weingarten at the Cambridge Family Institute. We live in an age where our senses of community and individuality are threatened by the dominance of an increasingly monolithic global culture. For Weingarten, Roth, and other narrative therapists, gathering stories and pursuing people's life histories provides, to paraphrase Deana Metzger (1992), a bulwark against the erosion of our personal and collective energies.

5. Psychoanalysts D. W. Winnicott (1965, 1971), Christopher Bollas (1992, 1995), Roy Schafer (1976, 1981, 1983, 1992), and Donald Spence (1982, 1987), who bridge the gap between the personal and social worlds of experience. These analysts, although oriented to Freud, listen to postmodern voices. Schafer, along with Spence, introduced the concept of narrative into psychoanalytic discourse. Their rereading of traditional psychoanalytic concepts as "interpretive storylines" opposed to scientific principles undercuts the claim to objectivity of the psychoanalyst and the therapeutic hour. These analysts join their postmodern psychoanalytic feminist cousins, Jessica Benjamin (1988), Evelyn Fox Keller (1983, 1992), and Jane Flax (1983, 1990a. 1990b, 1993; Keller & Flax, 1988), who, using the lens of gender, call for an end to psychotherapy's love affair with the concept of a unified, autonomous, and independent self. Collectively, throughout the chapter, these therapists and their work serve as a kind of "analytic reflecting team," helping me deconstruct my rendition of narrative therapy and ideas. By showcasing the work of these analysts and its application to narrative practices, I hope to demonstrate how psychoanalytic concepts can be used in all sorts of clinical encounters in highly innovative ways—even in single, sometimes decisive exchanges, rather than confining these ideas to the luxury of long-term psychotherapy or the slow unfolding process of an analysis.

6. Above all, the protagonist of this story is Australian family therapist Michael White, who along with his associate from New Zealand, David Epston, has given new force and fresh twists to the term *narrative* as he applies it to therapy. White and Epston's ideas serve as moorings for many therapists trying to develop a postmodern narrative orientation or attitude toward therapy.

In addition to the disavowal of Western concepts of the self, the work of all these therapists underscores two other key elements of postmodern theory. The first is its emphasis on respecting difference, and the second is—to borrow the real-estate mantra—"location, location, location" (i.e., the importance of specificity when discussing postmodernism or any other theory).

The implications of these ideas for clinical social workers and other clinicians is that no specific theory ever captures the entire picture, or what Gadamer (1960/1975) called our *"horizon of understanding.* Every theory brings certain aspects of culture into view and leaves out others. As Cushman (1995) wrote, "A specific theory articulates the local truth of a specific set of people in a specific moment in history" (p. 202).

This brief overview of the history of these ideas reminds us just how artificial are the boundaries and different languages we use to distinguish one form of practice from another. In actuality, there are no such entities as narrative, social constructionist, deconstructive, or postmodern therapies. Like Freud's typography of the mind—the id, ego, and superego—these are imaginary worlds we create that shape our thinking about therapy and help us make sense of our own and our clients' experiences. Therapy is always about a relationship between two people (or parties); it is not a technique. Theories have meaning and purpose only to the extent that they serve to deepen and strengthen those relationships.

Narrating the Unconscious

A question asked of Michael White and other presenters at every postmodern family therapy gathering I've attended is, "Do you believe in the unconscious?" For me, the answer is simple, like for Starhawk (1987, 1989), who when asked if she believes in the Goddess replied that she believes in the goddess in the same way she believes in rocks. She doesn't "believe in" either god or rocks—she "connects with" them. I do not believe in the unconscious; I connect with it. The unconscious, wrote Metzger (1992), is like a plumb line running through all our worlds:

Every time we speak, write, or act, we sacrifice completeness. Given that things will be omitted, moments will be truncated, experiences will, at best, be rendered partially, we learn to communicate through silences and absences as well as through disclosure. (p. 33)

Bollas (1992) described the unconscious as a kind of spirit place wrapped in language. In this sense, and from the standpoint of literary theory, we are all authors of our own inner worlds and idioms, creators of our own psychic genres.

The trouble with psychotherapy is not its belief in the unconscious but its need to diagnose it. The language of psychopathology and the language of psychotherapy are not the same. *Borderline* and *narcissistic personality disorder, co-dependency, enmeshed families*—these terms function as linguistic straitjackets that strip us of our personhood. Psychotherapy, it seems to me, is more about mystery and wonder—matters of the heart and soul— and our language should reflect those practices. While expressing a clear preference for the lexicon of narrative family therapy over psychoanalytic forms of discourse, I believe neither approach has exclusive rights to compassionate or dehumanizing methods of practice.

When consulting with people, all theories about therapy—including the narrative and postmodern ideas presented here—do violence to relationships with clients. They create distance between people by dividing the parties into observers and subjects. This leaves many in the helping professions in a bind. Therpists need theories and stories about therapy. More like flotation devices than navigational equipment, theories and stories help therapists stay afloat and remain calm in the face of great pain and injustice. Postmodern family therapists say we can engage in this kind of conversation and hold on to our theories about therapy if we need to, so long as we make ourselves more aware of what socially, and in fact morally and ethically, we are doing in our talk. It is a clinical version of the judgment of Solomon: those willing to give them up are awarded the privilege of keeping them. The challenge is to allow ourselves space to engage in psychological wisdom and thinking without forgetting the harm that our psychological theories and language practices have done historically to the people we are trying to help.

KEY THEORETICAL CONSTRUCTS

Philosophy as Therapy

Prior to turning to some of the issues these ideas raise for clinicians using postmodern and narrative approaches to therapy, I would like to appropriate a parable from my own ethnic heritage to help make a point. A grandson tells his Jewish grandmother his great news. "Grandma, I am going to become a doctor of social work!" His grandmother replies, "That's wonderful! So tell me, what kind of disease is social work?" In its original telling, it is a degree in philosophy that is called into question, but Austrian-born philosopher Ludwig Wittgenstein would approve of either version, as he viewed philosophy as sick and in need of treatment (Rorty, 1982). Wittgenstein's work serves as a kind of scaffolding for postmodern philosophy and therapy. For Wittgenstein (1958, 1966, 1974; Kenny, 1994), meaning takes place in language. Words and their meanings are social constructions, part of a language game one learns to play, the rules and practices of which allow members of a community to understand one another, linking them to the larger culture.

Words, then, are not pictures of the world, and they are derived not from private ideas in the mind but from social practice. Consequently, Wittgenstein's grammatical investigations are not like scientific investigations, "concerned with finding the hidden reality behind appearances, with finding the supposed causes in the past that will explain the occurrence of present circumstances" (Shotter, 1994, p. 5). He abandoned the search for universal truths and absolutes—grand narratives that hold explanations of events and phenomena together—in favor of closely knit associations and connections he called *family resemblances*. (This concept bears a strong resemblance to Gregory Bateson's [1991] expression, *syllogisms in the grass*, a rather mystifying term he used to describe cause by association rather than logic.) Wittgenstein has argued that, although people may be tempted to search for causal explanations "to penetrate phenomena," this is missing the point. Our investigations, he has argued, should be directed "towards the 'possibilities' of phenomena" (Shotter, p. 5).

Wittgenstein viewed philosophy as a form of therapy. Therapists who advocate for more postmodern and narrative approaches to social work wish therapy would come to view itself more like a form of Wittgenstein's philosophy—exploring the possibilities of people's lives. Unfortunately, social workers, psychiatrists, and psychologists collectively appear to have assumed philosophy's prominent role as the modern-day carrier of the virus of rationality, objectivity, and validity.

According to postmodern and narrative perspectives, the tragedy of psychotherapy has been in the ways in which people's stories are categorized and arranged like aisles in a supermarket. Words and behaviors have significance in terms of the categories and the systems in which they are placed, as opposed to their relevance to the therapeutic relationship and meaning they have to the client.

The work of the narrative therapists, to be taken up in the next section, provides an alternative. These therapists make a strong case against the use of expert knowledges and metanarratives in psychology and social work, knowledges that "totalize" people's experience (i.e., professions that impose the same dominant cultural framework or narrative on every client's own unique individual story) and specify the buried and hidden truth of their lives (by subscribing to theories that view human nature as fundamentally destructive and pathological and describe human beings as characterologically flawed, psychologically tortured, unhappy, conflicted creatures). These differences cannot be attributed to their creators simply cleaning up the demeaning and depersonalizing language of psychotherapy. The differences are the result of some very fundamental changes in various therapists' orientation toward their work.

A Therapy of Literary Merit

The following represents a brief overview of various narrative practices and techniques advanced by White and Epston. I have tried to glean the main tenets of their re-authoring approach to therapy—more specifically, their application of Michel Foucault's ideas about power and knowledge as well as their use of letters in work with individuals and families.

In a recent issue of the *Family Therapy Networker* that profiled White's narrative therapy, Gene Combs commented on the difference between the "clinical zeitgeist suggested by the standard family therapy metaphors of cybernetics and systems theory" and White's approach:

> You have to think more in anthropological, sociological metaphors; you need to have pictures of ideas in your mind about how social and moral values, political and ethical practices are transmitted in a culture, and how they influence the way people are. When Michael talks about stories, he's not just talking about individual anecdotes, but the story of Western Civilization and how it has already "storied" our lives for us before we were born. (Wylie, 1994, p. 46)

In White and Epston's narrative therapy, the text analogy provides a frame that enables readers to consider the broader socio-political contexts of people's lives and relationships (White & Epston, 1990). They use historian Michel Foucault's analysis of power and knowledge and the deconstructive methods of philosopher Jacques Derrida to explore the nuances of this broader context. No aspect of White's work is more central to his approach, and no aspect is more understood (by critics and supporters) than his appropriation of the ideas of Foucault. A thorough analysis of Foucault's work is beyond the scope of this chapter.[1] However, building on some of the concepts already mapped out in previous sections, I explain some of the particular features of Foucault's ideas that White and Epston draw on and their relevance to a re-authoring therapy.

The Cultural Context

As one family therapist and author cautioned, "The project of reading Foucault should not be taken lightly ... his style is uncharitable and his

---

[1] Readers interested in a more in-depth examination of Foucault's ideas might start with *Feminist Knowledge: Critique and Construct* (Gunew, 1990). Also see White's own explanations (1990, 1991) as well as *The Foucault Reader* (Rabinow, 1984).

ideas yield but grudgingly to the reader (Luepnitz, 1992, p. 284). However, in an effort to simplify, I would be tempted to say that the essence of Foucault's thought is captured quite succinctly by two popular slogans frequently spotted on the bumpers of passing automobiles: "Information Is Power" and "Think Globally, Act Locally." These ideas stem from Foucault's concept of the inseparability of knowledge and power and his use of the term *power–knowledge* in their place. They also express the political currents that run through the work of White and Epston and others.

In contrast to analyses of the repressive and "negative" consequences of power, Foucault thinks of modern power as "positive" in its character and effects. He does not mean *positive* in the traditional sense—that is, something absolute or affirming—but sees power as constitutive and shaping of person's lives: "Through this power persons are subject to normalizing truths that shape their lives and relationships" (White, 1989c, p. 25).

Foucault was "intent on exposing operations of power at the micro-level and at the periphery of society" in, for example, our psychiatric, medical, and criminal systems, "the level of every-day, taken-for-granted social practices" (White, 1991, p. 137). It is at these local levels that the operations of power are perfected, are most evident, and are allowed to have their global effects (White, 1991).

In his early work, Foucault presented his ideas on discourse, what he called *archaeologies of knowledge*. In this realm of language, power is used to silence and oppress, legitimizing some people's ideas and knowledge while marginalizing others'. In his later work, he shifted his emphasis to how these "technologies of power operate on human bodies to shape, organize, and subscribe them" (Grosz, 1990, p. 86), which he called *genealogies of power*. Whereas the archaeologist looks at the history of knowledge, exposing the silences and voices left out of its stories, the genealogist examines how the culture produces objects for knowledge and "tries to put knowledge to work in local struggles" (Best & Kellner, 1991, p. 47). The term *power–knowledge* is a way to wed the two, to bind together the archaeological and the genealogical method.

Misinterpretations of Foucault hinge on the "conflation between power as omnipresent and omnipotent" and fail to recognize "his emphasis on the contingency and vulnerability of power" (Best & Kellner, 1991, p. 55). In a Foucauldian world, we are not helpless subjects and passive victims: "As soon as there is a power relation, there is a possibility of resistance. We can never be ensnared by power: we can always modify its grip in determinate conditions and according to a precise strategy" (Foucault, 1984, p. 123). The implication is that "knowledges, methods, procedures which at one time support forms of power, at another time or in a different context can act as sites of resistance, struggle and change" (Grosz, 1990, p. 89). In Foucault's (1980) words, "There is no locus of great Refusal, no soul of revolt, source of all rebellions, or pure law of the revolutionary. Instead there is a plurality of resistances, each of them a special case" (pp. 95–96).

The political task of the intellectual in Foucault's view of society (and the therapist in White's postmodern therapy) is to locate the specific place and time where "'regimes of truth' are produced, distributed, circulated, and consumed" (West, 1993, p. 142). As Foucault wrote, the aim is

> to criticize the workings of institutions which appear to be both neutral and independent; [and] to criticize them in such a manner that the political violence which has always exercised itself obscurely through them will be unmasked, so that one can fight them. (Quoted in Best & Kellner, 1991, p. 57).

White and Epston used Foucault's ideas to create a "blueprint for transforming people's problems into the forces of oppression and therapy into a resistance movement" (Hoffman, 1993, p. 105). Individuals and families are encouraged to view their dilemmas as a battle between oppressive institutions and problems, on the one hand, and their own subjugated knowledges, on the other.

For example, a man's abusive behavior might be described as a struggle of his own values—"I never imagined myself the kind of man who would hit a woman [in Charley's case, his daughter] in order to win an argument"—versus the values of patriarchy—women are men's property without rights of their own.

French philosopher Jacques Derrida, whose work comes under the rubric of deconstruction, is a more recent addition to White's conceptual collage. Like Foucault, Derrida sees Western philosophies as philosophies of violence and power. However, unlike Foucault, Derrida argues not for the end of philosophy but that it be read in a certain way.

Derrida analyzes or deconstructs many of the major texts within the history of philosophy and literature, the so-called canon of Western thought, to show how they secure a position of dominance and what "they must suppress [or] leave unacknowledged, for this dominance to be assured" (Grosz, 1990, p. 93). Since Plato, traditional philosophy has privileged speech and rhetoric over poetry and writing (what Derrida calls *phonocentrism*) and thought (i.e., mind) over matter. The binary logic that informs this kind of thinking structures concepts in such a way that one term is pitted against the other, as in *good–evil, black–white, man–woman, mind–body, sameness–difference, presence–absence,* or *culture–nature.* Consequently, one term is elevated to the status of knowledge while the other, its opposite, is ignored and marginalized. The way that one word or concept is presented in positive terms while the other is given a negative connotation is crucial to the workings of this system.

According to Derrida, Western philosophy and metaphysics is obsessed with this kind of dualistic thinking and its emphasis on the autonomous, all-present, conscious subject. It is a philosophy of sameness that wipes out differences and assumes a universal sense of subjectivity and experience of the world. Derrida (1976, 1978, 1981) calls this system of dichotomies and binary oppositions *logocentrism* (*logos* = speech, logic, reason, the word, God). White's deconstructive method attempts to expose these dichotomies in our thinking about therapy. He looks, for example, at the dominance of the surface–depth metaphor in Western therapies that value understanding and insight (i.e., logic and reason) into a person's unconscious states and inner world over people's passions and preferences (i.e., their lived experience). White tries to imagine what a therapy that does not privilege talk and speech might look like.

Following Derrida, White's strategy is to construct alternative narratives whose rhetorical force can displace the dominant understanding of a story. A person's lived experience provides the repertory from which alternatives—*preferred outcomes*—are selected. White's primary, and most original, technique for accessing this experience is to externalize the problem.

Externalizing Discourse

Externalizing the problem involves a process White (1989e) calls *relative influence questioning*—what I think of as a form of circular questioning (originally developed by the Milanians) for the masses. How does the problem influence their lives? How do they influence the life of the problem? How have they organized their lives around it? What has been the nature of its "career," its success? White goes on to ask about other more "sympathetic" and previously neglected aspects of a person's life— exceptions to the usual patterns, what he refers to as *unique outcomes*. What in the past accounts for this new behavior? How can people resurrect these "subjugated knowledges" to help them in the struggles they are currently waging?[2] In the case of those whose accounts of their lives are not problem saturated but mundane and uneventful, therapists could "encourage persons to identify the 'sparkling facts' of their career in life" (White, 1989e, p. 28).

Through the process of externalization, people gain a reflexive perspective on their lives. New options become available to them that help them challenge the "truths" that they have experienced as defining and specifying of themselves and their relationships. This helps them "refuse the objectification or 'thingification' of themselves and their bodies through knowledge" (White & Epston, 1990, p. 30). Externalizing problems in this

---

[2]For more on this technique, see "The Process of Questioning a Therapy of Literary Merit" (White, 1989e).

advocates that ordinary everyday speech replace the professional vernacular of the field. White believes therapists should challenge their expert views "by continually encouraging persons to evaluate the effects of the therapy in their lives and relationships, and to determine for themselves to what extent these effects are preferred effects and to what extent they are not" (White & Epston, 1992, p. 144). White and Epston describe this reflexive posture in therapy as a "condition of transparency":

> This transparency of practice provides a challenge to the commonly accepted idea that for therapy to have its desired effects its workings need to be kept secret; the idea that if persons know what the therapist is up to then it won't work. (pp. 144–145)

More recently, narrative therapists have been using the term *accountability* to emphasize the need to focus on developing more respectful and ethical forms of practice (White, 1995).

Listening, caring, relationship, and affect are the heart of the narrative approach: listening to people's stories, expecting competence, respecting differences, and when people's stories break apart, recognizing the pain and suffering and searching for health within the broken fragments. In other words, we have faith and trust that conversations and stories can be healing for both therapist and client. The importance of the postmodern lens and packaging that narrative therapy comes with is its ability to free therapists and clients from constraints that limit conversation, preclude listening, and lead towards diagnosis rather than growth.

TREATMENT OF CHOICE

The question for narrative therapists is not "For what type of 'clinical population' is this approach most appropriate?" but "For what kind of problem formation is the approach most appropriate?" The answer is "most kinds." Literature applying narrative therapy to a range of problems, diagnoses (sic), and human dilemmas in a variety of settings is beginning to surface. These include (but are not limited to) child therapy (Freeman & Lobovits, 1993; Freeman, Epston, & Lobovits, 1997), group therapy (O'Neil & Stockwell, 1991), couples therapy (White, 1986/1987), collaborating with schools (McLean, 1995; Morgan, 1995), schizophrenia (White, 1989d), AIDS/HIV (White, 1992a), anorexia (White, 1989a), violence against women (Jenkins, 1990; White, 1989b), sexual abuse and trauma (Durant & White, 1991), and problems encountered by families with adolescents and teenagers (Dickerson & Zimmerman, 1993).

Critiques of White and Epston's early work have focused on their reliance on metaphors of protest and resistance. However, as Freeman and

Lobovits (1993) observed, White and Epston use metaphors of protest and resistance that encourage personal agency for more oppressive and intractable problems such as anorexia and men who are violent. However, letter writing and other "narrativizing" practices (White, 1991), as demonstrated, can be applied to situations where metaphors of relationship, celebration, and ritual, not protest, are more applicable.

Freeman and Lobovits, inspired by relational theory and Jean Baker Miller's concept of "power in relation to" instead of over others, have explored narrative metaphors of nonviolence, civil disobedience, and other "forms of relatedness between persons and their problems" (1993, p. 220). Blending aspects of Eastern philosophy and Japanese culture with the concepts of White and Epston's externalizing conversation, Tomm, Suzuki, and Suzuki (1990) wrote about metaphors that promote compromise and coexistence with problems, not ones of resistance and struggle against them.

Additionally, narrative therapy provides an opening for exploring people's spirituality and experience of intimacy and connection as well as their histories of protest and resistance. Narrative therapy offers therapists an opportunity to explore how people's spirituality—the power of love and faith—is socially constructed.

THE THERAPEUTIC PROCESS

A Storied Therapy

This section explores in more detail the application of several narrative themes and ideas to the Shore's case. These include defining the problem, examining the culture and politics of therapy, the use of the reflecting team and reflexivity in therapy, and reauthoring stories of trauma and violence. From the standpoint of narrative therapy, the Shore family provides an excellent venue for such an exercise because its members are rich in lived experience. However, the act of extrapolating a set of universal principles from a single case, although a useful teaching tool, clearly goes against the grain of postmodern practice. Similarly, applying narrative or postmodern ideas in a generic or prescriptive manner to another person's story is also counterintuitive.

In a postmodern world therapists are more akin to artists and storytellers than scientists and researchers, pattern makers in contrast to pattern finders (Spence, 1987). Narrative therapists view their interpretations and ideas as artistic creations that find a narrative home in a client's therapy judged on the basis of their aesthetic appeal. These therapists do not enter a family's story or swoop down on a text, armed with a hypothesis searching for instances of what they hope will be the right explanation. From the standpoint of postmodern and narrative therapies, to read and comment on people's experiences outside the context of the relationships in which they took place feels depersonalizing and disrespectful at best— exploitative at worst—especially when this effort is undertaken to advance our understanding of a theory. It makes me uncomfortable.

The only way I found to overcome this awkwardness was to imagine the Shores' story as a work of fiction that I could infuse with my own experiences, feelings, and imagination. I do not know how any of the Shores would respond to these ideas or how my version of postmodern and narrative therapy and practices would mesh with their experience of their lives. I can only try to create a sense of what some of the possibilities might be by drawing on my personal experiences and from therapies I have conducted with other families.

Collectively, the Shores' story represents what White and Epston would refer to as an archaeology of therapy written in a "grammar of agency," transforming the family's experience from the passive to the active voice. From the standpoint of postmodernism, both volumes of this narrative (i.e., *Paradigms of Clinical Social Work*) served the Shores much as the journal serves the writer or the poem serves the poet. In Myerhoff's (1982) words, it provided "a frame surrounding internal chaos," a clinical hope chest in which the most precious items are placed for safekeeping (p. 353). Therapy at these moments is about restoring—or, from the standpoint of writing, restorying—clients' capacity for concern and faith in their own humanity, a process described by analyst Hans Loewald and expanded on by Schafer (1992) of "safeguarding a future for that person" (p. 307).

There is at the heart of the Shores' experience a profound sense of loss and sadness. Each family member expressed a deep sense of sorrow, anguish, and grief. These feelings evolved around time not spent with a parent whose life was ravaged by drinking (as in Charley's experience) or around the sense of loneliness and emptiness created by their having to cope with the emotional injury of having actually been given up, left, or lost (as in Rena's and Nancy's situations). For the child of an alcoholic, a divorce, or adoption, the question "Why did they leave?" always includes, as Hope Edelman (1994) said, the appendix *me*. For Nancy, and my client Miranda, grief also stemmed from the loss of self. Fragmented and discordant story lines were a predominant theme in Nancy's life, as they were for Miranda, whose grief stemmed from just imagining the absence of a drink or drug.

Again, from the standpoint of postmodern and narrative family therapies, recounting past experiences in the form of a narrative, for all clients, results in their discovering and making available a myriad of "lost or forgotten knowledges" of themselves in the fashion White (1989f) described in his article "Saying Hello Again." Certainly Rena and many other women have had the experience of having their grief labeled as *pathological mourning*. Rena's conversations and the ideas they generated about her relationships appear to have allowed her to incorporate different and less pathological views of her grief and sadness. Also, circulating these newly discovered and preferred stories of herself in groups with people up against similar troubles seems to have been a crucial (as well as frustrating) aspect of her healing.

In the case of the Shores, I like the way in which narrative therapy's radically transparent and democratic techniques nest with 12-step epistemology and other self-help approaches to treatment—to which I am strongly committed. I could, if given the opportunity to consult with the Shores, imagine inviting Nancy and Charley to explore and bring specific aspects of their past and current relationships to these rooms.

In its current form, what I and other narrative therapists are proposing is a tapestry or patchwork quilt of ideas about therapy that contrasts with more systematic theories of human development. Using the narrative the Shore family shared with us, the remainder of this chapter presents a list of principles, biases, and assumptions that will help map out some of the landscape covered and illustrate how narrative and postmodern ideas can change the way we conceptualize and think about the process of therapy.

One final note of caution. As any practitioner or social work student can tell you, therapy is a disorderly and chaotic process. Similar to White's (1991) reflections on his efforts to write about his work, readers will find in these accounts a simplicity that cannot be found in therapy.

Defining the Problem

Current metaphors for mental illness and addiction adopt the terminology of medicine and science. Practitioners are encouraged to view the emotional struggles and problems people face as forms of pathology that can be diagnosed and treated like various strands of a virus. The narrative family therapist prefers to see clients suffering from these types of troubles as "stuck." Put another way, nurturing a postmodern approach to therapy means paying more attention to how we position ourselves in relation to problems rather than how we define or label them.

A disease or biological model can be a useful metaphor for families trying to break out of the cycles of shame and blame that grip people facing problems with drugs and alcohol or bouts of bipolar depression that affect a person's brain functioning. However, none of these ideas explain the complexity of the phenomenon we call *addiction* or *mental illness*. When it comes to treating alcoholism, addiction, or mental illness, narrative therapy is more interested in knowing what sort of person has a disease than what sort of disease a person has. Michael's asthma offers a good example of the way labels can become totalizing of one's identity—that is, how a person's sense of self and his or her relationships with others can become crystallized and organized around an illness. Michael is seen by his family and himself as an asthmatic first, and a scout, athlete, student, and young man second.

Stories of Gender and Justice Revisited: The Culture and Politics of Psychotherapy

We need to recognize that the culture of therapy and recovery does not have a "privileged location outside of the culture at large," as Michael White argued in a 1992 workshop (1992b). According to White, "A review of the history of the culture of therapy suggests it has played a significant role in the production and reproduction of the ideologies of the dominant culture, particularly through the pathologizing of people's lives and relationships." Can we, as James Hillman (1972) challenged us, imagine the psyche without this language—without *psychopathology, psychosis, dysfunctions,* and *disorders*?

The Shores are a good illustration of the negative impact and constricting effects that gender stereotypes, expectations, and roles imposed by the larger culture can have on relationships. In this instance it is too convenient and simplistic to label Nancy's behavior as *co-dependent* or *overinvolved* and her relationship with her family as *dysfunctional*. This stance, in addition to being disrespectful and demeaning, ignores the complex lace-work of cultural, familial, and psychic factors that influence the events of people's lives. As Bepko and Krestan (1991) cautioned, these terms—initially meant to help people identify behaviors that were interfering with their enjoyment and ability to take responsibility for their own lives—can become just another oppressive discourse, "another tool in the oppression of women, fostering denial of male accountability" (p. 51).

Similarly, assuming that the Shores were suffering from a "hierarchical imbalance of power" (Lappin, 1988) is also problematic. Although meant to improve the possibilities of the Shores' lives, continued efforts to get Charley more involved in family life could have met with alarming results. The incident in which Charley battered and assaulted his daughter made this point clearer. A family therapy approach to get Charley more involved in his daughter's life is missing the point by placing too much emphasis on a point of view that sees families without an active and involved father as incomplete and difficult to change. Rena and Nancy obviously needed help in managing their relationship with Charley. However, the essential point here was that these relations were still characterized primarily by the abuse of power, not the absence of it. Intervening in families with fathers who behave violently towards others is a risky and scary business. It is easy to join family members in their silence and understandable desire to minimize the severity of the problem or make excuses for and rationalize the violent person's behavior.

Homophobia, racism, sexism, and other forms of oppression must be addressed in therapy and recovery. Clients who do not receive help in coping with these societal problems in treatment are at a much greater risk for relapse. We are often wasting work when we address a person's emotional, mental, and spiritual needs but fail to identify and assist them with the sociopolitical and economic challenges they face. This means viewing therapy as a political as well as clinical process by providing clients with a safe space in which to learn about homophobia, racism, and sexism and by actively modeling effective resistance to oppression in our own lives.

As Schafer (1992) pointed out, from the standpoint of writing—for Nancy and many others—women are the pages on which men write their stories of power. Nancy's experience of oppression as a woman has colored her experience of her relationship with anxiety, food, and her body. Helping Nancy recognize and understand her need to connect with other women would be an integral part of her therapy. In other words, Nancy needs a safe haven from the effects of both sexism and overeating and family crises.

Helping clients develop and become involved in an active and politically conscious social network is an important aspect of narrative therapy and is good social work practice. Political activity is another way for each of us to develop a stronger sense of self and connection to community. Encouraging Nancy to bring her problems to a group—a gathering of other women, in particular—would be important role-modeling on my part, reinforcing the message that I always try to give women clients about the need for a female presence and voice in their work.

Reflexivity and Reflecting Team Work with Multistoried Families: "Take What You Need and Leave the Rest"

The use of the reflecting team in family therapy is a way of offering families an array of ideas, thoughts, and reflections about their problems from which to choose. It complements many narrative and postmodern principles that emphasize cultural diversity, specificity, and respect for local customs and practices. An innovation in the use of the two-way mirror in family therapy, pioneered by Norwegian family therapist Tom Andersen, was adapted and expanded on in this country by Lynn Hoffman, Bill Lax, and their colleagues at the Brattleboro Family Institute (Anderson, 1991; Hoffman, 1993; Miller & Lax, 1988). Andersen offered the following definition of *reflexivity* as it is applied in this context: "Reflecting refers here to the same meaning as the French word *reflexion* (something heard is taken in, thought over, and the thought is given back) and not the English meaning (replication or mirroring)" (Andersen, 1992, p. 62). These postmodern innovations and approaches break with more systemic—that is, modern—forms of practice that rely on "prescriptions," "paradoxes," "interventions," and other directives, delivered by a team of experts hidden behind a one-way screen.

After observing a consultation between a family and a therapist, the team trades places with the family. This gives family members the opportunity to observe the therapy team and listen to team members' thoughts and feelings regarding the family's predicament. The two groups trade places a second time and the consulting therapist facilitates a conversation in which participants sift through the team's offerings and pick and choose (i.e., reflect back) those they found most useful or that resonate with their own experience. In other words, the family decides which ideas fit with their own experience and story about themselves. The process may be repeated several times during the course of an interview. As a result of this process, the family members often describe feeling a strong sense of connection—what Epston and White describe as a sense of *communitas*—with the therapist and the team members.

Therapy that makes use of such reflections resembles the call and response of a jazz concert. Ideas are shared in a give-and-take process that avoids methods that cause us to "practice down" to the people we see or to organize or present our thoughts hierarchically or in a fashion that weighs the therapist's voice more heavily than the client's. Hoffman (1993) feels that the process dramatically alters the family's position in relation to the professionals they come to see by introducing more equality between consultant and client and generating more freedom for clients to accept or reject a thought or idea. Hoffman described a process that creates more "horizontal" and positive ways of working with families and responded to Hillman and White's call for a depathologizing language of the psyche:

> People talking in front of a family had to abandon the clinical language that was usually used to describe family or individual dynamics. Phrases like "enmeshed family," "over-involved mother," "projecting," "controlling," and the like were not appropriate to this situation. Thus, the use of a reflecting team was as much of an influence on the professionals as on the family. For the first time in the history of psychotherapy, as far as I knew, a constraint against this blameful in-house discourse was put into place. (p. 59)

Deconstruction, with its sensitivity to the contextual dimensions of texts and marginalization of voices, has played an instrumental part in these de-

velopments. Seeing therapy as a collection of cultural narratives and personal stories encourages therapists to view their role within a process of
moving from center to edge rather than moving up and down a hierarchy
(i.e., being "one up" or "one down"). Sometimes the therapist is a more
central character in the drama of people's lives; other times the therapist
rests at the perimeter of their stories. There is no canon, no story, that applies universally to all client experience.

Letters allow therapists working alone, without the benefits of a reflecting team, to share their thoughts with people in a similar fashion, thus
allowing clients to pick and choose ideas they find useful. Written correspondence creates a space in which I can offer my own thoughts on clients'
addictions (and other dilemmas) to be tossed about, digested, or discarded,
away from direct exchange and the need for normal personal defenses. In
this sense, the letters and the fate they meet are a bit like the paper toys
Winnicott made for children when they left his consulting room. Like these
parting gifts, Winnicott viewed all his thoughts and interpretations as subjective objects that were meant to be played with, "kicked around, mulled
over, torn to pieces." He would put them to his clients as objects between
client and therapist, as one possible version of their story, "rather than as
official psychoanalytic decodings of the person's unconscious life" (Bollas,
1983, p. 7).

I also find letter writing a refreshing change from the conventional discharge summaries written in the cryptic discourse of our field. When I have
had to write these documents to meet the requirements of a client's insurance plan or agency regulations, I write them as though clients are the audience. A letter to the Shores, for example, might be used to thicken some of
the thin descriptions of their lives presented in their narrative. Such a correspondence might, for example, inquire about Nancy's mother's attempts,
some successful and some not, to reach out to her grandchildren—Rena, in
particular—and the strong culture of connection created by grandmothers
and granddaughters in Nancy's family. Or it could be used to focus more
attention on the stories of pride the Shores may feel about their family and
each of their childhoods.

Reflexivity, however, does not just mean looking at how our experience impacts on our clients' stories but means looking at how our clients'
knowledge shapes and colors our own narratives. This is what psychoana-
lytically oriented therapists call *countertransference*. I have never been comfortable with this term or its companion expression, *transference*, as both
seem to suggest that the client is solely responsible for the kinds of spells
we fall under, as well as the intense emotional states that surface in the
therapy relationship. They are false dichotomies that divide therapy relationships into observers and subjects. This chapter makes a case for the role
of *countertranspondence* in psychotherapy. Regardless of what one calls it, it

is crucial that therapists remain open to exploring both their own and their clients' experience of therapy.

Transference relationships and other unconscious experience can be invaluable sources of knowledge about past relationships and can provide future opportunities for healing. Dismissal of this classical analytic concept in contemporary postmodern and narrative therapy is in vogue today. This is a mistake. Exploring these feelings in therapy can serve as a relational time capsule that offers insight into past traumas and experiences.

Rewriting Stories of Trauma and Loss

Trauma comes from the Greek word meaning a wound or hurt. As Sanville (1991) wrote, "It refers not to what inflicted the injury but to the effect on that person. What is wounding to one person may not be to another, or what is hurtful at one age might not be at a later age" (p. 151). When retelling traumatic stories about our lives in therapy, it is inevitable that we also revisit some of the painful and frightening feelings associated with those experiences. This is particularly true when the constellation of gender and age differential between client and therapist parallel those of the perpetrator and victim at the time the abuse occurred.

Sackvitne and Pearlman (1995) use the phrase *vicarious traumatization* to describe the range of emotions and feelings that therapists experience when collaborating in therapy with clients trying to rewrite stories of sexual abuse, trauma, and loss. These experiences often leave people desperately trying to change something about their past that is not changeable. They are trying to resolve what was an impossible situation, such as trying to love someone or something that seems to be causing the person's spiritual death. Often this results in a person's seeking out impossible situations—what family therapy theory refers to as *double binds*—in adult life that recreate these feelings and the experience of the abuse or abandonment. (For an explanation of double binds, see Bateson, Jackson, Haley, & Weakland, 1956). These dynamics may have contributed to Miranda's drinking, Nancy's attempts to master and control her eating, and Charley's violent behavior.

Miller (1994) talks about a transitional period in a person's recovery, where the therapeutic relationship "substitutes" for the client's symptoms. The client then develops a myriad of feelings towards the therapist— feelings that previously had been attached to the client's problems. This might include making impossible demands on the therapist's time, demeaning the therapist's work, or subjecting the therapist to intense bouts of anger and rage. These phases of therapy do not have to be destructive to the client, therapist, or relationship. Indeed, they can strengthen people's resiliency and resolve to put the trauma behind them, so long as the therapist is aware of the impossibility of the requests and does not get into an impossible situation by trying to resolve the client's dilemmas.

The use of laughter and humor—what Bollas (1995) would call *cracking up* the Shores' self-deprecating image of themselves—is another strategy I might use. Humor often creates a safe space where clients and therapists can use their creative imaginations to crack up seemingly immovable objects—fixed stories—in their lives, replacing them with more affirming, less destructive ones.

Although comic relief, an indispensable part of any serious or tragic drama, helps us through many trying moments in therapy, it cannot crack them all up. Sometimes the silence, "the blank nothing" created by trauma, can be deafening (p. 114). Stories like the Shores' (and others more brutal in their imagery and graphic descriptions of violence) can sometimes have this kind of traumatizing effect on family members and therapists alike. I often find myself not knowing what to think or say and having to look away for a moment when family member's narratives present the facts of the deeds done to them.

"Profound facts," Bollas wrote, "are wrapped in their own traumatic space" (p. 114). They are shocking and arresting. Neither client nor therapist can think about them when they are presented in sessions, so a client's recurrent telling of them and a therapist's recurrent noting of them becomes an important stage in both the client's and the therapist's recovery from the shocking facts of the person's life. Therapy is what happens after the fact; it is a process of unpacking the trauma and wrapping a story around it. This concept is especially applicable to experiences of family violence and abuse. It explains why, for the Shores and other families, identifying and naming their experiences can be both traumatizing and liberating. Everyone is traumatized when confronted by the facts of his or her abuse, neglect, or addiction. However, when wrapped in a narrative, fashioned into a story, and given new meaning, the trauma becomes detoxified and loses its grip on the person's life.

For Rena, perhaps the act of writing helped facilitate this process by transforming her hurt and pain into performances of meaning. As discussed in this chapter's introduction, telling our stories (either verbally or through writing) can bring us from silent isolation into language and community. It gives meaning to our experience by putting words to previously indescribably terrible events and feelings—what Bollas (1992) calls the *unthought known* and child analyst Melanie Klein named our *unthinkable agonies*. No activity is more essential to a person's recovery from pain and trauma than the act of naming (i.e., putting words to) one's traumatic experience. It enhances and deepens our connection with ourselves and with others.

Cultural anthropologist Barbara Myerhoff (1982) observed that letter writing and journaling in groups (therapy techniques, she notes, that owe their origins and much of their form to the women's movement) appear to transform experiences and emotions of derision and shame into gifts to be shared with others, who in turn are transformed and often feel privileged to witness them.

Telegrams From God

In this chapter, we have focused a great deal of our attention on the use of written productions in narrative therapy. However, the most powerful introduction to these concepts I have experienced in my life took place in my own therapy, in my participation in Al-anon, and from a piece of correspondence never written or sent.

My mother has suffered from alcoholism throughout much of my childhood and adult life. When I decided to marry Dana, my partner of many years, my mother's drinking became the source of much stress and anxiety for me, as it had on numerous other occasions. Unsure about how to handle the presence of alcohol at my wedding and concerned about her alcoholism, I sought a personal consultation with my colleague, Roget. After listening patiently to my dilemma, Roget asked me to entertain the following scenario: "Imagine, Jon, if tomorrow morning you went out to your mailbox and discovered a telegram, and when you opened it, it read, 'Dear Jonathan, I am sorry it is not in the stars for your mother to get better. Love, God.'" I fought back tears when I heard/read these words (not yet realizing at the time that *not* fighting tears was an option!). Their message led to a profound shift in my relationship with my mother from one of grieving for the past to one of living for the present. My mother's alcoholism, while still active, is in the midst of a process that I have come to describe as "bottoming up." With so much love, care, and change in her own life and the lives of people around her, the alcoholic cannot help but feel better about herself and her circumstances.

This imaginary telegram had a greater impact on my life story than any real correspondence or letter I have ever received. I have since passed this intervention on to numerous clients. I found myself revisiting it again when reading about Rena's ongoing search for her birth mother and her hopes for that relationship upon finding her. I have also not missed the irony (or, in literary terms, *poetic justice*) in discovering that my own "higher power" (in 12-step speak) often channels her communiqués through my most challenging and difficult relationships.

These ideas about trauma carry over to generational issues of abuse and neglect in families as well. Destructive and unhealthy parenting styles are often passed from one generation to the next. Finding good role models for parenting is essential to arrest the cycle of abuse (Miller, 1994). For example, Charley, like many other physically abusive fathers I have worked with, may have experienced envy and anger at his children, who were receiving from Nancy a kind of caring and protection his own mother and father could not provide him with. Charley's behavior towards his daughter, bad as it was (judging from his reports), was still a vast improvement on the way he was treated by his father. Many parents find that their worst rages are often triggered by a sense that their children (who have no reason to feel otherwise) do not appreciate what they have and take their parents' love for granted.

Prior to discussing the strengths and limitations of a narrative context for psychotherapy, I want to address some of the recklessly essentialist questions the Shores' narrative raised for me about the role drugs and alcohol might have played in Charley's life. As Caroline Knapp (1996) wrote, "Alcohol travels through families like water over a landscape, sometimes in torrents, sometimes in trickles, always shaping the ground it covers in inexorable ways" (p. 28). In Charley's family, alcohol appears to have washed over an entire generation in a very dramatic fashion. However, drinking can take a much more subtle path and still have a profound effect on people's actions and behaviors.

Clearly, Charley's father's addiction had a very destructive impact on Charley's childhood and current family relationships. This reality, coupled with his history of underemployment, grandiosity, and "emotional breakdowns," make Charley an extremely strong candidate for developing a drinking or drug problem of his own. Although not mentioned in their story, I might invite Charley and Nancy to have a conversation with me about these concerns.

Unfortunately, many of my colleagues in the narrative community will find themselves at odds with this perspective as well as my integration and use of 12-step knowledge and practices in my work. They are writing about the "mythologizing" stories of addiction that they feel pathologize clients by encouraging them to view their drinking problems as part of a disease or illness (a metaphor I do not personally embrace but appreciate and—in the case of addictions—have deep respect for). I think this is unfortunate, if not dangerous. It feels like a knee-jerk reaction to the fact that alcoholism is recognized by the medical community and in the *Diagnostic and Statistical Manual of Mental Disorders* (*DSM–IV*; American Psychiatric Association, 1994) as a "legitimate" illness and diagnosis. But the story and culture of alcoholism and 12-step programs have a unique history of their own, different than many of the other diagnoses found in the *DSM–IV*—more akin, for example, to the story of posttraumatic stress disorder (PTSD) than the recent controversies over the use of pejorative labels like *borderline personality disorder*.[4]

As Judith Herman (1992) documented in her groundbreaking study on trauma, the most common posttraumatic stress disorders are not suffered by men in war but by women in civilian life. In the case of PTSD, the women's movement created a political context that recognized that the syndromes seen in survivors of rape, domestic battery, and incest were essentially the same as syndromes of survivors of military battles. It has, as Herman observed, never been possible to advance the study of psychological trauma without the context of a political movement. When this kind of support does not exist, history teaches us that knowledge can disappear— as it did earlier in this century when Freud, pressured by his peers in the medical establishment, abandoned his own trauma theory and betrayed his patients' disclosures of sexual abuse (Masson, 1984).

LIMITATIONS OF THE MODEL

Hermeneutist or Heretic?

One of the few conclusions I have arrived at after studying this body of thought is that ideas that make for good postmodern theory do not necessarily translate into good psychotherapy. As a consequence, the work presented in this chapter, my own included, is riddled with contradictions. It relies heavily on what I refer to as *old ways of knowing*, learned from experience in the field, that are crucial aspects of effective psychotherapy and healing. In cases of violence and trauma, for example, these practices— many drawn from object relations theory and classical analysis—help people create the kind of safe and protective boundaries they need in their lives in order to overcome the harsh realities of abuse and trauma. I have also tried to avoid some of the pitfalls of postmodern forms of practice, "ignoring the past in an effort to focus more on the present, moving too quickly to solutions, exonerating the bad, and not bearing witness to people's anger and pain" (L. Hoffman, personal communication, 1994).

---

[4] From the standpoint of postmodernism, narrative theory, and other reconstructive knowledges (e.g., feminism, social constructionism), the significance of Alcoholics Anonymous (AA) is in large part due to its ability to provide healing without healers (i.e., professionals), spirituality (i.e., faith and hope) without religion (religious institutions in particular), and solidarity and community without organization and bureaucracy. As one colleague puts it, "AA is more like an 'un-organization.'" It does not seek approval, legitimacy, or money and does not adhere to a dominant political ideology. Its purpose for being could be summed up as helping its members (whose ranks include heterosexuals, gays, lesbians, people of color, Caucasians, conservatives, liberals, radicals, people living/dying with AIDS, men and women, young and old) face their feelings with more courage, think more clearly, and experience life with more reckless abandon (and less alcohol). Further, although an interest in narrative and storytelling as a metaphor for human growth and development has been experiencing a renaissance in the psychotherapy community and so many other disciplines, Alcoholics Anonymous has lived in story, and by story, since its inception in 1935. Today the telling of stories remains the heart of the program, and writing is part of its lifeblood.

Postmodern concepts, in general, emphasize therapy and theory that rejects edifying philosophical and clinical concepts. I have, in turn, attempted whenever possible to draw connections between specific therapeutic practices and the philosophical traditions they stem from. This was an effort on my part to make my values and beliefs more transparent in my writing, as well as rendering more accessible the narrative and other kinds of theories and approaches discussed. It is my attempt to show that, as a fortune cookie recently reminded me, "The philosophy of one generation is the common sense of the next." Author Jay Efran (1991), in his article "Constructivism in the Inner City," echoed these pragmatist concerns about philosophy's elitist reputation and practices, "the idea that philosophy is the aloof contemplation of trivialities, basically useless when it comes to solving blood and guts issues in the real world" (p. 51). Contrary to this image, Efran sees philosophy and its practices as a crucial part of any effort to help people with the problems they face in therapy:

> I consider the dilemmas of homeless people, rape victims, addicts and welfare mothers no less philosophical because their worlds may be filled with brutality and danger. In fact, philosophical clarity is often what bolsters the courage and resolve of those faced with great adversities. (p. 51)

The history of philosophy, said T. W. Adorno, is the history of forgetting. As Russell Jacoby (1975) observed in another context, problems and ideas once examined fall out of sight and out of mind only to resurface later as novel and new. It would sadden me if narrative therapy were to establish its own history of forgetting when it comes to understanding the experience of trauma and addiction, as well as the important ways that psychoanalysis and narrative's other clinical ancestors have contributed to the development of postmodern family therapy.

The therapists whose work is surveyed in this chapter serve as touchstones for me. All of these authors have a teleology of one kind or another at work in their writing. There is a search, and they have faith that they will find what they are looking for. "There is always a history of struggle and protest—always," said White (Wylie, 1994, p. 43).

Reinventing Postmodernism

Hundreds of years from now, when writers and psychohistorians are studying the origins of their own thoughts and language practices, they will trace the story of the end of oppressive and pathologizing descriptions of people's lives to a certain type of wild knowledge located in the twentieth century and misnamed postmodern theory. When they examine the ideas that stem from this relic of twentieth-century knowledge more closely, they will hopefully reveal an uncanny, almost visionary, understanding of the violence perpetrated by psychological theories on clients. And as crude as the shape and form these ideas will be in when they are found in print (another relic), these intellectual time travelers will still be able to recognize a historic rupture—a moment—in the discourse that permanently changed the culture of therapy.

As ontologically problematic as some of White and Epston's version of moral discourse may be, it remains important for several reasons. Umberto Eco (1990) has written, "There is nothing more meaningful than a text that asserts there is no meaning" (p. 7). Every text tells a political story and contains within its covers its own unique cultural and moral history. What I appreciate about White and Epston's writing is that they are very clear about what biases, values, and beliefs they bring to their work as well as the kind of political story they are trying to tell. I also appreciate that they present their moral assumptions as their own and take responsibility for that ownership and all its contradictions and idiosyncrasies.

Our goal should not be to sanitize therapy of all its moral implications, an impossible task and perhaps the most treacherous moral position of all. We need more, not fewer, moral visions reflected in our therapies, so that larger numbers of people from different cultural and socioeconomic backgrounds and ethnic groups can hear their own voices and see their identities reflected in our practices.

White and Epston's ideas meet my desire to be part of a culture of therapy that sees itself as needing to take both clinical and political responsibility for the impact our beliefs and choices have on individuals and the community as well as for the complexity these choices generate. In other words, narrative and postmodern therapy in general, and White and Epston's work in particular, help me feel connected to myself, to others, and to the world around me.

RESEARCH

Stories in science are judged meaningful if they are thought to be true, whereas in psychotherapy and the other human sciences stories are often thought to be true if they are meaningful (Parry, 1993). Veracity in both cases does not come easy. Like the character in the old folk tale, first we shoot holes in the fence and then we paint the bulls-eyes around them. In the context of this volume, and narrative research in general, the question posed is not "How can I prove, or disprove, a researcher's findings?" but "How did this experience move me and how can I use it to move others?"

This chapter, like its subject matter, was a creative literary endeavor. I hope it inspires studies that emphasize narrative metaphors over biological ones for psychotherapy and other human sciences. However, I am not advocating that we abandon or ignore biology, physiology, or brain functioning and other neurological research. This would be impossible in the case of problems such as schizophrenia, bipolar depression, and addictions, and ill-advised in any effort to understand human beings whose bodies produce, every moment, thousands of chemical reactions independent of any foreign substances introduced into them. In fact, recent developments in medicine and science confirm that these aspects of human experience are all part of the same larger story—or, as philosopher Richard Rorty (1982) reminds us, facts are dead metaphors.

Developments in brain research demonstrate how the mind constructs rather than mirrors images and that the mind does not process but narrates information (Edelman, 1992). Memories are "not akin to a reshowing of a movie but something more like the second or fiftieth performance of a Broadway play" (Levy, 1994, p. 71). According to these theories, our minds function less like a computer and more like an ecosystem (Edelman, 1992; Maturana & Varela, 1987).

It would be foolish to ignore the stories generated by science because when you ignore something you are not allowing its story to be part of the larger one. Narrative and scientific studies that emphasize the importance of the mind–body connection in coping with stressful illness and psychological trauma abound in the literature (Roud, 1994; Seigal, 1986; van der Kolk, 1987, 1994). I simply feel, along with Metzger (1992) that "at the end of what we might call the century of psychology, it is not theory but stories that are informing us about human nature" (p. 68) and that psychotherapy's specific contribution to this understanding is more literary than medical. However, the two are not mutually exclusive.

In Tillie Olson's (1978) groundbreaking study *Silences*, and Catherine Bateson's (1989) rich collection of life histories *Composing a Life*, both authors asked, what are the social forces that uplift—or silence—the voice of an artist? In a sense, this question was implicit in my discussion of clients' stories and my treatment of postmodern and narrative theory. However, I would like to see further studies that pose this same question, explicitly, of therapists.

Finally, I would like to see more work that attempts to bridge narrative analytic and family therapy perspectives—perhaps a revival of Freud's case studies, not necessarily written in the genre of the detective mystery that Freud preferred but where the emphasis was on telling a good story and sharing mysteries instead of solving them.

SUMMARY

In a piece he wrote for the *Family Therapy Networker*, Garrison Keillor (1991) said it is "an author's fate—to write the books and then go and live them" (p. 68). In this story, the narrator and main character, Al Denny, a self-help guru and millionaire a hundred times over, confessed that he had nothing left to say about his area of expertise, as he had said everything there was to say about the subject before he knew anything about it. The destiny of this chapter and its author is not unlike that of the protagonist in Keillor's story. Its ending, as the reader who has made it this far will soon discover, is anticlimactic.

Roland Barthes, discussing the increasingly popular topic of interdisciplinary work, observed that such study is not about confronting already constituted disciplines: "To do something interdisciplinary it's not enough to choose a 'subject' and gather around it two or three sciences. Interdisciplinarity consists in creating a new object that belongs to no one" (quoted in Clifford & Marcus, 1986, p. 78). Putting my postmodern politics and narrative sensibilities aside for a moment, my unspoken desire for the ideas and written productions that my clients and I co-construct in therapy (as well as the relationships themselves) was for them to constitute such creative "objects."

However, given this chapter's cautions about the dangers of grand or universal theories of any kind, fortunately, my discussion of the Shores' situation and Miranda's story, borrowed from my own practice, did not advance my dream of becoming part of the new canon of narrative psychotherapy. Instead, these examples read more like a series of short stories, each presenting a theme, its own unique version of a narrative concept or practice. Collectively, these ideas function like a prism reflecting the colors of a person's life. Some of the many hues cast include (a) defining the problem; (b) ideas about the politics and culture of recovery; (c) the notion of reflexivity in written correspondence and dialogue in narrative therapy; and (d) patterns of relationship between client and therapist that are unique to work with families with a history of trauma, violence, and addiction.

Loss of fulfillment, or loss of the possibility of fulfillment, was a significant theme in every family's story. Each person described experiencing intense feelings of abandonment and grief when letting go of or imagining letting go of their relationship to past and current trauma. These moments in therapy when a person feels truly alone with his or her pain remind me of Audre Lorde's (1978) words, "for the embattled there is no place that cannot be home nor is" (p. 55).

My own experience and relationship to the themes raised in the Shores' story is also an integral part of this process. Writing this chapter has made me aware of how deeply mutual the shared grief-work of clients relinquishing their pain (or any other part of their identity) truly is. Healing is a process of learning to live with the loss, not under it—to, as Edelman (1994) said, let it become our companion rather than our guide.

In the end, all of us have something broken, some aspect of our lives that can't be mended or put back together. For Nancy and Charley, it was the loss of their relationships with their fathers (to alcoholism and other women) and possibly their marriage and the dreams they had for it; for

Rena, it was the loss of her birth mother; and finally, for Michael, it was the loss of the connection to his body. On some people, it doesn't show. In today's times the less broken have to take care of the more broken. I've learned that from my clients.

REFERENCES

American Psychiatric Association. (1994). *Diagnostic and statistical manual of mental disorders* (4th ed.). Washington, DC: Author.

Andersen, T. (1987). The reflecting team: Dialogue and meta-dialogue in clinical work. *Family Process, 26*, 415–428.

Andersen, T. (Ed.). (1991). *The reflecting team: Dialogues, and dialogues about the dialogues.* New York:. Norton.

Andersen, T. (1992). Reflections on reflecting with families. In S. McNamee & K. Gergen (Eds.), *Therapy as social construction* (pp. 54–68). London: Sage.

Andersen, T. (1993). See and hear, and be seen and heard. In S. Friedman (Ed.), *The new language of change: Constructive collaboration in psychotherapy* (pp. 303–322). New York: Guilford.

Anderson, H. (1991). Thinking about multi-agency work with substance abusers and their families: A language systems approach. *Journal of Strategic and Systemic Therapies, 10*, 20–35.

Anderson, H. (1993). On a roller coaster: A collaborative language systems approach to therapy. In S. Friedman (Ed.), *The new language of change: Constructive collaboration in psychotherapy* (pp. 323–344). New York: Guilford.

Anderson, H. (1994). A collaborative language systems approach to therapy: Postmodern systems theory. In R. Mikesell, D. D. Lusterman, & S. McDaniel (Eds.), *Family psychology and systems theory.* Washington, DC: American Psychological Association.

Anderson, H., & Goolishian, H. A. (1988). Human systems as linguistic systems: Preliminary and evolving ideas about the implications for clinical theory. *Family Process, 27*(4), 371–393.

Anderson, H., & Goolishian, H. A. (1992). The client is the expert: A not-knowing position for family therapy. In S. McNamee & K. Gergen (Eds.), *Therapy as social construction* (pp. 25–39). London: Sage.

Aponte, H. (1976). Underorganization in the poor family. In P. Guerin (Ed.), *Family therapy theory and practice.* New York: Gardner.

Bateson, C. (1989). *Composing a life.* New York: Penguin.

Bateson, G. (1991). *Sacred unity: Further steps to an ecology of mind.* New York: Harper Collins.

Bateson, G., Jackson, D., Haley, J., & Weakland, J. (1956). Toward a theory of schizophrenia. *Behavioral Science, 1*, 251–264.

Belenky, M., Clinchy, B., Goldberger, N., & Tarule, J. (1987). *Women's ways of knowing: The development of self, voice and mind.* New York: Basic Books.

Benjamin, J. (1988). *The bonds of love.* New York: Pantheon.

Bepko, C., & Krestan, J. (1991). Codependency and the social reconstruction of female experience. In C. Bepko (Ed.), *Feminism and addiction* (pp. 49–66). New York: Hawthorne.

Best, S., & Kellner, D. (1991). *Postmodern theory.* New York: Guilford.

Black, E. (Ed.). (1993). *Secrets in families and family therapy.* New York: Norton.

Black, E. I., Roberts, J., & Whiting, R. (Eds.). (1988). *Rituals in family therapy.* New York: Norton.

Bollas, C. (1983). Expressive uses of countertransference. *Contemporary Psychoanalysis, 19*(1), 1–34.

Bollas, C. (1992). *On being a character.* New York: Hill & Wang.

Bollas, C. (1995). *Cracking up: The work of unconscious experience.* New York: Hill & Wang.

Bruner, J. (1986). *Actual minds, possible worlds.* Cambridge, MA: Harvard University Press.

Clifford, J., & Marcus, G. E. (Eds.). (1986). *Writing culture: The poetics and politics of ethnography*. Berkeley: University of California Press.

Cushman, P. (1991). Ideology obscured: Political uses of the self in Daniel Stern's infant. *American Psychologist, 46*, 206–219.

Cushman, P. (1995). *Constructing the self, constructing America: A cultural history of psychotherapy*. New York: Addison Wesley.

Derrida, J. (1976). *Of grammatology*. Baltimore: Johns Hopkins University Press.

Derrida, J. (1978). *Writing and difference*. London: Routledge & Kegan Paul.

Derrida, J. (1981). *Positions*. London: Athlone Press.

Dickerson, V., & Zimmerman, J. (1993). A narrative approach to families with adolescents. In S. Friedman (Ed.), *The new language of change: Constructive collaboration in psychotherapy* (pp. 226–250). New York: Guilford.

Durant, M., & White, C. (1991). *Ideas for therapy with sexual abuse*. Adelaide, Australia: Dulwich Centre.

Eco, U. (1990). *The limits of interpretation*. New York: Routledge.

Edelman, H. (1994). *Motherless daughters: The legacy of loss*. Reading, MA: Addison-Wesley.

Edelman, M. (1992). *Bright fire, brilliant fire*. New York: Harper & Row.

Efran, J. (1991). Constructivism in the inner city. *Family Therapy Networker, 15*(5), 51–52.

Epston, D. (1994). Extending the conversation. *Family Therapy Networker, 18*(6), 30–39, 62–63.

Flax, J. (1983). Political philosophy and the patriarchal unconscious: A perspective on epistemology and metaphysics. In S. Harding & M. Hintikka (Eds.), *Discovering reality* (pp. 245–282). Dordrecht, Holland: Riedel.

Flax, J. (1990a). *Thinking fragments: Feminism and postmodernism in the contemporary west*. New York: Routledge.

Flax, J. (1990b). Postmodernism and gender relations in feminist theory. In L. Nicholson (Ed.), *Feminism and postmodernism*. New York: Routledge.

Flax, J. (1993). *Disputed subjects: Essays on psychoanalysis, politics, and philosophy*. New York: Routledge.

Foucault, M. (1980). *Power/knowledge: Selected interviews and other writings*. New York: Pantheon.

Foucault, M. (1984). What is enlightenment? In P. Rabinow (Ed.), *The Foucault Reader* (pp. 32–50). New York: Pantheon.

Freeman, J., Epston, D., & Lobovits, D. (1997). *Playful approaches to serious problems*. New York: Norton.

Freeman, J., & Lobovits, D. (1993). The turtle with wings. In S. Friedman (Ed.), *The new language of change: Constructive collaboration in psychotherapy* (pp. 188–227). New York: Guilford.

Gadamer, H. (1975). *Philosophical hermeneutics*. Berkeley: University of California Press. (Original work published 1960)

Gadamer, H. (1986). *Truth and method*. New York: Cross Road. (Original work published 1960)

Gergen, K. (1985). The social constructionist movement in modern psychology. *American Psychologist, 40*, 266–275.

Gergen, K. (1988). If persons are texts. In S. B. Messer, L. A. Sass, & R. L. Woolfolk (Eds.), *Hermeneutics and psychological theory* (pp. 28–51). New Brunswick, NJ: Rutgers University Press.

Gergen, K. (1989). Warranting voice and the elaboration of self. In J. Shotter & K. J. Gergen (Eds.), *Texts of identity*. London: Sage.

Gergen, K. (1991). *The saturated self*. New York: Basic Books.

Gergen, M. (1988). *Feminist thought and the structure of knowledge*. New York: University Press.

Gilligan, C. (1982). *In a different voice*. Cambridge, MA: Harvard University Press.

Grosz, E. (1990). Contemporary theories of power and subjectivity. In S. Gunew (Ed.), *Feminist knowledge: Critique and construct* (pp. 59–120). London: Routledge.

Gunew, S. (Ed.). (1990). *Feminist knowledge: Critique and construct*. London: Routledge.

Herman, J. (1992). *Trauma and recovery*. New York: Basic Books.

Hillman, J. (1972). *The myth of analysis*. Chicago: Northwestern University Press.

Hoffman, L. (1993). *Exchanging voices: A collaborative approach to family therapy.* London: Karnac Books.

Hoffman, L. (1994, July 19–20). *Narrative therapy.* Workshop presented at Smith College School for Social Work, Northampton, MA.

Jacoby, R. (1975). *Social amnesia.* Boston: Beacon Press.

Jenkins, A. (1990). *Invitation to responsibility: The therapeutic engagement of men who are violent and abusive.* Adelaide, Australia: Dulwich Centre.

Keller, E. F. (1983). The mind's eye. In S. Harding & M. Hintikka (Eds.), *Discovering reality* (pp. 207–224). Dordrecht, Holland: Riedel.

Keller, E. F. (1992). *Secrets of life and death: Essays on language, gender, and science.* New York: Routledge.

Keller, E. F., & Flax, J. (1988). A feminist critique of psychoanalysis. In S. B. Messer, L. A. Sass, & R. L. Woolfolk, (Eds.), *Hermeneutics and psychological theory* (pp. 334–366). New Brunswick, NJ: Rutgers University Press.

Kenny, A. (1994). *The Wittgenstein reader.* Cambridge, MA: Blackwell.

Keillor, G. (1991). A short story: Al Denny. *Family Therapy Networker, 15*(5), 66–68.

Knapp, C. (1996). *Drinking a love story.* New York: Delta.

Laird, J. (1989). Women and stories: Restorying women's self-constructions. In M. Mc-Goldrick, C. Anderson, & F. Walsh (Eds.), *Women in families* (pp. 427–450). New York: Norton.

Lappin, J. (1988). Family therapy: A structural approach. In R. Dorfman (Ed.), *Paradigms of clinical social work* (pp. 220–252). New York: Brunner/Mazel.

Levin, S. (1992). *Hearing the unheard: Stories of women who have been battered.* Unpublished master's thesis, The Union Institute, New York, NY.

Levy, S. (1994, May 2). Dr. Edelman's brain. *New Yorker, 70,* 62–73.

Lorde, A. (1978). School note. In *The black unicorn* (p. 55). New York: Norton.

Luepnitz, D. A. (1992). Nothing in common but their first names: The case of Foucault and White. *Journal of Family Therapy, 14*(3), 281–284.

Masson, J. (1984). *The assault on truth.* New York: Harper-Collins.

Maturana, H., & Varela, F. (1987). *The tree of knowledge.* Boston: New Science Library.

McLean, C. (1995). Schools as communities of acknowledgment: A conversation with Michael White. *Schooling & education: Exploring new possibilities, Dulwich Centre Newsletter* (2/3), 51–66.

McNamee, S. & Gergen, K. J. (Eds.). (1992). *Therapy as social construction.* London: Sage.

Metzger, D. (1992). *Writing for your life: A guide and companion to the inner worlds.* San Francisco: Harper Collins.

Miller, D. (1994). *Women who hurt themselves.* New York: Basic Books.

Miller, D., & Lax, W. D. (1988). Interrupting deadly struggles: A reflecting team model for working with couples. *Journal of Strategic and Systemic Therapies, 7*(3), 16–22.

Miller, J. B. (1976). *Toward a new psychology of women.* Boston: Beacon.

Morgan, A. (1995). Taking responsibility: Working with teasing and bullying in schools. *Schooling & education: Exploring new possibilities, Dulwich Centre Newsletter* (2/3), 16–28.

Myerhoff, B. (1982). The journal as activity and genre. In J. B. Ruby (Ed.), *A crack in the mirror: Reflexive perspectives in anthropology* (pp. 341–360). Philadelphia: University of Pennsylvania Press.

O'Hanlon, W. (1994). The third wave. *Family Therapy Networker, 18*(6), 19–29.

Olson, M. (1995). Conversation and writing: A collaborative approach to bulimia. *Journal of Feminist Family Therapy, 6*(4), 21–44.

Olson, T. (1978). *Silences.* New York: Delacorte.

O'Neil, M., & Stockwell, G. (1991). Worthy of discussion: Collaborative group therapy. *Australian and New Zealand Journal of Family Therapy, 12*(4), 201–206.

Ong, W. (1982). *Orality and literacy.* New York: Norton.

Parry, A. (1993). Preparations for postmodern living. In S. Friedman (Ed.), *The new language of change: Constructive collaboration in psychotherapy* (pp. 428–459). New York: Guilford.

Penn, P. (1992). Letters to ourselves. *Family Therapy Networker, 15,* 43–45.

Penn, P., & Schienberg, M. (1991). Stories and conversations. *Journal of Strategic and Systemic Therapies, 10*(3/4), 30–37.

Rabinow, P. (Ed.). (1984). *The Foucault reader*. New York: Pantheon.

Roberts, J. (1988). Use of ritual in "redocumenting" psychiatric history. In E. I. Black, J. Roberts, & R. Whiting (Eds.), *Rituals in family therapy* (pp. 307–330). New York: Norton.

Roberts, J. (1994). *Tales of transformation: Stories in families and family therapy*. New York: Norton.

Rorty, R. (1982). *Philosophical papers* (Vols. 1 & 2). Princeton, NJ: Princeton University Press.

Roth, S., Chasin, L., Chasin, R., Becker, R., & Herzig, M. (1992). From debate to dialogue: A facilitating role for family therapists in the public forum. *Dulwich Centre Newsletter* (2), 41–48.

Roud, P. (1994). *Making miracles*. New York: Harper & Row.

Sackvitne, K., & Pearlman, L. (1995). *Trauma and the therapist*. New York: Norton.

Sanville, J. (1991). *The playground of psychoanalytic therapy*. London: Analytic Press.

Schafer, R. (1976). *A new language for psychoanalysis*. New Haven: Yale University Press.

Schafer, R. (1981). *Narrative actions in psychoanalysis*. Worcester, MA: Clark University Press.

Schafer, R. (1983). *The analytic attitude*. New York: Basic Books.

Schafer, R. (1992). *Retelling a life: Narration and dialogue in psychoanalysis*. New York: Basic Books.

Seigal, B. (1986). *Love medicine and miracles*. Boston: G. K. Hall.

Shotter, J. (1994). *Making sense on the boundaries: On moving between philosophy and psychotherapy*. Unpublished manuscript. The University of New Hampshire.

Spence, D. (1982). *Narrative truth, historical truth*. New York: Norton.

Spence, D. (1987). *The Freudian metaphor: Toward paradigmatic change in psychoanalysis*. New York: Norton.

Starhawk. (1987). *Truth or dare: Encounters with power, authority and mystery*. San Francisco: Harper & Row.

Starhawk. (1989). *The spiral dance*. New York: Harper & Row.

Tomm, K., Suzuki, K., & Suzuki, K. (1990). The Ka-No-Mushi: An inner externalization that enables compromise? *Journal of Australian and New Zealand Family Therapy, 11*(2), 104–107.

van der Kolk, B. (Ed.). (1987). *Psychological trauma*. Washington, DC: American Psychiatric Press.

van der Kolk, B. (1994). The body keeps the score: Memory and the evolving psychobiology of posttraumatic stress. *Harvard Review of Psychiatry, 1*, 253–265.

Waldegrave, C. (1990). "Just therapy." *Dulwich Centre Newsletter, 1*, 6–46. (Available from Dulwich Centre Publications, Adelaide, Australia).

West, C. (1993). *Prophetic thought in postmodern times*. Monroe, ME: Common Courage Press.

White, M. (1986/1987, Summer). Couple therapy: "Urging for sameness" or "appreciation of difference." *Dulwich Centre Newsletter*, pp. 11–13.

White, M. (1989a). Anorexia nervosa: A cybernetic perspective. In M. White, *Selected papers* (pp. 65–76). Adelaide, Australia: Dulwich Centre.

White, M. (1989b). The conjoint therapy of men who batter. In M. White, *Selected papers* (pp. 101–106). Adelaide, Australia: Dulwich Centre.

White, M. (1989c). The externalizing of the problem and the re-authoring of lives and relationships. In M. White, *Selected papers* (pp. 5–28). Adelaide, Australia: Dulwich Centre.

White, M. (1989d). Family therapy & schizophrenia: Addressing the "in the corner lifestyle." In M. White, *Selected papers* (pp. 47–58). Adelaide, Australia: Dulwich Centre.

White, M. (1989e). The process of questioning a therapy of literary merit. In M. White, *Selected papers* (pp. 37–46). Adelaide, Australia: Dulwich Centre.

White, M. (1989f). Saying hello again. In M. White, *Selected papers* (pp. 29–36). Adelaide, Australia: Dulwich Centre.

White, M. (1989g). Pseudo-encopresis: From avalanche to victory, from vicious to virtuous cycles. In M. White, *Selected papers* (pp. 110–124). Adelaide, Australia: Dulwich Centre.

White, M. (1991). Deconstruction and therapy. In M. White & D. Epston, *Experience, contradiction, narrative, & imagination: Selected papers of Michael White and David Epston* (pp. 109–151). Adelaide, Australia: Dulwich Centre Publications.

White, M. (1992a). A conversation about AIDS and dying. In M. White & D. Epston, *Experience, contradiction, narrative, & imagination: Selected papers of Michael White and David Epston* (pp. 27–36). Adelaide, Australia: Dulwich Centre Publications.

White, M. (1992b, October). "Narrative Therapy." Workshop presented at the Family Therapy Center of Burlington, Burlington, VT.

White, M. (1995). *Reauthoring lives: Interviews and essays*. Adelaide: Dulwich Centre.

White, M., & Epston, D. (1990). *Narrative means to therapeutic ends*. London: Norton.

White, M., & Epston, D. (1992). *Experience, contradiction, narrative, & imagination: Selected papers of Michael White and David Epston*. Adelaide, Australia: Dulwich Centre.

Winnicott, D. W. (1949). Hate in the countertransference. *International Journal of Psychoanalysis, 30*(2), 69–74.

Winnicott, D. W. (1965). *The maturational environment*. New York: Basic Books.

Winnicott, D. W. (1971). *Playing and reality*. London: Tavistock.

Winnicott, D. W. (1989). *Psychoanalytic explorations*. Cambridge, MA: Harvard University Press.

Wittgenstein, L. (1958). *The blue and brown books*. Oxford: Blackwell.

Wittgenstein, L. (1966). *Lectures and conversations on aesthetics, psychology and religious beliefs*. Oxford: Blackwell.

Wittgenstein, L. (1974). *Tractus logico-philosophicus*. London: Routledge and Kegan Paul.

Wylie, M. (1994). Panning for gold. *Family Therapy Networker, 18*(6), 40–46.

PART III
Metaparadigms

9

The Feminist Approach to Clinical Social Work

Helen Land, Ph.D.

INTRODUCTION

The feminist approach to clinical social work is best described as a phi-losophy of psychotherapeutic intervention or as a stance or clinical lens used to guide practice. In that sense it is a metaparadigm. Drawing from a wide variety of traditions, clinical social workers who are feminist in their practice may assess and intervene from a variety of theoretical orienta-tions and use any number of treatment modalities (e.g., individual, cou-ple, group, advocacy, therapeutic case management). In fact, those calling themselves feminist clinicians have published from widely diverse theo-retical orientations, including cognitive–behavioral (Mancoske, Standifer, & Cauley, 1994), psychodynamic (Chodorow, 1978; Eichenbaum & Or-bach, 1983; Gould, 1981; Jordan & Surrey, 1986), psychosocial (Ruderman, 1986), task centered (Worell & Remer, 1992), family systems (Ault-Riche, 1986; Luepnitz, 1988; Robbins, 1983), constructivist (Neimeyer, 1993), and transpersonal (Cowley, 1993). Although feminist clinical social work en-compasses a diversity of treatment interventions, there are core principles and an important body of theory that guide practice. Feminist theory (or the feminist way of seeing the world) has been greatly influenced by cer-tain scholars and historical events that gave rise to feminist orientations to the psychotherapeutic process. This chapter discusses the historical back-drop of feminist clinical practice and the core theoretical constructs of prac-tice as well as the phases of intervention, aspects of the therapeutic process, limitations of the model, and issues in its efficacy.

227

CONCEPT OF THE PERSON AND THE HUMAN EXPERIENCE

Current feminist theory and practice has its origin in the civil rights and women's liberation movements of the 1960s. During that time, consciousness-raising groups evolved, and with them a new way of seeing the world with different methods of problem solving. Meeting in groups, many women began to understand that they often shared similar experiences and a common agenda. Through talking with one another and sharing experiences, feelings, thoughts, and behaviors, there developed what Belenky (Belenky, Clinchy, Goldberger, & Tarule, 1986) called "a different way of knowing." Women began to make sense out of what often seemed to be a senseless enigma, those situations fraught with gender oppression, stigma, and—ultimately—disabling outcomes. Women began to enunciate new understandings of their experiences, and they also began to recognize how internalizing the patriarchal mentality and structured gender role sets of society often resulted in a negative sense of identity, self-doubt, and few choices for change. Through these groups and other methods of exchange, feminist theory evolved in the social sciences.

Feminist theories elucidate varied ways of viewing and understanding the lives and experiences of women and men—in particular, the nature and impact of inequality between genders and the structuring of gender role sets. Such theories have emerged from and are tied to movements to stem the oppression and disenfranchisement of women and men. Much of feminist theory centers on the connections among gender, privilege, value, social class, culture, sexuality, and the concept of the self.

HISTORICAL PERSPECTIVE

Although much of current feminist practice grew out of the women's movement of the 1960s, these approaches to problem solving can be traced to the value base of social work, enunciated by those who first developed the profession. Many of the early leaders in social work were women and could be called feminists because they defined problems and many of the concerns of women as being rooted in social forces interacting with interpersonal and psychological issues. For example, early visionaries such as Jane Addams attempted to provide social support services for the newly immigrated in an effort to ease the acculturation process (Fisher, 1971). Mary Richmond (1917) viewed problems as requiring a social diagnosis and enumerated the importance of recognizing issues in the family's ecology and its impact on the family's ways of interacting. Of particular concern to her were women who had been abandoned by their spouses and women who were mentally ill (Perlman, 1971). Others such as Bertha Reynolds (Hollis, 1971) brought socialistic precepts to practice, and Gordon

Hamilton (1951) elucidated the important links among social casework, social welfare services, the economic factors pressing against families in distress, and the need for social action and advocacy (Hollis, 1970, 1971). These were women who developed approaches to ameliorate problematic conditions embedded in the daily lives of the clients, problems that are alarmingly similar to those faced by social work practitioners today as they approach the new millennium: the feminization of poverty, family discord and violence, inadequate social resources for immigrant groups, undereducation of the urban poor, homelessness, minimal health care resources for vulnerable groups, and children at risk for physical and psychological problems.

Adding a structural–social component to problem definition and its amelioration, these women developed a stance toward practice that collided with the positions of other helping professions. Largely concerned with disenfranchised groups and women's issues, historical social work leaders saw problem evolution differently than colleagues in other disciplines. As a result, they drew fire from established fields. In large part, social work was responsible for delineating social problems, especially those problems rooted in inequity. In fact, Abraham Flexner (1915) at the National Conference on Charities and Corrections questioned the very validity of social work because he felt it lacked an emphasis on individual responsibility in welfare and provided only a mediating service—what we know today as *therapeutic case management*. Thus, our early feminist pioneers were motivated to define the principles that would lead to cardinal constructs of today's clinical social work practice: the biopsychosocial approach, the person-in-situation paradigm, and empowerment practice. Yet much in the same way that they were questioned about the uniqueness and validity of their practice, feminist clinicians today are queried about what constitutes feminist theory and what is so unique about feminist practice.

KEY THEORETICAL CONSTRUCTS

Validating the Social Context

Those practicing feminist clinical social work hold as primary the analysis of the effects of the social context on difficulties of the client as they are jointly assessed by the client and the practitioner. Such a stance is not new to social work. However, in this perspective, particular attention is given to environmental pressures that press on *gender-role enactment* (i.e., those roles normatively enacted by men or women) and discrimination. Such a scenario may greatly affect clients' experience of stress and may impact their cognitive structures, patterns of interpersonal behavior, self-concept, and—ultimately—identity formation (Brodsky, 1980; Day, 1992).

Feminist practice theory proposes that theories of human behavior must be understood within the broader social context and that clinical interpretations of behavior must attend to the impact of external realities on clients' internal processes (Brown & Brodsky, 1992). For example, symptoms of depression may be validated and interpreted as a reaction to depressing conditions rather than being primarily conceived as a pathological reactive disorder related to an ambiguous set of circumstances. Hence clinicians with a feminist orientation would investigate factors such as environmental inequity, interpersonal stress, biological changes and determinants, and issues related to self-concept and world view that might result in a depressive condition. Subsequently, those factors fostering the depression are investigated mutually by the client and clinician in order that the symptoms might be alleviated.

Recognizing How the Personal Is Political

Feminist practitioners often acknowledge ways in which the personal issues of their clients are ultimately political in nature and may reflect power inequities in relationships with others. Sexual harassment is an obvious example. Many times, the components of the political context are multifaceted, covert in nature, and defined by those in power positions as problems residing within the individual rather than within the system. Common issues include the often cited experience that individuals at the workplace may not speak with one another in languages other than English. Such a work environment results in an inability for workers to communicate with each other, to identify problematic work conditions, and to problem solve. The consequence may be immobilization. These forces ultimately culminate in stress and anger, which may then be internalized and lead to depressive symptoms. In this situation, feminist clinicians might help clients speak with one another, vocalize how their individual and personal situations are politically based problems, and organize a plan of action.

Other issues reflecting how the personal experience is political in nature involve the examination of the allocation of labor, power distribution, entitlement, value definitions and rewards, and the ways in which such factors interact within interpersonal relationships experienced by couples and families (Laird, 1995). For example, one common theme with which couples often struggle involves the replication of the hierarchy in employment status positions in the couple relationship. In other words, value, worth, and subsequent rewards associated with power allocations on the job are mirrored in the couple relationship. When inequity exists in employment status, it is commonly replicated in relationships, causing conflict between the partners.

Rebalancing Perceptions of Normality and Deviance

At times in the history of the psychotherapeutic professions, what was considered deviant was a reflection of the behavior of less privileged groups such as women, people of color, poor people, older adults, and gay men and lesbians. Some diagnostic disorders once published in the *Diagnostic and Statistical Manual of Mental Disorders* (e.g., American Psychiatric Association, 1994) have been more frequently seen in female clients; such is the case with neurasthenic personality disorder. This now-invalidated disorder, whose symptoms included malingering behavior, complaints of lack of energy, and fatigue, was probably more closely related to chronic fatigue syndrome, an immune disorder more commonly seen in women. Recently, feminist members of the American Psychological Association blocked the inclusion of the diagnostic disorder "self-defeating personality disorder" because they felt it defined certain groups of women as pathological. They pointed out that no attempt has been made to include a category for "dominating personality disorder," a set of behaviors that may be seen with greater frequency in men. Hence, many feminist practitioners emphasize the need to reexamine conceptions of morality and deviance in order to prevent the stigmatization, marginalization, or exclusion of certain groups.

The Inclusive Stance

The inclusive stance seeks to include the experiences related to gender in all formulations of human experience and to stem the dominance of male assumptions in the generation of theories. Those in feminist practice are interested in understanding and changing the processes that keep men and women thinking and acting within patriarchal frameworks (Walters, Carter, Papp, & Silverstein, 1988). In addition, the inclusive stance seeks to stem the assumption that Western cultural models must predominate in current thinking; therefore, the inclusive stance in psychotherapeutic efforts mandates a reexamination of many Anglocentric assumptions and embraces the expanding mentality of pluralism in U.S. society (Land, 1995). For example, the strength of the kinship system among women of African American and Latin American cultures provides social support and stress resistance. However, from an Anglocentric perspective, such family and friendship networks may be interpreted as signifying an enmeshed, collusive, matriarchal family system that ultimately operates toward dysfunction.

Moreover, feminist clinicians support an inclusive determination of function and dysfunction. That which is seen as indicating psychopathology in the occidental model may be a culture-bound phenomenon of which little is known. Such is the case with *embrujado* (Koss-Chioino & Canive,

1993), *susto* or *ataque de nervios* (Guarnaccia, De La Cancela, & Carillo, 1989; Martinez, 1993), and belief in spiritualism (Suarez, Rafaelli, & O'Leary, 1996).[1] Western medicine has been slow to acknowledge the existence of culture-bound syndromes and slow to validate their alternative treatments that are often relied on by culturally indigenous caregivers. Hence, feminist practice seeks to include knowledge that is often marginalized by the medical model of practice.

The Deconstructive Stance

Deconstruction, first elaborated by Derrida (1976) and others (e.g., Bakhtin, 1981; Foucault, 1980), places value on that knowledge which, they assert, has been subjugated. Assuming a deconstructivist stance, feminists assess how culture- and gender-bound definitions of right and wrong and correct and incorrect behaviors are mediated through *occidental hegemony* (i.e., Western domination), thus, such assumptions require reexamination and reconceptualization. Deconstruction eschews or dismantles dualistic thinking and choices so prevalent in Western society and favors the exploration of pluralistic ones. This perspective, first outlined by Nietzsche (1964), has now been embraced by a growing number of scholars within the psychotherapeutic community (e.g., Andersen, 1991; Goldner, 1991; Hare-Mustin, 1988; Laird, 1995; Luepnitz, 1988; McGoldrick, Giordano, & Pearce, 1996; Walters, Carter, Papp, & Silverstein, 1988).

When applied to feminist therapy, the deconstructivist stance examines conceptual barriers to understanding. These barriers especially operate through the use of language as language defines experience (McCannell, 1986). What is given power, what is seen as devalued, what is recognized as valuable, and what is worthy of historical documentation is often reflected in the language of the patriarchy. Feminist therapy is concerned with locating the subjugated voice, with questioning hegemonic knowledge and truths, and with understanding whether narratives are potentiating or subjugating to individuals who seek treatment. Hence feminist psychotherapeutic practice can inform and unite disparate ideas and meanings, especially by exploring with clients how these ideas have been shaped in relationship to the power hierarchy with which clients live (Laird, 1995).

This position, in part, explains why feminists attend to language and sexist usage, because language is often a defining experience, one that reflects the power structure in which it was born. The deconstructive clinical

---

[1] *Susto* is a culture-bound syndrome and involves symptoms of anxiety and depression following a fright and involving possible soul loss. *Ataque de nervios* is a type of anxiety panic condition existing in Latin cultures. *Embrujado* involves bewitchment. Spiritualism or *espiritismo* encompasses efforts to communicate with the spirits of the dead.

stance seeks to take apart and reexamine the structural use of language and experience in order to stem its debilitating effects (Land, 1995).

Narratives

Narratives and stories by which people live their lives become quite important in feminist therapy. Some theorists assert that problems are socially constructed in language-determined systems (Anderson & Goolishian, 1992). The use of language and metaphor in narratives often reflects the *zeitgeist* or world view of the individual seeking help. Moreover, personal and societally determined narratives are often intimately connected, whereas other narratives are silenced (Foucault, 1980; Laird, 1995). By discussing the meaning of narratives, and the making of their meaning (Gergen & Kaye, 1992), feminist clinicians help their clients to deconstruct limiting, problem-saturated narratives—voice narratives that have been silenced—and reconstruct narratives that nourish self-growth and actualization (White, 1993; White & Epston, 1990).

Revaluing Positions Enacted by Women

Many feminist practitioners feel that mainstream psychotherapies have benefited the more economically and socially privileged in society. As a result, those stances and activities that have been pursued by men tend to be conceived of as normative and valuable. For example, striving toward upward mobility in a competitive manner is often valued because this sort of behavior has been successful in economically advancing White men. Conversely, behaviors that are often performed by women, such as compromising, cooperating, seeking consensus, providing nurturance to others, and the many aspects of care-giving, are often devalued, ostensibly because they reflect a female experience (Freedberg, 1993; Hare-Mustin & Maracek, 1988). Feminist clinicians support such behaviors and assert that they are vitally important to the well-being of society, as they often result in positive behavioral outcomes. Hence these behaviors should receive greater value in this pluralistic society (Morrison Dore, 1994).

Recognizing Difference in Male and Female Experience

The results of Carol Gilligan's (1982) insightful research on the difference in courses of human development in male and female children is an example of a theory that suggests men and women often have different experiences but that only one experience has been validated while the other is unknown or undervalued. Although some have criticized Gilligan on methodological grounds, her contribution to feminist theory is significant. Prior to the publication of her study, little attention had been given to female developmental life. Theorists assumed that all development reflected the experience of the male child with his parent figures. Gilligan elucidates the relationship patterns that female children have with their care-giving figures and how their subsequent socialization and consequent behavioral actions may take different courses than those of their male counterparts. Specifically, because female children are socially permitted to have more intimate contacts (especially with their mothers) for sustained periods of time throughout life, they reap the effects of the closer parental relationship in terms of both personality development and socialized behavior patterns that reflect parenting norms and concerns. These patterns may include attention to the well-being of others before the needs of self, assumption of importance of care-giving, use of group cooperation, and collaborative problem solving. In addition, closeness of attachment to caregivers for longer periods of time may result in greater comfort with intimacy and negotiation of the affectual world. Although many developmental theories do not attend to gender differences over the course of human development, such differences are of central importance to feminist theories. Feminist scholars assert that to understand the internal psychic structure of women and women's concepts of self, we must examine the effects of the near family environment patterns (i.e., the impact of significant others and family forces) that interact with the oppressive social structures. These forces culminate in a psychological milieu that impacts female development (Ault-Riche, 1986; Braverman, 1988; Laird, 1994).

Challenging Reductionistic Models

Although feminists recognize the importance of behaviors traditionally enacted by women and acknowledge the impact of gender role socialization, most feminist clinicians eschew theories of sex-role modeling such as the notion that the division between women and men is that women are the social and emotional caretakers while men assume the instrumental roles in family life. Such reductionistic models that seek to codify societal expectations of sex-role stratification are seen as limiting and nonproductive for both genders. Attending to a balance between autonomy and relationship competence for both genders is a key component in feminist clinical practice. Knowledge of limitations of such reductionistic models, coupled with knowledge of the differences in gender development, assist in understanding how the therapeutic relationship can best address the needs of clients (Day, 1992).

Aspects of the Therapeutic Relationship

Attention to the power dynamics in the relationship

This precept attends to the value of client–clinician equity and to power dynamics manifested within family and couple systems. Many feminist clinicians believe that the historical asymmetry in the psychotherapeutic relationship between therapist and client is inimical to the goals of feminist clinical practice. Development of an egalitarian relationship is a desired goal. Empowerment models (see, e.g., Levine, et al., 1993; Solomon, 1976) that seek to harness client strengths in self-advocacy, self-determination, and problem solving particularly support the stance of egalitarianism. Other approaches such as constructivist and narrative traditions seek to locate the subjugated voice within the client and define—at the vortex of therapy—the client's meaning and definition of the conflict (Neimeyer, 1993). Other perspectives such as client-centered approaches and the intersubjective stance within self psychology are attuned to the mutuality of experience in the treatment process and the rebalancing of power dynamics within the therapeutic relationship.

Partnering stance

Whereas traditional psychotherapy discourages the practice of therapist self-disclosure except in rare instances, feminist clinicians believe that their clients may learn from the clinician's experience as a person living in a male-dominated society. Hence elements of self-disclosure, especially in situations where the personal is political, are used with greater frequency in feminist clinical practice. The therapeutic relationship is viewed as a partnership in which both parties are affected by and affect the course of the involvement.

Empowerment practice

Although the means for psychotherapeutic growth may vary among feminist clinicians, almost by definition feminist clinical practice is empowerment practice. Within this tradition, therapeutic goals for clients are generated mutually between clinicians and clients. The focus is often on empowering clients to change the negative social, interpersonal, and political environments that reduce well-being instead of helping them adapt to an oppressive social context. During this process, feminist clinicians may use interventions derived from a number of practice theories, including examining intrapsychic concerns, untangling interpersonal issues, reviewing perspectives on the sociocultural contexts that affect life, and suggesting new behavioral actions such as skills-building and advocacy work (Brown

& Liss-Levinson, 1981). The modalities used may include individual, couple, family, and small-group experiences. Group counseling, in particular, remains a valued tradition within feminist clinical practice because of the therapeutic and empowering effects of group cohesion and support, universality, and the corrective emotional experiences gained in group settings. In empowerment practice, the social work clinician uses *experience-near* language (White, 1993)—that is, language that does not offend the client's self-narrative and that is empowering.

ASSESSMENT

In the assessment phase, feminist clinical social workers use precepts of feminist theories of psychotherapy in concert with a psychosocial assessment as elaborated by social work scholars (see, e.g., Hepworth & Larson, 1996; Meyer, 1983).

The following assessment questions are particularly related to feminist theory:

- How does the social context support the current problematic situation of the client? To what extent do sociopolitical gender issues encumber the client's capacities? Are gender stereotypes affecting the allocation of labor, power, and rewards?
- In what way is the client's personal experience embedded in the political context? What is the effect on the client?
- What conceptions of normality and deviance are operating in the client system, and are they embedded in the traditions of patriarchy? Are they supportive or encumbering of potentials?
- What narratives are operating for the family as a whole and for particular family members? To what extent do they restrict growth?
- What can be valued in each family member? Have certain conceptions of self been devalued because of gender issues and stereotyping?
- How are male and female experiences in this family different? What do family members believe about masculinity and femininity and gender issues as they relate to labor, power, desires, worth, values, and entitlement? Are family members satisfied with the current distribution of these factors?
- What are the power dynamics in this family with particular respect to issues of gender roles?

These questions illustrate how the feminist perspective provides a lens through which specific gender issues can be addressed. The following material provides examples of how such issues are addressed in the Shore family case.

The Social Context

The Shore family presents a set of complex issues operating at multiple levels. Here is a family facing chronic unemployment for both parents, consequent financial strain, and chronic physical illness in the mother and son. The father, Charley, has suffered from bipolar depression, and the wife, Nancy, lacks solid information about the extent of her husband's limitations. Nancy has endured anxiety attacks, agoraphobia, and depression, and she has been struggling with an eating disorder. The daughter, Rena, a young adult, has few role models. She is currently searching for her birth parents and struggles with an uncertain future and sporadic depression. The younger child, Michael, is challenged with problematic peer interactions, questionable mental stability, a waning learning disability, and a seizure disorder. The family has limited social supports. Extended family in the grandparents' generation have been felt to be generally problematic by the parents, and in any case these family members are now deceased. No other relatives or friends currently support the family. The family's only outside contact appears to be with social service providers; otherwise the family seems to be socially isolated. No mention is made of ethnicity or race.

Although daunting, this family scenario is not an atypical one for social workers. In the assessment phase, a feminist clinician would recognize and validate the burdensome social context. From this tradition, a clinician would seek to examine how these forces have interacted with the mentality of the family as a whole, as well as its individual members. For example, the father's bipolar depression and his chronic unemployment place him in a low status position for males in this society and may feed his feelings of inadequacy in his roles as spouse, father, and societally designated breadwinner. The numerous crises of the family may render the mother anxious, emotionally paralyzed, and physically exhausted. These tensions may play into her chronic back problems. She has been designated the family caregiver, a frequently assumed gender role for women. In this capacity she endures role overload and feelings of role captivity (Aneshensel, Pearlin, Mullan, Zarit, & Whitlatch, 1995; Land, 1992; Pearlin, Aneshensel, & LeBlanc, 1997). Common to many female caregivers, she gains satisfaction in her care-giving competencies. However, such family burdens have limited her dream of opportunities to advance in her career.

Rena, age 18, is socially isolated and faces few supports or access to opportunities for young women from a financially limited family. The environmentally chaotic nature of family life, and her exposure to few affirming female role models, have partially contributed to feelings that she herself brings crises to her life and forces others to abandon her. Such ownership of problems is commonly seen among women seeking help. Although intellectually bright, she has been validated only for her entertainment-performance skills.

Michael's poor physical capabilities, seizure disorder, and remaining learning disability make it difficult for him to live up to male peer-group expectations. Moreover, the relationship between stress and somatic conditions such as asthma has been well documented. Therefore, one might conclude that environmental stress may well contribute to his difficulties.

For all members of this family, societal forces and gender constructs embedded in patriarchy have resulted in limiting identities and access to opportunity and privilege. One can readily see the many social forces that are impinging on a family identity of marginality, with resultant encumbrance of self-concept.

Conceptions of Normality and Deviance

Entrenched conceptions of deviance are operating on each family member. The father is deemed deviant by society, his family, and himself because of his mental health status, lack of employment stability, and interpersonal difficulties. The mother is bound by her anxiety, depression, and eating disorder. Rena carries an identity of a quitter and a rejected child who is responsible for her own abandonment. Her adoptive status has been poorly incorporated into her self-identity. Michael feels like he belongs in a different world. These multiple conceptualizations of deviance for each member of the family point to a family definition of abnormality and poor potentiality. Such identities often play a part in maintaining problem-saturated scenarios because of the lack of self-defined potential.

The Deconstructive Stance and Evident Narratives

In the assessment phase, practitioners using the deconstructive stance seek knowledge that has been subjugated by the family and its members. Moreover, the deconstructive approach advocates examining conceptual barriers to understanding, especially as manifested through the use of language. Often, narratives are embedded in the language of the societal power structure and in the patterns of family traditions that have become limiting. Many examples are evident in the Shore family. Charley operates from a history of being beaten and teased, never feeling as though he were the center of anyone's positive regard. He has been called names at work. He has learned to cope in the world by clowning and by being self-effacing. He must put on a false self (see, e.g., Kohut 1977) in his comedy act as Joe Penn, but he is rewarded for this and therefore values it. He speaks of missed opportunities as if to say classically, "I could have been a contender." He fears he cannot solve the family's problems. He mentions suicide and getting on disability. He worries about his wife's rejection of him as he enters the house. All these narratives culminate in a disempowered, inadequate sense of self in relation to the world. The case provides some clues for accessing subjugated knowledge. There is a voice within Charley that admits limitations, but he attends a rehabilitation program. There is an effort to maintain a medication regimen so as to be stable, a voice that would rather die than accept disability payments and that values his wife but resents being parented by her. There is part of Charley that nurtures; here is someone who sensitively rubbed his mother's feet as she took a break from scrubbing floors.

Similarly, Nancy's history has impacted her current internal narratives. Although Nancy was valued by her maternal aunt and grandmother, her mother was said to be narcissistic, and Nancy is convinced that she was unwanted by her mother. She remembers that in high school her mother was competitive with her; she was the ugly duckling. Food has taken on a central meaning to her because she has fond memories of her father's love being connected to bringing home food for the family. As a result, food is tied to family cohesion. Her father was an unstable presence in her life, and in the end she felt unloved and replaced by his other children. Such a history reveals a family situation of emotional instability and lack of consistent affirmation of Nancy by her significant others. In self-psychological terms, her self remains fragmented due to lack of sufficient mirroring, idealizing, and partnering in selfobject relations (Kohut, 1977). She has internalized negative object figures (Mitchell, 1988). Nancy's internal narratives support such theories. She refers to herself today as "grossly obese." She comes from a disempowered stance, saying that she worries about the family but there is nothing she can do about the state of affairs. She says that she would rather people "walk on her" than vice versa. She is forgetful and cannot concentrate. She has become the family worrier, and she feels that no one gives a damn. Yet other voices exist. Here, feminists would look to her consistent capability to function well in family crises and her ability to take control of life, her dream of something better, her love of nursing, her capacity to have insight into her daughter's psychological difficulties, and her ability to persist through difficult times. Thus her potentials as a mother, wife, and nurse are far more evident and efficacious than Nancy's dominant narratives reveal.

Rena's developmental history repeats patterns of her adoptive mother. Like Nancy, she got along better with adults and had few peer relationships. She was emancipated prematurely and engaged in independent living at age 13. The death of her maternal great-grandmother signifies the loss of an attachment to the only perceived adult nurturing figure in Rena's life. At age 12, when a person is facing adolescent identity issues, such a loss can be considered quite significant. She has endured child abuse and appears to be struggling with depression. It is evident that these historical issues have scripted Rena's narratives, many of which point to issues of very poor self-esteem. She feels that somehow she deserves abandonment, even forces it, and that she is repeating patterns of her birth mother by dropping out of high school. Although she is searching for her birth mother, she wonders about her approval because her birth mother has rejected her before. Rena dreams of performing for her. She speaks of her own shame. Through it all, subjugated voices reveal a young woman who seeks to discover more about her roots and actualize her many gifts, even though she may face pain.

Michael mirrors his father's wish to be good at something. The case history addresses bizarre behavior, suggesting that he may be manifesting some signs of mental illness. His mother feels that he was born unlucky. He speaks of his difference and alienation from others, saying that he feels like he belongs in another country or in another time zone. He wishes he could start his life over again. He feels that God has put a scar on him and that he must overcome this scar before life will be better. But there is a glimmering of an alternative voice. This is a child who gains strength from his patriotism and values authenticity. He is knowledgeable about current events. He sympathizes with those who are vulnerable. Against many odds, he persists in interacting with his peer group and is sure he will someday find his special talent.

This is a family that has developed narratives that are ubiquitously problem saturated. Defeatist voices are evident in each family member. The deconstructive stance seeks the underdeveloped voices and would explore those narratives that are more potentiating in each member and in the family as a whole (White & Epston, 1990). In addition, feminist clinicians would explore how socioeconomic disadvantage and the potential of racial, cultural, and gender prejudices play into the defeatist voices that resound in the Shore family.

Recognizing Difference in Male and Female Experience

Feminist clinical assessment pays particular attention to the differences in male and female experience with regard to development and the current making of meaning in the lives of each client. A regular part of the assessment is being attuned to the meaning of male and female, as well as heterosexual and homosexual experiences. What is Charley's experience as a man, as a husband, and as a father? What does he think of Nancy's experience of him in these roles? What is Nancy's meaning of womanness; what is her experience as a woman, a wife, a mother? What does she think of Charley's conceptualization of her as a woman? What is it like for Rena to be a young adult in today's world? What is her experience as a daughter, a granddaughter, a girlfriend? What does she want for herself as a woman? What does she think of her parents' ideas of her in these capacities? Similarly, what is Michael's experience as a 12-year-old male adolescent in his microculture? Does he have any ideas of how his parents see him, relative to how he sees himself? In what way do factors such as the labor, power, and reward structure in the family impact their internal narratives? Addressing such issues gives the clinician a better understanding of the gender identities, value, worth, and self-concept issues for each family member. Although some of this material had been explored in other parts of the assessment, many of the answers to these questions remain elusive and would be explored directly with each client as well as with the family as a whole.

Challenging Reductionistic Models

Often, reductionistic models document disorders while failing to document strengths. This part of the feminist assessment process challenges the clinician to think beyond models that are often pathology-based and limiting in their scope of human experience. Although many members of this family are coping with very real difficulties—the father's bipolar disorder; the mother's panic disorder, depression, and chronic back condition; the daughter's depression; the son's asthma and behavioral difficulties—the clinician must strive to use a strengths–needs approach and to assess beyond the documentation of disorder. The clinician needs to be cognizant of what the family will be likely to expect from the clinician, given their history with other helping professionals and their seeming failure to feel improvement from that help. What solutions have been closed off because of potentially sexist orientations?

Moreover, the feminist clinician is sensitive to gender issues within the therapeutic relationship during the assessment process. These issues may include the family's receptivity to the therapist's gender, as well as if and how the family perceives therapist vulnerability (Laird, 1995).

Power Dynamics

The assessment phase is delicate because it is the first time the family will experience the therapeutic relationship; therefore, attention to power dynamics is crucial as one commences treatment. Here the clinician must be attuned to the use of the partnering stance and assess the family's reaction to it. Relationship formation, although frequently constructed as part of the treatment phase, begins in assessment. At times, those clients who have experienced substantial interaction with service providers reflexively assume a patient role as opposed to a partnership stance. Such clients may initially expect a more hierarchical arrangement within the client–clinician relationship. Hence the reception of the partnership is seen as diagnostically valuable in and of itself.

Assessing power dynamics within the family system is complicated because power allocation may take on many faces. At first glance, we attend to issues of entitlement, value, allocation of labor, and the current reward system in the family. Here, Nancy assumes heavy work allocations that appear to be burdensome, but she gains a sense of competence in this role. No one in this family appears to exhibit aspects of overt entitlement, as self-esteem is quite precarious for all members. Still, power is held and enacted in different ways by all family members. For example, Charley has been deemed ineffective in his roles as parent, partner, and economic breadwinner. This ineffectiveness has freed him from the responsibility to enact adult roles; hence, he holds the power to make others assume what should be his responsibilities. Nancy holds the power of decision-making and care-giving but feels disempowered to effect positive change and growth within the family. Rena holds power through her runaway behavior and failure to succeed; her parents worry about her and thus she gains a certain type of attention through this process. Michael feels scarred and ineffectual but is able to create a disaster scenario with his periodic asthma attacks, bizarre behavior with peers, and chronic school problems. Although this family does not fit a classic patriarchal mold with regard to power distribution, each member holds power in characterological form.

As in other traditions of assessment, the following issues would be addressed in this family in this phase. Many members of this family appear to be quite depressed; much of the case material suggests the potential of suicide risk in Rena and Charley and possibly in Nancy. As in any other psychosocial assessment, clinicians using this model would also conduct an assessment of substance abuse and subsequent referral for medication evaluation for affective disorders and anxiety. Moreover, the clinician would assess the possibility of any member of the family having experienced sexual abuse. Material in the case, such as Rena living alone with her grandfather, her premature emancipation coupled with running-away behavior, and Michael's peer vulnerability and bizarre behavior all point to the possibility of previous child sexual abuse for these siblings. In addition, a pain evaluation for the mother may well be in order.

Thus, in the assessment phase, the feminist clinician examines all these issues—but in particular how gender mediates the pressures, wishes, and relationships that culminate in the evolution of the clients' perception of problems and their solutions.

TREATMENT OF CHOICE

Feminist therapy is exceedingly applicable to this family for a number of reasons. Much needed is attention to social context, particularly the way in which environmental stresses press on gender role enactment and discrimination. Such an evaluation goes hand in hand with recognizing differences in male and female experiences. To date, nowhere in the history of their treatment has anyone engaged this family in an examination of these sociocontextual and gender-based issues. To ignore or minimize them in either the assessment or treatment phase would be a great disservice to this family. Similar issues relate to assessments of normality and deviance. Throughout the case, each member reveals feelings of difference and even deviance. Although this family has been seen by a number of service providers for disorders in each member, issues surrounding the conception of normality and deviance and its impact on family and self-identities have remained unaddressed. These conceptions may directly relate to the narratives so poignantly drawn in the case material and to the enactment of the power dynamics in the family. Deconstruction, with its emphasis on taking apart conceptual barriers to understanding, may be extremely helpful, given the family's emphasis on problem-saturated narratives. One method with high probability of success involves helping members to examine their subjugated voices, explore more potentiating scenarios, and externalize problems. Hence, in exploring theoretical treatment choices, both the clinician and the family are pressed to go beyond reductionistic models that perpetuate identities embedded in deviance and pathology. Because of this tenacious tendency evident in the history of both the family and their professional helping community, feminist therapy is quite applicable.

THE THERAPEUTIC PROCESS

Modalities

The choice of therapeutic method in feminist clinical practice may vary considerably depending on the theoretical orientation of the clinician. However, methods used should flow directly from the assessment and follow the precepts of feminist theory. In the Shore case, the assessment reveals that a number of modalities may be helpful in stemming the multiple problems evident in the family and furthering the family in self-growth. The clinician should be sensitive to not overwhelming the family with interventions, because this process may have the effect of further fostering a sense of disorder and pathology within the family. Although the sequencing of the modalities throughout the treatment process is flexible, the clinician may very well want to see the family as a whole in the beginning, in order to establish relationships with all members and to gain insight into the operation and dynamics of the family system. Family-oriented practice may uniquely address the ingrained patterns of relating that culminate in a family self-identity embedded in pathology. The therapist may then proceed to negotiate with family members in determining what other modalities they may find helpful. For example, individually oriented feminist therapy would likely help both the mother and daughter, who appear to be good candidates for examining the many inhibiting narratives that impede a healthy sense of self. At some point, mother and daughter may be seen conjointly to discuss women's issues in this family. In addition, therapeutic support groups would further the potentials of a number of family members during the course of treatment. For instance, Michael may make good use of a therapeutic peer group intervention for male adolescents in order to foster better peer-group interactions and exposure to male role models. Likewise, Charley may benefit from a social skills support group for men—hopefully, one that is connected to his rehabilitation program. Often such groups help people to cope with self-esteem issues as they relate to the experience of having a mental disorder such as bipolar depression. Both of the women in the family could make use of age-appropriate feminist-oriented support groups for women. Nancy is socially isolated from other women and could benefit from the support for coping with depression, anxiety, an eating disorder, and low self-esteem. Similarly, Rena might benefit from talking with other young women who are facing the challenges of adulthood or a group of adult adoptees who are engaging in the search process. Groups are excellent sources of information on how others see clients as opposed to how they see themselves. As a result, some of the destructive narratives carried by members of this family might be reworked in group.

In addition, when appropriate, referrals may be indicated for adjunct services such as pain evaluation for the mother and medication evaluations for mother, daughter, and son, as previously mentioned. At some point in the treatment process, the clinician should have information to rule out a neurological or other psychiatric disorder in Michael. Negotiating this referral with the parents and son may be a sensitive process because of the multiple difficulties the son has experienced with school systems and his history of being tested for learning disorders. However, having such information may be greatly beneficial for everyone, even if the process involves more contact with professional service providers. During the treatment process, the therapist should examine the family's interaction with its community, as social connections with supportive institutions have been well-documented (Hartman & Laird, 1983; Land, 1995). Thus, over time, the feminist clinical social worker composes, with the family, a comprehensive and overarching plan that addresses the particular concerns of each family member and his or her ecological milieu.

Therapeutic Relationship and the Partnering Stance

The clinician's first goal is to attend to the formulation and maintenance of a therapeutic alliance and subsequent relationship with the clients. Attention to the therapeutic relationship can not be overly emphasized in feminist clinical therapy because the relationship is at the crux of the therapeutic process. If the therapeutic relationship violates the precepts of self-determination and egalitarianism, the process can no longer be deemed feminist or therapeutic in nature. As with other practical theories, the therapist has specific skills, educational credentials, and experiences that are unique to assisting in the helping process, and with this background goes the responsibility to assist the client in achieving desired goals. In feminist theory, the clinician is considered a partner or guide in this process. Importantly, in no instance should the therapeutic relationship replicate the inequity experienced by clients in the hierarchy of the social context in which they live. This possibility should be checked in the therapeutic dialogue on an ongoing basis. Consequently, less emphasis is placed on essentialism and universal theory as applied to the therapeutic relationship, while more attention is paid to the local truths and the unique subjective experience of client and clinician (Meinert, Pardeck, & Sullivan, 1994).

Within this stance, feminist theory is in synchrony with a number of therapeutic traditions in their discussions of the therapeutic relationship. For example, Rogers's (1986a, 1986b) concepts of genuineness, congruence, and the two-person relational approach, and Carkuff's (1986) elaboration of the therapeutic core fit well with the co-creative, partnering stance within feminist theory. Likewise, scholars of self psychology, such as Stolorow, Atwood, and Branschaft (1992), speak of unique organizing principles by which people react day-to-day. Self psychologists also speak of *intersubjectivity*—that is, the necessity for clinicians to reflect on the involvement of their own subjective experience in therapeutic interaction. Similarly, the relational school within psychoanalysis is addressed by Mitchell (1988; Aron, 1996) and Stern (1996), who emphasize the innate nature of the two-person system in therapy and the mutuality of the therapeutic process. These traditions all address mutuality in therapeutic relationships as a co-creative process (Kahn, 1996). As the client experiences the relationship, so does the therapist. Thus, importance is placed on how the relationship is experienced by client and therapist in a partnership and how this partnership generates progress and meets goals that are codefined by client and clinician.

Treatment Methods

Stemming directly from feminist theory, feminist-oriented methods of psychotherapy seek to engage clients in a reflection of those forces that impede growth. The treatment stance embraces feminist psychotherapy concepts that are introduced in the assessment phase. These methods are wide ranging and may vary considerably; a few that are in synchrony with feminist clinical practice are listed below. A review of the assessment reveals a number of areas that may be experienced as being psychologically damaging to the Shore family and therefore may require their attention.

Validating the social context

Here the clinician might explore with the family members how their social context supports their problematic situations. For example, unemployment for both parents is one factor that may impact a number of issues: the grind of day-to-day poverty, lack of access to opportunity and benefits for the family, lack of contact with a peer group, and diminished sense of efficacy within the self. The case suggests that both parents are experiencing constriction in gender roles associated with employment. Thus the clinician might see the couple alone to determine if and how these scenarios are operating. Is the couple burdened by gender-role stereotyping? How does each one see himself or herself as architects of the family? Unemployment for men in U.S. society can be especially devastating, given socialized gender-role expectations. If this is the case, Charley's involvement in a rehabilitation program can be framed as his work and contribution to the family. Similarly, Nancy's care-giving and nursing of family members is one type of work that should be revalued and validated, as should the stress it engenders. In addition, the therapist can work with the family to obtain their views about the multiple crises and the degree to which these crises have led to an entrenched identity of pathology. Because of the chronic nature of crises and their tendencies to proliferate (Pearlin, 1997), the clinician may involve the family in some psychoeducation about stress reduction and reframing of crises. Moreover, the clinician might help each partner look for positive functioning in the self and in his or her spouse. Subsequently, over time, the couple may be helped to look to each other for support in family difficulties rather than be stuck in prescribed roles. Such work relates to other issues in treatment such as conceptions of normality and deviance, the examination of narratives, and working with the power dynamics in the family. Eventually, it is hoped, the parents could realize some of their life plans and respond less as the recipients of environmentally oriented stress and more as the framers of their future.

Conceptions of normality and deviance

As discussed in the assessment, identities of deviance in the self and in the view of one's family members maintain problem-saturated narratives and limit potential. These conceptions may be operating on multiple levels in this family—at the individual level (in terms of self-identities), on the couple level (in terms of how the spouses see each other and how these views relate to expectations of self and other), and on the family level (pertaining to how the parents view their children and vice versa). Treatment would focus on each of these systems in a reflective process regarding how these conceptions operate and their effect on well-being. For example, if Charley sees himself as hopelessly ineffectual, others (such as Nancy) will selectively tune in to this identity and not acknowledge other possibilities. If Rena sees herself as a rejected child and as a failure, her parents and others may habitually screen out all other behavior in order to fit this identity. To help members of this family drop their toxic identities, individual, couple, and family work is in order. Here the clinician could help the family members as a unit to notice and support their definitions of self in their loved ones.

For example, the case states that Nancy is depressed and paralyzed with anxiety, but she is able to competently manage a complex set of medical regimens when Michael suffers from an asthmatic attack. In fact, she enjoys taking control and is good at managing the family's precarious budget. Still, such behavior is relatively unsupported by others. Furthermore, family care-giving and nursing responsibilities are not the principal defining identities that Nancy holds of herself. Similarly, the family is more likely to see Michael as born unlucky rather than as a somewhat unusual child who is particularly good at conversing about world events, politics, and business. For this part of his character, he could be much supported and rewarded. Individual work may involve the exploration of narratives as they relate to the evolution of self-identities and the deconstruction of limiting forces as discussed below.

Deconstruction and the narrative approach

Following the assessment of narratives in the family, the feminist clinician would follow up on exploring and empowering those subjugated voices in the Shore family. For example, Nancy sees her failure to maintain a nursing career, but—paradoxically—she is already nursing. This potential could be harnessed in a variety of ways outside the home, if she desires it. Many nursing careers, such as visiting nurses associations and outpatient-care nursing, demand less strenuous work. Thus the therapist would listen for glimmers of a will toward empowerment and actualization and would foster those voices within Nancy. Psychodynamic feminist therapists would engage the family members in a discussion to explore the ways in which historical and current forces in their lives have contributed to their current narratives. For instance, Nancy may have internalized a rejecting self-object due to her mother's competitive and rejecting demeanor. Many of her narratives reflect this sense of inadequacy; other more subjugated ones point to more potentiating scenarios. Similarly, Rena's feelings that she forces abandonment and failure on herself might be tied to unre-solved issues pertaining to her adoption history. Quiet but emerging voices reveal the quest for healthy identity formation. Cognitive–behavioral feminist therapists might concentrate on life schemas that support inhibiting narratives, on Nancy's tendency to catastrophize, on dichotomous think-ing and automatic thoughts that perpetuate problem-saturated narratives, and ultimately on examining the evidence that opposes negative outcomes. Hence, the use of narratives can be quite helpful and can be integrated with other theoretical traditions.

Recognizing differences in male and female experiences

Drawing from the assessment phase, the feminist clinician would seek to help clients answer those questions that pertain to male and female dif-ferences. A central tenet in the treatment phase is to validate rather than evade those defined differences in experiences that relate to gender dif-ference. Thus, the clinician would engage Nancy and Rena in exploring issues of worth and assist them in building healthy identities of wom-anness. Women in this family are often depressed and insecure in their self-concept. The clinician may wish to invite mother and daughter, both separately and together, to address this issue. Similarly, both Charley and Michael might be engaged in discussion that addresses those questions identified in the assessment phase. Male gender identities are less defined and less actualized in this family. The feminist clinician might want to see Michael and Charley together to discuss issues of maleness and its mean-ing or potential meaning in this family. These issues also directly relate to the construct of challenging reductionistic models. Are gender expec-tations restricting and limiting? In what ways? What can be done to re-lease family members from these reductionistic positions? Must Charley be the breadwinner? Must Michael only succeed in certain societally de-fined male-oriented behavioral expectations? A feminist clinician values inquiry into these issues.

Power dynamics

Once the dynamics of power have been identified in the family, the clin-ician may wish to see the family conjointly in order to address less inhibit-ing methods of meeting needs. The timing of such family work is a sen-sitive issue. It may be that the family will not feel safe enough to address these issues until some individual work or couple work is well under way. In addition, a solid therapeutic relationship with all family members is essential prior to attempting this discussion. Within feminist psychother-apy, therapists changing unhealthy power distributions and dynamics in the family should again make use of the partnering stance as opposed to attempting to evoke change that members are not ready to enact. Thus, although some family therapists may use confronting or paradoxical techniques, the feminist stance aims to enact such skills as validation and demystification (Goodrich, Rampage, Ellman, & Halstead, 1988).

For example, the exploration of family cultural metaphors, culled from story, myth, narrative, and rituals, gets closer to the family's lived experience (White & Epston, 1990). Exploring these metaphors may assist the family in grappling with power dynamics and their effects. Whereas some schools of family treatment have been criticized for manipulative and distancing intervention, feminist family practice makes use of less distancing and less hierarchical models (Laird, 1994). Although some traditions make use of deficit-describing metaphors, feminist perspectives tend to rely on ethnographic traditions that view the workings of the family—as well as inner psychological experiences—as being negotiated in the social and cultural world of meanings (Anderson & Goolishian, 1992). Therapy is conceptualized as a dialogic process in which new meanings and understandings are mutually evolved yet always restricted by culturally negotiated rules of meaning. Here, the family practitioner searches for the family's system of meaning and belief, its dominant symbols and metaphors, its spiritualities and identities, and its way of organizing itself in relation to its societal context (Laird, 1992). The process is not seen as linear. Rather, it is a reflexive one in which narratives, myths, and stories are visited and revisited, and in which all parties, including the practitioner, are changed.

Thus, in working with the Shore family, the feminist practitioner would explore current traditions and methods of needs attainment, as well as Nancy and Charley's family-of-origin traditions pertaining to power allocation and need attainment. For example, how were needs addressed between spouses in the families of origin? How was male and female power allocated in the parental pair? How did the spousal pair include or exclude both Nancy and Charley with regard to power, need, and worth? What was the expectation of meeting needs in the family? Were needs seen as burdensome to self and others? How do these traditions impact on current family functioning pertaining to need, worth, and power allocation? Some case material reveals that needs were inconsistently met for both Nancy and Charley, although both experienced value and nurturance from certain figures in their lives. Neither has a history of a stable parental pair; therefore, few models may exist on how couples successfully negotiate need and power distribution.

Discussion that is centered on the way in which needs are met and how they are addressed in the family may then proceed to a discussion of satisfaction with the current state and alternative methods of getting needs met. For example, do members of the family have the right to overtly ask for attention from one another? How is this experienced by the asker and the giver? Similarly, do members have the right to set limits with one another? How is this experienced by the asker? Is there a sense of judgment involved in asking and getting needs met? Are current patterns fair ones, or are there alternative methods of communicating need or discontent? In other words, the family has the right to create its own ritual and narrative with regard to need, value, worth, power, and gender.

The feminist approach to the treatment phase flows from the assessment phase and is seen as a recursive and reflexive process. This orientation in no way impedes the use of multiple modalities or multiple theoretical stances. The uniqueness of feminist practice during this phase points to the partnering stance and the central contract of the making of meaning with clients seeking change. Using an ethnographic lens, practitioners must come from an *emic* rather than *etic* stance.[2] Hence, they must become, in some way, a part of the family tradition enough to hear those voices that have been silent and to invite a hearing of them. The feminist tradition makes use of the full range of available complementary and collateral services in its pursuit of comprehensive social work practice.

LIMITATIONS OF THE MODEL

Clearly, feminist practice has many strengths and contributes significantly to the body of knowledge of practice theory. In fact, the embracing of some of its principles is long overdue in the psychotherapeutic professions. Still, some have challenged feminist practice with regard to a number of principles: the primacy of the gender construct, the cardinal principle of the use of the subjective stance, the emphasis on the importance of the making of meaning and deconstruction in clinical practice.

For some clients, gender issues may not take primacy, so should clinicians look for gender issues when clients do not? Feminists reject the stance of value-free psychotherapy. Many treatment traditions ignore issues pertaining to gender. Feminists feel that gender questions are often at the heart of how life is experienced and how identities are formed. Thus, although treatment directions are not forced, clients may not think to examine or raise gender issues, especially because such issues are often silenced by power structures.

With regard to the objective–subjective stance, others have stated that feminists place too much emphasis on subjectivity rather than on examining objectively those problems that clients face. For example, mental disorders such as schizophrenia and bipolar depression have well-documented histories and treatment programs; thus, they are not in totality a subjective

---

[2]The *emic* tradition examines behavior from within the cultural systems and is usually based on data from only one culture. Conversely, the *etic* approach studies behavior from outside the cultural system, examines data from many cultures, and extracts common elements across cultures.

experience. This criticism raises two questions: One involves the subjective stance; the other involves differential ways of knowing and knowledge building. To these criticisms, feminist theorists remark that it is not the validity of some disorders that is in contention; rather, it is the effects of living as a marginalized person that must be examined. The objective stance (i.e., well-documented and effective treatment programs) has been embraced by many feminists. Still, the subjective stance has often been forgotten in other psychotherapeutic theories. Listening to the subjective experience of the client can only help to foster growth and self-respect and ultimately enhance the well-being of those who are enduring difficulties. A coupling of objective with subjective stances is often in order.

With regard to knowledge-building in the occidental tradition, much of our history has been in quest of ultimate truths. Such pursuit of universal knowledge has, at times, led to gross errors in conclusions (see, e.g., Gould, 1981; Tavris, 1992). Although feminists as a group are not uniform in their methods of pursuing scientific inquiry, they are, however, unified in their belief that certain knowledge has not only not been pursued, it has been suppressed. Hence, it is not so much the method of knowing (objectivity or subjectivity) that is important as long as the method fits the parameters of the problem under scrutiny.

RESEARCH

There is a trend among feminist scholars to rely on and include both quantitative and qualitative methods, both process and product (i.e., outcome) in knowledge building. Moreover, many feminist scholars challenge the traditional assumption that science is objective. Thus, they see the need for including research agendas and seek to critically analyze and uncover androcentric bias both in lines of inquiry and in methodologies (Lott, 1985). Feminist clinical practice has been the impetus for developing lines of scholarship that seek to learn how culture constructs gender experience and scholarship on the formidable exigencies that face women in this society. These include the sequelae of personal violence and sexual assault, depression, eating disorders, and anxiety reactions and specific health issues related to women. In many therapeutic approaches, knowledge flows from quantitative empirical findings into clinical practice. By contrast, the feminist approach sees the value in a variety of scholarly traditions. A key principle of feminist clinical social work is noting and embracing the knowledge-building interplay between feminist scholarship and feminist clinical practice. To date, noteworthy work has been completed in a number of areas related to women, including research on female development and the myth of psychosexual stages (Jordan, Surrey, & Kaplan, 1983), differences between male and female mental health and health issues such as the course and treatment of substance abuse (Nadelson & Zimmerman, 1993), differences in responses to psychotropic and other drugs (Austrian, 1995), the particular experiences of women's reproductive health (Sayette & Mayne, 1990), and the development of interventions centered on women's family relationships with one another (Eichenbaum & Orbach, 1983; Rave & Larsen, 1990). Such lines of inquiry are much valued and supported by feminist theorists and impact the provision of clinical service in significant ways.

SUMMARY

Because of the field's increasing recognition of the diversity of ethnic and cultural groups in society, social work clinical practice must pursue principles of recognizing, understanding, valuing, and using nondiscriminatory practice styles. Inclusion ideology has always been a tenet of feminist practice. More recently, attention to gender-relational development across cultural and class groups has emerged in the clinical literature (Boyd, 1990; Bradshaw, 1990; Gaw, 1993; Ho, 1990; Palladino & Stephenson, 1990; Sears, 1990). Still, to date, the generation of most feminist theory, therapy, and research remains largely dominated by middle-class White women, as several feminist scholars have noted (Brown, 1990; Brown & Root, 1990; Kanuha, 1990). Moreover, just as views of human behavior have been influenced by patriarchy and occidental traditions, views of women's development have been influenced by the White female experience. This history suggests that therapists must continue to assess dominant norms and incorporate nondominant ones as a means of enlarging our comprehension of the experiences of women from nondominant groups.

If people are imbued with the language of the culture, as Daly (1983) and Johnson (1987) suggest, it will be difficult to envision a feminist perspective that is not an amalgam of influences of other theories and other cultures. This goal suggests that social workers must draw on multiple methods of knowledge building, as some have begun to do (Ballou, 1990; Belenky, Clinchy, Goldberger, & Tarule, 1986).

Historically, feminist treatment has largely been conceived of as a paradigm applicable to women only. But because feminists value an inclusive stance and many elucidate the needs of diverse populations, feminist clinical theory is ultimately highly applicable to the interactive concerns and realities of men and their gender issues. Hence feminist practice must continue to expand its definition to include gender-sensitive practice with men and women, boys and girls, as they negotiate issues pertaining to gender and difference throughout the life cycle. Work aimed toward understanding the intersubjective experience between genders is a crucial matter, given the problems that confront this society.

Toward achieving this goal, feminist social workers will need to become involved in both policy and clinical practice agendas within our field. Both of these traditions continue to develop and interact within the sociopolitical context, and both impact on client needs (Hagen & Davis, 1992; McCannell, 1986). Ultimately, feminist social work practice is embedded in the person-in-situation perspective. Should it lose this perspective, not only will women and men fail to receive the service they deserve, but the field of social work will not realize its ultimate goal of creating and maintaining a just society.

REFERENCES

American Psychiatric Association. (1994). *Diagnostic and statistical manual of mental disorders* (4th ed.). Washington, DC: Author.

Andersen, T. (1991). The reflecting team: Dialogue and metadialogue in clinical work. *Family Process, 26,* 415–428.

Anderson, H., & Goolishian, H. (1992). The client is the expert: A not-knowing approach to therapy. In S. McNamee & K. J. Gergen (Eds.), *Therapy as social construction* (pp. 25–39). Newbury Park, CA: Sage.

Aneshensel, C. S., Pearlin, L. I., Mullan, J. T., Zarit, S. H., & Whitlatch, C. J. (1995). *Profiles in caregiving: The unexpected career.* San Diego, CA: Academic.

Aron, L. (1996). *A meeting of minds: Mutuality in psychoanalysis.* Hillsdale, NJ: Analytic.

Ault-Riche, M. (Ed.). (1986). *Women and family therapy.* Rockville, MD: Aspen Systems.

Austrian, S. (1995). *Mental disorders, medication and clinical social work.* New York: Columbia University Press.

Bakhtin, M. M. (1981). *The dialogic imagination: Four essays by M. M. Bakhtin* (M. Holquist, Ed. & C. Emerson & M. Holquist, Trans.). Baltimore: Johns Hopkins University Press.

Ballou, M. (1990). Approaching a feminist-principled paradigm in the construction of a personality theory. In L. S. Brown & M. P. P. Root (Eds.), *Diversity and complexity in feminist therapy* (pp. 23–40). New York: Haworth.

Belenky, M., Clinchy, B., Goldberger, N., & Tarule, J. (1986). *Women's ways of knowing.* New York: Basic Books.

Boyd, J. A. (1990). Ethnic and cultural diversity: Keys to power. In L. S. Brown & M. P. P. Root (Eds.), *Diversity and complexity in feminist therapy* (pp. 151–168). New York: Haworth.

Bradshaw, C. K. (1990). A Japanese view of dependency: What can amae psychology contribute to feminist therapy? In L. S. Brown & M. P. P. Root (Eds.), *Diversity and complexity in feminist therapy* (pp. 67–87). New York: Haworth.

Braverman, L. (Ed.). (1988). *Women, feminism and family therapy.* New York: Haworth.

Brodsky, A. (1980). A decade of feminist influence on psychotherapy. *Psychology of Women Quarterly, 4,* 331–344.

Brown, L. S. (1990). The meaning of a multicultural perspective for theory building in feminist therapy. In L. S. Brown & M. P. P. Root (Eds.), *Diversity and complexity in feminist therapy* (pp. 1–22). New York: Haworth.

Brown, L. S., & Brodsky, A. M. (1992). The future of feminist therapy. *Psychotherapy, 29,* 51–57.

Brown, L. S., & Liss-Levinson, N. (1981). Feminist therapy. In R. Corsini (Ed.), *Handbook of innovative psychotherapies* (pp. 299–314). New York: John Wiley & Sons.

Brown, L. S., & Root, M. P. P. (1990). Introduction. In L. S. Brown & M. P. P. Root (Eds.), *Diversity and complexity in feminist therapy* (pp. i–xii). New York: Haworth.

Carkhuff, R. (1986). Learning in the age of information. *Education, 106*(3), 264–267.

Chodorow, N. (1978). *The reproduction of mothering.* Berkeley: University of California Press.

Cowley, A. (1993). Transpersonal social work: A theory for the '90s. *Social Work, 38*(5), 527–534.

Daly, M. (1983). *Pure lust: Elemental feminist philosophy.* Boston: Beacon.

Day, L. (1992). Counseling for women: The contribution of feminist theory and practice. *Counseling Psychology Quarterly, 5,* 373–384.

Derrida, J. (1976). *Of grammatology* (G. C. Spivak, Trans.). Baltimore: Johns Hopkins University Press.

Eichenbaum, L., & Orbach, S. (1983). *Understanding women: A basic feminist psychoanalytic view.* New York: Basic Books.

Fisher, J. (1971). Jane Addams. In R. Morris (Ed.), *Encyclopedia of social work* (16th ed., pp. 1217–1226). New York: National Association of Social Workers.

Flexner, A. (1915). Is social work a profession? *Proceedings of the National Conference on Charities and Corrections,* 576–590.

Foucault, M. (1980). *Power/knowledge: Selected interviews and other writings.* New York: Pantheon.

Freedberg, A. (1993). The feminine ethic of care and the professionalization of social work. *Social Work, 38,* 535–541.

Gaw, A. (Ed.). *Culture, ethnicity and mentalillness.* Washington, DC: American Psychiatric Press.

Gergen, K. J., & Kaye, J. (1992). Beyond narrative in the negotiation of therapeutic meaning. In S. McNamee & K. J. Gergen (Eds.), *Therapy as social construction* (pp. 166–185). Newbury Park, CA: Sage.

Gilligan, C. (1982). *In a different voice.* Cambridge, MA: Harvard University Press.

Goldner, V. (1991). Feminism and systemic practice: Two critical traditions in transition. *Journal of Strategic and Systems Therapy, 10,* 118–126.

Goodrich, T. J., Rampage, C., Ellman, B., & Halstead, K. (1988). *Feminist family therapy: A casebook.* New York: Norton.

Gould, S. (1981). *The mismeasure of man.* New York: Norton.

Guarnaccia, P. J., De La Cancela, V., & Carillo, E. (1989). The multiple meanings of ataques de nervios in the Latin community. *Medical Anthropology, 11,* 47–62.

Hagen, I., & Davis, L. (1992). Working with women: Building a policy and practice agenda. *Social Work, 32,* 495–502.

Hamilton, G. (1951). *Theory and practice of social casework.* New York: Columbia University Press.

Hare-Mustin, R., & Maracek, J. (1988). The meaning of difference: Gender theory, post modernism and psychology. *American Psychologist, 43,* 455–464.

Hartman, A., & Laird, J. (1983). *Family centered social work practice.* New York: The Free Press.

Hepworth, D. H., & Larson, J. A. (1996). *Direct social work practice: Theory and skills* (3rd ed.). Belmont, CA: Wadsworth.

Ho, C. K. (1990). An analysis of domestic violence in Asian-American communities: A multicultural approach to counseling. In L. S. Brown & M. P. P. Root (Eds.), *Diversity and complexity in feminist therapy* (pp. 129–150). New York: Haworth.

Hollis, F. (1970). The psychosocial approach to the practice of casework. In R. Roberts & R. Nee (Eds.), *Theories of social casework* (pp. 33–75). Chicago: University of Chicago Press.

Hollis, F. (1971). Social casework: The psychosocial approach. In R. Morris (Ed.), *Encyclopedia of social work* (16th ed., pp. 1217–1226). New York: National Association of Social Workers.

Johnson, S. (1987). *Going out of our minds: The metaphysics of liberation.* Freedom, CA: Crossing Press.

Jordan, J., & Surrey, J. L. (1986). Self in relation: a theory of women's development. In T. Bernay & D. W. Cantor (Eds.), *The psychology of today's woman: The psychoanalytic vision* (pp. 81–104). Cambridge, MA: Harvard University Press.

Jordan, J., Surrey, J. L., & Kaplan, A. G. (1983). *Women and empathy.* Wellesley, MA: Stone Center for Working Papers Series.

Kahn, E. (1996). The intersubjective perspective and the client-centered approach: Are they one at their core? *Psychotherapy, 33*(1), 30–42.

Kanuha, V. (1990). The need for an integrated analysis of oppression in feminist therapy ethics. In H. Lerman & N. Porter (Eds.), *Feminist ethics and psychotherapy* (pp. 24–36). New York: Springer.

Kohut, H. (1977). *The restoration of the self.* New York: International Universities Press.

Koss-Chioino, J. D., & Canive, J. M. (1993). The interaction of popular and clinical diagnostic labeling: The case of embrujado. *Medical Anthropology, 15,* 171–188.

Laird, J. (1992). Women's secrets—Women's silences. In E. Imber-Black (Ed.), *Secrets in families and in family therapy* (pp. 243–267). New York: Norton.

Laird, J. (1994). Lesbian families: A cultural perspective. In M. P. Mirkin (Ed.), *Women in context: Toward a feminist reconstruction of psychotherapy* (pp. 118–148). New York: Guilford.

Laird, J. (1995). Family-centered practice: Feminist, constructionist and cultural perspectives. In N. Van Den Bergh (Ed.), *Feminist practice in the twenty-first century* (pp. 20–40). Washington, DC: N.A.S.W. Press.

Land, H. (1995). Feminist clinical social work in the twenty-first century. In N. Van Den Berg (Ed.), *Feminist practice in the twenty-first century* (pp. 3–19). Washington, DC: N.A.S.W. Press.

Land, H. (Ed.). (1992). *AIDS: A complete guide to psychosocial intervention.* Milwaukee, WI: Families International Press.

Levine, O., Britton, P., James, T., Jackson, A., Hobfoll, S., & Lavin, J. (1993). The empowerment of women: A key for HIV prevention. *Journal of Community Psychology, 21,* 320–334.

Lott, B. (1985), The potential enrichment of social/personality psychology through feminist research and vice versa. *American Psychologist, 40,* 155–164.

Luepnitz, D. A. (1988). *The family interpreted: Feminist theory in clinical practice.* New York: Basic Books.

Mancoske, R. J., Standifer, D., & Cauley, C. (1994). The effectiveness of brief counseling services for battered women. *Research on Social Work Practice, 4*(1), 53–63.

Martinez, C. (1993). Psychiatric care of Mexican-Americans. In A. Gaw (Ed.), *Culture, ethnicity and mental illness* (pp. 431–466). Washington, DC: American Psychiatric Press.

McCannell, K. (1986). Family politics, family policy and family practice: A feminist perspective. Women and mental health [Special issue]. *Canadian Journal of Community Mental Health, 5,* 61–71.

McGoldrick, M., Giordano, J., & Pearce, J. (1996). *Ethnicity and family therapy II.* New York: Guilford.

Meinert, R. G., Pardeck, J. T., & Sullivan, W. P. (1994). *Issues in social work: A critical analysis.* Westport, CT: Auburn House.

Meyer, C. (1983). *Clinical social work in the eco-systems perspective.* New York: Columbia University Press.

Mitchell, S. A. (1988). *Relational concepts in psychoanalysis: An integration.* Cambridge, MA: Harvard University Press.

Morrison Dore, M. (1994). Feminist pedagogy and the teaching of social work practice. *Journal of Social Work Education, 30,* 97–106.

Nadelson, C. C., & Zimmerman, V. (1993). Culture and psychiatric care of women. In A. Gaw (Ed.), *Culture, ethnicity and mental illness* (pp. 501–516). Washington, DC: American Psychiatric Press.

Neimeyer, R. (1993). An appraisal of constructivist psychotherapies. *Journal of Consulting and Clinical Psychology, 61,* 221–234.

Nietzsche, F. (1964). In W. Kaufmann (Ed.), *Basic writings of Nietzsche.* New York: Modern Library.

Palladino, D., & Stephenson, Y. (1990). Perceptions of the sexual self: Their impact on relationships between lesbian and heterosexual women. In L. S. Brown & M. P. P. Root (Eds.), *Diversity and complexity in feminist therapy* (pp. 231–254). New York: Haworth.

Pearlin, L., Aneshensel, C., & LeBlanc, A. (1997). The forms and mechanisms of stress proliferation: The case of AIDS caregivers. *Journal of Health and Social Behavior, 38,* 223–336.

Perlman, H. (1971). Social casework: The problem solving approach. In R. Morris (Ed.), *Encyclopedia of social work* (16th ed., pp. 1206–1216). New York: National Association of Social Workers.

Rave, F. J., & Larsen, C. (1990). Development of the code: The feminist process. In H. Lerman & N. Porter (Eds.), *Feminist ethics and psychotherapy* (pp. 14–23). New York: Springer.

Richmond, M. (1917). *Social diagnosis.* New York: Russell Sage Foundation.

Robbins, J. (1983). A legacy of weakness: Unresolved issues in the mother-daughter arrangement in a patriarchal culture. *Women Changing Therapy, 2,* 41–50.

Rogers, C. (1986a). Client-centered therapy. In U. L. Kutash & A. Wolf (Eds.), *Psychotherapist's casebook* (pp. 197–208). San Francisco: Jossey-Bass.

Rogers, C. (1986b). Rogers, Kohut and Erikson: A personal perspective on some similarities and differences. *Person-Centered Review, 1,* 125–140.

Ruderman, E. (1986). Gender-related themes of women psychotherapists in their treatment of women patients: The creative and reparative use of countertransference as a mutual growth experience. *Clinical Social Work Journal, 14,* 103–126.

Sayette, M. A., & Mayne, T. J. (1990). Survey of current clinical and research trends in clinical psychology. *American Psychologist, 45,* 1263–1266.

Sears, V. L. (1990). On being an only one. In H. Lerman & N. Porter (Eds.), *Feminist ethics and psychotherapy* (pp. 102–105). New York: Springer.

Solomon, B. (1976). *Black empowerment.* New York: Columbia University Press.

Stern, D. (1996). *Unformulated experience.* Hillsdale, NJ: Analytic.

Stolorow, R. D., Atwood, G. E., & Brandschaft, B. (1992). *Contexts of being: The intersubjective foundations of psychological life.* Hillsdale, NJ: Analytic.

Suarez, M., Rafaelli, M., & O'Leary, A. (1996). Use of folk-healing practices by HIV-infected Hispanics living in the United States. *AIDS CARE, 6,* 683–690.

Tavris, C. (1992). *The mismeasure of woman.* New York: Touchstone.

Walters, M., Carter, B., Papp, P., & Silverstein, O. (1988). *The invisible web: Gender patterns in family relationships.* New York: Guilford.

White, M. (1993). Deconstruction and therapy. In S. Gilligan & R. Price (Eds.) *Therapeutic conversations* (pp. 22–61). New York: Norton.

White, M., & Epston, D. (1990). *Narrative means to therapeutic ends.* New York: Norton.

Worell, J., & Remer, P. (1992). *Feminist perspectives in therapy: An empowerment model for women.* New York: John Wiley & Sons.

10

Meaning-Making as a Metaframework for Clinical Practice

Hugh Rosen, D.S.W.

It would be possible to describe everything scientifically, but it would make no sense. It would be a description without meaning—as if you described a Beethoven symphony as a variation of wave pressure.—Albert Einstein (Calaprice, 1966, p. 224)

INTRODUCTION

In my view, no therapeutic model of practice has cornered the market on absolute truth, that much admired virtue so desperately sought after, yet rarely attained—some would say never attained. At the beginning of the history of psychotherapy, classical psychoanalysis reigned supreme. With the passage of time, not only has psychoanalysis splintered into many variations, but virtually hundreds of other models have emerged and been put into practice. Many of their adherents have embraced their chosen way with religious fervor, even going to such extreme lengths as shunning those members of their therapeutic community who attempted major modifications of the model or rejected it in favor of an alternate approach to helping. Still others possess the wisdom to recognize that their adopted clinical theory and practice constitute only one school out of a wide-ranging spectrum of schools of therapy. While respecting pluralism in the world of psychotherapy, they have exercised their right to make a commitment to the one school that holds the most meaning for them. This provides them with a single clear and coherent map to guide them in their efforts to help others.

Yet, to date, there exists no compelling evidence that one therapeutic model is consistently superior in treating all psychosocial disorders (Lambert, 1992). In fact, one frequently advanced explanation for why a variety of therapeutic models have demonstrated equal efficacy in treating psychological and interpersonal problems is that certain common variables cut across all schools and account for the change in clients rather than the specific or unique techniques of any one school (Frank & Frank, 1991). Be that as it may, all therapeutic models have their limitations, as do individual practitioners. Many practicing clinicians who started out as advocates of a single school eventually turn to other approaches to borrow ideas, methods, and techniques for use in their current practice. Thus, over the years, a new sphere of activity focusing on both eclecticism and integration has evolved (Gold, 1996; Norcross, 1986; Rosen, 1988; Strickler & Gold, 1993). *Eclecticism* essentially means borrowing what appear to be the best procedures from a wide range of models and putting them into practice on behalf of one's clients. What constitutes the "best procedures" is a matter of clinical judgment in each case, including, to some extent, the data garnered from empirical research. Some would regard the procedures based on empirical data as the ideal, but in actual practice it is doubtful that this is strictly adhered to. Integration involves taking two or more models and finding compatible conceptual linkages that when successfully intertwined produce a synergistic model of greater therapeutic power than is provided by any one of the models in operation alone. However, therapeutic models with opposing epistemological premises do not lend themselves readily, if at all, to this endeavor. Not surprisingly, at least not to the constructivist mind, the eclectic and integrationist movements have led not to one unifying approach that all can agree on, but rather to a proliferation of second-order models of therapy in their own right. Hence both beginning and experienced therapists are now faced with an even more bewildering array of choices than they previously had.

Before going any further, I would like to assert that all therapeutic models, whether *first-order* (single models) or *second-order* (eclectic and integrationist models), offer us ways of talking about and construing psychotherapy, but they never have and never will provide us with absolute, immutable truths. What is of utmost significance is the meaning they hold for therapists and clients—and, ultimately, their instrumental viability for effecting desired change for those persons seeking help (Mahoney, 1991). This is equally true for the discussion to follow on meaning-making as a metaframework for clinical practice. Notice that this signifies a transition into the realm of paradox and contradiction, for even as I speak of the absence of immutable absolutes, I am also asserting what is "true." The world is fraught with these phenomena, and the maturing mind acquires the dialectical ability to deal with them (Basseches, 1984; Pascual-Leone, 1990).

In this chapter, meaning-making is presented as a unifying and superordinate concept that threads its way through all psychotherapies. Thinking in meaning-making terms can serve as a guiding metaphor for all clinicians, regardless of what therapeutic model drives their clinical work and on what level they practice (first-order or second-order). It is more an orientation and a way of looking at their work, as well as a philosophical way of viewing both themselves and their clients, than a source for manufacturing clever techniques. This is not to say, however, that there are no practice implications to a meaning-making orientation. As a caveat, meaning-making does not constitute a single model of practice. It is a monolithic concept, like a multifaceted jewel that radiates out in various directions even though its brilliance stems from the same source. Those directions include such movements as constructivism, social constructionism, narrative theory, postmodernism, and developmental constructivism (Rosen, 1996).

It is important to state at this juncture that because this chapter is more philosophical in tone, given its metatheoretical emphasis, and because it does not offer specifically concrete techniques for application, I do not make direct references to the case of the Shore family.

THE CONCEPT OF THE PERSON AND THE HUMAN EXPERIENCE

This chapter is predicated on the premise that an essential defining characteristic of all persons is that they, above all creatures on Earth, make meaning out of their internal and external experiences—out of the personal events they pass through historically; out of their evolving self and interpersonal relationships; out of their social and physical worlds; out of their spiritual yearnings and development; and out of their memories, their present existence, and their projected futures. In other words, people are not passive recipients of static internal or external stimuli, but they proactively construct and organize meaning from the raw data of their experiences (Mahoney, 1988a; R. A. Neimeyer, 1987). Further, there does not exist only one way of construing experience, for what can be construed in one way can always be construed in alternative ways (Kelly, 1955). It is often the very fact of being locked into only one way of construing a situation, or being embedded in a single set of meanings, that brings clients into the consulting office. With this in mind, psychotherapy can be viewed as a process in which therapists create the conditions and facilitate the process through which their clients can construct new meanings and transform old meanings. It can also lead to a new and transformative understanding of meaning itself (Gergen, 1994). This view differs from Frankl's logotherapy, in which clients are said to experience an existential vacuum that is remedied by discovering meaning in the real world. Dyck (1987) stated, "Frankl is wrong in presuming that meaning has an objective existence. Meaning cannot be considered objective because it is never independently verifiable; meaning is inextricable from the thinking of the person who experiences it" (p. 159). Hence the acquisition of meaning is an invention or creation of the person's own making, and this "made meaning" is not immutable but is subject to historical and developmental reconstruction throughout an individual's life. Furthermore, because individuals are embedded in a social matrix, meanings are also socially constructed in dyadic, familial, communal, and cultural contexts. The role of language is an essential component of socially constructed meaning and is discussed at greater length in another section of this chapter. Because psychotherapy is conducted in a social setting and language is the primary medium of exchange in the process (visual cues and voice tones notwithstanding), psychotherapy may be viewed as a co-construction of meaning between client and therapist. Although clients are of primary importance in such exchanges, this view does not preclude the process of meaning-making occurring for therapists also. Indeed, therapists who are genuinely "alive" and emotionally "connected" in the presence of their clients will inevitably construct new meanings and reconstruct old meanings in the course of their clinical careers.

From a philosophical perspective, the meaning-making orientation has demonstrated considerable interest in the nature of knowing (*epistemology*) and being or reality (*ontology*). Although the two are conceptually distinct, they are operationally linked, for the question of knowing is about what, if anything, people can know about the real world and how they come to know whatever it is that they can know. The question of ontology deals with the very issue of whether the world even exists independently of one's mind and, hence, whether it even makes sense to talk about a real or objective world. The discussion in this chapter will dispense with arcane arguments about whether the world actually exists beyond the realm of the mind and will adopt the common-sense position that it does, indeed, exist without assistance from the mind. With respect to the epistemological question of whether people can ever know anything about the real world as it exists objectively, my position is that people can know some facts about the world, physical and social, but that meaning-making activity is a process involving interpretations and construals of those facts, as well as value-laden constructions that transcend facts. This activity takes place at both conscious and nonconscious levels. Furthermore, much of what is taken for "fact" in one historical era is reinterpreted as fiction in another (e.g., The world is flat). This is no less true ontogenetically during the developmental life span of an individual. It follows that much of what people take for reality is actually a construction or co-construction of human minds. This, coupled with the statement that what has been constructed can be reconstructed, is something that all therapies rely on, even though it may not be explicitly articulated in a therapy's undergirding theory. It should be noted that even though knowledge is a human construction, it does not follow that such knowledge necessarily fails to tell people something about the way the world operates. For instance, inferentially constructed concepts such as gravity, electricity, morality, and the nonconscious, although neither apprehensible to the senses nor materially extant in an objective world, nevertheless have explanatory power and prove to have pragmatic value in interacting with that world. There are numerous books on this subject, and one would do well to consult the works of Kelly (1955), Piaget (Gruber & Vonèche, 1977), and Popper (1979) for diverse but relevant and interrelated views. Personal belief systems that have low explanatory power and prove to have little pragmatic use in helping people navigate through life often bring the holders of such beliefs into social workers' offices for therapeutic services. In the ensuing process, such beliefs and ascribed meanings are identified, explored, challenged, renegotiated, and changed.

HISTORICAL PERSPECTIVE

In this section, I identify the major historical and contemporary figures who, in one way or another, have advocated the use of a meaning-making orientation in the field of psychotherapy. This metatheoretical framework does not have a single originator and has not run a pure course of linear development, which is why this subject must be discussed from a variety of perspectives. The main purpose here is to provide the reader with some of the major reference sources in the various directions in which the meaning-making concept radiates. The exposition of ideas and implications for practice follow in appropriate sections ahead.

The Early Constructivists

Mahoney (1988a) traces the first systematic presentation of constructivist thinking (a key meaning-making approach) to the philosopher of history Giambattista Vico (1725/1948). As Mahoney (1988a) stated, "Vico's contribution to constructive metatheory stems from his recognition that 'knowing' is not a form of disembodied intellectual reflection but, rather, an active and embodied engagement with life's challenges" (p. 16). For Vico, as with all constructivists, the world we come to know is the world we construct within ourselves. Other major philosophers along the path to constructivism are Immanuel Kant and Hans Vahinger. Vahinger holds that thoughts and beliefs tend to be more self-constructed fictions than mental representations of reality, although these fictions may prove to be of great use in adapting to life's circumstances. Believing and behaving as if something were true, even though it may not be, can sometimes have instrumental value (Mahoney, 1988a). Adler adopted the notion that psychological fictions fuel people's personal understanding of the world and guide their behavior in it, but these fictions may not always be adaptive, in which case treatment aims to change maladaptive into adaptive fictions. One way of accomplishing this is for the client to act as if the more functional fiction has already been accepted. Watzlawick (1984), through his edited book *The Invented Reality*, has made a major contribution towards a current understanding of the philosophy and psychology of constructivism.

George Kelly

More directly related to the field of personality theory and psychotherapy has been the innovative work of George Kelly (1955), an American psychologist whose psychology of personal constructs is traced developmentally by R. A. Neimeyer (1985). Kelly's work is vast and complex, but as Neimeyer wrote, "Kelly's most fundamental assumption about the nature of human beings was that they were essentially interpretive, always in the process of attributing meaning to their ongoing experience" (1987, p. 4). These attributed meanings are always subject to revision and alternative constructions or meanings. Kelly had adopted the metaphor of individuals as personal scientists who devise theories about themselves and their world—theories that serve as a basis for anticipating outcomes of their actions and making predictions about their lives in the world. When these anticipations and predictions are not confirmed, the adapting individuals modify their theories, leading to a reconstruction of personal meaning. Although not completely neglectful of social interaction, Kelly's main emphasis was on the individual's construction of meaning. Mascolo (1994) proposes a neo-Kellian social constructivist psychology, stating

> Whereas Kelly's theory implies an active child and a relatively passive world, a social constructivist view implies an active child and an active social world. The child constructs meaning socially by relating to others who help structure and define his or her social and physical world. (p. 96)

Jean Piaget

Throughout his lifetime (1896–1980), Jean Piaget offered a voluminous body of theory and research in the form of his science of genetic epistemology. (In psychological circles, this is more commonly presented as a theory of cognitive development.) His work offers a comprehensive constructivist–developmental approach to the growth of knowledge in the individual, to which he also drew parallels to the growth of knowledge from ancient to modern times in civilization (Piaget & Garcia, 1983/1989). Piaget emphasized the sequential development of universal cognitive structures, leading to the acquisition of necessary—and qualitatively more adequate—knowledge (Smith, 1993). This differs from Kelly's form of constructivism, which emphasized the idiosyncratic and personal construct system of each individual. For Piaget, the individual is a meaning-making organism whose made meanings are delimited by the particular stage of cognitive understanding where he or she is at during any given period of development. For this reason, knowledge or meaning is considered to be a relationship between the knowing subject and the known object. Kohlberg (1981, 1984) focused on extending Piaget's orientation into the domain of moral meaning-making. Gonçalves (Gonçalves & Ivey, 1993), Guidano (1987, 1991), Ivey (1986), Keating (Keating & Rosen, 1991), Kegan (1982, 1994), Rosen, (1985, 1989), and Selman (1980; Selman, Brion-Meisels, & Wilkins, 1996) are other contemporary figures whose work builds on Piaget's and who might be of interest to clinical social workers. Despite Piaget's enormous impact in this area, I say little else about him here, but I refer the reader to my chapter on his constructivist-developmental model in Volume 1 of *Paradigms of Clinical Social Work* (Rosen, 1988).

Social Constructionism

Social constructionism differs from constructivism in its singular emphasis on the social matrix within which reality and meaning are co-constructed. The seminal work in this area is that of Berger and Luckmann (1966), who produced "a treatise in the sociology of knowledge." Their message has flourished more recently through the efforts of Gergen (1985, 1994), McNamee (McNamee & Gergen (1992), and Shotter (1993). Much more is said about this topic in a later section. (See Gergen, 1985, for an in-depth presentation on the background of social constructionism.)

Narrative

A burgeoning area in the field of clinical practice is that of narrative theory and therapy. Narrative, or storytelling, most likely has its origins in ancient times, beginning with the ability of humans to communicate through language. From a therapeutic perspective, a brief but highly influential book by White and Epston (1990) set in motion a flurry of other works on narrative therapy. Among these are books by Freedman and Combs (1996), Freeman (1993), Monk, Winslade, Crocket and Epston (1997), Parry and Doan (1994), and Zimmerman and Dickerson (1996). For the most part, these forays into narrative therapy adopt a postmodern outlook, as is equally true of most constructivists and social constructionists. Schafer (1992) and Spence (1982) are most notable among those writing on narrative from a psychoanalytic reference point. Sarbin (1986) is still another trailblazer dealing with narrative and human conduct.

The narrative approach is a metaphor about how people's lives have been co-authored by society, culture, family, friends, and lovers, as well as authored by the people themselves. The primary aim is to regain agency by becoming the senior author and rewriting the story in a way that has the most value and meaning for each individual while living the revised story within an ethical framework that is fair to others. Being fair, however, does not always mean that others will necessarily be spared pain.

KEY THEORETICAL CONSTRUCTS

In the current literature, therapies that are predicated on constructivist, social-constructionist, and narrative orientations are most commonly viewed by their proponents through a postmodern lens. Already in the use of my language I have violated a postmodern tenet, for there is no single lens that encompasses postmodernism. In fact, postmodernism itself is fraught with contradiction, irony, fragmentation, and paradox. The postmodern world is one in which the distinction between reality and fiction has become blurred; a world in which fictions are often mistaken for objective reality and where what was once taken for objective reality is deconstructed into the fictitious. Many of the most prominent "postmodernists" have never labeled themselves as such but have been so labeled by others who have studied their writings. Be that as it may, some of the most highly influential writers who have contributed to the postmodern zeitgeist are Derrida (1967/1976), Foucault (1972, 1973), Lyotard (1984), Rorty (1979), and Wittgenstein (1958) in his later work.

Postmodernism rejects the notion of bedrock foundational knowledge. There are no absolute, universal, and certain truths that can be obtained by human minds or societies, regardless of how strong the propensity to try to achieve them. Knowledge and meanings are subjectively or communally constructed, primarily through language and dialogue (Wittgenstein, 1958). They are historical, localized, and contextualized stories that individuals tell themselves and co-construct with others. This leads to a relativistic and neopragmatic outlook (Rorty, 1991), which in psychotherapy translates to giving central importance to the adaptability and viability of the client's beliefs rather than to their validity or truthfulness (Mahoney, 1991; von Glaserfeld, 1984). For critical commentary on postmodernism, readers may wish to review Held (1995) and Rosen (1996, pp. 40–43). Furthermore, it should be borne in mind that although Piaget's constructivist–developmental paradigm shares some epistemological postulates with those of postmodernism, there are fundamental variances in this area that constitute radical differences (Kuehlwein, 1996a; Rosen, 1996). From the postmodern viewpoint, there are no totalizing "grand narratives" (Lyotard, 1984) that hold true, transcending all cultures across time and space. Progress does not follow an impeded line of advance, and science is considered to be only one narrative among many, no matter how compelling or powerful a story it may seem to be. Postmodernism emphasizes how marginalized and submerged voices come into being through power relations and hierarchical structures. Hence, as social constructionist Kenneth Gergen (1994) stated, "Not only does the discourse of objectivity generate and sustain unwarranted hierarchies of privilege—along with an accompanying array of prejudices, hostilities, and conflicts—but it excludes many voices from full participation in the culture's constructions of the good and the real" (p. 180). For this reason, postmodernism advocates the demarginalization of these voices and the emergence of those that have been silenced (Foucault, 1972, 1973). Assumptions and beliefs that have been reified into objective and absolute truths are subject to a process of deconstruction (Derrida, 1981), in which beliefs are dismantled and hidden premises, contradictions, and presuppositions are exposed. (See Karasu, 1996, for a discussion on the deconstruction of psychotherapy, and Parker, Georgaca, Harper, McLaughlin, & Stowell-Smith, 1995, on the deconstruction of psychopathology.) At its best, the deconstructing process is not a nihilistic exercise in futility. Instead, it leads to a recognition of the limitations of one's own beliefs and assumptions, a respect for the pluralism of other ways of meaning-making, and a reconstruction of new meanings, when appropriate, within one's own personal or cultural knowledge paradigm (Kegan, 1982). Modernism—with its emphasis on reason, science, technology, empiricism, objectivity and progress—is not the reigning paradigm among postmodernists. Observers are not neutral and detached from what is observed, but instead there is a feedforward mechanism at work (Mahoney, 1991), such that their personal theories and beliefs guide what they see and how they interpret what they experience. Hence, in large measure what is observed is governed by the preexisting theory-laden and meaning-saturated observers. In the absence of some accommodation to the newly observed, the observed is totally assimilated into the story that an observer brings to the task of making sense out of what is being encountered.

Psychopathology in Dispute

Despite exhortations to view normalcy and psychopathology along a continuum, people have come to dichotomize these socially constructed phenomena—in the process driving a wedge between two artificially created classes of people. Indeed, I would venture to say that many clients in psychotherapy lead richer and more satisfying lives than their psychotherapists do. The *Diagnostic and Statistical Manual* of the American Psychiatric Association (APA), the gold standard for diagnosing psychopathology, with its ever-widening labeling of human behavior as disordered, is itself a socially constructed product. It has evolved not simply by bringing scientific evidence to bear but through social discourse, often involving sharp differences and heated debate. One has only to think of the earlier compromise vote to remove homosexuality as a disorder from the manual unless it is experienced as "ego dystonic" by the individual. The social discourse occurred not only within professional circles, where the political factor is no stranger, but also between professionals and gay activists, further bringing political influence to bear. But somehow, in the minds of many, despite its evolving and social constructionist history, the *DSM* (now the *DSM–IV*; APA, 1994) is regarded as an absolute and objectified set of truths. I would like to make clear here that I think it is perfectly natural for the human mind to draw distinctions and devise classification systems. However, this tells little about the personhood of the individual, and people must be wary of reifying and objectifying the classification systems they socially construct. (See McNamee, 1996, for an interesting discussion on the social construction of psychotherapy itself, and Watzlawick, 1996, for a discussion of clinical "realities" as human constructions.) Rogers and Kegan (1991) illustrate this very well by presenting research that shows that psychiatric patients with the same diagnosis but who are at a different stage of meaning-making from one another have much less in common with each other than they do with others who have different diagnoses but who are in the same stage of meaning-making as they engage in the activity of evolving a self. Similarly, a patient diagnosed with a more severe disorder, such as schizophrenia, can be more developmentally advanced than one with a less severe disorder, from the standpoint of a self-structured meaning-making orientation. (See Kegan, 1982, for an in-depth discussion of his meaning-making orientation, and Rosen, 1991, for an amplification of the implications of Kegan's ideas as they apply to understanding psychotherapy.) By way of a caveat, let it be said that postmodernists do not look kindly on the idea of a developmental stage theory in which each stage constitutes a hierarchical advance over the preceding one.

Meaning-making orientations tend to depathologize the client. Illness and cure are not central to viewing or working with clients. Psychiatric diagnoses are de-emphasized. Labeling, stereotyping, and categorizing the client are avoided. The notion of the therapist as expert (in the sense of knowing what is necessarily best for the client) is rejected. Postmodernists actually engage in deconstructing the very idea of psychopathology itself (Parker et al., 1995). Despite how maladaptive the client's behavior may appear to the "objective" observer, there is an inner coherence, logic, and meaning to it from the perspective of the client. The individual's quest for personal meaning and its reconstruction is continuous (Guidano, 1991). As Gergen (1994) has suggested, "The ultimate challenge for therapy ... is not so much to replace an unworkable narrative with a serviceable one, but to enable clients to participate in the continuous process of creating and transforming meaning" (p. 245). For many, the reauthoring of one's life story and participating in the scripting and narrative action of the next chapter in one's own life, rather than repetitively living the same story over and over again, amounts to the creation and transformation of meaning. Another perspective on depathologizing the client is advanced by Lyddon (1993): "Far from being indicators of pathology, psychological problems are construed as important precursors to healthy growth and development" (p. 387). This is consonant with Mahoney's (1991) position that disorganizing and destabilizing experiences and their accompanying intensification of emotion offer opportunities to achieve further growth by constructing "higher-order patterns and capacities" (Lyddon, 1993, p. 387). In an extreme view, but one consistent with postmodernism, Becvar and Becvar (1996) draw out the implications of Humberto Maturana's radical constructivist epistemology in stating, "All systems do what they do, and what they do is not pathological unless we so define it" (p. 123). Clearly these ways of talking about psychotherapy step outside of the pathologizing framework that has been the hallmark of historical and traditional treatment circles. It may be one of those paradoxes of life that even if one were to grant some sanction to standardized diagnostic nomenclature, the helping process would be most readily facilitated by working with the client through a predominantly depathologizing orientation. Be that as it may, the dialectical clinician, in my opinion, will not throw the baby out with the bath water. Instead, he or she will use the diagnostic approach for what it is worth, while retaining a meaning-making metaframework in conducting psychotherapy. For example, the advances and advantages in biological psychiatry for treating certain specified disorders are too persuasive to be ignored—and they will not be ignored, except by the most entrenched ideologues sharing an anti-medication bias. Furthermore, the ethics of keeping one's client in the dark about such options because of the clinician's own biases or ignorance of what is available are highly questionable. Having said this, I would like to assert that I do not see diagnosis and medication as substitutes for the values of a meaning-making orientation, regardless of what school of therapy one practices.

The Process of Change and Transformation

The process of what brings about change in psychotherapy is obviously of critical significance. To many psychotherapists, it is undoubtedly the result of the efficacy of the techniques they introduce from the model they practice. This is surprising, given the fact that Lambert (1992) ascribed approximately only 15% of the influence in therapy to techniques and the model they derive from. But many clients are less impressed with their therapist's theories and techniques and ascribe more importance to the perceived personality of the therapist and the quality of the relationship that is established. For some therapists a good therapeutic alliance is viewed as a necessary but not sufficient condition for successful outcomes. For others, such an alliance is regarded as both necessary and sufficient. The common-variables hypothesis, alluded to in an earlier section, offers another route to explain successful outcomes despite the plethora of models in contemporary psychotherapy. Perhaps at the heart of successful change in therapy there lies a mystery, a suggestion that will probably please no one, least of all researchers in the field and dogmatic adherents to any one particular theory or model of practice.

Maturana (1988, Maturana & Varela, 1987) is a radical constructivist who believes there is a *multiverse* of realities rather than a single existing universe. In his view, the nervous system is a closed system that does not take data directly from the outside without transforming it in a manner that is determined by the structure of the organism's own mind (Efran, Lukens, & Lukens, 1990). Each mind constructs its own universe of understandings and meanings. Hence, Efran and Greene (1996) referred to Maturana's notion of "the myth of instructive interaction." In a therapeutic context, what the therapist says is not what the client hears. Translating this into terms of therapeutic change and transformation, Ruiz (1996) stated

> Any change emerging in human systems from the intervention of a psychotherapist is always to be understood as a reorganization of the experience of the patient determined by the patient himself or herself and not by the therapist. Thus, the therapist can only generate *perturbations* in the patient that may trigger his or her mental reorganization but never specify it. (p. 285)

Despite significant epistemological differences, the use of the term *perturbations* immediately brings to mind Piaget's equilibration model (1975/1985). As I have written elsewhere

> As long as the individual's knowledge system is adequate to the tasks and problems at hand, a state of equilibrium can be maintained. However, cognitive conflict generated by perceived incongruity, discrepancy, or contradiction sparks the perturbation experience, which sets

in motion a re-equilibrating process. What constitutes a perceived contradiction or disturber to one individual may not be perceived in this way by another, since the experience will be influenced by the present cognitive-structural-developmental formation of the person. The re-equilibration of cognitive-structural organization will lead to a new and improved balance of knowledge. (Rosen, 1993, p. 421)

Developmental constructivist William J. Lyddon is another who suggests that the bedrock mechanisms of contrast and contradiction are the foundation for change in all effective therapies, regardless of the model being practiced. As he has stated

It is the experience of discrepancy and its concomitant emotional arousal that, in experiential terms, can provoke a "creation of meaning event"—a therapeutic episode in which the client specifies the discrepancy, evaluates the tenability of the cherished belief, and puts forth a "key symbolization" or personal hypothesis as to how the particular belief came to be valued and why it is no longer viable. (Lyddon, 1993, p. 386)

Lyddon went on to suggest that the revision of old meanings and the creation of new ones brought on by perturbating experiences (those that precipitate a state of disequilibrium in the knowing subject) will help clients deal with a wider—and, I would add, a more complex—range of circumstances. (See Rosen, 1985, 1989, 1991 for further discussion of the generic effects of perturbating experiences across all psychotherapies.)

ASSESSMENT

In view of the fact that a meaning-making metaframework is an attitude, a philosophical orientation, a way of conceptualizing practice across all schools, and a cluster of metaphors and radiates out into a pluralistic range of domains, it is not possible to identify a single set of assessment methods that are representative of it. It is probably safe to say that many who adopt a purist meaning-making orientation and who do not embrace a preexisting therapeutic model out of which they operate, do not conduct any kind of formal assessment. Emphasis ranges from the phenomenologically made meanings of the individual client to the socially and culturally co-constructed meanings achieved through social interaction and dialogue. In constructivist therapies, the assessment focus is on "exploration of personal narratives, autobiography, and personal and family construct systems and hierarchies" (R. A. Neimeyer, 1995, p. 17, Table 1). G. J. Neimeyer and R. A. Neimeyer (1993) have articulated some essential observations about constructivist assessment. One cardinal belief is predicated on the premise that specific constructions or meanings of the client may best be comprehended not in a vacuum but within the broader and more complex meaning system in which they are embedded. The Neimeyers refer to this as *semantic holism* (p. 13). (See also Bruner, 1990, for an application of this principle within a cultural context.) Furthermore, they construe assessment not as a singular isolated activity but rather as an intervention that may lead to a change in the very construct or meaning being assessed. Thus, looked at in this manner, "*Assessment* is inherently a change-generating process that can be harnessed and directed toward promoting personal reconstructions" (p. 12). Mahoney (1988b) allowed that, in the assessment procedure, constructivists may very well acquire a developmental history, but that this history constitutes a subjective reconstruction and not an accurate, absolute, linear, and objective accounting of the client's life story. This viewpoint is very much in keeping with Spence's (1982), in which, coming from a psychoanalytic perspective, he interprets the patient's story of his life as a reconstructed narrative truth rather than historical truth grounded on an objective foundation.

Another approach to assessment—the assessment of progress in therapy—can be gleaned from a creative chapter titled "Metaphor, Meaning-Making and Metamorphosis" (Carlsen, 1996). Carlsen's seminal thought in this work is that clients' expressions of metaphors throughout the course of psychotherapy reflect their evolutionary meaning-making progress. Although acknowledging that certainly not all clients spontaneously produce changing metaphors throughout the series of sessions that make up a therapeutic experience, Carlsen has found it fruitful to vigilantly take note of those who do. For example, one client started in therapy by describing herself as "like a china doll, like a child" (Carlsen, 1996). As the process continued, she realized that she had not been seeing herself as a "whole person" but as one made up of "scattered pieces." Later in therapy, she began to experience herself as "growing toward wholeness." These metaphors not only served as a basis for assessing her perception of herself and her progress in moving through therapy, but also as springboards for discourse around issues of concern and meaning.

In summary, assessment in a constructivist mode is a holistic approach occurring within a hierarchically constructed meaning matrix. Assessment itself is seen as a form of intervention capable of producing change. This approach views the client's life story told during assessment as a subjectively reconstructed narrative rather than an objectively stated sequence of historically true events. It invokes the capacity to make meaningful use of client-generated metaphors. This rendition is basically a qualitative one, as opposed to either a diagnostic or psychometric form of assessment.

TREATMENT OF CHOICE

Because the meaning-making concept and process is being presented in this chapter as a metaframework for clinical practice, it is not being considered as a single theoretical model in itself, but rather as an orientation that can be adopted by practitioners across many, if not all, kinds of therapeutic models. Furthermore, because its superordinate definition of human beings is that they are organisms engaged in the proactive process of making or constructing organized patterns and meaning out of experience, there are practically no individuals to whom this metaframework is not applicable, except perhaps those in the tragic state of being brain-dead. Perhaps this can best be expressed in the words of Kegan (1982), who with a slight twist has stated, "It is not that a person makes meaning, as much as that the activity of being a person is the activity of meaning-making" (p. 11).

An anecdote that makes the rounds in therapeutic circles describes a visit by Milton Erickson to a state hospital, where he was to exhibit his renowned creative ability to help people in distress. Wishing to put him to the test with a serious challenge, his colleagues and hosts presented him with a severely disturbed patient diagnosed with schizophrenia who labored under the delusion that he was Jesus Christ. He was a very passive patient who, unlike many of his peers in the hospital, refused to perform any tasks or accept work assignments on the grounds. Erickson apparently chose not to confront or attempt to dispel this young man's delusion of being Jesus Christ. Instead, in the course of talking with him, Erickson commented that he understood that the young man was a pretty good carpenter (as was true of the historic Jesus). It seems, as the story goes, that Erickson had hit the nail on the head. The patient not only agreed, consistent with his delusion, but before long he had become a hard-working carpenter on the hospital grounds. Through talking with the patient, Erickson facilitated his capacity to generate new meaning out of his delusion, leading to markedly changed behavior. (See Matthews, 1996, for a constructivist formulation of Erickson's practices in psychotherapy.) Although suffering from a severe case of schizophrenia, the patient was still a person, and as I have already mentioned, "The activity of being a person is the activity of meaning-making" (Kegan, 1982, p. 11).

THE THERAPEUTIC PROCESS

Therapy is, indeed, process oriented. In particular, meaning-making orientations, with their shared anti-objectivist epistemology, have emphasized process over technique in their literature on conducting psychotherapy (Neimeyer & Mahoney, 1995; Rosen & Kuehlwein 1996). As Carlsen (1988) stated, "Therapy is a doing rather than a fixed package of theory and technique" (p. 91). Farther on in her book she suggested, "*In process:*

these words are absolutely key in this whole business of change—a willingness to *not* have everything neatly defined and settled once and for all" (p. 100). The central core of her conception of psychotherapy is linked to her definition of meaning-making itself:

> I interpret *meaning-making* as the forming and reforming of intention and significance; of what one has in mind and *how* one has in mind; and of the succession of synergies or gestalten of personal knowledge and meaning. And, if living *is* meaning-making—as Angyal, Kegan, and Fowler suggest—then the vital focus for therapy is also meaning-making. (Carlsen, 1988, p. 23)

Although coming from a distinctly psychodynamic orientation, Saari (1991) reflected much the same sentiment. Restating the old social work dictum of "starting where the client is," Saari suggested that what this tells us, in effect, is that the client's meaning system is what the clinical social worker is to be concerned about. For her, "The purpose of treatment is to help the client practice the creation of meaning" (Saari, 1991, p. 145). Elsewhere she defined even basic identity as "a personal meaning system that is created over the course of the individual's experience with the world and is organized primarily in narrative form" (Saari, 1996, p. 144).

What has been said so far in this section may create the impression of a coherence among meaning-making theorists. This would convey a false impression, for there is much divergence among them. Even among those who regard themselves as constructivists there exists a pluralism of voices (R. A. Neimeyer, 1997). They are certainly united in their sharing of an anti-foundational epistemology; the implied relativism (but not solipsism) of this; and their rejection of the idea that universal, immutable, absolute truths are attainable. But despite this shared epistemology, there are differences among them. For this reason I present separately some comments on constructivism, social constructionism, and narrative. Keep in mind that postmodernism is a leitmotif that runs across each of the three preceding orientations and that although there are differences among them, they also overlap in significant ways.

Constructivism

In a book on constructivism written expressly for social workers, Fisher (1991) stated

> There is no one right way of doing things. To the contrary, there are many ways. Each way of doing things has some utility under certain conditions. Thus, constructivism is a pragmatic epistemology, but this

is constrained by a powerful ethic. That is, we are responsible for the meanings we give to events and, in an immediate sense, for the actions that flow from these constructions. (p. 5)

I think that these words serve well as an anchor-point not only for openly avowed constructivist therapists but for all psychotherapists. They suggest the practical implications of constructivism and, felicitously, are embedded in an ethical posture.

Although not preoccupied with techniques in a cookbook fashion, constructivists certainly do use various techniques and methods, including homework assignments, as they proceed with the therapy. From a constructivist perspective, however, it is not the technique that does something to the person in therapy. Rather, what matters is what the client does with the technique (G. J. Neimeyer, 1993). As Guidano (1995) so aptly put it, "The therapist can only try to set 'conditions' capable of triggering a reorganization, but she or he cannot determine or control either when or how clients organize the final outcome of the reorganization" (p. 104).

Mahoney (1988b), while respectful of the client's presenting problem, tries to move away from repetitively working on the client's day-to-day crises in favor of getting at deeper structures and the patterned way in which these deeper structures tend to govern the client's emotions and behavior. (See also Guidano, 1987, 1991; Guidano & Liotti, 1983.) Mahoney referred to his most basic focus as the process level of therapy. In working at this level, he has found the gestalt, experiential, and humanistic–transpersonal models of therapy especially helpful. He stated, "Beyond changes in their [clients'] symbolic conceptualizations of self and world, *process* work invites deeply felt and intensely emotional experiments in being" (Mahoney, 1988b, p. 305). Although painful to the patient, negative emotions are not viewed as the problem, but rather as potentially transitional states that can lead from having a disorganizing and destabilizing effect on the client to a reorganized and more adaptive state. Resistance is to be expected in this process as a natural attempt on the part of the self to avoid change of core constructs. Mahoney views this not as something the therapist should oppose, but rather as something to be worked with and even regarded with respect. The relationship that the process is predicated upon is not essentially different from other approaches. It should offer a safe, secure, and caring context that serves as a springboard for the client to try out new behaviors and roles both within and outside of the therapy. As Mahoney (1988b) put it

A bond of caring and trust is developed, and the therapeutic relationship becomes an interpersonal context in and from which the client is encouraged to examine, explore, and experiment with personal constructions of their identity, reality, values, and capacities. (p. 308)

Lastly, it is always vital to remain cognizant of and work within clients' present phenomenological frameworks of assumptions, premises, and beliefs while working toward modification and replacement of those that have become obsolete and maladaptive. Nevertheless, rigidly entrenched clients may sometimes need to be confronted with a radically different paradigmatic way of knowing-and-being in the world in order to shake them loose from their moorings. (For further elaboration of Mahoney's views about constructivist psychotherapy, see also Mahoney, 1991; in press).

R. A. Neimeyer (1996) has developed a constructivist-based taxonomy of process interventions, although he reminded his readers that constructivism, far from being a separate school of therapy, is a mind-set that can be adopted by therapists of various theoretical orientations. Space does not permit elaborating on each of his crafted interventions, which he acknowledges to be works in progress, but I do want to emphasize what he sees as the driving force behind them as I understand him. Neimeyer started his early career as an adherent of the work of George Kelly. Although his roots remain with Kelly, he has broadened his own meaning-making base and embraced the postmodern zeitgeist (with some reservation) along his own developmental journey. He has moved toward an increasing appreciation of the role of language in the construction of meaning and alternative realities, much as is emphasized in the work of social constructionists. Nevertheless, he wishes to eschew what appears to be the excessive theorizing about language in social-constructionist circles without sufficient evidence of the concretization in real therapeutic situations that would lead to connection and engagement between client and therapist. (Some of these concerns may have been remedied with the publication of Anderson's book, *Conversation, Language, and Possibilities: A Postmodern Approach to Therapy*, in 1997, and Gergen's 1994 book, *Realities and Relationships: Soundings in Social Construction*, as well as that of McNamee & Gergen's 1992 book, *Therapy as Social Construction*.) To prepare for the task of developing his taxonomy, Neimeyer reflected thoughtfully about his own practice so that he could "unpack the conversational artistry that typifies psychotherapy" (R. A. Neimeyer, 1996, p. 382). As he further stated, "One alternative that has particular appeal to me is therapy as an exercise in *rhetoric*, understood as an artful use of discourse to accomplish pragmatic ends" (p. 382). It becomes clear that Neimeyer is attempting to restore the tarnished connotation of the word *rhetoric* to its earlier heights as a respectable form of conversation—in this case, therapeutic conversation through which "the utility of rhetoric as a symbolic discursive form of reality construction may now be possible" (p. 382). Neimeyer's taxonomy consists of 10 conversational strategies that he uses with his clients as he engages them in the intersubjective process of mutual meaning-making. These 10 strategies in no way constrict or exhaust the full range of his therapeutic repertoire, however.

Social Constructionism

In dyads, groups, communities, and societies, people construct social realities through the use of language in discourse. This is a perfectly natural process and outcome of the human condition. What is problematic is the all-too-frequent practice of universalizing these socially constructed realities into absolute and objective truths, such that alternative versions of reality constructed by different groups from other localities and contexts are pronounced as patently wrong. The tendency is to take a socially constructed reality that is, of necessity, historically and locally bound and reify it so that it is accorded the status of a "thing" or truth that crosses and transcends historically and locally bounded situations. It should not go unnoticed that therapists with a faithful allegiance to only one model of practice are often, but not always, engaging in this very same absolutizing tendency.

For social constructionists, "Humans do not have a basic, fundamental, pure human nature that is transhistorical and transcultural" (Cushman, 1995, p. 17). Similarly, "There is no universal, transhistorical self, only local selves; there is no universal theory about the self, only local theories" (p. 23). Despite some common ground, the social constructionists seek to sharply distinguish themselves from constructivists. Although constructivists have an appreciation for the role of language and sociality in meaning-making, they tend to emphasize the individual as the primary agent who constructs meanings. For social constructionists, dialogue and the relationship within which it occurs take priority over the conception of a private self, with its personal, intrinsic motivations and intentions. As Gergen (1994) stated, "The view of the private self as the source of art and literature, practical decisions, moral deliberation, emotional activity, and the like is no longer viable" (p. 181). There is no essential self that exists or develops in a cohesive organized fashion over time. For someone who has not made the shift to a postmodern mind-set, this will surely be a difficult proposition to accept. However, is the difficulty inherent in accepting this assertion due to one's embeddedness in the socially constructed modern Western concept of an individual self? This is the question to ponder. For Gergen (1991)

> Meaning is born of interdependence, and because there is no self outside of a system of meaning, it may be said that relations precede and are more fundamental than self. Without relationship there is no language with which to conceptualize the emotions, thoughts, or intentions of the self. (p. 157)

Even emotions are viewed as social constructions, not hard-wired tendencies of the human species (Harré, 1986). As Nunley and Averill (1996) stated, "Whenever individuals learn a new emotional concept, they also learn how to be emotional in a way appropriate to the culture" (p. 225). A vivid illustration of this can be seen in an account by Tofani (1996) of torture in Tibet under the government of China, which occupies the country. A Tibetan Buddhist monk was tortured by having a hot, burning shovel placed on his stomach. He was also shocked with an electric cattle prod. What were his reactions to this, beyond the obvious pain he endured? For one thing, he consoled himself by thinking that he was suffering for a cause, the cause of the Tibetan people. Beyond that, however, he experienced emotions of compassion and sorrow for the Chinese police officer inflicting the pain. He thought to himself that while the Chinese people are good, it is their government that is evil. The police officer, he believed, was only carrying out his orders and would lose his job if he failed to do so. According to the article, based on interviews, what the monk felt and thought were derived from the beliefs specific to Tibetan Buddhist religion and culture. I would submit that this is not the same reaction or set of emotions that would be elicited from those of other cultures not steeped in the ways of the Tibetan Buddhist monk.

As therapists enter the consulting room, where does social constructionism, informed by postmodernism, lead them? It might be instructive to begin with the evolving ideas of family therapist and social worker Lynn Hoffman (1993). Her ideas traversed through cybernetics and systems thinking to constructivism and then on to social constructionism and postmodernism. She has come to embrace the view that "The postmodern therapist comes into the family without any definition of pathology, without any idea about what dysfunctional structures to look for, and without any set ideas about what should or should not be changed" (Hoffman, 1990, p. 10). At the same time, this should not be misconstrued to mean that Hoffman believes that the therapists encounter the family bereft of any ideas of their own. Therapists, however, should be aware of these ideas and not seek to impose them unilaterally: "In therapy, we listen to a story and then we collaborate with the persons we are seeing to invent other stories or other meanings for the stories that are told" (Hoffman, 1990, p. 11). The medium of therapy is that of conversations that produce realities that have no objective basis in the world at large but derive their sanction from the social consensus of the participants in the dialogue (Hoffman, 1990).

Hoffman was heavily influenced by the work of Anderson and Goolishian (1988, 1992), which emphasizes the role of language and dialogue in the creation of meaning during the therapeutic session. Anderson (1995) refers to therapy as "generative conversation" (p. 31). This is a form of conversation based on a collaborative and egalitarian discourse, which is neither hierarchical nor power-based in the kind of relationship it offers. What emerges out of the dialogical exchange is new meaning, new possibilities for understanding and action, and new alternatives for living. Empathic and receptive listening by the therapist is as important as is speaking, for in large measure it helps to bring forth and develop the very stories that clients must disclose and recreate. Anderson (1995) advocated that the postmodern therapist adopt a stance of "not-knowing." "*Not-knowing* refers to the attitude and belief that the therapist does not have access to privileged information, can never fully understand another person, and always needs to learn more about what has been said or not said" (p. 34). This stance de-emphasizes the tendency of therapists to set up a hierarchically structured relationship in which they listen for what they want to hear and presume to inform clients, based on preexisting ideas, how they should live their lives. It engenders a climate for discourse that enables therapists and clients to co-construct alternatives that are congruent with the clients' own present and evolving feelings, beliefs, and circumstances. It is a stance that is predicated on the conviction that the client is the expert on the client. The questions asked by therapists embracing a not-knowing attitude do not derive from a content-based theory (e.g., such concepts held in mind as id, ego, and superego), which are likely to lead to a distortion of what clients say and an omission of what they might have said. Furthermore, in therapy of this sort, the idea behind the role of language is not simply that it is used to express the realities people believe in, but that language in social discourse brings forth new and multiple realities, however context-bound they may be. In brief, for Goolishian and Anderson, language is regarded as generative and is seen "as the essence of dialogue, and therefore the *essence* of the therapeutic process" (Anderson, 1993, p. 343). The reader wishing to pursue further the social-constructionist approach to psychotherapy would do well to consult Friedman (1993) and McNamee and Gergen (1992).

Narrative Therapy

Although stories are only one way of talking about their lives, it can be said that people live in and through stories. People can become trapped in stories, their own and even those of others. They can also, however, become liberated by extricating themselves from the roles they play in others' stories, when they no longer wish to have a part in them, and by reauthoring their own stories. In literature, perhaps the greatest dramatic example of this is Ibsen's (1965) famous and controversial play *A Doll's House* (controversial, at least, during the historical period when it was first introduced). For 8 years of married life, Nora, the heroine, has lived a story consonant with the societal mores of the day, in which she has played the part of a dutiful wife and mother, subjugated to the dominance of her loving husband. She has done this without questioning the appropriateness of the arrangement. Her ideas and behavior have been molded by her husband, her pastor, and her father (before her marriage). In the last scene, however, a disillusionment with her husband materializes, along with a deeply significant realization that she has never been permitted (or even allowed herself) to think or to make decisions independently. She has been married to a man who treats her as a child, however lovingly; who treats her as a china doll. She has remained in a marriage without reciprocity, one built upon the socially sanctioned pattern of a hierarchically structured relationship of power and dominance. In a rare and bold act of independence, she makes a firm decision to emancipate herself. With no way of being sure of the outcome, she announces that she will leave home, leaving behind her husband and three children. She will venture forth alone into the world to experience it through her own eyes and to educate herself, to think her own thoughts, to come to conclusions on her own. The last thing the audience hears is the door slamming behind her as Nora leaves the "doll's house" behind. Nora, in other words, has adventurously decided to leave one story and to create another; she has decided to re-story her life.

It will come as no surprise to the constructivist mind that there are several versions of narrative theory and therapy. A sampling of these can be found in the works of Gergen and Kaye (1992); Gonçalves (1994, 1995); Howard (1991); Parry and Doan (1994); Russell and Wandrei, (1996); Schafer (1992); and White and Epston (1990). The common theme that "our practice of meaning-making involves us as constructive narrators at every turn" (Russell, 1991, p. 246) threads through these works. According to Gonçalves (1994):

> The objective of every therapy should be to orient the client into new life narratives, bringing with it a sense of acting and authorship. ....
> The venture into the unknown, the world of possibility, is indeed the final objective of therapy. (p. 119)

When Nora left the doll house behind, it was precisely a step into the unknown and the world of possibility that she was taking. She ventured forth into the realm of uncertainty and new possibilities to re-author her life; to make new meanings of it for herself.

The various narrative therapies are not separate from the themes of constructivism, social constructionism, and postmodernism. Rather, they interlock with them. Although they consist of differing emphases and techniques, they each belong to the family of a meaning-making orientation. Nora left her old story behind and ventured forth to create a new one, without benefit of a therapist. With a little imagination, however, one might say that she had the help of a therapist who was sensitive to her subjugated existence and who co-authored her liberation. His name was Henrik Ibsen. In actual therapy (notice the postmodern blurring of lines between fiction and reality), the therapist is witness to the disclosure of the old story and—through discourse, dialogue, and questions—participates with the client in the exploration and co-construction of new ones. There is no one right story for the client to live, nor is there a single absolute truth for the client to cling to. Instead, a multiplicity of narrative possibilities await the client as author to bring form, plot, and character to one or more of them. Please do not mistake this as a facile rendition of the application of a narrative metaphor to the process of therapy. There is pain and struggle and loss in this process. Intertwined with this, however, there is gain and excitement and the joy of living new narratives of one's own making. Co-constructed though the narratives may be, the client is always the senior author. For Freeman (1993), "The very act of existing meaningfully in time . . . the very act of making sense of ourselves and others, is only possible in and through the fabric of narrative itself" (p. 21).

LIMITATIONS OF THE MODEL

The term *constructivism* is often used in the broad sense of being equatable with a meaning-making orientation and thus encompassing such relevant areas as personal construct therapy, narrative constructivism, developmental constructivism, postmodern trends, and social constructivism, although proponents of the last of these would prefer to be known as social constructionists. With this in mind, it may be suggested that "*constructivism* may not imply a unique therapeutic style. It may instead represent a set of assumptions that influence individual therapists within their more traditional frameworks" (Vasco, 1994, p. 12). At the same time constructivism is not a monolithic theory-driven orientation nor is it subject to the "tyranny of technique" (Mahoney, 1986). Vasco (1994) suggests that therapists with a more constructivist mind-set are likely to be "more creative, allowing themselves to experiment with a wider array of therapeutic methodologies and to develop more individualized and personalized therapeutic styles" (p. 13). Constructivism points to a more exploratory and less directed type of therapy, emphasizing the therapeutic process itself over specified goals and outcomes. Depending on the reader's personal outlook, these observations may or may not appear to be limitations. However, when contextualized in the present managed health care environment, with its insistence on accountability, such observations are likely to be looked on with either indifference or disfavor. An openly avowed meaning-making orientation is not likely to succeed in getting a therapist on the referral list of any managed care system. Of course, this is not a limitation intrinsic to a constructivist approach, but a relational one with respect to the presently evolved health care system. I hasten to add, however, that I am an advocate of seeking brief and effective ways of conducting psychotherapy.

Another limitation, which is not inherent to constructivism itself, is the potential for the misguided interpretation that phenomena such as poverty, racism, crime, domestic violence, and AIDS can be ignored, or at least de-emphasized. There is a real world out there, some philosophical protestations to the contrary notwithstanding. The issue is the meaning people make of such phenomena, how meanings fit into their value structure, and the attitudes and actions that are governed by made meanings. Schwartzberg (1996), speaking of the effects of trauma on people, stated, "How we previously made sense of the world is no longer valid or useful. And this is the central challenge of trauma—to reestablish life's meaning in a dramatically changed world" (p. 24). Depicting the lives of men who have been diagnosed with HIV, he wrote, "Each of these men is attempting to meet the challenge of holding onto life's meaning in a changed reality. They follow different paths, but have all found a way to integrate their infection into a meaningful life narrative" (p. 25). A diagnosis of HIV can lead to many varying revisions of meaning and accompanying behaviors. These range through such possible narratives as committing suicide out of the belief that life is no longer worth living, a conviction that one is being punished by God for sins committed, a commitment to living life more intensively and adventurously, a reawakened appreciation of one's own consciousness and existence, a deeply profound spiritual transformation, dedication to a life of service to others, and a shift from passivity to an engagement in social activism. In other words, the same event or condition can lead to many disparate ways of making meaning out of it and to vastly different actions with either negative or positive consequences.

R. A. Neimeyer (1997) has indicated that constructivism, broadly defined to embrace a wide range of meaning-making orientations, clearly lacks a single cohesive paradigm. As he stated, "Any close listening to the postmodern chorus reveals a polyphony of voices, not all of which are singing in the same key" (p. 55). To add to the confusion, he pointed out how even such psychotherapists as Ellis and Meichenbaum, known for their more rationalist and objectivist views, have begun to recast themselves within constructivist and narrative terminologies. Furthermore, a case has been made for highlighting the constructivist components of Beck's empirically based cognitive therapy (Kuehlwein, 1996b; Rosen, 1993). In fact, Alford and Beck (1997) have gone so far as to suggest, "The theoretical framework of cognitive therapy constitutes a 'theory of theories'; it is a formal theory of the effects of personal (informal) theories or *constructions of reality*" (p. 11, emphasis added). Neimeyer (1997) is hopeful, however, that future critical analysis of the diverse voices among the family of constructivists will lead to forging a foundational theoretical integration based on the common ground of their shared epistemological beliefs.

Another limitation discussed by R. A. Neimeyer (1997) is the general level of abstraction at which constructivist discourse is aimed, often leading to heightened expectancy and excitement on the part of therapists, yet leaving them with too little in the way of technical procedures and methods to actually apply in practice. However, Neimeyer pointed out that there has recently been a strong trend toward greater specification of clinical assessment and treatment procedures in the field. To help remedy this situation, he suggested accelerating the publication of more case studies and focusing more on specific types of problems, such as various anxiety disorders, depression, and bereavement. G. J. Neimeyer (1993, p. 18) also listed some specific interventions derived from constructivist approaches. In addition, a forthcoming book by Mahoney (in press) on the principles and practices of constructive psychotherapy should prove to be instructive and should go a long way toward remedying the limitation under discussion here. (See also Duncan, Solovey, & Rusk, 1992; R. A. Neimeyer & G. J. Neimeyer, 1987.)

In summary, although an honest critique of the meaning-making orientation does indeed reveal limitations, it seems that these limitations are in the process of being resolved, and interested parties can anticipate the promise of greater elaboration of procedural methods.

RESEARCH

Experimental research in the area of the meaning-making orientation has tended to be sparse and concentrated mostly in a very narrow range of the full possibilities. Impediments to research include the very nature of the concept, its high level of conceptual and epistemological abstraction, and its use more as an integrating framework for clinical practice (Neimeyer & Feixas, 1990) than as a unique model of practice in itself.

Nevertheless, personal construct theory, one major variation among the voices of constructivism, "has been remarkably fertile in generating empirical research, with more than 60% of the nearly 2000 publications using personal construct concepts or methods consisting of studies of the structure of personal meaning systems and their development" (R. A. Neimeyer, 1997, p. 63). Much of this research has been pitched not to measuring atomistic quantitative changes in behavior but to investigating systemic conceptual changes in meaning over the course of therapy, determining those factors that contribute to the client's therapeutic improvement, and exploring the ways in which both client and therapist view the very process of therapy itself. Of course, this type of research could be brought to bear on any model of therapeutic practice.

Bruner (1986) identified two forms of cognitive thought, the paradigmatic or logico-scientific one and the narrative mode. The two represent opposing ways of thinking and bringing about causal explanations, and scientific research is usually associated with the logico-scientific form.

Toukmanian and Rennie (1992) edited a book with the underlying theme that both modes of explanation proposed by Bruner are germane to human science and are currently to be found in research on process psychotherapy. They compare the two modes this way: "While paradigmatic explanation is deductive, demonstrative, and quantitative, narrative explanation is inductive, hermeneutical, and qualitative. ... Narrative explanation is constructive rather than objective" (Rennie & Toukmanian, 1992, p. 235). The paradigmatic mode has been more traditionally applied in psychotherapy research, but Rennie and Toukmanian assert that the narrative mode, although relatively new in psychotherapy process research, is more appropriate to apply because by its very nature it deals with meaning construction at "the level of the person" (p. 235). Nevertheless, they do not denigrate the paradigmatic mode. In fact, they recommend applying both modes to psychotherapy process research and propose a synthesis of the differing epistemologies of the two modes, bringing information derived from one approach to bear in explaining information coming from the other approach. However, they plead that the narrative approach to psychotherapy process research not be required to be subject to the demands of the more traditionally scientific method of the paradigmatic mode. The paradigmatic method draws upon an objective "third-party perspective" (p. 246), whereas the narrative mode focuses on human will, intentionality, and self-reflexivity of both client and therapist within the context of the dialogical relationship between the two. In the words of Stiles (1994)

> Because it is linguistic, empathic, contextual, polydimensional, and nonlinear, qualitative [narrative] research adopts a more tentative epistemology than that of hypothesis-testing research. It shifts the goal of quality control from the truth of statements to understanding by people. It does this by revealing rather than avoiding personal involvement in the process of observing and interpreting and by evaluating interpretations according to their impact on people. (p. 159)

With its implication for the construction of meaning, it may well be that the qualitative research of the narrative mode is more suitable for process-oriented psychotherapy, particularly for those therapies characterized by a meaning-making orientation. Although it has yet to be fully put to the trial in the crucible of such research endeavors, qualitative research has already taken some promising steps.

SUMMARY

This chapter has focused on presenting a metaframework for clinical practice through a plurality of lenses in order to engage the reader with the significant concept and process of meaning-making. The lenses chosen have been those of constructivism, social constructionism, narrative, and postmodernism. But even within each of these overlapping and interlocking domains that both radiate from and converge on meaning-making, there exists a multiplicity of voices. The scope of this material has been vast, has multiple perspectives, and is certainly not integrated into a single pattern. The material has dealt more with subjects such as epistemology, dialogue, narrative as a metaphor for how people author and re-author their lives, and the construction and reconstruction of meaning than it has with what techniques therapists can apply during the next session with any of their clients.

Although the chapter is coming to an end, I doubt that there will be any sense of certainty or closure on the reader's part. What I do confidently believe at this point, however, is that you, the reader, will continue with your end of the dialogue that has been taking place between us. Regardless of my intentions, you will construct your own meaning out of it, just as your clients will do as you engage them in the therapeutic process. This is how it should be, and it is the primary message of the chapter.

REFERENCES

Alford, B. A., & Beck, A. T. (1997). *The integrative power of cognitive therapy*. New York: Guilford.

American Psychiatric Association. (1994). *Diagnostic and statistical manual of mental disorders* (4th ed.). Washington, DC: Author.

Anderson, H. (1993). On a roller coaster: A collaborative language systems approach to therapy. In S. Friedman (Ed.), *The new language of change: Constructive collaboration in psychotherapy* (pp. 323–344). New York: Guilford.

Anderson, H. (1995). Collaborative language systems: Toward a postmodern theory. In R. H. Mikesell, D-D Lusterman, & S. McDaniel (Eds.), *Integrating family therapy: Handbook of family psychology and systems theory* (pp. 27–44). Washington, DC: American Psychological Association.

Anderson, H. (1997). *Conversation, language, and possibilities: A postmodern approach to therapy*. New York: Basic Books.

Anderson, H., & Goolishian, H. (1988). Human systems as linguistic systems: Preliminary and evolving ideas about the implications for clinical theory. *Family Process, 27*, 371–393.

Anderson, H., & Goolishian, H. (1992). The client is the expert: A not-knowing approach to therapy. In S. McNamee & K. J. Gergen (Eds.), *Therapy as social construction* (pp. 25–39). Newbury Park, CA: Sage.

Basseches, M. (1984). *Dialectical thinking and adult development*. Norwood, NJ: Ablex.

Becvar, D. S., & Becvar, R. J. (1996). *Family therapy: A systemic integration* (3rd ed.). Needham Heights, MA: Allyn & Bacon.

Berger, P. L., & Luckmann, T. (1966). *The social construction of reality*. New York: Bantam Doubleday Dell.

Bruner, J. (1986). *Actual minds, possible worlds*. Cambridge, MA: Harvard University Press.

Bruner, J. (1990). *Acts of meaning*. Cambridge, MA: Harvard University Press.

Calaprice, A. (Ed.). (1996). *The quotable Einstein*. Princeton: Princeton University Press.

Carlsen, M. B. (1988). *Meaning-making: Therapeutic processes in adult development*. New York: Norton.

Carlsen, M. B. (1996). Metaphor, meaning-making, and metamorphosis. In H. Rosen & K. T. Kuehlwein (Eds.), *Constructing realities: Meaning-making perspectives for psychotherapists* (pp. 337–368). San Francisco: Jossey-Bass.

Cushman, P. (1995). *Constructing the self, constructing America: A cultural history of psychotherapy.* New York: Addison-Wesley.

Derrida, J. (1976). *Of grammatology* (G. C. Spivack, Trans.). Baltimore, MD: Johns Hopkins University Press. (Original work published 1967).

Derrida, J. (1981). *Dissemination.* Chicago: University of Chicago Press.

Duncan, B. L., Solovey, A. D., & Rusk, G. S. (1992). *Changing the rules.* New York: Guilford.

Dyck, M. J. (1987). Cognitive therapy and logotherapy: Contrasting views on meaning. *Journal of Cognitive Psychotherapy, 1,* 155–169.

Efran, J. S., & Greene, M. A. (1996). Psychotherapeutic theory and practice: Contributions from Maturana's structure determinism. In H. Rosen & K. T. Kuehlwein (Eds.), *Constructing realities: Meaning-making perspectives for psychotherapists* (pp. 71–113). San Francisco: Jossey-Bass.

Efran, J. S., Lukens, M. D., & Lukens, R. J. (1990). *Language, structure, and change: Frameworks of meaning in psychotherapy.* New York: Norton.

Fisher, D. D. V. (1991). *An introduction to constructivism for social workers.* New York: Praeger.

Foucault, M. (1972). *The archeology of knowledge.* New York: Pantheon.

Foucault, M. (1973). *Madness and civilization.* New York: Vintage Books.

Frank, J. D., & Frank, J. B. (1991). *Persuasion and healing: A comparative study of psychotherapy* (3rd ed.). Baltimore: Johns Hopkins University Press.

Freedman, J., & Combs, G. (1996). *Narrative therapy: The social construction of preferred realities.* New York: Norton.

Freeman, M. (1993). *Rewriting the self: History, memory, narrative.* New York: Routledge & Kegan Paul.

Friedman, S. (Ed.). (1993). *The new language of change: Constructive collaboration in psychotherapy.* New York: Guilford.

Gergen, K. J. (1985). The social constructionist movement in modern psychology. *American Psychologist, 40,* 266–275.

Gergen, K. J. (1991). *The saturated self: Dilemmas of identity in contemporary life.* New York: Basic Books.

Gergen, K. J. (1994). *Realities and relationships: Soundings in social construction.* Cambridge, MA: Harvard University Press.

Gergen, K. J., & Kaye, J. (1992). Beyond narrative in the negotiation of therapeutic meaning. In S. McNamee & K. J. Gergen (Eds.), *Therapy as social construction* (pp. 166–185). Newbury Park, CA: Sage.

Gold, J. R. (1996). *Key concepts in psychotherapy integration.* New York: Plenum.

Gonçalves, O. F. (1994). Cognitive narrative psychotherapy: The hermeneutic construction of alternative meanings. *Journal of Cognitive Psychotherapy: An International Quarterly, 8,* 105–125.

Gonçalves, O. F. (1995). Hermeneutics, constructivism, and cognitive-behavioral therapies: From the object to the project. In R. A. Neimeyer & M. J. Mahoney (Eds.), *Constructivism in psychotherapy* (pp. 195–230). Washington, DC: American Psychological Association.

Gonçalves, O. F., & Ivey, A. E. (1993). Developmental therapy: Clinical applications. In K. T. Kuehlwein & H. Rosen (Eds.), *Cognitive therapies in action: Evolving innovative practice* (pp. 326–352). San Francisco: Jossey-Bass.

Gruber, H., & Vonèche, J. (Eds.). (1977). *The essential Piaget: An interpretive reference and guide.* New York: Basic Books.

Guidano, V. F. (1987). *Complexity of the self: A developmental approach to psychopathology and therapy.* New York: Guilford.

Guidano, V. F. (1991). *The self in process: Toward a post-rationalist psychotherapy.* New York: Guilford.

Guidano, V. F. (1995). Constructivist psychotherapy: A theoretical framework. In R. A. Neimeyer & M. J. Mahoney (Eds.), *Constructivism in psychotherapy* (pp. 93–108). Washington, DC: American Psychological Association.

Guidano, V. F., & Liotti, G. (1983). *Cognitive processes and emotional disorders: A structural approach to psychotherapy*. New York: Guilford.

Harré, R. (Ed.). (1986). *The social construction of emotions*. New York: Basil Blackwell.

Held, B. S. (1995). *Back to reality: A critique of postmodern theory in psychotherapy*. New York: Guilford.

Hoffman, L. (1990). Constructing realities: An art of lenses. *Family Process, 29*, 1–12.

Hoffman, L. (1993). *Exchanging voices: A collaborative approach to family therapy*. London: Karnac Books.

Howard, G. S. (1991). Culture tales: A narrative approach to thinking, crosscultural psychology, and psychotherapy. *American Psychologist, 46*, 187–197.

Ibsen, H. (1965). A doll's house. In H. Ibsen, *A doll's house and other plays* (pp. 147–232). New York: Penguin.

Ivey, A. E. (1986). *Developmental therapy*. San Francisco: Jossey-Bass.

Karasu, T. B. (1996). *Deconstruction of psychotherapy*. Northvale, NJ: Jason Aronson.

Keating, D. P., & Rosen, H. (Eds.). (1991). *Constructivist perspectives on developmental psychopathology and atypical development*. Hillsdale, NJ: Erlbaum.

Kegan, R. (1982). *The evolving self*. Cambridge, MA: Harvard University Press.

Kegan, R. (1994). *In over our heads: The mental demands of modern life*. Cambridge, MA: Harvard University Press.

Kelly, G. A. (1955). *The psychology of personal constructs* (2 vols.). New York: Norton.

Kohlberg, L. (1981). *Essays on moral development: Vol. 1. The philosophy of moral development*. New York: Harper Collins.

Kohlberg, L. (1984). *Essays on moral development: Vol. 2. The psychology of moral development*. New York: Harper Collins.

Kuehlwein, K. T. (1996a, September). Piaget, postmodernism, and psychotherapy: Epistemological assumptions and praxis. In L. Bizzini (Chair), *Some contributions of Piagetian thinking to psychotherapy theory and practice*. Symposium conducted at the Growing Mind Centennial of Jean Piaget's Birth, Geneva, Switzerland.

Kuehlwein, K. T. (1996b). Interweaving themes and threads of meaning-making. In H. Rosen & K. T. Kuehlwein (Eds.), *Constructing realities: Meaning-making perspectives for psychotherapists* (pp. 491–512). San Francisco: Jossey-Bass.

Lambert, M. J. (1992). Psychotherapy outcome research: Implications for integrative and eclectic therapists. In J. C. Norcross & M. Goldfried (Eds.), *Handbook of psychotherapy integration* (pp. 94–129). New York: Basic Books.

Lyddon, W. J. (1993). Contrast, contradiction, and change in psychotherapy. *Psychotherapy, 30*, 383–390.

Lyotard, J. (1984). *The postmodern condition: A report on knowledge*. Minneapolis: University of Minnesota Press.

Mahoney, M. J. (1986). The tyranny of technique. *Counseling and Values, 30*, 169–174.

Mahoney, M. J. (1988a). Constructive metatheory: I. Basic features and historical foundations. *International Journal of Personal Construct Psychology, 1*, 1–35.

Mahoney, M. J. (1988b). Constructive metatheory: II. Implications for psychotherapy. *International Journal of Personal Construct Psychology, 1*, 299–315.

Mahoney, M. J. (1991). *Human change processes: The scientific foundations of psychotherapy*. New York: Basic Books.

Mahoney, M. J. (in press). *Constructive psychotherapy: Explorations in principles and practices*. New York: Guilford.

Mascolo, M. F. (1994). Toward a social constructivist psychology: The case of self-evaluative emotional development. *Journal of Constructivist Psychology, 7*, 87–106.

Matthews, W. J. (1996). Ericksonian approaches to psychotherapy: From objective to constructed reality. *Journal of Cognitive Psychology, 10*, 205–218.

Maturana, H. R. (1988). Reality: The search for objectivity or the quest for a compelling argument. *Irish Journal of Psychology, 9*, 25–82.

Maturana, H. R., & Varela, F. J. (1987). *The tree of knowledge: The biological roots of human understanding*. Boston: New Science Library.

McNamee, S. (1996). Psychotherapy as a social construction. In H. Rosen & K. T. Kuehlwein (Eds.), *Constructing realities: Meaning-making perspectives for psychotherapists* (pp. 115–137). San Francisco: Jossey-Bass.

McNamee, S., & Gergen, K. J. (Eds.). (1992). *Therapy as social construction.* Newbury Park, CA: Sage.

Monk, G., Winslade, J., Crocket, K., & Epston, D. (Eds.). (1997). *Narrative therapy in practice: The archeology of hope.* San Francisco: Jossey-Bass.

Neimeyer, G. J. (1993). The challenge of change: Reflections on constructivist psychotherapy. *Journal of Cognitive Psychotherapy, 7,* 183–194.

Neimeyer, G. J., & Neimeyer, R. A. (1993). Defining the boundaries of constructivist assessment. In G. Neimeyer (Ed.), *Constructivist assessment: A casebook* (pp. 1–30). Newbury Park, CA: Sage.

Neimeyer, R. A. (1985). *The development of personal construct psychology.* Lincoln: University of Nebraska Press.

Neimeyer, R. A. (1987). An orientation to personal construct therapy. In R. A. Neimeyer & G. J. Neimeyer (Eds.), *Personal construct therapy casebook* (pp. 3–19). New York: Springer.

Neimeyer, R. A. (1995). Constructivist psychotherapies: Features, foundations, and future directions. In R. A. Neimeyer & M. J. Mahoney (Eds.), *Constructivism in psychotherapy* (pp. 11–38). Washington, DC: American Psychological Association.

Neimeyer, R. A. (1996). Process interventions for the constructivist psychotherapist. In H. Rosen & K. T. Kuehlwein (Eds.), *Constructing realities: Meaning-making perspectives for psychotherapists* (pp. 371–411). San Francisco: Jossey-Bass.

Neimeyer, R. A. (1997). Problems and prospects in constructivist psychotherapy. *Journal of Constructivist Psychology, 10,* 51–74.

Neimeyer, R. A., & Feixas, G. (1990). Constructivist contributions to psychotherapy integration. *Journal of Integrative and Eclectic Psychotherapy, 9,* 4–20.

Neimeyer, R. A., & Mahoney, M. J. (Eds.). (1995). *Constructivism in psychotherapy.* Washington, DC: American Psychological Association.

Neimeyer, R. A., & Neimeyer, G. J. (Eds.). (1987). *Personal construct therapy casebook.* New York: Springer.

Norcross, J. C. (Ed.). (1986). *Handbook of eclectic psychotherapy.* New York: Brunner/Mazel.

Nunley, E. P., & Averill, J. A. (1996). Emotional creativity: Theoretical and applied aspects. In H. Rosen & K. T. Kuehlwein (Eds.), *Constructing realities: Meaning-making perspectives for psychotherapists* (pp. 223–251). San Francisco: Jossey-Bass.

Parker, I., Georgaca, E., Harper, D., McLaughlin, T., & Stowell-Smith, M. (1995). *Deconstructing psychopathology.* Thousand Oaks, CA: Sage.

Parry, A., & Doan, R. E. (1994). *Story re-visions: Narrative therapy in the postmodern world.* New York: Guilford.

Pascual-Leone, J. (1990). Reflections on life-span intelligence, consciousness, and ego development. In C. N. Alexander & E. J. Langer (Eds.), *Higher stages of human development* (pp. 258–285). New York: Oxford University Press.

Piaget, J. (1985). *The equilibration of cognitive structures.* Chicago: University of Chicago Press. (Original work published 1975)

Piaget, J., & Garcia, R. (1989). *Psychogenesis and the history of science* (H. Fieder, Trans.). New York: Columbia University Press. (Original work published 1983)

Popper, K. R. (1979). *Objective knowledge: An evolutionary approach* (rev. ed.). New York: Oxford University Press.

Rennie, D. L., & Toukmanian, S. G. (1992). Explanation in psychotherapy process research. In S. G. Toukmanian & D. L. Rennie (Eds.), *Psychotherapy process research: Paradigmatic and narrative approaches* (pp. 234–251). Newbury Park, CA: Sage.

Rogers, L., & Kegan, R. (1991). Mental growth and mental health as distinct concepts in the study of developmental psychopathology: Theory, research and clinical implications. In D. P. Keating & H. Rosen (Eds.), *Constructivist perspectives on developmental psychopathology and atypical development* (pp. 103–147). Hillsdale, NJ: Erlbaum.

Rorty, R. (1979). *Philosophy and the mirror of nature.* Princeton, NJ: Princeton University Press.

Rorty, R. (1991). *Objectivity, relativism, and truth.* Cambridge: Cambridge University Press.

Rosen, H. (1985). *Piagetian dimensions of clinical relevance*. New York: Columbia University Press.

Rosen, H. (1988). Evolving a personal philosophy of practice: Toward eclecticism. In R. Dorfman (Ed.), *Paradigms of clinical social work* (pp. 388–412). New York: Brunner/Mazel.

Rosen, H. (1989). Piagetian theory and cognitive therapy. In A. Freeman, K. M. Simon, L. Beutler, & H. Arkowitz (Eds.), *Comprehensive handbook of cognitive therapy* (pp. 189–212). New York: Plenum.

Rosen, H. (1991). Constructivism: Personality, psychopathology and psychotherapy. In D. Keating & H. Rosen (Eds.), *Constructivist perspectives on developmental psychopathology and atypical development* (pp. 149–171). Hillsdale, NJ: Erlbaum.

Rosen, H. (1993). Developing themes in the field of cognitive therapy. In K. T. Kuehlwein & H. Rosen (Eds.), *Cognitive therapies in action: Evolving innovative practice* (pp. 403–434). San Francisco: Jossey-Bass.

Rosen, H. (1996). Meaning-making narratives: Foundations for constructivist and social constructionist psychotherapies. In H. Rosen & K. T. Kuehlwein (Eds.), *Constructing realities: Meaning-making perspectives for psychotherapists* (pp. 1–51). San Francisco: Jossey-Bass.

Rosen, H., & Kuehlwein, K. T. (Eds.). (1996). *Constructing realities: Meaning-making perspectives for psychotherapists*. San Francisco: Jossey-Bass.

Ruiz, A. B. (1996). The contribution of Humberto Maturana to the sciences of complexity and psychology. *Journal of Constructivist Psychology, 9*, 283–302.

Russell, R. L. (1991). Narrative in views of humanity, science, and action: Lessons for cognitive therapy. *Journal of Cognitive Psychotherapy, 5*, 241–256.

Russell, R. L., & Wandrei, M. L. (1996). Narrative and the process of psychotherapy: Theoretical foundations and empirical support. In H. Rosen & K. T. Kuehlwein (Eds.), *Constructing realities: Meaning-making perspectives for psychotherapists* (pp. 307–335). San Francisco: Jossey-Bass.

Saari, C. (1991). *The creation of meaning in clinical social work*. New York: Guilford.

Saari, C. (1996). Relationship factors in the creation of identity: A psychodynamic perspective. In H. Rosen & K. T. Kuehlwein (Eds.), *Constructing realities: Meaning-making perspectives for psychotherapists* (pp. 141–165). San Francisco: Jossey-Bass.

Sarbin, T. R. (1986). *Narrative psychology: The storied nature of human conduct*. New York: Praeger.

Schafer, R. (1992). *Retelling a life: Narration and dialogue in psychoanalysis*. New York: Basic Books.

Schwartzberg, S. (1996). *A crisis of meaning: How gay men are making sense of AIDS*. New York: Oxford University Press.

Selman, R. L. (1980). *The growth of interpersonal understanding: Developmental and clinical analyses*. San Diego, CA: Academic.

Selman, R. L., Brion-Meisels, S., & Wilkins, G. G. (1996). The meaning of relationship in residential treatment: A developmental perspective. In H. Rosen & K. T. Kuehlwein (Eds.), *Constructing realities: Meaning-making perspectives for psychotherapists* (pp. 455–488). San Francisco: Jossey-Bass.

Shotter, J. (1993). *Conversational realities: Constructing life through language*. Newbury Park, CA: Sage.

Smith, L. (1993). *Necessary knowledge: Piagetian perspectives on constructivism*. Hillsdale, NJ: Erlbaum.

Spence, D. P. (1982). *Narrative truth and historical truth: Meaning and interpretation in psychoanalysis*. New York: Norton.

Stiles, W. B. (1994). Views of the chasm between psychotherapy research and practice. In P. F. Talley, H. H. Strupp, & S. F. Butler (Eds.), *Psychotherapy research and practice: Bridging the gap* (pp. 154–166). New York: Basic Books.

Strickler, G., & Gold, J. R. (Eds.). (1993). *Comprehensive handbook of psychotherapy integration*. New York: Plenum.

Tofani, L. (1996, December 8). Bodies scarred, spirits unbroken. *The Philadelphia Inquirer*, A1, A24–A27.

Toukmanian, S. G., & Rennie, D. L. (Eds.). (1992). *Psychotherapy process research: Paradigmatic and narrative approaches.* Newbury Park, CA: Sage.

Vasco, A. B. (1994). Correlates of constructivism among Portuguese therapists. *Journal of Constructivist Psychology, 7,* 1–16.

Vico, G. (1948). *The new science* (T. G. Bergin & M. H. Fisch, Trans.). Ithaca, NY: Cornell University Press. (Original work published 1725)

von Glaserfeld, E. (1984). An introduction to radical constructivism. In P. Watzlawick (Ed.), *The invented reality: How do we know what we believe we know? Contributions to constructivism* (pp. 17–40). New York: Norton.

Watzlawick, P. (Ed.). (1984). *The invented reality: How do we know what we believe we know? Contributions to constructivism.* New York: Norton.

Watzlawick, P. (1996). The construction of clinical "realities." In H. Rosen & K. T. Kuehlwein (Eds.), *Constructing realities: Meaning-making perspectives for psychotherapists* (pp. 55–70). San Francisco: Jossey-Bass.

White, M., & Epston, D. (1990). *Narrative means to therapeutic ends.* New York: Norton.

Wittgenstein, L. (1958). *Philosophical investigations* (3rd ed.; G. E. M. Anscombe, Trans.). New York: Macmillan.

Zimmerman, J. L., & Dickerson, V. C. (1996). *If problems talked: Narrative therapy in action.* New York: Guilford.

11

Prescriptive Eclectic Psychotherapy

John C. Norcross, Ph.D., Larry E. Beutler, Ph.D., and John F. Clarkin, Ph.D.

INTRODUCTION

The need to match patient and treatment has been recognized from the beginning of psychotherapy. As early as 1919, Freud introduced psychoanalytic psychotherapy as an alternative to classical analysis on the recognition that the more rarified approach lacked universal applicability and that many patients did not possess the requisite psychological mindedness (Liff, 1992). He referred the majority of so-called unanalyzable patients for a psychotherapy based on direct suggestion.

As the field of psychotherapy has matured, the genesis of therapeutic change has been properly recognized as more complex and multifaceted than ever. The identical psychosocial treatment for all patients is now recognized as inappropriate and, in selected cases, even unethical (Norcross, 1991). The efficacy and applicability of psychotherapy will be enhanced by tailoring it to the unique needs of the client, not by imposing a single conforming system onto unwitting consumers of psychological services. Prescriptive matching is embodied in Gordon Paul's (1967) famous question: "*What* treatment, by *whom*, is most effective for *this* individual with *that* specific problem, under *which* set of circumstances?"

Recently, the rapid evolution of health care delivery and the encroaching dominance of managed care have given increased urgency to the task of tailoring time-limited psychological interventions to the client and his or her unique situation. Brief therapies, in turn, demand integrative, explicit, and empirically based models of treatment selection. Within 6 or 12 or 26 sessions, the practitioner is expected to diagnose psychosocial or mental disorders, select specific technical and interpersonal methods to remediate those disorders, apply those methods in sequences or stages over the course of treatment, and then rapidly terminate the efficacious treatment while preventing relapse (Norcross & Beutler, 1997).

Our respective approaches to psychotherapy closely resemble each other in addressing these challenges, as expressed in their titles: *prescriptive eclectic therapy* (Norcross, 1994), *systematic eclectic psychotherapy* (Beutler, 1983), and *systematic treatment selection* (Beutler & Clarkin, 1990). This form of integrative psychotherapy (Norcross & Goldfried, 1992) attempts to customize psychological treatments and therapeutic relationships to the specific and varied needs of individual patients. It does so by drawing on effective methods from across theoretical camps (*eclecticism*), by matching those methods to particular cases on the basis of empirically supported guidelines (*prescriptionism*), and by adhering to an explicit and orderly model of treatment selection (*systematic*). The result of such a systematic and prescriptive eclecticism is a more efficient and efficacious therapy that fits both the client and the clinician.

On the face of it, virtually every psychotherapist endorses prescriptive matching. After all, who can seriously dispute the notion that psychological treatment should be tailored to fit the needs of the individual patient in order to improve the outcome of psychotherapy? However, systematic and prescriptive eclecticism goes beyond this simple acknowledgment in at least four ways:

1. Our basis of prescriptive matching is derived directly from outcome research, rather than from the typical theoretical basis.
2. We adopt an integrative or transtheoretical basis that acknowledges the potential contributions of multiple systems of psychotherapy, rather than working from within a single theory.
3. The guidelines for prescriptive matching are culled from multiple diagnostic and nondiagnostic client variables, in contrast to the typical reliance on the single, static variable of patient diagnosis.
4. Our aim is the research-informed and practice-tested selection of technical interventions and interpersonal stances, whereas most previous prescriptive efforts focused narrowly on the selection of disembodied techniques (Norcross & Beutler, 1997).

In this chapter, we present our prescriptive eclectic model for selecting and sequencing the therapy formats, methods, and relationships of choice, using the case of the Shore family as an illustration. To begin, we trace the underlying philosophy, history, and key constructs of our model. We then demonstrate our typical process of assessment, treatment selection, and therapeutic process, again taking the Shore family as an illustration. We conclude by addressing several limitations of the model and by reviewing the extensive empirical research conducted on the prescriptive matching guidelines underlying the model.

THE CONCEPT OF THE PERSON AND THE HUMAN EXPERIENCE

Eclectic models of personality development and the human experiences are predictably broad and inclusive. People, functional and dysfunctional alike, are the products of a complex interplay of their genetic endowment, social-learning history, and physical environment. By the same token, our eclectic paradigm views psychological disturbances as resulting from numerous influences.

Consider the apparently simple case of specific phobias. The psychoanalytic view, as demonstrated in Freud's (1909) well-known study of phobic 5-year-old "Little Hans," holds that phobias nearly always have unconscious significance and usually result from the displacement of hostile or erotic impulses. The behavioral view, as exemplified by Watson and Rayner's (1920) case of the 11-month-old "little Albert" rendered fearful of furry objects, holds that phobias nearly always have their origins in conditioning and are usually compounded by subsequent avoidance behavior. The psychological formulations embodied by the benchmark cases of Little Hans and Little Albert are insufficient for eclectics. The dichotomy between the psychoanalytic and behavioral views has retarded clinical progress. More complex conceptualizations and multimodal treatments are required for phobias and other behavioral disorders (Lazarus, 1991).

Our eclectic approach is principally concerned with remediating psychopathology, not with explaining it. Behind every eclectic is a vague or inclusive theory of personality. Instead, the central focus is on the content and process of change, a shift in clinical attention that we and other eclectics heartily endorse.

HISTORICAL PERSPECTIVE

In one sense, all treatments—psychotherapeutic or otherwise—are eclectic. No model evolves in a vacuum, and all models reflect at least an implicit process of assimilating, accommodating, and reprioritizing concepts that have been used before. Freud integrated concepts from philosophy, religion, and neurology; Sullivan integrated concepts from psychoanalysis, sociology, and anthropology; Perls integrated concepts from experimental Gestalt psychology, psychoanalytic theory, and dramatic art; and the list goes on. But there are two major historical differences between the development of most psychotherapy theories and that of prescriptive eclecticism.

First, the integration that is a part of the evolution of traditional psychotherapeutic approaches is serendipitous; it is an inevitable aspect of development that nothing arises *de novo* from the head of Zeus. The integration is neither intentional nor terribly desirable. The ascendance of these single-system approaches, however, is accomplished by emphasizing their differences compared to other approaches. By contrast, prescriptive eclectic models thoughtfully and explicitly incorporate methods from other theories. They emphasize their similarities to single-system approaches in addition to their differences.

Second, the nature of prescriptive eclectic psychotherapy is more directly focused on the application of interventions and strategies than on the theoretical constructs of how problems and psychopathology develop. Beginning with Freud, most theories of psychotherapy are also theories of psychopathology. This is not true of the preponderance of prescriptive eclectic models, and certainly is not true of our model. Prescriptive eclectic psychotherapy is more pragmatic than theoretical and also more empirical than theoretical, independent of the theory of psychopathology that underlies them. In other words, if the procedures work, even if the theory is inaccurate, they may be used in a pragmatic and prescriptive manner.

That is not to say that eclectic approaches are *a*theoretical. Indeed, none are. But eclectic theories rarely specify how psychopathology develops. Eclectic theories stay closer to the data and focus on how and what procedures may be combined to the greatest clinical advantage.

Historically, there have been numerous pathways toward the integration of the psychotherapies (Mahrer, 1989; Norcross & Newman, 1992). The three most popular routes have been theoretical integration, technical eclecticism, and common factors (Arkowitz, 1989; Norcross & Grencavage, 1989). Although all three paths are intent on increasing therapeutic effectiveness and efficiency by looking beyond the confines of single-school approaches, they do so in rather different ways and at different levels.

In the pathway known as *theoretical integration,* an effort is made to develop a new approach by integrating two or more old ones. These approaches are concerned with melding theories, including the identification of how psychopathology develops and the mechanisms of change. They assume that techniques and strategies of treatment will best arise from a theoretical understanding of people. The earliest and best example of theoretical integration was that of Dollard and Miller (1950). In their classic book, these authors translated psychoanalytic concepts into behavioral principles and extrapolated the divergent implications for treatment that arose from this amalgamation. This tradition asserted that the most productive level of integration was to blend concepts of two or more theories.

From this blending, a new but vaguely familiar theory would evolve. This general movement was followed by other early efforts to integrate at this level, including a particularly interesting adaptation of exposure therapy and psychodynamic theory called *implosive therapy* (Stampfl & Levis, 1967). In more modern traditions, the effort to bridge theories and blend them into a new one is represented by the work of Wachtel (1977) and Arkowitz and Messer (1984).

A second pathway to integration is known as *technical eclecticism* (Lazarus, 1967; Norcross, 1986). Frederick Thorne (1967) is, probably rightly, credited with being the father of technical eclecticism. Persuasively arguing that any skilled technician should come prepared with more than one tool, Thorne emphasized the need for clinicians to fill their tool boxes with procedures from many different theoretical models. He likened contemporary psychotherapy to a plumber who would use only a screwdriver in his work. Like such a plumber, traditional psychotherapists apply the same treatment to all people regardless of individual differences and expect the patient to adapt to the therapist rather than vice versa. Thorne's admonitions went largely ignored but were followed more than a decade later by a similarly little-noticed book by Goldstein and Stein (1976) that first identified *prescriptive psychotherapy*. This book, also far ahead of its time, outlined treatment programs for different people based on the nature of their problems and aspects of their living situations. In more recent renditions of this form of merging treatments, Lazarus (1967, 1989) has been the most noted and articulate spokesperson, and he was joined by others soon afterward (Beutler, 1983; Frances, Clarkin, & Perry, 1984; Norcross, 1986).

Goldfried and Padawer (1982) argued for a third integrative pathway between the high level of abstraction occupied by global theories and the low level of abstraction occupied by specific techniques. These common factors, or *change processes,* emphasize the understanding of stable principles for combining interventions, which can guide the development and application both of new techniques and the combination of old ones, in order to meet the needs of new situations and events. Goldfried (1980, 1995) as well as Prochaska (1984; Prochaska & Norcross, 1994) have been stalwart proponents of this level of integration.

In the evolution of our own prescriptive eclecticism, we have been influenced by all three pathways to integration, but principally technical eclecticism and change principles. Although our personal and professional histories have led us each in somewhat different directions, we have maintained a core commitment to the central tenet of all eclectic and prescriptive paradigms (Lazarus, Beutler, & Norcross, 1992)—namely, that empirical knowledge and scientific research are the best arbitrators of these differences (Lazarus, 1989). We remain suspicious of global theories of psychotherapy that evolve from other theories, may only reflect the strong opinions of their originators, and consist of descriptions of psychopathology rather than mechanisms of change. Thus a consistent value of prescriptive eclecticism is faith in the scientific method, not as an infallible guide to truth but as the most reliable and valid method available by which to evaluate the value of any psychotherapy, integrative or otherwise.

KEY THEORETICAL CONSTRUCTS

The ultimate goal of psychosocial treatment is symptom relief, whether it be one or a constellation of symptoms or conflicts. In order for the mental health professionals operating on a clinical basis to make the initial probes required to determine a treatment plan and to make a judgment about prognosis, they must focus on patient symptoms and diagnosis, the natural course of those symptoms, the personality of the patient in whom the symptoms reside, and process and mediating goals of the therapy. Throughout this chapter, we refer to certain key treatment planning factors. These include the patient's diagnosis and related problem areas, and mediating and final goals of treatment.

Diagnosis and Problem Areas

We organize our treatment planning in part around the disorders as described in the *Diagnostic and Statistical Manual of Mental Disorders, 4th edition* (*DSM–IV;* American Psychiatric Association, 1994). Although diagnosis alone is not sufficient for treatment planning, there are practical reasons why diagnosis is necessary. First, insurance companies demand a diagnosis, and utilization review is done in reference to diagnosis. Second, treatment research is usually organized around specific diagnostic groups. In order to profit from this research, one must know the patient's diagnosis. Third, the accumulation of knowledge in some areas in which diagnosis has specific and limiting characteristics (e.g., agoraphobia with panic) has been paralleled by the development of empirically supported specialized treatment procedures and treatment manuals.

The diagnoses are related to treatment planning by (a) indicating the outcome criteria of treatment as directly related to altering dysfunctional behavior (e.g., reducing depression); (b) highlighting mediating goals indirectly related to reduction of the criterion (e.g., changing cognitions related to depressive affect); (c) suggesting mediating goals related to coping with the criteria; (d) suggesting mediating goals related to improving social skills that overcome isolation with the disorder (e.g., social skills training for schizophrenic patients); and (e) indicating mediating goals related to modifying the environment of the patient (e.g., lowering of family expressed emotion for the schizophrenic patient).

At the same time, there are many reasons why diagnosis alone is not sufficient for treatment planning (Beutler, 1989; Beutler & Clarkin, 1990). The criteria sets for the disorders are multiple and ever-changing and select different groups of patients. Thus we emphasize the mediating goals of treatment that are somewhat unique in their combination for each individual patient. Axis I patients may also have comorbid Axis I disorders, in addition to one or more Axis II disorders. One formulates treatment planning for individuals, not for isolated disorders.

We focus on Axis I and Axis II disorders for treatment planning. However, the combination of all five axes—a large array of possibilities—must be taken into account in treatment planning for the individual. Given the multiaxial nature of *DSM–IV*, the diagnosis is not limited to just Axis I (symptoms) and Axis II (personality disorders) considerations, but also to environmental stress (Axis IV) and level of overall functioning (Axis V). This is why there should be no surprise that several patients with the same Axis I disorder could and should receive quite different treatments. The Axis V or Global Assessment of Functioning (GAF) rating may be of particular importance in treatment planning. Independently of the particular Axis I (and Axis II) diagnosis, the relative level of the GAF score may relate to the nature and process of differential treatment planning.

Let us briefly use each treatment decision point in reference to the members of the Shore family. From a diagnostic point of view, it seems important to note Mr. Shore's diagnosis of bipolar depression. The case description is not clear, but because the term *bipolar* is used and since he is on maintenance lithium, it suggests that he has had at least one manic episode in his lifetime. Mrs. Shore is obese, and although the diagnosis is not clearly made, there are indications that she has anxiety or panic attacks, and suggestions that she has probably suffered from major depression (gained 50 pounds, sleeps poorly, cannot concentrate). Son Michael appears to have a learning disability.

Mediating and Final Goals of Treatment

The alleviation or elimination of a particular problem is the typical final goal of treatment. However, the mediating goals of treatment—those intermediate goals or subgoals that must be reached in order to achieve the final goals—are not always so obvious. They are dictated by the model of the symptom picture, problem area, or successive steps to health and will depend on the particular problem area, the theoretical orientation of the assessor, and current understanding of the particular diagnosis or problem area in question. The nature and extent of these mediating goals provides the indications for the various therapeutic settings, formats, strategies or techniques, somatic treatments, and treatment durations. Therefore, in the evaluation and treatment planning phase for any case, the clinician must be as precise as possible about the mediating goals of treatment.

The complexity of the patient's problem and the patient's readiness for change are the primary variables that go into selecting treatment goals and subgoals. Complexity is defined as the degree to which the problem represents an isolated or continuing problem. Complex problems are chronic, recurrent, affect many life functions, and usually reflect a recurrent interpersonal theme or pattern. Concomitantly, complex problems require a focus on more thematic and systemic goals than the symptomatic ones that are appropriate to a situational problem.

Usually an assessment of complexity begins with a determination of the problem for which the patient (or family) is seeking help. If it is identified as complex, the therapist proceeds to a determination of what interpersonal pattern is present in their collective interactions. Changing this pattern is then included as a treatment objective, along with symptom amelioration and improved functioning. The information that is contained in the narrative about the Shore family is incomplete for some of our purposes. Even with only the information provided, however, it seems safe to assume that the problems of the Shore family are quite complex. They are recurrent, persistent, and life-involving. They seem endemic to the nature of the life function and environment. Probably, therefore, they require an intensive treatment focused on changing the interpersonal patterns and themes that sustain the problems.

The next step is to identify the particular pattern on which work is needed. Here, the incomplete narrative description is a decided handicap. Although it provides information about each person within the family, it does not outline the sequential pattern of family interaction with respect to demand and withdrawal, systemic motives, and coping strategies. We must not simply know that Charley is fragile and depressed, that Nancy is searching for control, that Rena is rebelling and unsettled in her family identification, and that Michael is poorly socialized and inappropriate. We also must know the orchestrated interactions that describe when each of these people display these behaviors. That is, we must know when the behaviors are displayed and in what juxtaposition they exist to the behaviors of other family members. A systematic evaluation, based largely on observational and interview methods, would help define this theme.

There are many ways of formulating problems. One may be as good as the next, but it is important that a pattern of interactions be defined that can serve as a thread to pursue in changing the meaning and repetition of the complex problem. Usually, the evaluation includes direct observations from which questions are developed that allow the clinician to construct a working model of how the family interacts. This model will probably include at least three aspects that describe each person's role in times of crisis: (a) the wants of each individual that press to be met at the crisis moment, (b) the expectations and fears that each family member experiences should he or she express these wants directly, and (c) the consequential behaviors and introjects that represent the compromises made by the family system to balance wants and expectations.[1]

Let us assume that we have conducted such observations and interviews, and that we have determined the following pattern of interactions: Nancy plays the role of sentry. She is in an *action mode* (stage of readiness for change) and demands that others change in her environment. That is, she is the vigilant and responsible one who alerts the family to trouble from within or without. This vigilant role is a logical one for her since Charley seems bent on denying problems until they overtake him, and because both Rena and Michael are disengaged from the family, either by virtue of geographic distance or by lack of emotional awareness and maturity.

We may determine that when Nancy plays her role of identifying impending harm, her primary want is to protect her family from harm and herself from the experience of vulnerability and incompetence. Thus, she sees her role as central to family safety and may bemoan that no one else can perform this function in the family. We may also determine that she usually directs the alarm to Charley, trying to motivate him to action. She sees Charley as the one who could and should protect the family, but she expects that he will not do so and that instead he will be unresponsive and unavailable. Charley, in turn, is not at the action stage of readiness but is still somewhere between contemplation of changes and avoiding the idea all together (*precontemplative*). Thus, he usually complies with Nancy's negative expectations of passivity, which only further excites Nancy's efforts to motivate him to take action as she sees the situation worsen. We may also find that this continued demand by Nancy is ultimately followed by Charley's withdrawal—he leaves on the pretense of searching for the illusive job that will fix things up—and depression. Charley wants safety and recognition; he expects that the recognition he will receive, however, will only be negative and critical; he concludes the pattern by engaging in self-depreciation and behavioral withdrawal to avoid this criticism.

Michael, we might find, wants to preserve his parents' relationship. He expects danger and abandonment should their arguments continue. Michael vacillates between a contemplative and an action state of readiness, protecting the family by diverting members' focus to his own inappropriate behavior at school. This may keep Nancy and Charley united in a joint but futile effort to "fix" Michael.

Rena's situation is somewhat different. She is out of the family and developmentally attempting to establish an independent role. She has taken

---

[1]*Editor's note:* An introject is that which was once external to the person but has now been "taken in" or internalized as a means of coping with or adapting to a threatening situation.

some action and seems ambivalently to be preparing for more (preparation phase), seeking her identity as an adult and as a person independently of her family. She expects that family crises will prevent or interfere with these efforts, and she responds by becoming more withdrawn and hopeless. She adopts the low level of functioning that will keep her tied to and dependent on her family as a compromise between her need for others and her own desire for individuation.

As the pattern is enacted, each member of the family has developed his or her own explanation for the recurrence and failure of the pattern to meet their individual needs. These explanations will range from assigning blame to Charley's "condition," to Rena's laziness, to Michael's "learning problem," and Nancy's failure to be sufficiently vigilant. Family work may now be initiated with the goals of changing the identified family theme. There may be some additional individual themes that need attention— for example, Rena's struggle to disengage from her family and establish a sense of identity separate from it.

ASSESSMENT

Clinical assessment in prescriptive eclecticism is relatively traditional— with one large exception. The assessment interview(s) will entail collecting information on clients' presenting problems, relevant histories, treatment expectations and goals, as well as building solid rapport and a working alliance. As psychologists, we also typically request or conduct psychological testing as a means of securing additional data and normative comparisons for Axis I and Axis II disorders. We recommend that social workers and other non-psychologists thoroughly ground themselves in the use of symptomatic rating forms (e.g., Beck Depression Inventory, Symptom Checklist–90R) and, as clinically indicated, routinely refer clients for more extensive psychological testing. The large exception to this traditional assessment process is that—from the outset—prescriptive eclecticism systematically collects information on multiple patient dimensions that will guide treatment selection.

One of the central challenges to prescriptive eclectic psychotherapies is the identification of productive patient dimensions that relate to treatment decisions. The complexity of this task can be grasped by enumerating the variety of potential combinations of patient, therapist, and treatment variables that may be included in a comprehensive model of psychotherapy. Even conservatively identifying the variables that are known to have an effect on psychotherapy, there are still millions of potential permutations and combinations that could contribute to relevant systematic treatment planning (Beutler, 1991). The very contemplation of such an extensive array of variables is daunting, made more so by managed health care systems that have historically eschewed the use of formal psychological testing. Elsewhere, we (Beutler, Kim, Davison, Karno, & Fisher, 1996; Harwood et al., 1997) have argued for a new approach to psychological assessment, one that is highly focused and targeted on those dimensions of the patient and environment that are most predictive of differential treatment response.

Within the large list of important patient variables, research has enabled us to select a smaller number that are most promising as prescriptive guidelines. In various combinations and with different amounts of emphasis, each of us has acknowledged the promising nature of multiple patient characteristics in treatment planning. We focus on six that we have found to be of primary importance:

1. diagnosis/symptoms,
2. functional impairment,
3. coping style,
4. resistance potential,
5. readiness for change/stage of change, and
6. preferences for certain methods or relationships.

It is still not clear how to rank-order these different patient characteristics, ascertain how they interact, or verify their independence. Nonetheless, each of these client variables has been found to affect psychotherapy outcomes. In their most refined form, these can be used to differentially predict the rate and magnitude of change accompanying different forms of treatment (see Beutler & Berren, 1995; Beutler, Kim et al., 1996; Frances, Clarkin, & Perry, 1984; Gaw & Beutler, 1995; Groth-Marnat, 1997; Prochaska, Norcross, & DiClemente, 1994).

Several years ago, Beutler and Clarkin (1990) suggested some methods of measuring each of these dimensions. More recently, Groth-Marnat (1997), Beutler and Berren (1995), and Beutler and Harwood (1995) have specifically identified a variety of psychometric tests and clinical methods that may be used to assess these dimensions, along with methods of identifying the treatments for which each may be a prescriptive guideline. Unlike traditional, broad-band evaluations that do not focus directly on treatment implications, our assessments attempt to derive a clinically focused, empirically supported, and relationship-based treatment plan. The assessment task in prescriptive eclectic psychotherapy is to identify the most reliable predictors of differential treatment response.

The problems with this assessment tack have always been that the sheer number of variables are beyond the capacities of clinicians to use consistently, and that the way that these variables would be balanced and weighted has not been established empirically. However, the advent of the computer has introduced the capacity to manage large numbers of patient, therapist, and treatment variables and to identify predictive patterns that are objective and independent of therapists' personal preferences. With to-day's computers, it is now possible to rapidly extract relationships that will allow highly individualized and precise predictions of the effects of differ-ent therapists and different therapeutic procedures. Beutler and Williams (1995; Beutler, Kim, et al, 1996) have introduced computer software that is designed to help clinicians summarize information gathered from nu-merous, individualized sources of data into stable judgments that can then apply a number of patient, treatment, and therapist dimensions to reach empirically derived predictions of what procedures, therapists, and treat-ments will be most likely to yield good effects.

TREATMENT OF CHOICE

Prescriptive eclecticism is a meta-model that attempts to enhance the ef-fectiveness, efficiency, and applicability of psychotherapy by tailoring it to the particular needs of clients, settings, and situations. Accordingly, our in-tegrative model is designed to transcend the limited applicability of single-theory or *school-bound* psychotherapies. Put another way, rather than re-stricting itself to select situations or imposing a theoretical Procrustean bed onto all situations, prescriptive eclecticism ascertains the treatment (and relationship) of choice for each individual patient.

THERAPEUTIC PROCESS

Treatment Decisions

Prescriptive eclectic clinicians are concerned with treatment planning as well as the therapist–client relationship. Treatment planning invariably in-volves five interrelated decisions:

1. treatment setting,
2. treatment format,
3. strategies and techniques,
4. treatment intensity, and
5. choice of somatic treatments.

Treatment setting

The therapeutic setting is where the treatment occurs—a psychothera-pist's office, a psychiatric hospital, a halfway house, an outpatient clinic, a medical ward, and so on. The choice of setting depends primarily on the relative need for restricting and supporting the patient due to the severity of psychopathology and the level of support in the patient's environment.

Each treatment decision is related to the treatment decisions considered below, as well as to certain patient variables, which will be considered later in this chapter. For example, the optimal treatment setting is partially affected by level of symptomatic impairment and partially reflects resistance level. Those clients who are most impaired and resistant (i.e., dangerous) have the greatest need for a restrictive environment. The optimal treatment format for other clients may well reflect client preferences and adequacy of social support.

Ambulatory treatment is always preferred. Hospitalization may be needed infrequently for Charley if his manic behavior and suicidal ideation get out of control. Otherwise, there are no other pressing indications for a setting other than outpatient care.

Treatment format

The therapeutic format describes who directly participates in the treatment. Each of the typical treatment formats—individual, group, and family—is characterized by a set of treatment parameters, all determined largely by the number and identities of the participants (e.g., patient, parents, spouse, siblings).

Because the individual format is familiar, private, relatively flexible, and built on the basic trust inherent in a dyadic relationship, it remains the most prevalent format of psychosocial treatment. Over the past 40 years, as the limitations of an individual format have become more widely appreciated and as the field has shifted toward theoretical models that emphasize interpersonal rather than intrapsychic dynamics, clinicians have increasingly used family–marital and group treatment formats.

The choice of a particular treatment format is determined, in part, by the way in which the patient–family and the clinician defines the presenting problem. Some couples apply to a family clinic for marital treatment for what they perceive as an interpersonal problem or conflict. In another couple with the same situation, the wife may call a clinic and ask for an appointment for herself. From the clinician's point of view, the treatment of a spouse with depression can vary depending on whether it is viewed (etiology aside) as a current adaptation to a larger problem involving the family unit (suggesting a need for family intervention) or as the patient's personal adaptation to a unique biological, social, and historical situation (suggesting individual or group treatment). The mediating and final goals of treatment will vary accordingly. Although therapeutic strategies and techniques are influenced by treatment format, these can vary independently of format and in accordance with the clinician's theoretical system.

The distress level in the Shore family is high, concomitant with the level of family disruption. Here, the Shore family must be considered as both a unit and a collection of individuals—that is, as both psyches and systems. We would give priority to family intervention in view of the paucity of support that each member of the family is receiving from others inside and outside the family. Thus we would intervene first and most strongly at the interpersonal and systems levels of functioning. Family therapy will likely be valuable in facilitating and enhancing the availability of support in ways that will provide a platform of security for further individual exploration, if such exploration continues to be indicated.

Most members of this family will probably receive direct and helpful assistance through the medium of family therapy. Unless any of them have strong and persuasive reasons for preferring individual therapy, family treatment may even obviate the need for other psychosocial interventions. This conclusion reflects our tentative assumption that most of the major problems for this family are central to and provoked by family dysfunction, since the major evidences of individual psychopathology seem to have occurred either within the family system or in response to it. Further evaluation of the relationship between personal psychopathology (the psyches) and family functioning (the system) is needed in order to predict the degree to which personal problems will be responsive to therapeutically induced changes in the family environment.

Let us assume that individual therapy would be initiated once family functioning has achieved some stability and has manifested sufficient support. Individual psychotherapy may well be indicated for Charley and perhaps for Nancy and Rena as well. In Rena's case, intermediate goals would be providing support and encouragement; in the case of Nancy and Charley, intermediate goals would be enhanced coping and improved social functioning. Charley is the one who most obviously can be expected to benefit from individual psychotherapy, and this format could productively focus on expanding his available work and social skills. The nature of their respective individual therapies, however, must take into account factors beyond the therapy format, including each individual's coping style and resistance level.

Strategies and techniques

The choice of psychotherapeutic strategies and techniques depends on the mediating goals of treatment that are considered paramount. *Technique*—what a clinician actually does with a patient—most closely reflects the clinician's view of the etiological and maintaining factors of mental disorders. The selection and use of therapeutic techniques and strategies are the most controversial components of the prescriptive model. Proponents of different theories have decidedly different views of what appear to be the same techniques, and any given technique can be used in vastly different ways. Thus rather than focusing on the selection and use of specific techniques, we have adopted the strategy of prescribing general principles or strategies of change. These strategies can be implemented in a number of ways and with a diversity of specific techniques. For example, by mixing and matching procedures from different treatment manuals (see below), we attempt to tailor the treatment and the therapist's roles to address the particular but distinguishing mediating goals and objectives for a given patient.

Clinical research has indicated strategies and techniques that are effective with specific patient problem areas. Manuals are now being written to guide research and training in the techniques of the various schools (dynamic, behavior, cognitive) for diverse patient populations, for example, anxiety (Beck & Emery, 1985), depression (Beck, Rush, Shaw & Emery, 1979), schizophrenia (Falloon, Boyd, & McGill, 1984), interpersonal problems (Luborsky, 1984; Strupp & Binder, 1984), and suicidal behaviors (Linehan, 1993). These manuals explicate the treatments and illustrate their similarities (despite different theories and theoretical languages) and their differences. These manuals describe particular strategies and techniques in detail and discuss when best to use them.

We are conservative in our approach and emphasize only those classes of technique that have a long history (such as psychodynamic and experiential) or that are supported by substantial outcome research (such as behavioral, cognitive–behavioral, and systems family techniques). In addition, we have tried to classify techniques with the goal of treatment planning specifically in mind. In this situation, the clinician must determine specific mediating goals for each particular patient, given his or her unique diagnosis, social environmental situation, and personality assets and liabilities. From this point of view, our categorization includes so-called psychoanalytic techniques that have the mediating goal of insight and conflict resolution; behavioral techniques, with the mediating goals of specific behavioral changes; cognitive techniques, with the mediating goals of change in conscious thought processes; experiential techniques, with the immediate goals of increased awareness that is more fully integrated into the patient's personality; and systemic techniques with the mediating goals of restructuring family interactions.

As we have noted, most therapists cannot keep in hand more than three or four variables at once. Rather than address each of the many dimensions that we have addressed, we will illustrate the use of only the six patient variables we discussed above as applied to the Shore family: diagnosis and symptoms, functional impairment, coping style, resistance potential, readiness for change or stage of change, and preferences for certain methods or relationships.

The selection of psychotherapy methods must be done within the context (setting, intensity, and format) of treatment. They must also be considered within the context of the psychotherapeutic relationship. Somewhat different methods will be used when the therapist–family relationship is supportive and stable as opposed to when it is characterized by instability and hostility. We will discuss these relationship issues shortly. For the moment, we will assume that the therapist has spent initial time developing a working relationship with each family member, has established a contract for the treatment within the context of this relationship, and has been able to overcome the initially expected distrust and fear by establishing himself or herself as a caring and attentive person.

In this relationship-building phase, the goals of treatment are identified, both for the individual patients and for the family; the level of intervention is identified; and the therapeutic relationship is established. There are other aspects of treatment, of course, but these three components of the treatment package will serve to illustrate the use of prescriptive eclectic models.

The level of intervention may vary from behavioral to insight and from individual to interpersonal. The level of treatment must be consistent with the coping style developed and used most dominantly in the family. Coping style varies from being externalized and impulsive to cyclic and unstable to avoidant, internalized, and self-punitive. Research is increasingly suggesting that the level of externalization drives the decision as to whether one will intervene at the level of behavior or insight. Although insight-oriented therapies may do well for internalizing individuals, the presence of externalizing behaviors—those that move against people—mitigate this influence (Beutler, Engle, Mohr et al., 1991; Beutler, Mohr et al., 1991).

One can see in both Nancy and Rena a tendency to use action-oriented defenses and coping strategies, although Rena appears to also use some internalizing and self-reflective coping strategies. She probably represents an unstable cyclic pattern of coping, partially consistent with her developmental level. These patterns of Nancy and Rena stand in contrast to Charley's avoidant style (low internalizing and low externalizing tendencies). Michael seems to be a less socialized variant of his father and is characterized by both some externalization and avoidance.

Both the general pattern of being outgoing (Nancy) and the pattern of directly avoiding conflict (Rena) indicate the presence of a moderate to high level of externalization in this family. This viewpoint is reinforced by the action-oriented stage of change that seems to characterize both Nancy and Rena. These patterns of externalization indicate that direct control of disruptive behaviors is needed. At least initially, we focus on the behavioral level of change, beginning our interventions, therefore, by using behavioral and cognitive–behavioral strategies. Accordingly, we would share our formulation of the family pattern with the family members and then would begin to facilitate an effort among family members to identify the signal behaviors that seem to stimulate the initiation and escalation of this pattern. We would initiate some homework tasks, probably first working to identify and tabulate the frequency of certain key events (crises). We might progress to the use of techniques that are designed to increase the level of positive reinforcement and affective tone in the family environment—for example, noting with Nancy that she seems to be trying too hard to prevent dissolution and pain. We may suggest that she seems to be very optimistic about getting Charley to take charge in spite of her repeated failures to do so. We might suggest that a change of tactic from criticism to reward would be interesting to try. Using a token system for signaling when members of the family are criticizing, punishing, and ignoring others, we could encourage family members to begin having short family conversations in which they practice more positive strategies.

In the latter half of therapy, the behavioral focus might also shift to the area of skill development. Communication, work, study, and job-hunting skills all appear to be lacking in one or more members of the family. Homework assignments and the use of role playing could facilitate the development of insight and understanding.

As homework and in-session interventions are tried, and as they reduce the level to which family members, especially Nancy, attempt to control other people by criticism and attack, the focus may change to be more insight oriented. Certain family members, such as Rena, may benefit from understanding each family member's contribution to the overall family theme. Now the shift will be toward stimulating understanding, but this might be of most advantage to Rena, whose development seems most compatible with these insight goals. If so, some individual therapy might be indicated to help her solidify her separation.

Treatment intensity

The *intensity* of a psychosocial treatment is the product of the duration of the treatment episode, the length of a session, and the frequency of sessions. Treatment intensity should depend on the technical requirements and goals of the treatment and the severity of the disorder. Brief treatments are obviously not for everyone, and many patients need long-term treatment or lifetime care, but the clinical research attention to brief therapy has pushed differential treatment planning forward by clarifying which patient conditions can profit from planned treatments of relatively brief duration.

The treatment duration is more multifaceted. The major reference is to the duration of the *treatment episode*—that is, the time from evaluation to termination of this particular treatment period. Alternatively, one could consider the duration of each *aspect* of the total treatment package. For example, the total treatment package for one episode of a disorder may include different treatment settings (inpatient followed by outpatient), treatment formats (individual and family therapy), medications of various durations, and different strategies. Finally, treatment can be lifetime—that is, involving many episodes of treatment throughout the lifetime of a patient who has a chronic psychiatric condition such as schizophrenia or bipolar disorder.

The Shores' disorders imply a chronic course (i.e., bipolar disorder and major depression), and it is no wonder that the family seems to require continual care. This appears to be a family that is coping, albeit somewhat ineffectively, with chronic affective disorder. Brief treatments for crisis in the context of long-term maintenance care (i.e., maintenance medication for Charley) would be indicated.

Choice of somatic treatments

The clinician has two major questions to answer regarding somatic treatment: Is a somatic treatment (psychotropic medication and electroconvulsive therapy) indicated and, if so, how should it be prescribed (which drug in which dosage at which frequency and for how long)? The answer to the first major question is quite easy when the patient clearly has an impairment amenable to a somatic intervention. At other times, however, the decision is uncertain. Because research has not yet determined precisely when a somatic treatment should be introduced in conjunction with a psychosocial treatment, this decision will be greatly influenced by the individual preferences of the pharmacologist and patient. To date, psychopharmacological research has been more systematic in answering the second major question confronting the consultant. Once a decision is made to use a somatic treatment, many studies are available to guide the consultant in the choice, dosage, frequency, and duration of the drug.[2]

It seems clear that because of his diagnosis of bipolar disorder Charley should be maintained on medication. There are treatment guidelines for this condition, and one of the many psychoeducational packets (e.g., Frances, Docherty & Kahn, 1996) about the disorder could be given to and shared with the family.

It is less clear, but quite possible, that the severity of Nancy's major depression may indicate a positive response to an antidepressant medication. This is a treatment option that we would certainly discuss with her, before and during the psychotherapy.

The foregoing pages demonstrate the step-by-step selection of therapeutic strategies and the complex process of determining the optimal course of treatment for the Shore family. It would be a colossal misunderstanding, however, to view prescriptive eclecticism as endorsing a disembodied,

---

[2]*Editor's note:* Social workers are not physicians and thus are not sanctioned to prescribe or advise clients about psychopharmacological treatments. However, they commonly refer their clients to psychiatrists for evaluation and often work in conjunction with psychiatrists if their clients are taking medication or are receiving other somatic treatments.

technique-oriented model of psychotherapy. Prescriptive eclectic clinicians attempt to customize not only therapy techniques but also their relationship stances to individual clients. One way to conceptualize the matter, paralleling the notion of "treatments of choice" in terms of techniques, is how clinicians determine "therapeutic relationships of choice" in terms of interpersonal stances (Lazarus, 1993; Norcross, 1993).

In the case of the Shore family, we would probably tailor the therapeutic relationship to their interpersonal preferences and to their patient resistance. When ethically and clinically appropriate, we prefer to accommodate a client's relational preferences—when to be warm, tepid, or cool; when to be active or passive; and so on. As is unfortunately the case in most clinical presentations, the information presented about the Shore family does not indicate their relational preferences—what they would like from the therapist in terms of level of activity, formality, closeness, structure, and so forth. By contrast, the case presentation does provide some hints of their level of resistance. The level of resistance can be seen both for the family as a unit and for the individual members; in this family, one might expect that resistance levels are moderate or high. High resistance indicates the need for nondirective, self-directed, or paradoxical interventions, whereas low resistance indicates the patient's accessibility to a wider range of interventions, including therapist-controlled ones (Beutler, Sandowicz, Fisher, & Albanese, 1996).

The nature of individual levels of resistance varies from being passive (Charley and Michael) to active (Rena) and ambivalent (Nancy). As with level of intervention, the level of directiveness and control established by the therapist must be adapted to the individual with the highest level of trait-like resistance potential. This is especially critical since, in this case, we have selected a behavioral level of intervention, and this ordinarily suggests a high level of therapist control. Such directiveness is contraindicated in the case of highly resistant individuals.

Self-help books and self-monitoring may be useful in the development of homework assignments, particularly for the most resistant members (probably Charley and Nancy). Paradoxical instructions directed at Nancy to avoid making or instigating changes too rapidly, and even prescribing or predicting a period of time in which no change should occur, may be particularly helpful. The therapist who assumes the role of family consultant rather than expert or guide may successfully circumnavigate the hazards of noncompliance. Thus the behavioral contracts might be initiated by the patient, following the suggestion that he or she read certain materials on how to establish behavioral self-control. Contract negotiation and behavioral exchange procedures may supplement these procedures—for instance, interpersonal contracts that offer to trade positive behaviors, such as less demand by Nancy being exchanged for more physical availability by Charley. Therapists must be careful to avoid making demands or relying on their own expertise that would give Nancy and Charley a reason for rebellion and non-cooperation. The therapist who maintains a consultant role as an observer and commentator regarding family dynamics, rather than as an agent of change, may prove to be most helpful.

Resistance is also a state-like quality and is responsive to the level of safety present in the therapeutic environment. Thus, as the environment becomes safer, a therapist may be able to increase the level of directiveness used. Therapists often find that they can be directive with one patient in the family but not with another. These forces must be constantly monitored and the therapists' stance adjusted accordingly.

LIMITATIONS OF THE MODEL

Our prescriptive eclectic model has developed largely in response to the realities of clinical practice and to the limitations of older forms of technical eclecticism. As described earlier, the historical limitations of eclectic models—relying on the single, static variable of patient diagnosis to select a particular technique—have been rectified in contemporary, prescriptive eclectic models of psychotherapy. We have indeed learned from cogent criticisms.

This leaves us with the dilemma of either positing limitations of all psychotherapy models (e.g., the need for additional research) or of letting others speak to the limitations in our model. We will briefly do both.

So far, research and training have been limited (Lambert & Bergin, 1992; Norcross, 1997). We need to conduct further prospective outcome research that demonstrates the differential effectiveness of these nondiagnostic treatment markers with diagnostically heterogeneous patients. We also require the establishment of training programs that will insure a modicum of competence in prescriptive eclecticism or in differential referral. To date, training in psychotherapy integration has largely been idiosyncratic and unreliable.

Other psychotherapeutic systems have also found problems with prescriptive eclecticism. In the integrative spirit of entertaining multiple perspectives on any clinical matter (even though we disagree with them), let us share some of the common criticisms (adapted from Prochaska & Norcross, 1994). From a psychoanalytic perspective, adding behavioral, cognitive, and systemic interventions bespeaks impatience with the necessarily gradual alteration in historically situated intrapsychic conflicts. From a behavioral perspective, *eclecticism* usually means that therapists beg, borrow, and steal from the leading systems of psychotherapy. Rarely do eclectics create new therapeutic interventions or theoretical constructs. To the extent they are creative, it is in the way they put together their bag of tricks rather than in creating new concepts that others could borrow. From a humanistic perspective, *psychotherapy* is an encounter between two people in a helping relationship; for some eclectics, psychotherapy is more a technical enterprise. Clients may disappear in case presentations, partitioned into segments in the quest for prescriptive guidelines and then repaired in segments with precise surgical interventions. And from a contextual perspective, as each psychotherapeutic door opens, another closes. There are always trade-offs in the service of psychotherapy integration. In recommending action along with psychic exploration, eclectics can close off some avenues to deeper meaning and intention. In bringing cognitive and affective factors into the behavioral purview, eclectics may reduce the appeal to measurable objectives and tangible contingencies (Messer, 1992).

RESEARCH

The outcome research supporting prescriptive eclectic psychotherapy comes in two guises. First and most generally, the entire body of empirical research on psychotherapy informs our treatment decisions and key constructs. This is the basis from which we have systematized our process of treatment selection. A genuine advantage of being an eclectic is the vast amount of research attesting to the efficacy of psychotherapy and pointing to its differential effectiveness with certain types of disorders and patients. Eclectic therapy tries to incorporate state-of-the-art research findings into its open framework, in contrast to developing yet another system of psychotherapy.

Second and more specifically, ongoing programmatic research has supported the value of systematic treatment planning according to several client variables. All the interrelationships among these patient qualities that predict differential treatment response have to be determined, but considerable evidence indicates each of the patient variables we have described is conducive to predicting a differential treatment response. Although a full review of research available on this topic is not possible here, aspects of it have been summarized elsewhere (Beutler & Clarkin, 1990; Beutler, Kim et al., 1996; Gaw & Beutler, 1995; Harwood et al., 1997; Lazarus, Beutler, & Norcross, 1992; Norcross, 1994; Norcross & Beutler, 1997; Prochaska, Norcross, & DiClemente, 1994). The following established relationships suggest directions for enhancing the efficacy and efficiency of psychotherapy:

1. Among the more important achievements of psychotherapy research is the demonstration of the differential efficacy of a few therapies with specific disorders (Lambert & Bergin, 1992). Although we can not match them all up with certainty, some "marriages" between disorder and treatment seem to do well—for example, mild to moderate

depressions seem to be particularly responsive to cognitive therapy or interpersonal therapy; specific phobias and trauma to some form of exposure; panic attacks and childhood aggression to cognitive–behavioral therapy; and marital discord to conjoint treatment (Barlow, 1994; Chambless et al, 1996; Lambert & Bergin, 1992).

2. Patient externalizing coping style is probably a differential predictor of responsivity to symptom-focused interventions and may contraindicate the use of insight interventions (Beutler, Engle, Mohr, et al., 1991; Beutler, Machado, Engle, & Mohr., 1993; Beutler, Mohr, et al., 1991).

3. The severity of symptoms or the degree of functional impairment is a probable predictor of response to medication and may even indicate the relative value of psychopharmacological versus psychological interventions (Beutler & Baker, in press; Elkin, 1994; Elkin, Gibbons, Shea, & Shaw, 1996).

4. Level of resistance potential is probably a specific indicator of using highly directive or nondirective, self-directed, and even paradoxical interventions (Beutler, Sandowicz, Fisher, & Albanese, 1996; Shoham-Salomon & Hannah, 1991).

5. Level of patient arousal may interact with the use of procedures that heighten or directly reduce arousal and distress (Beutler, Kim, et al., 1996; Burgoon et al., 1993).

6. Level of patient social support and investment in social attachments may be predictive of the value of interpersonally focused and family therapies (Elkin et al., 1989; Sotsky et al., 1991).

7. Patient readiness for change, as represented in the stages of change, is probably predictive of response to type of change processes and interpersonal stance (Prochaska, DiClemente, & Norcross, 1992; Prochaska, Norcross, & DiClemente, 1994; Prochaska, Rossi, & Wilcox, 1991). Specifically, clients in the contemplation stage respond best to awareness-inducing, self-reevaluation, emotional processing, and a therapist stance akin to a nurturing parent and a Socratic teacher. By contrast, clients in the action stage respond best to the change processes of contingency management, counterconditioning, and stimulus control and to a therapist stance characterized as an experienced coach.

All of this is to say that the science and art of psychotherapy has progressed to the point where clinically relevant and readily assessable patient characteristics can systematically inform specific treatment plans and thereby enhance the efficacy and efficiency of our clinical work (Beutler & Berren, 1995; Beutler & Clarkin, 1990; Groth-Marnat, 1997; Norcross, 1994).

SUMMARY

Although necessarily simplified and condensed, this chapter outlines our prescriptive eclectic model of psychotherapy. Our aim has been to demonstrate the process of systematic treatment selection, a process that applies knowledge from multiple theoretical orientations on both diagnostic and nondiagnostic variables to the optimal choice of technical and interpersonal methods. Prescriptive eclectic psychotherapy posits that many treatment methods and therapeutic stances have a valuable place in the repertoire of the contemporary psychotherapist. The particular and differential place they occupy can be determined by outcome research and seasoned experience that places individual client needs at the center of the clinical enterprise. In the future, psychotherapy will be enhanced by selecting among existing technical and interpersonal processes in specific circumstances. Herein may ultimately lie the promise of the scientific and human enterprise known as psychotherapy.

REFERENCES

American Psychiatric Association. (1994). *Diagnostic and statistical manual of mental disorders* (4th ed.). Washington, DC: Author.

Arkowitz, H. (1989). The role of theory in psychotherapy integration. *Journal of Integrative and Eclectic Psychotherapy, 8,* 8–16.

Arkowitz, H., & Messer, S. B. (Eds.). (1984). *Psychoanalytic and behavior therapy: Is integration possible?* New York: Plenum.

Barlow, D. H. (1994). Psychological interventions in the era of managed competition. *Clinical Psychology: Science and Practice, 1,* 109–122.

Beck, A. T., & Emery, G. (with Greenberg, R.). (1985). *Anxiety disorders and phobias: A cognitive perspective.* New York: Basic Books.

Beck, A. T., Rush, A. J., Shaw, B. F., & Emery, G. (1979). *Cognitive therapy of depression: A treatment manual.* New York: Guilford.

Beutler, L. E. (1983). *Eclectic psychotherapy: A systematic approach.* New York: Pergamon.

Beutler, L. E. (1989). Differential treatment selection: The role of diagnosis in psychotherapy. *Psychotherapy, 26,* 271–281.

Beutler, L. E. (1991). Have all won and must all have prizes? Revisiting Luborsky, et al.'s verdict. *Journal of Consulting and Clinical Psychology, 59,* 226–232.

Beutler, L. E., & Baker, M. (in press). The movement towards empirical validation: At what level should we analyze and who are the consumers? In K. S. Dobson & K. D. Craig (Eds.), *Best practice: Developing and promoting empirically validated interventions.* Newbury Park, CA: Sage.

Beutler, L. E., & Berren, M. (Eds.). (1995). *Integrative assessment of adult personality.* New York: Guilford.

Beutler, L. E., & Clarkin, J. (1990). *Systematic treatment selection: Toward targeted therapeutic interventions.* New York: Brunner/Mazel.

Beutler, L. E., & Harwood, T. M. (1995). How to assess clients in pretreatment planning. In J. N. Butcher (Ed.), *Clinical personality assessment* (pp. 59–77). New York: Oxford University Press.

Beutler, L. E., Engle, D., Mohr, D., Daldrup, R. J., Bergan, J., Meredith, K., & Merry, W. (1991). Predictors of differential response to cognitive, experiential and self-directed psychotherapeutic procedures. *Journal of Consulting and Clinical Psychology, 59,* 333–340.

Beutler, L. E., Engle, D., Shoham-Salomon, V., Mohr, D. C., Dean, J. C., & Bernat, E. M. (1991). University of Arizona: Searching for differential treatments. In L. E. Beutler & M. Crago (Eds.), *Psychotherapy research: An international review of programmatic studies* (pp. 90–97). Washington, DC: American Psychological Association.

Beutler, L. E., Kim, E. J., Davison, E., Karno, M., & Fisher, D. (1996). Research contributions to improving managed health care outcomes. *Psychotherapy, 33,* 197–206.

Beutler, L. E., Machado, P. P. P., Engle, D., & Mohr, D. (1993). Differential patient x treatment maintenance among cognitive, experiential, and self-directed psychotherapies. *Journal of Psychotherapy Integration, 3,* 15–30.

Beutler, L. E., Mohr, D. C., Grawe, K., Engle, D., & MacDonald, R. (1991). Looking for differential effects: Cross-cultural predictors of differential psychotherapy efficacy. *Journal of Psychotherapy Integration, 1,* 121–142.

Beutler, L. E., Sandowicz, M., Fisher, D., & Albanese, A. L. (1996). Resistance in psychotherapy: Conclusions that are supported by research. *In Session: Psychotherapy in Practice, 2,* 77–86.

Beutler, L. E., & Williams, O. B. (1995, July/Aug.). Computer applications for the selection of optimal psychosocial therapeutic interventions. *Behavioral Healthcare Tomorrow,* 66–68.

Burgoon, J. K., Beutler, L. E., Le Poire, B. A., Engle, D., Bergan, J., Salvio, M. A., & Mohr, D. C. (1993). Nonverbal indices of arousal in group psychotherapy. *Psychotherapy, 30,* 635–645.

Chambless, D. L., Sanderson, W. C., Shoham, V., Johnson, S. B., Pope, K. S., Crits-Christoph, P., Baker, M., Johnson, B., Woody, S. R., Sue, S., Beutler, L. E., Williams, D. A., & McCurry, S. (1996). An update on empirically validated therapies. *The Clinical Psychologist, 49*(2), 5–14.

Dollard, J., & Miller, N. E. (1950). *Personality and psychotherapy: An analysis in terms of learning, thinking and culture.* New York: McGraw-Hill.

Elkin, I. (1994). The NIMH treatment of depression collaborative research program: Where we began and where we are. In A. E. Bergin & S. L. Garfield (Eds.), *Handbook of psychotherapy and behavior change* (4th ed., pp. 114–139). New York: Wiley.

Elkin, I., Gibbons, R. D., Shea, M. T., & Shaw, B. F. (1996). Science is not a trial (but it can sometimes be a tribulation. *Journal of Consulting and Clinical Psychology, 64,* 92–103.

Elkin, I. E., Shea, T., Watkins, J. T., Imber, S. D., Stotsky, S. M., Collins, J. F., Glass, D. R., Pilkonis, P. A., Leber, W. R., Docherty, J. P., Fiester, S. J., & Parloff, M. B. (1989). National Institute of Mental Health Treatment of Depression Collaborative Research Program. General effectiveness of treatment. *Archives of General Psychiatry, 46,* 974–982.

Falloon, I. R. H., Boyd, J. L., & McGill, C. W. (1984). *Family care of schizophrenia.* New York: Guilford.

Frances, A., Clarkin, J., & Perry, S. (1984). *Differential therapeutics in psychiatry.* New York: Brunner/Mazel.

Frances, A., Docherty, J. P., & Kahn, D. A. (1996). The expert consensus guideline series: Treatment of bipolar disorder. *Journal of Clinical Psychiatry, 57*(12A), 5–88.

Freud, S. (1909). Analysis of a phobia in a five-year-old boy. In *Sigmund Freud: Collected Papers* (vol. 3). New York: Basic Books.

Gaw, K. F., & Beutler, L. E. (1995). Integrating treatment recommendations. In L. E. Beutler & M. R. Berren (Eds.), *Integrative assessment of adult personality* (pp. 280–319). New York: Guilford.

Goldfried, M. R. (1980). Toward the delineation of therapeutic change principles. *American Psychologist, 35,* 991–999.

Goldfried, M. R. (1995). *From cognitive-behavior therapy to psychotherapy integration.* New York: Springer.

Goldfried, M. R., & Padawer, W. (1982). Current status and future directions in psychotherapy. In M. R. Goldfried (Ed.), *Converging themes in psychotherapy* (pp. 3–49). New York: Springer.

Goldstein, A. P., & Stein, N. (1976). *Prescriptive psychotherapies.* New York: Pergamon.

Groth-Marnat, G. (1997). *Handbook of psychological assessment* (3rd ed.). New York: Wiley.

Harwood, T. M., Beutler, L. E., Fisher, D., Sandowicz, M., Albanese, A. L., & Baker, M. (1997). In J. N. Butcher (Ed.), *Personality assessment in managed care: A practitioner's guide.* New York: Oxford University Press.

Lambert, M. J., & Bergin, A. E. (1992). Achievements and limitations of psychotherapy research. In D. K. Freedheim (Ed.), *History of psychotherapy* (pp. 360–389). Washington, DC: American Psychological Association.

Lazarus, A. A. (1967). In support of technical eclecticism. *Psychological Bulletin, 21,* 415–416.

Lazarus, A. A. (1989). *The practice of multimodal therapy.* Baltimore: The Johns Hopkins University Press. (Originally published in 1981)

Lazarus, A. A. (1991). A plague on Little Hans and Little Albert. *Psychotherapy, 28,* 444–447.

Lazarus, A. A. (1993). Tailoring the therapeutic relationship, or being an authentic chameleon. *Psychotherapy, 30,* 404–407.

Lazarus, A. A., Beutler, L. E., & Norcross, J. C. (1992). The future of technical eclecticism. *Psychotherapy, 29,* 11–20.

Liff, Z. A. (1992). Psychoanalysis and dynamic techniques. In D. K. Freedheim (Ed.), *History of psychotherapy* (pp. 571–586). Washington, DC: American Psychological Association.

Linehan, M. M. (1993). *Cognitive-behavioral treatment of borderline personality disorder.* New York: Guilford.

Luborsky, L. (1984). *Principles of psychoanalytic psychotherapy. A manual for supportive-expressive treatment.* New York: Basic Books.

Mahrer, A. R. (1989). *The integration of psychotherapies.* New York: Human Sciences.

Messer, S. B. (1992). A critical examination of belief structures in integrative and eclectic psychotherapy. In J. C. Norcross & M. R. Goldfried (Eds.), *Handbook of psychotherapy integration* (pp. 130–165). New York: Basic Books.

Norcross, J. C. (1986). *Handbook of eclectic psychotherapy.* New York: Brunner/Mazel.

Norcross, J. C. (1991). Prescriptive matching in psychotherapy: An introduction. *Psychotherapy, 28,* 439–443.

Norcross, J. C. (1993). The relationship of choice: Matching the therapist's stance to individual clients. *Psychotherapy, 30,* 402–403.

Norcross, J. C. (1994). *Prescriptive eclectic therapy.* Videotape in the APA Psychotherapy Videotape Series. Washington, DC: American Psychological Association.

Norcross, J. C. (1997). Emerging breakthroughs in psychotherapy integration: Three predictions and one fantasy. *Psychotherapy, 34,* 86–90.

Norcross, J. C., & Beutler, L. E. (1997). Determining the therapeutic relationship of choice in brief therapy. In J. N. Butcher (Ed.) (1997)., *Personality assessment in managed care: A practitioner's guide* (pp. 42–60). New York: Oxford University Press.

Norcross, J. C., & Goldfried, M. R. (Eds.). (1992). *Handbook of psychotherapy integration.* New York: Basic Books.

Norcross, J. C., & Grencavage, L. M. (1989). Eclecticism and integration in counseling and psychotherapy: Major themes and obstacles. *British Journal of Guidance and Counselling, 19,* 227–247.

Norcross, J. C., & Newman, C. F. (1992). Psychotherapy integration: Setting the context. In J. C. Norcross & M. R. Goldfried (Eds.), *Handbook of psychotherapy integration* (pp. 3–45). New York: Basic Books.

Paul, G. L. (1967). Strategy of outcome research in psychotherapy. *Journal of Consulting Psychology, 31,* 109–119.

Prochaska, J. O. (1984). *Systems of psychotherapy: A transtheoretical analysis* (2nd ed.). Homewood, IL: Dorsey.

Prochaska, J. O., DiClemente, C. C., & Norcross, J. C. (1992). In search of how people change: Applications to addictive behaviors. *American Psychologist, 47,* 1102–1114.

Prochaska, J. O., & Norcross, J. C. (1994). *Systems of psychotherapy: A transtheoretical analysis* (3rd. ed.). Pacific Grove, CA: Brooks/Cole.

Prochaska, J. O., Norcross, J. C., & DiClemente, C. C. (1994). *Changing for good.* New York: William Morrow.

Prochaska, J. O., Rossi, J. S., & Wilcox, N. S. (1991). Change processes and psychotherapy outcome in integrative case research. *Journal of Psychotherapy Integration, 1,* 103–120.

Shoham-Salomon, V., & Hannah, M. T. (1991). Client-treatment interactions in the study of differential change processes. *Journal of Consulting and Clinical Psychology, 59*, 217–225.

Sotsky, S. M., Glass, D. R., Shea, T. M., Pilkonis, P. A., Collins, J. F., Elkin, I., Watkins, J. T., Imber, S. D., Leber, W. R., Moyer, J., & Oliveri, M. E. (1991). Patient predictors of response to psychotherapy and pharmacotherapy: Findings in the NIMH Treatment of Depression Collaborative Research Program. *American Journal of Psychiatry, 148*, 997–1008.

Stampfl, T. G., & Levis, D. J. (1967). Essentials of implosive therapy: A learning theory-based psychodynamic behavioral therapy. *Journal of Abnormal Psychology, 72*, 496–503.

Strupp, H. H., & Binder, J. L. (1984). *Psychotherapy in a new key.* New York: Basic Books.

Thorne, F. C. (1967). The structure of integrative psychology. *Journal of Clinical Psychology, 23*, 3–11.

Wachtel, P. L. (1977). *Psychoanalysis and behavior therapy.* New York: Basic Books.

Watson, J. B., & Rayner, R. (1920). Conditioned emotional reactions. *Journal of Experimental Psychology, 3*, 1–14.

12

Clinical Social Work in the 21st Century: Behavioral Managed Care Is Here to Stay!

Sonia G. Austrian, D.S.W.

Managed care developed as a consequence of the spiraling costs of health care in the United States[1] and the government's decision that there be more accountability in the provision of health services. Stated most succinctly, it was designed to curtail unnecessary use of health care services through case management review and financial incentives to limit services.

Behavioral managed care (a subset of managed care) was created for the management of treatment for mental disorders and substance abuse. As such, it will be the most important factor in determining intervention plans for people suffering from mental disorders and chemical dependence, at least in the foreseeable future. The number of Americans enrolled in behavioral managed care plans in 1995 was 107 million, up from 86 million in 1992 (Austad, 1996). Many more will be enrolled in the future. Decisions regarding who can have treatment, who will provide it, duration of treatment, and even diagnosis will be affected by this phenomenon. It is no longer possible for mental health practitioners to ignore the ways in which managed care has impinged on their ability to practice autonomously. Managed care entities are overseeing care in both the pri-

---

[1]The cost of health care in the United States is approaching $1 trillion a year, representing about 15% of the gross national product (Shortell, Gillies, & Devers, 1995).

vate and public sectors. Only those who pay for treatment out of pocket can enjoy a therapeutic relationship with a provider free from interference.

Many issues must be considered by social workers providing services in the behavioral managed care context. Among them are facing possible reductions in income, learning ways of meeting a client's needs while satisfying the managing company, dealing with ethical issues involving confidentiality, and providing the necessary training, in professional schools as well as in continuing education programs, to cope with the new therapeutic environment.

Providers, payers, and clients have a number of concerns about managed care. Providers fear that managed care will mean major limitation of choice of provider, poor quality of intervention, limits on the amount of care, and mounting bureaucratic demands on their time. Payers seek to lower the cost of care for mental disorders and substance abuse, want providers to be more accountable and to have reliable outcome measures, and want easier administrative procedures. Consumers want to have quality care for both acute and chronic conditions. As I discuss below, these goals may not always be complementary.

Two major challenges to social workers are (a) how to adhere to the mission of the profession—that is, to enhance the well being of clients—when managed care is reluctant to provide services for the chronically mentally ill, and (b) how to practice within the ecosystem perspective, with its emphasis on person-in-environment, when the behavioral managed care focus reflects the medical perspective of symptom relief rather than the more complex and subtle forms of intervention typical of social work.

Adhering to a psychosocial perspective distinguishes social workers from all other mental health disciplines (Meyer, 1992). Beginning in the 1970s, in response to the publishing of Harriet Bartlett's (1970) seminal book, *The Common Base of Social Work Practice,* there was recognition that intervention should be determined by knowledge of case phenomena and professional skills, rather than a particular methodology. With this notion came a shift in the orientation of practice from the linear, causal approach, with its emphasis on specific methodology, to the more inclusive ecosystems perspective, with its emphasis on biopsychosocial assessment, which considered each case holistically, leading to a case-indicated choice of method. The ecosystems perspective is a unifying, conceptual construction that provided a framework for examining and understanding the complexity of a case while focusing on the interaction and reciprocity of person and environment. It requires thorough assessment, consideration of interrelated phenomena, and intervention based on contextual considerations. It is a framework not linked to any methodology. Thus, it allows the clinician to use the appropriate intervention based on a thorough assessment of the person-in-environment.

Social workers trained to look at cases through the broad lens of the ecosystems perspective may have difficulty accepting a return (under managed care) to a more linear, medical-model approach to case planning. Because obtaining authorization for intervention is frequently based on evaluation of a client's level of functional impairment (Axis V), social workers who prefer cognitive and behavioral methodologies will probably have less difficulty adhering to the demands of managed care than will those who prefer a psychosocial or psychodynamic approach. Short-term-focused intervention is being touted as the preferable methodology, which raises the important question of how people with long-standing character pathology will be offered case-indicated treatment. Another question, which has wide-spread societal implications, is what will be done to help the chronically mentally ill (a population served more often by social workers than by any other group of mental health professionals)? Untreated and undertreated mental disorders and chemical dependency can lead to public health problems, including medical overuse, school problems, domestic violence, lateness, absenteeism, lessened productivity, crime, and marital or family problems.

HISTORY

To some extent, managed care for mental health services has been with us for a long time. In the private sector, insurance companies have mandated exclusions, have identified certain professional disciplines that they will reimburse, have determined reimbursement rates, and have authorized care for predetermined length of intervention. In the public sector, state departments of mental health have controlled much of the care for the chronically mentally ill and the poor.

Behavioral managed care as it is now known—the industrialization of mental health care—came about because of the high costs of health and mental health care and the inability (or lack of interest) of the providers to police services with regard to both cost and duration of interventions. Employers (payers) balked at the rise in premiums, thus opening the door to businesses that promised to control cost and theoretically produce a system under which more people would receive services without an increase in total costs. Behavioral managed care has evolved since World War II.

Psychiatry became more widely accepted in the 1940s and 1950s, when many individuals suffering from battlefield emotional injuries were treated with short-term interventions and returned to active service. Erick Lindemann's theory of crisis intervention developed as a result of the Coconut Grove fire in Boston in 1943, where many were killed or injured and many more suffered from the trauma. The 1950s saw the impact of Freudian theory and the growing popularity of psychoanalysis. Health insurance began covering mental disorders and substance abuse in the 1960s. At that time, clients chose their providers. The need for and type of intervention was determined by the provider and the client. There was no mechanism for quality assurance, and the providers were not required to accept assignment (*assignment* is the fee determined by the payer for service, based on length of session, treatment modality, and professional discipline of the provider).

The community mental health center (CMHC) movement, created through the Comprehensive Mental Health Act in 1963, made psychotherapy available to most of the population without much regard to cost. Free community-based clinics were established, some of which included paraprofessionals and volunteers on staff. Many levels of service were provided to support the goal of deinstitutionalization. There was a great interest in psychosocial factors, and many clients did not want long-term intervention. Traditional psychiatrists were threatened by these ideas. Many chose not to work in CMHCs, thus opening the door to intervention by a broader range of mental health professionals, especially social workers. A required component in the design of a CMHC was program evaluation, recognizing the importance of cost accounting and quality assurance.

The 1970s ushered in greater interest in cognitive–behavioral interventions based on the works of B. F. Skinner, Carl Rogers, and Fritz Perls. During the Nixon administration, there was a shift away from community-based services. The charges were that they were not cost-effective or were not generating enough revenue. Demands were made for increased provider accountability, and substance abuse was seen as the province of law enforcement (Cornell, 1996). In 1972, Congress created the Peer Standards Review Organization (PSRO) to ensure proper utilization of health care services. The Health Maintenance Act of 1973 paved the way for private enterprise to develop and market all forms of health care for profit. It was designed to provide settings offering affordable, quality health care. In the 1980s, with deregulation, for-profit groups invested in hospitals, nursing homes, and outpatient facilities. Health care costs continued to rise, thus leading to the concept of managed care as a way to control costs and increase profits. In addition to intervention provided at Community Mental Health Centers, during the 1970s through the early 1980s mental health and substance-abuse benefits were provided for many employees as part of health-benefit packages that offered indemnity insurance plans (with small deductibles). These were fairly liberal, especially for inpatient treatment, with respect to duration of intervention and the amount reimbursable. There appeared to be no concern about cost. The "market" was unregulated, and it was during this era that nonmedical entrepreneurs opened chains of for-profit hospitals that provided psychiatric and substance abuse treatment in competition with large nonprofit teaching hospitals, which had larger overheads.

Beginning in the 1980s, there was greater concern about the rise in cost of all health care, in both the private and the public sectors. In 1982, the Tax Equity and Fiscal Responsibility Act led to the establishment of the diagnostic-related groups (DRGs), effective in 1983, which determined reimbursement rates for Medicare in-hospital patients. This resulted in greater attention being paid to all medical costs, including inpatient behavioral health care for employed persons, although it was clear that there was no way to apply DRGs to psychiatric disorders that are more idiosyncratic. Mental health providers cannot approach their cases as surgeons or internists do, although managed care organizations would like to develop similar guidelines. In mental health treatment, there is rarely a specific disease entity with a specific, proven intervention and a predictable road to recovery. Length of treatment for a medical disorder is fairly uniform, and thus predictable, whereas length of psychotherapy for a given emotional disorder or for substance abuse involves too many variables to be uniform. These variables include the personality of the client; co-morbidity (i.e., other factors that may contribute to the problem); and the competence, experience, and orientation of the provider.

As utilization review became more commonplace, managed care companies that offered to help control costs began to blossom. Initially, they offered preauthorization and utilization review, which resulted in fewer and shorter inpatient psychiatric stays. Having established some control over inpatient services, some of the managed care companies shifted their marketing from inpatient treatment to networks offering lower cost out-patient services. Beginning in 1990, some managed care companies began limiting clients' choice of clinicians by establishing formal networks of providers. Benefits were capped in terms of expenditure per patient per year. By 1992, as health care costs made up 14% of the gross national product (England, 1994)—with mental health costs rising even faster than health costs, particularly for the private sectors—employers welcomed the marketing of behavioral health care companies who promised quality care at less cost.

Although nonprofit managed care plans such as the well-known Kaiser Permanente plan continue to exist, for-profit plans with the stated goal of containing costs now control the health–mental health industry. As of January 1995, 58.2% of Americans with health insurance were enrolled in some form of managed mental health or behavioral health plan that determined the course of intervention for mental disorders or substance abuse (Geller, 1996). In addition, individuals who belong to health maintenance organizations (HMOs) and preferred provider organizations (PPOs) also have managed care that restricts their choice of provider and duration of intervention.

Behavioral health care companies began as private group practices or as informal networks of providers in the early 1980s. In the last decade, they grew rapidly. Company profits were not adequate to fund the operational infrastructure. Thus, venture capital was needed. The consequence was that the provision of behavioral health care became a major growth industry (Geller, 1996). Insurance companies—and, more recently, pharmaceutical companies—began to buy some of the managed care companies. Other companies remained independent of insurance companies but eventually merged to form larger organizations. The business strategy of driving competitors out of business or buying them out now characterizes the health care industry. Managed care has become "managed competition" as companies market themselves as able to provide "acceptable" outcomes at the cheapest price. Managed care that began as an effort to control access to care and the cost of care has moved toward controlling the delivery of services. Although it was originally developed to service the private sector, behavioral managed health care has expanded to cover Medicaid patients in many states and is being considered for people covered by Medicare. Providers, insurers, and state and federal health care agencies continue to debate over who should be treated under behavioral managed care contracts, which clients should not receive care or have benefits terminated, and which should be covered under government programs or insurance plans. Much of the decision-making is determined by the chronicity and severity of the disorder.

TERMINOLOGY

Managed care is a system of providing health care that is paid for, all or in part, by a third party and one in which decision-making about treatment rests with the managing entity and not with the consumer or provider. The proportion of American workers in managed care plans has grown to 74% in 1996, up from 55% in 1992 (Toner, 1996). Over the years, employers have reduced the number of plans offered to their workers; a recent survey indicated that 52% of midsized companies offer only one plan (Toner, 1996). The purpose of managed care is to manage resources and time, provide alternatives to costly inpatient hospitalizations, and—in the case of behavioral health care—require accountability for every dollar spent on treatment of mental disorders and chemical dependency. Under managed care, authorization of expenditures is limited to only those services determined to be "medically necessary." The basic strategy is to lower premiums and to enroll as few chronically ill or high-risk individuals as possible. Financial, organizational, administrative, and monitoring systems are designed to minimize use of resources and (theoretically) maximize efficiency and quality of care. The goal is cost savings for those who pay for care, thus making cost a crucial variable in clinical decision-making. Behavioral managed health care companies market themselves as offering interventions that are least intensive, least extensive, least intrusive, and least costly. Their financial success depends on doing as little as possible.

Proponents of managed care maintain that it can control the constantly rising costs of mental health care by providing the "consumer" with the right treatment, in the right setting, by the right provider, for the right duration, and at the right cost. They see the focus as not on cost per se, but on preventing overuse of service. On the other hand, critics view managed care as providing the cheapest care, with limited concern for quality—"acceptable" outcomes at the lowest price. They claim that these decisions are often made by persons who do not know the client, who do not have training in mental health or substance-abuse treatment, and whose main concern is cost containment. They fear that well-established professional and ethical standards, sound assessment, and appropriate intervention planning will suffer in the interest of profit. Critics also note that although rendering concrete services and making collateral visits—both often needed in interventions with children, the aged, and the chronically mentally ill—are deemed too costly and are often not reimbursable, the average remuneration package for CEOs of the seven largest for-profit HMOs was $7 million in 1994 ("Nation's Big," 1995).

Behavioral health care is provided through a network of providers who have contracted with a managed care company. Standardized pretreatment and treatment planning instruments are often required as well as outcome reviews.

Medical necessity governs decisions made by managed care reviewers, thus further equating intervention for mental disorders and substance abuse with treatment of medical illnesses. In keeping with the emphasis on the medical model, this term is used in place of the more appropriate *medical and/or psychosocial necessity* or even *clinical necessity*. Medical necessity is not nearly as clear for mental disorders as it is for medical problems. Furthermore, diagnosis may differ from one clinician to another. There are no standard biological indicators for mental disorders or substance abuse, except in cases where medication is essential (e.g., bipolar disorder). In addition, studies confirming the efficacy of differential interventions are limited (Glazer, 1992).

Nevertheless, medical necessity is the major factor in allocating public and private insurance funds as it establishes the criteria for treatment planning. (In other words, it is the gatekeeper.) It is often defined as

1. need for adequate and essential services to assess or treat a disease defined by standard diagnostic nomenclature such as the *DSM–IV* (American Psychiatric Association, 1994) or ICD–10 (World Health Organization, 1978),

2. reasonable expectation for improvement of the condition or of the person's level of functioning,
3. services in keeping with professional practice standards and empirical evidence of efficacy, and
4. most cost-effective services. (Rodriguez & Gibson, 1994)

Clearly, danger to oneself or others would render intervention as medically necessary. Behavioral managed care supports intervention for symptoms that if left untreated would result in serious impairment of functioning. This concept, however, makes it particularly difficult to obtain approval for treating people with Axis II disorders, especially if the presenting problem is impaired interpersonal relationships.

Health Maintenance Organizations (HMOs) began to appear toward the late 1970s. They are capitation arrangements (see below for a definition of *capitation*) whose original goal was to provide health promotion and comprehensive health care. However, in most cases, this preventive aspect has not materialized to the degree anticipated. Individuals can join HMOs independently or through an employer. There is pre-payment for each member on a monthly basis, with perhaps a small co-pay, for all needed services. The gatekeeper for these services, including behavioral health care, is still the primary care physician. Because there is a financial incentive to undertreat, questions have been raised about whether clients of HMOs face barriers to accessing treatment.

There are two models of HMOs: (a) those made up of providers who are salaried staff members, and (b) providers who are in group practices under a single administrative management who provide the needed range of general and behavioral health services.

Preferred Providers Organizations (PPOs) developed in the early 1980s. They consist of groups of clinicians who contract to serve a defined population on a discounted fee-for-service basis with little or no utilization control or fee management. While working well for the providers, they have not controlled costs to an appreciable degree and thus have not been attractive to employers.

Network is the term used for a group of providers who are joined together by managed care companies to offer a range of services. They have proliferated with the move from less inpatient care to more outpatient intervention. As behavioral managed care companies expand their control, providers feel pressure to join the networks that can limit the number of providers by profession and often have "closed panels" (when the company feels it has a sufficient number of specialists and thus will not accept applications from interested providers).

Managed behavioral care carve-out programs are programs contracted for by employers apart from their regular managed care health benefits. They are devoted to providing services for mental illness and substance abuse. The employer decides what type of behavioral health benefits will be offered, the benefits are purchased from a behavioral managed care company, and this company then contracts with providers on a set fee-for-service basis. These programs are designed to provide a range of services at a discounted fee. Employers usually pay a fixed per-capita rate for all covered workers—and, in some cases, their dependents. Most programs are staffed through contracts with providers from all mental health and substance abuse disciplines. Although employees of the behavioral managed care company review cases in terms of initial treatment plan, ongoing treatment, and outcome, the risk may be shared by the company and the provider or, in many instances, may be the sole responsibility of the provider. When cost is the primary concern, these arrangements have proven most appealing to employers and have prospered in this decade.

Managed behavioral care carve-in programs are group model programs such as HMOs and independent practitioner associations (IPAs). All needed services are available at one site, with a goal of integrating services. There is concern that these programs lead to undertreatment of persons with mental disorders or who have problems with chemical dependency, because the primary care physicians are the gatekeepers and may not make referrals either due to lack of training in identifying these problems or because of financial incentives to control referrals for specialized services.

Capitation is payment through a managed care contract on a per-person basis. The capitation rate is the amount of monthly or yearly reimbursement per employee in a capitated contract. For behavioral health care, inpatient care involves a flat discounted daily rate, regardless of diagnosis or case-indicated treatment. The assumption is that the fee will be greater than the cost of employee care: Although some patients may require more costly intervention, most employees will need only limited services or perhaps none at all. This can result in lower quality care (because the thrust is toward less costly care rather than case-indicated care) or, if indicated care is given, it may not be reimbursable. (If the intervention is not approved, it will not be reimbursed even if it is what the provider deems as appropriate and, at times, essential.) The incentive here is to avoid costly diagnostic or intervention procedures for inpatients. The result for many clients is a short stay to stabilize medication, often followed by additional brief hospitalizations. For outpatient treatment, the cost is set at a rate to cover all possible consumers. As few sessions as possible are offered for outpatient intervention, and the client may return for additional "episodes of service" at another time. In both instances, when a client re-enters care, the providers involved may be different than the ones involved in the past episode. Thus the case is "new," and the assessment process must begin again.

ISSUES OF CONCERN

Hospitalization

Managed care was first developed in response to the spiraling costs of inpatient hospitalization. In the 1970s, employees of major corporations might have up to a year's coverage. In some states, Medicaid covered from 4 to 12 months of inpatient treatment. Now stays have been reduced to an average of 3 to 21 days. The result has been symptom relief, often based on initiating or altering a course of medication. This frequently leads to rapid discharge followed by "recycling," with many people experiencing several brief hospitalizations.

Inpatient intervention for persons with substance abuse problems commonly involves a 5- to 7-day stay for detoxification, with very few people approved for a 22- to 30-day stay in an inpatient rehabilitation facility that has been proven most effective in maintaining sobriety.

Providers

The traditional solo mental health practice, in which clients were referred to providers by other practitioners and their own clients, is rapidly disappearing because nowadays providers must be on behavioral health care companies' panels in order to be reimbursed. Panels are often full. Even if they are not, the provider's profile may not conform to the panel's treatment policies and thus the provider may not be acceptable. If accepted, the clinician agrees to allow case managers employed by the behavioral managed care company to control who is treated, how, and for how long. If *efficiency* means treatment for as short a duration of intervention as possible, it follows that fewer providers will be needed because the "successful" ones will have a high turnover rate (i.e., fewer clinicians seeing a greater number of clients). Since the reimbursement rate is based on training, social workers with master's degrees will initially benefit. However, it is possible that they in turn will be replaced by still less expensive providers (e.g., persons with BSW degrees). These cheaper BSWs may be given more latitude in intervention planning, whereas the most costly providers—psychiatrists—are in many plans limited to dispensing medications. Negotiating fees and payment schedules, once considered part of the therapeutic process, are no longer a case-indicated decision but are determined by company policy.

Social workers who once had to learn to move from the linear language of study, diagnosis, and treatment to the ecosystems language of exploration, assessment, and intervention (Meyer, 1995) may now have to learn the managed care language. Some clinicians feel the need to "behaviorize" the language used in reports to satisfy the managed care companies—for example, changing "dealing with depression" to "affect management [of depression]" (Munson, 1996). The language is moving from terms familiar to mental health professionals to those used by business school graduates.

Providers are being pressured to show outcomes to justify their belonging to panels and to demonstrate effectiveness. This stems from the behaviorist approach followed by most behavioral managed care companies, with its emphasis on relief of symptoms. It is possible to observe indications of successful outcomes when medication is the treatment of choice for clients with depression and anxiety. It is also possible to determine abstinence from abusing substances. However, it is far more difficult, if not impossible, to evaluate change in persons with long-standing mental disorders or severe character pathology. What are viewed as successful outcomes for presenting problems often involve the treatment of related problems (e.g., social-skill deficits, vocational issues, time management) rather than underlying problems (e.g., character pathology) that will subsequently require additional intervention. When the emphasis is on identifying and treating the symptoms that have obvious indicators, clinicians run the risk of disregarding symptoms whose genesis may be intrapsychic and therefore less easy to identify (e.g., low-grade depression and low self-esteem). Short-term intervention and the use of medication are the interventions of choice for symptom relief. Long-term intervention with the goal of developing the client's potential is not usually reimbursable. Whether short-term intervention may actually do more harm than good is not addressed. Some clients may not have a positive response to the limited number of sessions and may come to view themselves as "failures," reactivating previous experiences of failure.

Confidentiality

Erosion of confidentiality has become a major problem in the practice of psychotherapy. The media relishes disclosures by former therapists about their treatment of celebrities such as Nicole Brown Simpson or the Menendez brothers. The general public can read transcripts of sessions such as those with poet Anne Sexton or with a psychotherapist charged with malpractice. Today, under behavioral managed care, a clinician can no longer assure a client that what is revealed in a session will remain between them. Assessments and diagnostic codes are shared with case managers from the behavioral health care company, may have been faxed to the company, and usually are stored in some fashion in computers. Thus many people unknown to the consumer and provider may be privy to what was once private information. In addition, initial authorization for treatment often is given when the consumer calls an 800 number and is asked to tell an unknown person over the telephone the most intimate details about the problem. Informal surveys have shown that when a case is managed by a behavioral health care company, at least 17 people may have some knowledge about the client's treatment (Munson, 1996). This violates the social work *Code of Ethics* that states that the social worker should "respect the privacy of clients and hold in confidence all information obtained in the course of professional service" (II. H), "share with others confidences revealed by clients, without their consent, only for compelling reasons" (II.H.1), and inform the client about what happens to information passed on to others (Meyer & Mattaini, 1995). The clinician has the impossible task of providing reviewers with sufficient information to gain authorization for intervention while still protecting the client's right to confidentiality. It should be noted that sharing information may result in either authorization of treatment or denial of needed intervention. Again, this is antithetical to the social work value of providing service to all who need and request it.

Consumers are entitled to know the parameters of confidentiality: what specific information will be shared, with whom, and for what purpose. They should give their consent in writing to protect themselves and to feel that they are part of the process.

Ethics

Managed care presents many ethical dilemmas for social workers. Clearly the most significant is that social workers believe that their primary responsibility is to deliver the best quality of service designed to enhance the welfare of their clients, whereas managed care changes their primary responsibility to adhering to the contractual agreements they make with the companies. Although social workers offer their services to the community at large, their unique strength is to advocate for and provide service for persons at greatest risk. In contrast, managed care seeks to limit the extent and type of intervention and does not appear to adequately meet the needs of the chronically mentally ill and the poor. There is a fiscal incentive toward under-diagnosis and thus undertreatment of severe and persistent mental illness while extending care to persons seen as having "transitional" mental health problems. As a result, the most needy are receiving less service or sometimes inappropriate service, often from persons with limited training.

The right of *self-determination*, a core value of the social work profession, is clearly violated when consumers no longer have control over whom they choose as a provider and for how long they feel that they need help. Control over these decisions, which formerly rested with the consumer and the provider, has now been taken over by the behavioral managed care company. Often the protocols on which these decisions are based are unknown to the clinician. As noted above, the client must contact the behavioral health care company for authorization. The company most often chooses the therapist (sometimes determined by zip code) and authorizes a preset number of sessions—usually one diagnostic session, followed by two to five treatment sessions. Additional sessions, usually three to six, require reauthorization. These determinations, which also encompass constant evaluations of the provider, are often made by nonprofessionals and are based on protocols, not client need. Because behavioral managed care companies rarely authorize treatment for more than 6 months, clients who do not respond and who thus have "poor outcomes" find themselves returning repeatedly for additional episodes of service. This may lead to feelings of failure and further lack of self-esteem, or clients may not return and may continue to suffer impaired functioning. In addition, because most carve-out contracts have a flat per-person fee, if treatment is extended to a point at which it exceeds the allotted cost per person, the company suffers. "Good" providers are those who ensure profit—or at least break even; providers who cannot adjust to these protocols will be dropped from the panel. The incentive is to keep the intervention short, not to make a case-indicated decision. This excessive reporting and review process "teaches" providers what is expected, and they learn to skew diagnoses and intervention reports in such a way as to have their interventions deemed medically necessary. Thus the client who is told to be honest and forthcoming with the clinician finds that these rules do not apply to the clinician!

The structure of behavioral managed care is an obstacle to establishing a secure therapeutic contract. The client–clinician relationship is key to the therapeutic process. Given the life experiences of many of our clients, problems often involve issues of trust, and a trusting client–clinician relationship only develops over time. Clients covered by behavioral health care companies may find payment denied, and thus treatment terminated, due to some administrative technicalities. For instance, if their employer changes companies, the client will be told to change to a therapist on the panel of the new company. The insistence on frequent review further undermines the therapist because of the implication that the case reviewer knows what is best for the client better than the clinician does.

Clients who are anxious and uncertain about the future of their contact with clinicians and who are aware of the limits of confidentiality may opt to bring to their sessions concerns that are superficial rather than deepseated. The threat to privacy may cause some in need of intervention to forgo it out of fear or humiliation. The importance of the relationship to effect change has been replaced by emphasis on assigning homework and tasks with expected, acceptable outcomes, based on apparently better day-to-day functioning and relief of symptoms.

That many contracts between providers and behavioral managed care companies absolve the company of risk, through a "hold harmless" clause, also raises an ethical question. If the company chooses the clinician, authorizes treatment, and sets the duration and type of intervention, then why, when something goes wrong, is it the provider's responsibility? This is a question that has involved, and will continue to involve, litigation, thus bringing yet another bureaucracy into the consumers' and providers' lives.

There is also the issue of who is and who is not "treatable." Is it ethical to refuse treatment to a person because any degree of resolution of the problem would not be cost effective? Can a client be viewed as "unresponsive" to intervention if the presenting problem(s) cannot be resolved through short-term intervention or medication?

Finally, in a further attempt to cut costs, a managed care company may not pay for filling a prescription as written, but will mandate substituting an older or cheaper "generic" drug. (Newer medications often are more expensive because they may initially be available only through one pharmaceutical house, yet they are often more effective and have fewer side effects.) A recent investigation found that drugs received by consumers, especially those enrolled in managed care plans, are increasingly not the ones initially prescribed or desired by the treating doctor. Although doctors are supposed to be consulted when prescriptions are changed, apparently this is often not done, and substitutions are frequently made without the doctor's knowledge (Freudenheim, 1996). Choices of allowable drugs are made by *pharmaceutical benefit managers* (PBMs) who work for companies that handle the purchase and distribution of drugs for many HMOs and other managed care plans. Because of the large volume of business they represent, they are able to negotiate discounts with pharmaceutical manufacturers (Herbert, 1996).

Intervention

Given the limited number of sessions authorized by behavioral managed care companies for psychotherapy and treatment for substance abuse, providers may have to rethink their approaches to intervention. Most behavioral managed care plans provide only brief treatment and will not treat chronic problems. Treatment is allowed for acute conditions with the goal of stabilization. This would never be acceptable as a criterion for medical intervention. It is of major concern that providers under behavioral managed care plans are often subjected to brief, anonymous guidelines that are designed to limit cost but are often unavailable to the provider and thus not subject to critical, professional review.

If this trend continues, inpatient treatment in the future will largely involve keeping individuals from harming themselves or others and stabilizing persons on medication. Less costly alternatives such as partial hospitalization and a range of day programs will replace long-term hospitalization.

Their effectiveness will have to be evaluated over time. Outpatient intervention planning will be based on focused assessment, resulting in precise goals that should be accomplished within the allotted number of sessions and time frame. Intervention will have a clear, fairly precise focus. The traditional weekly session may be replaced by weekly sessions initially, followed by the spacing out of sessions in order to allow the client to achieve the goals and to maximize the allotted benefit. Even more than in the past, there will be a need to identify what the client wants to work on and to accept the fact that accomplishing goals, rather than solidifying gains or promoting growth, is what will form the basis for authorizing additional sessions and evaluating outcomes of interventions, including the "skill" of the provider.

It is unlikely that people suffering from substance abuse will continue to be approved for the traditional 28-to-30-day detoxification–rehabilitation inpatient programs. Although inpatient detox may be approved in a few instances, outpatient detox followed by intensive outpatient care is the intervention most often approved by behavioral managed care reviewers. This is problematic for people who will return daily to their neighborhoods or families where abstinence may be difficult. People with dual diagnosis may also be allowed a short inpatient stay.

There is the distinct possibility that people needing extended psychotherapy will be directed toward superficial brief therapy, crisis intervention, or self-help programs. Medications may also be used as a "quick fix" requiring fewer or shortened visits. Because fast symptom relief can be achieved with medication, especially mood disorders, some anxiety disorders, and schizophrenia, this route is attractive to managed care. However, studies have shown that the combination of medication and psychotherapy, which might appear less cost-effective in the short run, will ultimately produce better long-term results.

Education

The *DSM–IV* is widely used as a basis for behavioral managed care reporting, although its approach is antithetical to the social work tradition of valuing the uniqueness of individuals and their situations, as well as the assessment process that is central to the ecosystems perspective. It uses a classification system that looks for group phenomena and relies on generalizations—highlighting similarities, overlooking differences, and disregarding context. Relying primarily on the *DSM–IV* might actually impede intervention because the categories provide no clues about what intervention in the environment may be essential, or at the very least what is important to enable better adaptation and coping. Classification systems may facilitate accurate communication across disciplines, but they can interfere with full understanding of a client's problems, which can only be obtained through exploration of aspects not listed in the criteria. Like following a cookbook, interventions directed by manuals follow from classification systems and make possible bureaucratic standards and forms for outcome data, as they dictate what the clinician must do.

Behavioral managed care promotes classification, labeling, and the use of manuals that prescribe interventions. This approach may appeal to inexperienced clinicians who feel it gives them a sense of control over a disorder even if its cause is unknown. However, it is important to recognize that treatment for mental disorders or substance abuse problems should not be determined by a knowledge of abstract statistical variables. Such knowledge alone does not help clinicians develop the skilled intuition necessary for appropriate assessment and intervention planning for complex and sometimes seemingly mysterious problems. First-rate interventions are grounded in assessment, based on engagement of a client. Schools of social work must not support an approach to intervention planning that is based on classification and statistically programmed service. It is hoped that these training institutions will continue to see that intervention based on rigorous assessment of person-in-environment defines the social work profession. The classification systems and diagnostic manuals that are available today are still too narrow to serve as more than an adjunct to this process. Therapists must never permit classification systems and intervention directed by manuals to let them lose sight of the uniqueness of clients and their environments. Commenting on the vast amount of information given in the *DSM–III–R* (American Psychiatric Association, 1987), Dumont (1987) likened the process of choosing a "cubicle" for a client to choosing from an "endless, infernal Chinese menu" (p. 11). Knowledge of classification systems and cognitive–behavioral techniques must remain only part of the education and repertoire of social workers.

To meet the demands of behavioral managed care, schools of social work must train their students to provide sharply focused assessment followed by focused short-term interventions with clearly defined goals. The emphasis must be on focus. A good grounding in developmental theory is also essential in order to understand the demands and stresses of different life-stages. A knowledge of resources, especially those deemed less intrusive and less costly, is needed to help solidify gains when sessions are discontinued. Psychoeducation will be important to help families identify when they must seek out intervention.

The faster turnover of clients and the additional paperwork brought about by managed care has added to the stress experienced by social workers in hospitals or agencies. It has also lessened their satisfaction with their jobs. As a result, many clinicians are reluctant to continue the long-held tradition of supervising graduate students in field placements. In addition, some managed care companies will not reimburse for services rendered by students—certainly not for the long-term interventions that have traditionally been part of training in a field-work placement. Thus agencies and schools will have to rethink their curricula and reassess what must realistically be offered as training.

Social work educators must be concerned about what will happen to their profession when behavioral managed care systems appear to prefer those less trained, professional judgment is not valued, and providers fear they will be "dropped" if they do not conform to behavioral managed care criteria. Experienced social workers are already demoralized, and this must affect their supervision and teaching. For those of us who believe in case-indicated decisions that may require intensive, long-term interventions, it is hard to switch to methods that are chosen primarily to please behavioral managed care companies.

CONCLUSION

Thus the goals of managed behavioral health care can be characterized as (a) seeing more clients for brief episodes of treatment, possibly throughout the life cycle rather than for a long-term treatment; (b) emphasizing symptom relief to promote functioning, instead of interventions with character pathology involving an emphasis on growth; and (c) providing services by the most cost-effective staffing.

In an ideal society, mental health professionals should not be "contract workers" or vendors. Clients are vulnerable, and they require relationships that are compassionate. They should not be exploited, nor should they be a source of profiteering. In the industrial and commercial realm, it may be accepted practice for workers with frozen salaries and limited job security to supply consumers with minimally acceptable goods and services while the CEOs of their companies profit. This cannot be acceptable when rendering service to vulnerable populations. Providers are losing control, and cheap labor will result in deprofessionalization.

Professional organizations have not taken the lead in protecting their members from the industrialization of behavioral health care. If anything, they appear to be trying to ignore it rather than to fight back. The National Association of Social Workers revised the *Code of Ethics* as recently as 1993 and made no changes in Section II H, which deals with "Confidentiality and Privacy," although, as noted above, the requirements of behavioral managed health plans do not permit strict adherence to the code with respect to confidentiality. In addition, there are problems with Section II F, "Primacy of Clients' Interest." Social workers cannot always "provide clients with accurate and complete information regarding the extent and nature of the services available to them" nor promise to "terminate service . . . when such services and relationships are no longer required or no longer serve the clients' needs or interests" nor promise not to "withdraw services precipitously only under unusual circumstances, giving careful consideration of all factors in the situation and taking care to minimize possible adverse effects" (Meyer & Mattaini, 1995, pp. 278–279). Perhaps social workers should consider the ethics of this stance and put more energy into advocating for confidential, case-indicated interventions based on thorough assessment and provided by well-trained professionals, not interventions based on profit. Closing inpatient units, limiting length of hospital stay, and dictating the terms of outpatient intervention will lead to major public health problems such as increased substance abuse, family dysfunction, homelessness, and a high recidivism rate. It would be wise for social workers to consider why some methods of intervention are currently valued, while others are devalued. They should courageously support what they feel will best use the strengths in the client and in the environment. Social workers must educate behavioral managed care companies about the nature of case management—that it consists of more than regulating the number of sessions and determining cost-effectiveness. Good case management not only focuses on identifying and providing concrete services. It also demands the establishment of a trusting relationship with a client over a period of several months before any significant change can occur. Industrialized behavioral health care, as it is now structured, denies both consumer and provider what neither can afford to lose—time and expertise.

Strategies must be developed to meet the needs of the three groups involved: providers, payers, and especially consumers. Initially, guidelines were brief and anonymous, and did little more than limit the number of sessions. Criteria for authorization and reimbursement were mostly unavailable and not subject to critical review. Given that managed care is probably here to stay, guidelines must still be established to assure not only cost containment, but the delivery of quality care as well. Based on the premise that clinical decisions should be made by properly trained and experienced clinicians, these guidelines must address the following issues: (a) the qualifications of providers, (b) the criteria for determining type and duration of intervention, (c) the availability of resources, and (d) the identification of appropriate levels of service.

A balance between cost-effective care and quality of care requires statutory protection for consumers (and sometimes providers). However, undue regulatory burdens and expensive mandates should be avoided. In order to create informed consumers and providers, legislation should do the following:

1. make available more detailed information regarding types of health insurance coverage and options;
2. establish standards for appeals and grievances by consumers and providers;

3. remove limitations imposed on providers' rights to advocate on behalf of consumers' needs without fear of reprisals;

4. assure that behavioral managed care companies maintain a sufficient range of providers and services to meet the needs of enrollees;

5. provide better access to needed specialty care, especially for the chronically mentally ill, the poor, the elderly, and children;

6. protect against inappropriate or insufficient services;

7. require that behavioral managed care companies make available to consumers and providers their criteria for approving or rejecting authorization of services, thus guarding against limitation of access to appropriate services;

8. require that behavioral managed care companies make available to consumers, providers, and payers their standards for accepting or dropping providers on their panels; and

9. protect the consumer's right to self-determination by requiring their full involvement in treatment decisions and ensuring the right to refuse inappropriate treatment.

Of course, the most urgent need is for legislation that will protect confidentiality. Currently, no federal law explicitly protects confidentiality of medical records, although there is a law protecting the confidentiality of video-store rental lists (Scarf, 1996)! Without this assurance of confidentiality, providers will find it almost impossible to adhere to the *Code of Ethics* and to core social work values. Contracts should be required between the behavioral managed care companies, the consumers, and the providers that clearly state (a) who has access to information obtained by the provider, (b) where this information is stored, (c) how long information will be kept, (d) what happens to the information if the consumer changes managed care companies, and (e) who is liable if information is not protected.

Because it appears that social workers must learn to live with behavioral managed care, it would make sense for us to take several steps. First, it is useful to try to develop a good working relationship with those individuals responsible for authorization (if they are identifiable) in order to understand each other's viewpoint and thus be able to work more cooperatively in trying to meet consumer needs. Second, social workers should develop research-study designs and measures that can inform us about who is served best by which specific intervention, and in what context. Third, the integrity of the profession can only be maintained if social workers place the needs of the client first and advocate having those needs appropriately met. Although it will place an added burden on overworked workers, social workers must fully document the consequences of instances when intervention plans have been denied and when inappropriate or inadequate service has been authorized. Limiting hospitalizations or out-patient intervention or refusing to authorize indicated treatment does not come without cost. These costs should be estimated. Due to high overhead costs that include marketing, utilization reviews, and elevated salaries (especially at the CEO level[2]), behavioral managed care may ultimately—and ironically—turn out to be more expensive than the system that preceded it. HMOs in New York estimate that they lost $285 million in 1997 as a result of higher than expected medical costs and employers' resistance to premium increases. The managed care plans are being forced to reevaluate service delivery and are considering the possibility of outsourcing some functions. Some HMOs have tried to renegotiate hospital contracts in order to shift costs to providers; however, they have met some resistance, due in part to an awareness of the salaries paid to CEOs, such as the $2.8 million paid to the CEO of Oxford (Benson, 1998).

There has been a backlash in the last few years as providers and consumers have become less passive in accepting the policies and procedures of managed care companies and the industrialization of medicine. Several groups have been formed with the mission of protecting consumers and providers by monitoring managed care and offering guidelines on how to work toward eliminating abuses. Two of the earliest were the National Coalition of Mental Health Professionals and Consumers, based in Commack, New York, and its affiliate in the Boston area, the Consortium for Psychotherapy. The latter organization created the American Mental Health Alliance (AMHA), an interdisciplinary nonprofit worker cooperative of licensed mental health professionals whose goal is to preserve choice of provider, type of intervention, range of fees, privacy, confidentiality, and the therapeutic relationship by making and managing contracts for behavioral health services. These groups seek to create a collaborative relationship between the providers and the plan, instead of an adversarial relationship based on authorizing, overseeing, and managing for profit.

In Massachusetts in 1997, an Ad Hoc Committee to Defend Health Care called for a moratorium on the corporate takeover of health services and curbs on the intrusion of HMOs into doctors' decision-making. While acknowledging the need for efficiency in providing health care, a group of 1,940 doctors, many of whom are connected with the Harvard Medical School, signed the committee's "Call to Action" protesting regulations that compromised the Hippocratic oath, the medical code of ethics that mandates putting patients first (Kilborn, 1997). Some doctors in California and Florida have joined unions to challenge HMO policies and procedures.

There have been a few other hopeful developments toward making managed care work for the consumers. For example, the National Health and Human Service Employees Union 1199, representing 120,000 health

---

[2]In 1996, the top 10 HMO executives split close to $399 million in salaries and options (Ginsburg & Demeranville, 1998).

care workers in New York State, has announced plans to market its own managed care health plan to the state's 2.5 million union members. This nonprofit health plan emerged out of anger and frustration when insurers such as Blue Cross moved from being nonprofit to being for-profit, limiting benefits while seeking profits. In Minneapolis, 24 companies are forming a consortium to set up their own managed care plan, which they hope will be more responsive to consumer needs (Rosenthal, 1996).

Nationwide, consumers and providers are calling for Congress and state legislatures to pass legislation that allows for "open access" to doctors, bypassing the HMO gatekeepers who control access to specialists, and establishes a "Bill of Rights" to set guidelines for arbitration of delays and denials of care. In 1997, following increased complaints by both consumers and providers, California began a major review of managed care systems aimed at tightening the government regulations. By mid-1997, 22 states had adopted some form of comprehensive consumer-rights bill, with additional bills pending in 11 other states. Most of these bills establish grievance procedures, ban the "gag orders" that limit what doctors can share with patients, require payment for all emergency room visits (even if later deemed unnecessary), curb financial incentives for doctors who deny treatment, and allow for direct access to certain specialists without authorization from a primary care doctor (Freudenheim, 1997, p. A1).

Candidates for Congress are finding that dissatisfaction with managed care and the need for regulations are major campaign issues. In response, some of the managed care organizations, insurance companies, and employers are forming coalitions to try to block some of the patients-rights proposals in Congress and respond to accusations. Commercials are being developed to "warn" consumers that regulation would result in higher premiums, loss of coverage, and layoffs of health care workers (Kilborn, 1998). The backlash is clearly gaining momentum.

The federal government has previously adopted a policy limiting the type of bonuses that can be paid to doctors for controlling the cost of services for Medicare and Medicaid patients. It is anticipated that this policy, which resulted from greater consumer awareness of the denial of necessary care, will eventually set standards for the entire managed care industry. Although these developments deal with managed care in the broadest sense, they also will undoubtedly have an impact on behavioral managed care plans and providers.

Behavioral managed care represents a major threat to basic social work values, social workers' commitment to serve those at greatest risk, and their professionalism. Social workers cannot ignore it and hope it will just go away. It will not, and thus the profession must move from complacency to commitment, advocating on behalf of itself and clients. It will not be an easy battle, but then social work is a profession that arose in response to societal challenges. This is just another, albeit difficult, challenge to tackle.

REFERENCES

American Psychiatric Association. (1987). *Diagnostic and statistical manual of mental disorders* (3rd ed., rev.). Washington, DC: Author.

American Psychiatric Association. (1994). *Diagnostic and statistical manual of mental disorders* (4th ed.). Washington, DC: Author.

Austad, C. S. (1996). *Is long-term psychotherapy unethical? Toward a social ethic in an era of managed care.* San Francisco: Jossey-Bass.

Bartlett, H. (1970). *The common base of social work practice.* Washington, DC: National Association of Social Workers.

Benson, B. (1998, May 11–17). Red ink drowns HMOs as losses hit $285 million. *Crain's,* pp. 1, 46.

Cornell, W. F. (1996). Capitalism in the consulting room. *Readings, 11*(1), 12–17.

Dumont, M. P. (1987). A diagnostic parable (first edition-unrevised). *Readings, 2*(4), 9–12.

England, M. J. (1994). From fee-for-service to accountable health plans. In R. K. Schreter, S. S. Sharfstein, & C. A. Schreter (Eds.), *Allies and adversaries* (pp. 3–8). Washington, DC: American Psychiatric Press.

Freudenheim, M. (1996, October 18). Not quite what doctor ordered. *New York Times,* pp. D1, D6.

Freudenheim, M. (1997, July 14). Pioneering state for managed care fights for change. *New York Times,* pp. A1, D8.

Geller, J. L. (1996). Mental health services of the future: Managed care, unmanaged care, mismanaged care. *Smith College Studies in Social Work, 66,* 223–329.

Ginsburg, C., & Demeranville, H. (1998, May 25). Nurses stand tall. *The Nation,* pp. 6–7.

Glazer, W. M. (1992). Psychiatry and medical necessity. *Psychiatric Annals, 22*(7), 362–366.

Herbert, B. (1996, December 27). Prescription switches. *New York Times,* p. A39.

Kilborn, P. T. (1997, July 1). Doctors organize to fight corporate intrusion. *New York Times,* p. A12.

Kilborn, P. T. (1998, May 17). Voters' anger at HMOs plays as hot political issue. *New York Times,* pp. A1, A22.

Lindemann, E. (1944). Symptomatology and management of acute grief. *American Journal of Psychiatry, 100,* 141–148.

Meyer, C. H. (1992). Social work assessment: Is there an empirical base? *Research on Social Work Practice, 2*(3), 297–305.

Meyer, C. H. (1993). *Assessment in social work practice.* New York: Columbia University Press.

Meyer, C. H. (1995). Assessment in social work: Direct practice. In *Encyclopedia of Social Work* (19th ed., pp. 260–270). Washington, DC: National Association of Social Workers.

Meyer, C. H., & Mattaini, M. A. (1995). *NASW code of ethics. The foundations of social work practice.* Washington, DC: National Association of Social Workers.

Munson, C. E. (1996). Autonomy and managed care in clinical social work practice. *Smith College Studies in Social Work, 66*(3), 241–60

Nation's big for-profit health maintenance organizations had banner year in 1994. (1995, April 11). *New York Times,* pp. D1, D5.

Rodriguez, A. R., & Gibson, R. W. (1994). Quality of care guidelines. In R. K. Schreter, S. S. Sharfstein, & C. A. Schreter (Eds.), *Allies and adversaries* (pp. 169–178). Washington, DC: American Psychiatric Press.

Rosenthal, E. (1996, December 17). Union plans to market own H.M.O. *New York Times,* pp. B1, B6.

Scarf, M. (1996, June 16). Keeping secrets. *The New York Times Magazine,* pp. 38–40.

Shortell, S. M., Gillies, R. R., & Devers, K. J. (1995). Reinventing the American hospital. *Milbank Quarterly 73*(2), 131–60.

Toner, R. (1996, November 24). Harry and Louise were right, sort of. *New York Times,* Section 4, p. 1.

World Health Organization. (1992–4). *International Statistical Classification of Disease and Related Health Problems. Tenth Revision.* Geneva: Author.

13

Paradigms and Long-Term Trends in Clinical Social Work

William J. Reid, D.S.W.

I examined the paradigms presented in this volume in relation to a number of long-term trends in clinical social work. These trends began to become visible during the early part of the post-World War II period and continued to emerge during the last half-century in the development of professional social work.

In a previous work (Reid, 1997a), I identified four trends that I thought to be of particular importance:

1. the increasing variety of interventions and the growth of eclectic practice,
2. the emergence and solidification of short-term modalities,
3. the development of action-oriented methods and their increasing integration with reflective-expressive approaches, and
4. the growing importance of research in practice theory and in practice.

To these I will add a fifth trend that is clearly seen in many of the paradigms in this volume: the change in perspective towards the practitioner–client relationship, which includes a shift toward greater practitioner–client egalitarianism and the view of the client as more competent and more responsible for directing change.

Obviously these trends are only a partial list of those that might be identified. I should note that the trends I have in mind are those that have developed over a number of decades. One sees in the paradigms in this book evidence of a variety of recent movements—for example, the development of new approaches based on postmodern epistemologies. Although such movements fit into certain of the trends I have identified, it remains to be seen if they themselves will become long-term trends of a different kind.

INTERVENTION VARIETY AND ECLECTIC PRACTICE

At the beginning of the past half-century, clinical social workers had few choices with respect to theories and methods of practice. Psychodynamic case work (the diagnostic school) was dominant, overshadowing the few alternatives that were available, such as the functional approach and the client-centered methods of Carl Rogers.

Since that time there has been an explosion of new practice paradigms. Over 400 systems of intervention have been identified in the field of psychotherapy alone (Bergin & Garfield, 1994), a number that does not include many systems designed expressly for social work. The proliferation shows no signs of abating. For example, the third edition of Turner's (1986) presentation of social work treatment systems covers 22 approaches, the fourth edition (1996) presents 28 systems. The majority of the models in the present volume are not found in either of the Turner books.

This growing variety has been the result of innovative responses to what have been perceived as shortfalls in existing systems. The process is well illustrated by the departures from classic psychoanalysis on the part of the founders of several of the paradigms presented in this volume. The originators of cognitive therapy, ego psychology, control-mastery theory, and self psychology were all trained in classical psychoanalysis. Each of these founders developed new theories in reaction to what they saw as limitations of the psychoanalytic model.

In general, new diagnostic and treatment theories arise from perceived insufficiencies of existing approaches. These insufficiencies come to light when it is realized that the theory is ignoring or misinterpreting some phenomenon. Theories are vulnerable to perceived insufficiencies because, by their very nature, they tend to focus on certain phenomena to the neglect of others and to view phenomena from their own vantage points. Moreover, in the helping professions, theories must guide practice. Thus they must be fused with notions of desirable goals of change, which contribute to sources of variation.

Thus, "unsatisfied with the relevance to the client's symptoms of the reported material produced in the session," Aaron Beck, the psychoanalyst, "began to suspect there was another level of cognition in his clients that existed just below their free associations" (Kuehlwein, chapter 6, p. 129) and went on to become Beck, the cognitive theorist and therapist. But in its preoccupation with the cognitive processes of the individual, Beck's theory may neglect a systemic view of human interaction, which, as Kuehlwein suggests, has given rise to new theoretical developments. When a domain is vast, complex, and lacking in hard knowledge, as is the case with human functioning and efforts to change it, one theory inevitably leads to another, spreading in all directions—hence the field's 400 (or perhaps 500?) systems with no end in sight.

What is the clinician to do with this "bewildering array of choices" (Rosen, chapter 10, p. 258)? Although some clinicians stick steadfastly to one system, many others appear to select ideas and methods from more than one. In this respect, clinicians are reacting much like the theorist who finds an existing approach insufficient. For the clinician, insufficiency arises when a given theory fails to supply what a case requires. The clinician typically responds not by developing a new theory but by incorporating elements from other theories that he or she thinks will be useful for the case at hand. In so responding, the clinician becomes an eclectic.

Indeed, most clinicians seem to practice within frameworks that might be considered eclectic (Bergin & Garfield, 1994; Jensen, Bergin, & Greaves, 1990). In their study, Jensen, Bergin & Greaves found that eclecticism was by far the leading orientation of the 423 clinicians surveyed. Over half the sample (56%) identified themselves as eclectic and an additional 12% indicated that they used more than one theoretical orientation. Over two thirds of the social workers in the sample were classified as eclectic by these criteria. Moreover, social work eclectics surpass those from other professional groups in respect to the average number (4.88) of orientations used. Still, among eclectics, certain orientations were used more than others. Among social workers, psychodynamic theory was the clear leader.

This very clear long-term trend toward increasing variety in treatment theories and the resulting rise of eclecticism has been viewed differently. As noted, Rosen sees the clinician faced with a "bewildering array of choices." Goldstein (1990), taking a much more negative position, laments that the profession has accumulated "a grab-bag of diverse and (in many instances incompatible) theories, methods, techniques, models, schools, and specializations" (p. 37).

I would take a more positive view. If one sees the increasing variety as providing a wider array of choices to both practitioners and clients— choices that may well result in better service to more clients—a proliferation can become a cornucopia. But like it or not, a pluralistic universe of treatment theories is here to stay for a while, and we need to find ways to come to terms with it. This is what Norcross, Beutler, and Clarkin (chapter 11) set out to do.

The prescriptive eclecticism presented by these authors provides a systematic way of combining methods from different intervention systems.

They provide a framework, principles, and guidelines for selecting the combination of methods that best suits the case. Prescriptive eclecticism appears to be a clear advance over the rather haphazard selections of diverse methods—*syncretism,* as Norcross and Newman (1992) have called it—that characterize much contemporary practice.

The integrationist movement (Castonguay & Goldfried, 1994) has been another response to the increasing variety of intervention systems and the growth of eclecticism. Integrationists seek to synthesize different systems into a new approach that presumably incorporates the distinctive strengths of the original systems. Wachtel's endeavors to synthesize psychodynamic, behavioral, and interpersonal theories provide a well-known example (Wachtel, 1977; Wachtel & McKinney, 1992). But as Rosen notes (chapter 10), the integrationist movement has produced a variety of "second-order models" that contribute to the proliferation of treatment systems. Or, as Weiner (1994) has commented, "We are seeing the emergence of as many brands of integrative psychotherapy as there are integrative psychotherapists" (p. 533).

These criticisms refer, however, to integration between different schools or systems of therapy without reference to particular clinical applications. A quite different kind of integration involves the synthesis of different approaches that is specific to a particular type of problem. In this kind of integration, methods from different systems are combined in ways to optimize treatment for a given problem type. The integration, guided by theoretical and diagnostic considerations, usually yields some form of written protocol as a guide to intervention. A growing number of examples can be found. Jensen (1994) combined cognitive–behavioral therapy and interpersonal psychotherapy in an approach to treating depression in women. The multisystemic family therapy of Henggeler and Borduin (1990) synthesizes family systems, behavioral, and other perspectives in a model for the treatment of adolescent behavior problems. A number of treatment approaches for bulimia combine cognitive–behavioral and psychodynamic methods (Hartmann, Herzog & Drinkmann, 1992). A review of integrative models for particular applications can be found in Albeniz and Holmes (1996).

Problem-specific integration (which can also include integration for types of clinical situations, such as schizophrenic patients living with their families) has much in common with prescriptive eclecticism. In the latter, the practitioner assembles an intervention package to suit the case at hand. In problem-specific integration, the package is assembled for a type of case. Both approaches to combining diverse treatments are needed and suggest paths that will help us turn our intervention diversity from an apparent failing to a source of strength.

SHORT-TERM MODELS

A second long-term development has to do with the rise of service models that are short-term by design. Such models may be arbitrarily limited, for example, to a certain number of sessions (usually 20 or fewer) or to a certain period of time (usually less than 6 months), or they may offer a brief service while avoiding arbitrary limits. Although such planned brief treatment approaches—and when I refer to brief treatment I will have the planned variety in mind—were available to clinical social workers at the beginning of the post-World War II period, they were generally confined to special settings such as Travelers Aid or to the practice of the small number of adherents of the functional school. The ideal was long-term treatment of a year or two, with the goal not just a resolution of clients' immediate problems but a thoroughgoing overhaul of whatever caused them to have problems in the first place. It was clear even then that most cases did not last beyond a small number of sessions (*unplanned* brief treatment) and that ambitious goals were seldom achieved. Nevertheless long-term treatment was the gold standard. Failure to achieve it was variously attributed to poor technique (e.g., not properly engaging or motivating clients) or to clients' recalcitrance or short-sightedness—resistance, premature termination, taking flight into health, and so on.

In the 1960s, brief treatment models began to achieve legitimacy in social work and related fields, notably in psychiatric and family settings, the bastions of long-term treatment. Use of these approaches has undergone a sustained period of growth. Brief treatment has become firmly established in social work practice, and the frequency of its use continues to be on the rise. It is also worth noting that most of the evidence of the effectiveness of psychotherapy and clinical social work (including psychodynamic approaches) that has accumulated in the past quarter-century is based on controlled experiments of brief treatment models.

The growth of brief service approaches has been driven by a combination of practical and clinical factors. Reduction of waiting lists, cost containment, disillusionment with accomplishments and client-holding capacities in open-ended treatment, the usefulness of time limits in focusing client and practitioner effort, and evidence of the effectiveness of brief treatment (Barber, 1994; Koss & Shiang, 1994)—all have played a part. Although brief treatment is perhaps reaching a position of dominance in the clinical services, it is "not for everyone," as Norcross, Beutler, and Clarkin point out (chapter 11, p. 305). It has been difficult, however, to establish research-supported criteria to suggest which clients might be better suited for longer forms of therapy.

As Steenbarger (1994) has suggested, there is evidence from a number of studies that the client's level of interpersonal functioning—for instance, ability to form attachments—may be a discriminating factor. For example, borderline clients who have difficulty in forming a therapeutic alliance may need treatment of longer duration in order to achieve any substantial benefits. In addition, the weight of the evidence supports use of long-term psychoeducational programs for schizophrenic clients living with their families (Hogarty, 1993). Finally, Koptka, Howard, Lowry, and Beutler (1994) provide some evidence for added benefits of treatment lasting up to a year for what they call *chronic distress symptoms,* although their findings must be interpreted with caution since their study did not satisfactorily separate the effects of the passage of time from the effects of treatment.

There has been a movement toward reconceptualizing the brief versus long-term dichotomy in terms of how much and what kind of intervention is needed for particular kinds of clinical situations (Bloom, 1992). To use a medical metaphor, how much of a dose of what treatment is required to achieve a sufficient outcome for the situation at hand? As a part of this reconceptualization, there has been increased advocacy for flexibility in the use of durational limits and other aspects of treatment dosage. As Bloom (1992) has commented, "Flexibility should be encouraged not only in duration of therapy but also in the frequency of therapy sessions, plans for follow-up interviews or return visits, and the use of alternatives to face-to-face interviews, such as contact by telephone or by letter" (p. 161). Flexibility would include combining episodes of brief intensive service with long-term case monitoring (Naleppa & Reid, in press; Reid, 1997b).

Such flexibility is reflected in the chapters in this book. In the solution-focused and Ericksonian approaches, fixed time limits are avoided in favor of a more flexible duration, which in the usual case is expected to be brief. Norcross, Beutler, and Clarkin (chapter 11) prescribe brief treatment for the Shores in the context of long-term maintenance care. Although Kuehlwein (chapter 6) does not address duration, most cognitive therapy tends to be planned for the short term (Moretti, Feldman, & Shaw, 1992), and his suggested treatment for the Shores could well fit into a flexible brief treatment structure.

In recent years, the growth of brief treatment has been driven by managed care, as Austrian's chapter (chapter 12) makes clear. Advocates of brief treatment, like myself, have mixed feelings about this development. On the one hand, managed care and other cost-containment initiatives have had some positive effects. One of them has been to place appropriate time and cost limits on behavioral health care that may be directed more at personal growth and self-enlightenment than at alleviating a mental health problem. Admittedly, this is a tricky distinction because it is often not at all clear when relieving a disability ends and the promotion of growth begins. And certainly I do not want to minimize the value of growth that may result from long-term treatment. The issue is who is to pay for it. Austrian comments, correctly, that "Long-term intervention with the goal of developing the client's potential is not usually reimbursable" (p. 325). The question is "Should it be?" One can argue that intervention with such a goal may be seen as a form of self-improvement similar to education rather than as treatment that should be covered by insurance.

On the other hand, fixed requirements that all clients be limited to a certain number of sessions regardless of problem or other considerations may do a disservice to those clients who genuinely need longer periods of service to successfully resolve the problems they are facing. Such decisions could be more confidently made if there were a better research base for specifying types of cases for which extended treatment might be more beneficial than brief treatment. As Austrian states, we need research "that can inform us about who is best served by which specific intervention, and in what context" (p. 333).

A somewhat different issue brought on by recent cost-cutting measures under managed care relates to how much short-term service can be reduced and still remain effective or even a service. Austrian gives the example of the move toward abbreviated hospital stays in inpatient psychiatric settings. This has resulted in very truncated brief service episodes, often ranging from a few days to a few weeks. Conventional brief treatment approaches with their 6 to 12 sessions are too long for such situations. As a result, there is pressure on service designers and staff to develop ever briefer models to produce ever greater miracles. Ironically, advocates of brief treatment may begin to sound like defenders of the long-term treatment faith, using the same arguments in pointing out that it takes time to develop a relationship, do a respectable assessment, and work out and implement an intervention plan with the client.

ACTION-ORIENTED METHODS

A third long-term development concerns a fundamental aspect of the helping process—the stimulation and guidance of actions clients might take to resolve difficulties in their own lives. Early social workers attempted to do this very directly and crudely—for example, by offering information and advice from their own perspectives. With the advent of psychodynamic casework, the emphasis shifted to facilitating the client's self-revelation and self-understanding. This mode of practice opened the way for social workers to explore the potential of more inwardly directed means of helping and to develop methods for doing it skillfully. For some clients, that was just what was needed. But for many others, especially those struggling with ordinary problems of living, this mode of helping was off the mark.

Many clients did not need self-discovery but rather needed to think of ways to act on the problems they were facing. Action-oriented forms of helping that were more psychologically sophisticated and more sensitive to the client's need for self-direction than simply giving advice were needed. Such methods began to emerge in the late 1940s in the work of Helen Harris Perlman (1949), who wrote of the value of helping clients rehearse problem-solving actions during the interview. In the next decade (Perlman, 1957), she developed a psychologically sophisticated, action-oriented approach to casework.

In the 1960s, action-oriented methods—behavioral social work, reality therapy, structural and strategic family therapy, the task-centered model among them—began to appear in force. Within two decades they became widely used in practice and formed the basis of much of the practice curricula in schools of social work (LeCroy & Goodwin, 1988). The growth of action-oriented methods was stimulated by the increased popularity of short-term approaches, which have traditionally tended to be more action-oriented, as well as by research that has demonstrated their effectiveness (see, e.g., Reid 1997c).

With the development of more varieties of action-oriented approaches, perhaps we need to rethink what they do and do not comprise. In such approaches, the client is helped to take specific problem-solving actions. Actions are usually learned or discussed in the session and undertaken between sessions. Many techniques are used—problem-solving with clients or enabling them to do their own problem solving in family or group situations; helping clients identify and correct the cognitive bases of dysfunctional actions; planning and reviewing specific actions; employing enactments and directives; reinforcing constructive behavior; and instructing them in new forms of action and then rehearsing those actions, as in parent-management, social skills, communications, and other such training programs.

Action-oriented methods can be contrasted with those that may be thought of as "reflective–expressive." These methods, which take place almost entirely within the session, rely on the expression of feeling and reflection about self, others, and one's situation to bring about internal changes. Such changes presumably will lead to change on a broad front of enhanced awareness and new modes of functioning without the necessity of specific action agendas. These methods are generally associated with the psychodynamic and humanistic practice schools.

The chapters in the present volume reflect both action-oriented and reflective–expressive approaches. In the former group we find cognitive, Ericksonian, and solution-focused models. We also note that the prescriptive eclectic application to the Shores draws heavily on action-oriented methods. Reflective–expressive approaches are found in the chapters on ego psychology, control-mastery theory, postmodern family therapy, feminist family therapy, and self-psychology.

Action-oriented methods have been shaped by a considerable amount of research and practice wisdom, both of which have added to their effectiveness. Most of us who espouse action-oriented methods have learned from both research and practice wisdom that these methods work best when used in the context of a strong therapeutic alliance. We have also learned that many clients need to tell their stories, need to grapple with issues from their pasts, and need help in achieving new perspectives before they can make use of action methods to resolve their difficulties.

On the other hand, as action-oriented practitioners have learned from reflective–expressive approaches, these approaches have increasingly begun to make use of action methods. The growing interpenetration of these two approaches is well illustrated by several of the chapters in this volume. In Kuehlwein's cognitive therapy, for example, behavioral methods, homework assignments, and other action-oriented approaches are used "as a means of reducing symptomatology, teaching and refining certain skills, and furthering cognitive change by experientially testing the validity and adaptiveness of certain beliefs". At the same time, helping the client decenter from "maladaptive constructions," especially at the level of schemas or core beliefs, makes use of insight-oriented methods and presumably can lead to extensive change on "all fronts" in a manner similar to the effect of the client's achieving experiential understanding of core conflicts in reflective–expressive therapy. Solution-focused therapy combines client reflection—about goals, strengths, and the future, among other things—with such action initiatives as encouragement, suggestions, and tasks. Ericksonian therapy, although primarily action-oriented, makes use of metaphor to "motivate, occupy, fixate, or interest the client's conscious frame of reference while generating an unconscious search for new or previously blocked experiences, meanings, or solutions" (Lankton & Lankton, chapter 7, p. 175). Ego psychological approaches bring together expressive–reflective (modifying) techniques with more action-oriented supportive efforts, which might include "learning and positive reinforcement of new behavior, skills, attitudes, problem-solving capacities, and coping strategies" (Goldstein, chapter 2, p. 37). (Here one notes the incorporation of some of the language of behavioral methods into a classically "non-behavioral" approach.) Prescriptive eclectic psychotherapy draws on experiential and psychodynamic methods (reflective–expressive) and cognitive–behavioral techniques (action-oriented). Finally, narrative therapy combines such reflective–expressive methods as story-telling with such action-oriented procedures as letter writing (Diamond, chapter 8).

The confluence of reflective–expressive and action-oriented approaches reflects a growing recognition of the multifaceted nature of the helping process. Most clients, particularly those seen by social workers, need help in devising and carrying out actions in their life situations, but at the same time such actions may not be possible, or may be short lived or poorly directed, unless they are a part of new self-understanding.

RESEARCH

Another trend concerns the evolution of the profession's research base, which includes not only research conducted under social work auspices but the far greater amount of research relevant to clinical social work emerging from cognate professions and disciplines. In the mid-1940s the amount of relevant research was too small to have much of an impact. In the ensuing half-century, the profession's research base has grown enormously. Research now exerts an influence on most aspects of practice. It has added to our understanding of most of the psychosocial problems we face in our work with clients. It has helped create a range of empirically tested methods. Research methods, such as assessment instruments, are being used increasingly in practice.

The current chapters provide an acid test of the growing importance of research as a base for social work practice. By the editor's design, the contributions are weighted toward psychodynamic and humanistic models, including some of the newer constructivist and postmodern approaches. These theories are not known for their strong research foundations. But even here there are signs of increasing attention to research. However, research may not be used in quite the way it is in more empirically based models, in which stress is given to testing effectiveness through controlled experiments. For example, in Wolmark and Sweezy's presentation of Kohut's self-psychology, there is little evidence of such testing. However, in their thoughtful critique of Kohut's thinking, the authors introduce recent research on infant behavior as a way of correcting some of the foundational assumptions of Kohut's theory. As they point out, "The classical psychoanalytic theory positing the infant's subjective perception of itself as omnipotent and as existing in symbiotic union with its mother is not upheld by empirical research" (p. 64). In a similar vein, Goldstein (chapter 2) refers to recent research on female development as a corrective to traditional object relations theory. (It should be noted that psychodynamic methods have also been subjected to an appreciable amount of effectiveness testing; see, e.g., Anderson & Lambert, 1995). Research on control-mastery theory has stressed single-case quantitative studies of change processes—that is, of factors relating to client change over the course of treatment. Rosen refers to the large amount of research on personal constructs as well as to newer qualitative methods, such as narrative explanation, for studying therapeutic processes.

In sum, the research growth in these psychodynamic and humanistic approaches—at least as reported in these chapters—may be related more to the study of underlying constructs and treatment processes than to more conventional effectiveness testing. We are seeing an increasing diversification in research strategies and methods that in some ways parallel the diversification in intervention approaches. For the long-term development of the influence of research it is important that different intervention approaches adapt their own investigative styles, even at the expense of a postponement in conventional effectiveness testing.

As we turn to other chapters in this book, we can see ample evidence of the rising influence of research in a more conventional sense. The growing use of cognitive therapy (chapter 6) has been driven in part by repeated demonstrations of its effectiveness for a wide variety of problems and populations (Reid, 1997c). In prescriptive eclectic psychotherapy, "The entire body of empirical research on psychotherapy informs ... treatment decisions." As the authors go on to state, "A genuine advantage of being an eclectic is the vast amount of research attesting to the efficacy of psychotherapy and pointing to its differential effectiveness with certain types of disorders and patients" (p. 309). Such a comment about the empirical base of helping methods would, of course, have been unthinkable a half-century ago. Finally, Austrian foresees a future dominated by managed care in which research will have an increasing role in documenting our effectiveness.

CHANGING VIEWS OF CLIENTS AND PRACTITIONERS

The final trend concerns changes in how social workers view clients and their helpers. As the profession evolved, social workers developed certain values about the people they served. Clients were seen as having inherent worth and dignity as human beings, and their right to self-determination was to be fostered. However, these convictions were colored by other perceptions, perhaps nurtured by social workers' roles as providers for the poor and by social work's love affair with psychoanalysis—clients were needy, dependent, and lacking direction and were prisoners of unconscious forces of which they were ignorant. Moreover, they were usually seen as suffering from some form of deep-set psychopathology. They could not be expected to have much of a conception of what was really good for them. Practitioners (social workers, psychotherapists) were viewed as the experts with the capacity to comprehend the client's hidden self and provide treatment guided by this understanding. Self-determination notwithstanding, practitioners were viewed as usually knowing what was best for clients. When clients balked at therapists' notions of what they needed, they were further labeled as "resistant." The chapters in this volume present a much different view of clients, who are now cast as more capable in setting their own directions and solving their own problems. Reciprocally, the role of the practitioner has been downstaged.

A number of the authors make a point of "depathologizing" clients' problems and emphasizing clients' strengths. This position emerges most clearly in the solution-focused approach and in postmodern and feminist family therapies, but it is also apparent in Rosen's "meaning-making" and in Goldstein's ego psychology. In discussing newer developments in ego psychology, Goldstein indeed refers to redefining women's behavior once seen as pathological into more normal terms (Goldstein, p. 31). For example, in these developments, lesbian object relations and self-development are viewed as a "variant of positive developmental experiences, in contrast to the traditional belief that they reflect arrested, immature, and undifferentiated object relations " (p. 33). This is a noteworthy shift in a theoretical tradition that has been criticized for its pathological interpretations of female development. In this vein we also note that in control-mastery theory, another psychodynamic approach, the unconscious has become "smart." Rather than a seething cauldron of primitive drives, it is "continuously engaged in complex, adaptive, problem-solving efforts" (p. 94).

As clients have begun to look healthier, practitioners have begun to appear more humble. Social workers have always given lip service to "helping clients help themselves" and other rhetoric of collaborative relationships with clients, but in these chapters one gets the sense that we have finally come to mean it. One illustration of this change can be seen in efforts to redefine impasses in therapy. The traditional way of viewing impasses, as client resistance, is explicitly disavowed in the cognitive, Ericksonian, and solution-focused approaches. In these models the notion of resistance is replaced with the idea that impasses result from the therapist's lack of knowledge of what the client wants, believes, or is up against. In short, the responsibility for the impasse shifts from the client to the practitioner.

Additional evidence of a shift in the power balance between clients and practitioners emerges in other chapters. In narrative therapies presented by Rosen (chapter 10) and Diamond (chapter 8), as well as in feminist family therapy (Land, chapter 9), the practitioner–client relationship is explicitly presented in egalitarian terms. In prescriptive-eclectic psychotherapy, the hypothetical therapist working with the Shores is advised to take on a "consultant role as an observer and commentator regarding family dynamics" (p. 306). Austrian (chapter 12) shows that under managed care "there will be a need to identify what the client *wants* to work on" (p. 327, emphasis added). In other words, the client's expressed concerns rather than the practitioner's vision of what the client needs will define the focus of the helping effort.

The redefinition of the practitioner–client relationship over the past half century appears to have been stimulated by a number of factors—the break-up of the psychoanalytic hegemony with its emphasis on underlying pathology; the rise of problem-focused, brief treatment, psychoeducational, and nonmedical practice approaches with their more optimistic assumptions about the client's coping capacities; the growth of client advocacy organizations; research challenging such client-blaming formulations as the schizophrenigenic mother (Anderson, Reiss, & Hogarty, 1986); a growing recognition on the part of practitioners about limits in their capacities to effect *fundamental* changes in clients' lives; and emerging emphases on client empowerment and client strengths.

This trend, of course, can be seen more clearly in theoretical writings about practice than in studies of practice itself. The field lacks data that might show how such things as practitioners' views of clients have changed over time. Regardless of what changes may have actually occurred, there is some evidence that clinical social workers may be lagging behind other professional groups. Thus in a study of "family-friendly" attitudes (Johnson & Renaud, 1997), which included measures of willingness to share information openly with parents and of not blaming parents for children's problems, social workers showed a "less friendly" perspective than either psychologists and psychiatrists. As Johnson and Renaud comment,

> This profile of clinical social workers is somewhat disturbing. Despite professional statements about compassion, empathy, nonjudgmental posture, egalitarianism, and consumer empowerment, the data consistently show this sample of clinical social workers to fare least well among the three disciplines in their beliefs on dimensions of a family friendly perspective. (p. 159)

The study does not say that the social worker's perspective is not "friendly" nor does it deny that changes toward greater "friendliness" may have occurred. It does suggest that social workers may not be the trend setters.

CONCLUSION

The presentation of such a variety of approaches as we have in this volume, most of them not contained in the most recent comprehensive anthology of treatment theories (Turner, 1996) in itself speaks to the continuing growth of pluralism in the development of our intervention systems. Prescriptive-eclecticism represents an advance in how to put this diversity to best use. The chapters on solution-focused and Ericksonian therapies present fruitful directions for determining optimal duration in brief treatment. These presentations, as well as those on prescriptive-eclecticism and cognitive therapy, offer new varieties of action-oriented approaches and new ways of integrating them with reflective–expressive methodologies. The role of research in challenging and correcting theories underlying treatment approaches, a role that is often neglected, emerges clearly in the papers on ego psychology and self-psychology. New forms of change-process research as a way of testing and developing treatment approaches are seen in the chapter on control-mastery theory.

New ways of viewing the interaction between clients and practitioners are evident in the egalitarian, client–empowering relationships one sees in the chapters on meaning-making and on postmodern and feminist family therapies. These chapters further advance the deemphasis on psychopathology in social workers' views of clients, a central factor in older conceptions of the practitioner–client relationship. The chapters on cognitive, solution-focused, and Ericksonian therapies add to existing rationales for abandoning the concept of resistance.

Finally, how will these trends be affected by managed care? From Austrian's chapter, one can surmise that some effects will be likely, but one cannot be certain how they will be played out. Managed care is likely to foster brief treatment and action-oriented modalities, intensify the influence of research on practice, and perhaps even strengthen some aspects of newer definitions of the practitioner–client relationship. But the danger is that it may do so in a way more responsive to fiscal concerns than the needs of the client or of the requirements of sound professional practice.

REFERENCES

Albeniz, A., & Holmes, J. (1996). Psychotherapy integration: Its implications for psychiatry. *British Journal of Psychiatry, 169,* 563–570.

Anderson, C. M., Reiss, D. J., & Hogarty, G. E. (1986). *Schizophrenia and the family.* New York: Guilford.

Anderson, E. M., & Lambert, M. J. (1995). Short-term dynamically oriented psychotherapy: A review and meta-analysis. *Clinical Psychology Review, 15*(6), 503–514.

Barber, J. P. (1994). Efficacy of short-term dynamic psychotherapy: Past, present, and future. *Journal of Psychotherapy Practice and Research, 3,* 108–121.

Bergin, A. E., & Garfield, S. L. (1994). Overview, trends and future issues. In A. Bergin & S. Garfield (Eds.), *Handbook of psychotherapy and behavior change* (4th ed., pp. 821–830). New York: Wiley.

Bloom, B. L. (1992). Planned short-term psychotherapy: Current status and future challenges. *Applied & Preventive Psychology, 1,* 157–164.

Castonguay, L. G., & Goldfried, M. R. (1994). Psychotherapy integration: An idea whose time has come. *Applied & Preventive Psychology, 3,* 159–172.

Goldstein, H. (1990). The knowledge base of social work practice: Theory, wisdom, analogue or art? *Families in Society, 71*(1), 32–43.

Hartmann, A., Herzog, T., & Drinkmann, A. (1992). Psychotherapy of bulimia nervosa: What is effective? A meta-analysis. *Journal of Psychosomatic Research, 36*(2), 159–167.

Henggeler, S. W., & Borduin, C. M. (1990). *Family therapy and beyond: A multisystemic approach to treating the behavior problems of children and adolescents.* Pacific Grove, CA: Brooks/Cole.

Hogarty, G. E. (1993). Prevention of relapse in chronic schizophrenic patients. *Journal of Clinical Psychiatry, 54*(3 suppl.), 18–23.

Jensen, C. (1994). Psychosocial treatment of depression in women, *Research on Social Work Practice, 4*, 267–282.

Jensen, J. P., Bergin, A. E., & Greaves, D. W. (1990). The meaning of eclecticism: New survey and analysis of components, *Professional Psychology: Research and Practice, 21*(2), 124–130.

Johnson, H. C., & Renaud, E. F. (1997). Professional beliefs about parents of children with mental and emotional disabilities: a cross discipline comparison, *Journal of Emotional and Behavioral Disorders, 5*,149–161.

Koptka, S. M., Howard, K. I., Lowry, J. L., & Beutler, L. E. (1994). Patterns of symptomatic recovery in psychotherapy, *Journal of Consulting and Clinical Psychology, 62*(5), 1009–1016.

Koss, M. P., & Shiang, J. (1994). Research on brief psychotherapy. In A. Bergin & S. Garfield (Eds.), *Handbook of psychotherapy and behavior change* (4th ed., pp. 664–700). New York: Wiley.

LeCroy, C. W., & Goodwin, C. C. (1988). New directions in teaching social work methods: A content analysis of course outlines. *Journal of Social Work Education, 24*, 43–49.

Moretti, M. M., Feldman, L. A., & Shaw, B. F. (1992). Cognitive therapy: Current issues in theory and practice. In R. A. Wells & V. J. Giannetti (Eds.), *Handbook of the brief psychotherapies* (pp. 217–237). New York: Plenum.

Naleppa, M. J., & Reid, W. J. (in press.) Task-centered case management for the elderly: Developing a practice model. *Research on Social Work Practice.*

Norcross, J. C., & Newman, C. F. (1992). Psychotherapy integration: Setting the context. In J. C. Norcross & M. R. Goldfried (Eds.), *Handbook of psychotherapy integration* (pp. 3–45). New York: Basic Books.

Perlman, H. H. (1949). Classroom teaching of psychiatric social work, *American Journal of Orthopsychiatry, 19*, 306–16.

Perlman, H. H. (1957). *Social casework: A problem-solving process.* Chicago: University of Chicago Press.

Reid, W. J. (1997a). Long-term trends in clinical social work. *Social Service Review, 71*(2), 200–213.

Reid, W. J. (1997b). Research on task-centered practice. *Social Work Research, 21*, 1–8.

Reid, W. J. (1997c). Evaluating the dodo's verdict: Do all interventions have equivalent outcomes? *Social Work Research, 21*, 5–18.

Steenbarger, B. N. (1994). Duration and outcome in psychotherapy: An integrative review. *Professional Psychology: Research and Practice, 25*(2), 111–119.

Turner, F. J. (Ed.). (1986). *Social work treatment* (3rd. ed.). New York: Free Press.

Turner, F. J. (Ed.). (1996). *Social work treatment* (4th ed.). New York: Free Press.

Wachtel, P. L. (1977). *Psychoanalysis and behavior therapy: Toward an integration.* New York: Basic Books.

Wachtel, P. L., & McKinney, M. (1992). Cyclical psychodynamics. In J. C. Norcross & M. R. Goldfried (Eds.), *Handbook of psychotherapy integration* (pp. 335–370). New York: Basic Books.

Weiner, I. B. (1994). Integration or diversity? [Review of the book *Comprehensive handbook of psychotherapy integration*]. *Contemporary Psychology, 39*, 532–533.

EPILOGUE

Rachelle Dorfman, Ph.D.

THE SHORES—TEN YEAR FOLLOW-UP

Almost 10 years later to the day, I find myself on the sidewalk in front of the Shore's house. As I approach the house, I remember that the last time I visited, their screen door was broken. It took a bit of finesse to get it open and not have it slap me in the behind as I entered. I wondered if 10 years later it had been repaired or was still "hanging on." The metaphor did not escape me.

Nancy

Nancy's demeanor remains fairly unchanged. At 54 she looks thinner but is still overweight. Her image may be the only constant in her life. For a year now, from Sunday to Friday, she has lived in a posh uptown residence with the family's benefactor, Aunt Flo. When Flo's husband Victor became terminally ill, Nancy stayed with the elderly couple to help out. Three weeks later, Uncle Victor was dead. Nancy remained because Flo was afraid to be alone. Nancy reasons that "Aunt Flo gave us our house, paid for Michael's college education, and has given us money over the years. This is a way to finally pay her back." On the weekend, Nancy lives with Charley, although she says it is more like a date than "living with" him: "We have sex. I take him to the movies, pour his medicine for the week, pay the bills, and make sure there is food in the house." She says it is a perfect arrangement. "In the beginning," Nancy explains, "I stayed with Aunt Flo for her sake. Now I am there for me. After 34 years of marriage, I just want to be away from Charley. I only make his life a living hell when I am there. We are each happier this way."

Nancy describes her new life as one enriched with theater, elegant dinners, and lively conversations with Aunt Flo. Because of her aunt's generosity, Nancy has a membership to a health club. She works out, walks 2 to 3 miles a day, and is more conscious of her diet. She has lost 31 pounds. Occasionally the old back injury acts up, only now she regards it as a minor annoyance she must live with. No longer is it "an excuse not to do anything." Nancy says, "Flo and I take care of each other. I have a purpose, and I finally have a companion."

The money problems that plagued the family have dissipated. Charley has secure employment, and in a few years he will retire with a pension. Nancy continues to receive monthly disability checks. They also have a steady rental income from the downstairs apartment.

Anxiety attacks are just an unpleasant memory for Nancy. Her chronic depression is managed by the antidepressant Zoloft. When she is with Charley for 2 days, she takes 100 mg. daily. The rest of the time she takes 25 to 50 mg. daily and is considering discontinuing the medication completely when she is uptown. She admits to occasionally worrying about other people's opinions, but being in the presence of the older woman's pragmatic and stoic nature has a calming effect. She is still troubled about Michael. Although she acknowledges his accomplishments, she says that she fears that he will never be happy. Nancy suspects that he has a bipolar disorder like his father and that he may have to have a breakdown before his life improves.

Nancy has not had social work treatment in 10 years. "I stopped going to therapy because the therapist was getting too close to the 'nitty gritty.' It seemed that the social worker wanted me to leave my husband so I panicked and left the therapy instead," she explains. Ironically Nancy attributes her improvements to "getting away from Charley." Although it is corny, she says, "repeating clichés helps a lot." Her favorites are "Take one day at a time," "What's the worst thing that can happen?" and "It will all work out."

As evidence of her new frame of mind, she divulges that, as a consequence of several recent falls, her doctor has made a referral for an evaluation for multiple sclerosis. She is unfazed. She says, "If I have it, it will not be so bad at my age, and anyway now I have a place to go." Her concern is that some other major family crisis could occur that would compel her to give up her new life.

Charley

Charley agrees that the new living arrangement is better than the old one, although his take on it is a bit different than his wife's: "We are sort of like separated—not really separated, but living apart. I could have made her stay. If I wanted to have her home, I could tell her. Her aunt is like her mother. She is the only niece."

At age 62, Charley has a very simple life. Because Nancy is content with Aunt Flo and there is more financial security, there is less arguing in the Shore house and thus less need for Charley to lie to his wife. He goes fishing, bowls, and cooks. He does the laundry for Michael and himself and watches hours of television a day. Every member of the family agrees that Charley just wants "not to be bothered."

His appearance has changed over the years. He looks noticeably older and suffers from arthritis and gout. He has a work-related back injury, and his hands tremble. He has difficulty staying on a topic. Charley is not unaware of these changes. He says, "The trouble when you are mentally disturbed is at times you start drifting. That's what I do." Indeed, he "drifts" frequently, often to memories of the "Hollywood days." Charley says that the doctor thinks his "limp" is related to his medication (Depakote and Lithium). According to Nancy, he is one of the 20 percent who do not respond to Lithium alone.

During the last 10 years, Charley has been hospitalized once—after he put a knife to his chest and told Nancy he was going to kill himself. He recalls that hospitalization fondly: "If they had a swimming pool I would have stayed longer. It was great. Three squares a day. Eat all you want." Nancy reports that his deterioration began with that hospitalization.

A city sanitation worker for 11 years, Charley was recently transferred to a new work site and a new supervisor. He complains, "My boss was nice at first, but now she takes out her frustrations on me. She always gives me a hard time. She says I curse and I don't wring out the mop right." On the one hand, he feels he is unjustly accused; on the other hand, he admits that during his 8-hour shift, "I sleep 6 and work 2." He daydreams about being a personal trainer for "fat old ladies" who don't want to exercise. He says, "I would charge $30 a half hour. Nancy won't let me do it." Charley claims that his night work keeps him from performing at the comedy club. Nancy argues that he couldn't do it anyway because his medication ruined any timing he ever had.

Charley is satisfied with his relationship with his daughter. He says, "It is decent. Our relationship depends on the mood she is in. Rena is a moody girl." Like the rest of the family, he tries to give his son advice. "I told Michael that one girl can louse up your whole life. See other girls and don't take it so hard when this one gives you a hard time [she threatens him if he says he wants to break up]. The girl is no good for him."

Charley says that Nancy doesn't know that he hit Michael about 3 months ago: "He said something to me that got on my nerves. We argued, then he started choking me. I got up and smacked him in the mouth with my closed fist. I said, 'Don't you ever pick up a hand to me again.' He said 'I'm sorry, Dad.' I said, 'I'm sorry too. I never want to hit you again.'"

Charley has had a great deal of counseling over the years, but he doesn't think that any of the counselors helped him. He says, "Psychologists are okay. Psychiatrists are nuts." He didn't offer opinions on social workers. He reports that what helps him most is working, relaxing, and watching television.

Rena

Rena has been a registered nurse for 5 years. At age 29, she is attractive, vibrant, and articulate. Although satisfied with her career accomplishments and her independence, she is still on a journey of self-improvement and self-discovery.

She likes providing nursing care to patients in their own homes. "I used to have a poor work history. I'd get bored and antsy, but that has changed," she reports. She is conscientious and responsible. Her remaining "rebelliousness," however, causes occasional problems. For example, she becomes infuriated when the "system" gets in the way of caring. She has said to her boss, "What do you mean I can't see this patient because insurance won't cover it? She needs continued care. Can't you work it out?" On another occasion she said, "I will not do Medicare fraud. I will not go and see a patient every day and bother her when she has a daughter that wants to take her out but can't because my employer wants me to make unnecessary visits." She laments that she is frequently too personally involved and tries to be a "rescuer."

Home-care work has been a source of personal growth. She says, "Seeing the pain and insecurities of others and witnessing the effect that their wounds have on their perception of themselves made me realize that I am not an 'alien' creature. Working with these patients helped me feel less different." She adds that many of her youthful feelings of alienation and difference stemmed from being adopted: "No one looked like me. No one had my problems, no one acted like me."

Two years ago, Rena learned that her biological father was dead, murdered by "a friend." She has few details about what happened. She has five half-brothers on her father's side, and each child has a different mother. Her biological mother, who never married, raised a younger daughter. Rena is the only child of all the children on both sides who has graduated from high school and has gone to college. Finding relatives helped her to understand herself. For example, she discovered that practically all the men on her father's side are auto mechanics, which seems to explain her mechanical ability. Meeting one of her half-brothers, "Little Jimmy, Jr.," who is 3 days younger than Rena, was a jolting experience. Jimmy is "very troubled and in and out of jail." Rena went to visit him in jail not long ago. She says that when she saw him, she saw herself. They looked at each through a glass partition and cried. She remembers, "He had the same face, the same hair, the same voice."

Locating her birth-mother turned out to be less dramatic than she thought. She reflects, "The fact that it didn't change my life, changed my life." Mother and daughter talk to each other about once a month. Rena describes her wheelchair-bound birth-mother as having many health problems and as being "lost." "My biological mother," she says, "is a 'topper'— she always tops everyone else's problems. No matter what you say, she has done it better in the negative sense. She always has it worse than anyone else. She personifies victimization and martyrdom. I have to work hard in the relationship so that I don't feel guilty. I try to keep her accountable for her own problems and not take them on as my own."

Rena no longer believes her adoption theory—that is, that being adopted caused her to get rid of people before they abandoned her. Instead she says that she fears and hates rejection no more than anyone else. She maintains that she "dumped" people in the past because of her low self-esteem, not as a result of her adoption history.

Rena asserts that her parents' living arrangement is more peaceful for all involved, but she adds that Michael feels abandoned by Nancy. "She left him with the ogre," Rena says. She adds, "I care about my father, but he is disturbing because he is so pathetic. I have shame issues about him. I am angry at him, but I should not be angry because he is sick. I try to work through my anger with him, but he is incapable of helping me—which only makes me more angry." One complaint is that Charley seems unable to give her the advice she longs for. She adds, "I would do anything to make him different. I would give him my kidney if that could fix him."

In contrast, Rena's relationship with Nancy is mutually satisfying. In the past, an angry Rena would not talk to her mother for weeks. Now disagreements and quarrels are resolved in a day or less, and they are soon on the phone agreeing that the tiff was ridiculous. Rena shares her mother's concern about Michael. She says that she tries to help him but he doesn't always want her help. They don't hang out together, but they do talk on the phone.

Rena has lost most of her ambitions to sing publicly. She had a boyfriend who did not want her to perform, and she recalls that relationship as one in which she gave up parts of herself in order to retain love. This past year she has taken opera lessons and did one performance in a club. Mainly, she sings only for friends. "Singing professionally plays havoc with my work schedule and is 'not conducive to my new more yuppie lifestyle,'" she says in jest. She denies being a "yuppie," saying, "My rebellious nature still despises pretension."

For the last year and a half, she has not dated because she decided to have a "hiatus" from men. "A lot of my issues are with men because I grew up in a very matriarchal family," she says. Recently she put the word out that she was willing to date again, and in the past 2 weeks she has been asked out by four different men.

A year after our last meeting, the journal that Rena kept was "violated and read," but she refused to say by whom. She threw that one away with others she had kept and did not write another word until 2 weeks ago, when she started a new journal with "Commitments to Myself" (see Exhibit 1). She says that at this point in her life she is on a spiritual journey, "fine-tuning," accepting some things about herself, and trying to change some lingering problems.

Rena says, "I used to look at people and almost feel subhuman by comparison. I thought that other people were perfect. The most important thing for me is not to repeat my family cycle or if I must repeat it, I hope that it will be in diluted form." Her goals include returning to school because she feels that she sold herself short on her education. She has not relinquished the wish to establish a more satisfying relationship with her father because she is convinced that she can't have a healthy relationship with a man unless she comes to terms with her father. Her last counseling experiencing was 2½ years ago.

Michael

"Overall," Michael says, "things are better than before because I am more aware than I was as a child. My mother sheltered me more than the average mother. Now I know how good things really are and I understand how bad things really are, but life is more complicated now."

On the one hand, Michael squirms under all the attention he receives from family members. On the other hand, he admits that he seeks out the opinions of others because he cannot think for himself, especially in matters of the heart. Nor, he says, can he evaluate his own or his family members' behavior.

At 23, he is in the "first relationship of intensity" in his life. His girlfriend is 19. He thinks that her intelligence makes her dangerous because she shows him things from a different perspective: "My parents are more controlling than I thought they were, but I only see this when my girlfriend points it out. When my girlfriend's views differ from my family's views, I don't know who to listen to. I don't trust my own opinion. Also, I don't know if I am really experiencing love or I am just enjoying being loved so much, being infatuated, enjoying the physical contact. I have been ruled by women most of my life. Even though they love me and care for me very much, sometimes I just want to get away." When Michael gets frustrated with all the women in his life, he fantasizes about being alone—which, he thinks, may be the only way he will find himself. He talks about running away to Wyoming where there is a lot of space and where there are relatively few people.

Michael longs for male role models and looks for them in television and books. Until now, he says, the only role models he has had have been scoutmasters, teachers, and professors. He says, "My dad hasn't been much of a role model. He just wants to come home from work with no responsibilities and watch TV. He never grew up. He never had a direction for himself just going from job to job never having a career." Michael has no problem with his parents' living arrangement.

Michael graduated from college with a B.A. in history and works as a substitute teacher as part of a program that allows people with bachelor's degrees to work in city schools. However, the job is not gratifying. He says it is just "baby-sitting." The pay is good, but there are no benefits. Michael's aspiration is to earn a graduate degree in library science. He took graduate courses at the local university and applied for admission but was told that the three Bs he earned did not meet their standards and his application was denied.

The most satisfying job he ever had was at college, where he worked for minimum wage in the library but nevertheless felt important. He states, "I have always been around books. People come up to me in libraries and ask me for help, and I am not even a librarian. Maybe it's part of my destiny to be a librarian. One of the highest points in my life was in college when I organized a study group. I tutored four or five people. One person in the group got an A, and I got an A–. I tutored her, and she got a higher grade than me. I was in charge, I was special, I was in control. I like when I am in control." Michael describes college as a fantasy world, "No ugly people there, just young people, every year a new crop."

After college, Michael went to Europe for a month. "If I could do one thing, it would be to earn enough money to travel." He traveled by himself, staying for a time with Nancy's half-sister in Denmark and in cheap hotels and hostels.

In our interview, Michael broke down recalling his childhood: "I always had the feeling that the medicine I took made me behave badly and never allowed me to grow up. I never learned how to act correctly. I'm learning now. It's sad. All through high school, I never had friends, I had acquaintances. People didn't dislike me, but they didn't like me enough to hang out with me outside of school." Michael talks of "missed opportunities" for peer relationships and his desire to reconnect with one girl he knew in high school. When he fantasizes about her, he imagines himself saying, "I wish I had taken the time to get to know you. I always wanted to get to know you. I never took the opportunity and I regret it." He adds, "I feel that it was my fault that I didn't have meaningful relationships in high school." He believes that he has to recapture some of these lost opportunities before he can move on.

Michael admits, "A lot of the accomplishments I achieved in high school [see Exhibit 2] were not as they appear. I volunteered because no one else wanted to do it. Take the recycling project, for example—it was a failure. A teacher started another more successful recycling program after I graduated. There was only one time where I competed and won. That was in an election for patrol leader."

"I've been in counseling on and off for 12 years," he says, "and I don't feel that it has done me much good. I didn't take much of what the social worker had to offer. Then again, I do feel better when I talk to someone. I search for validity; I need someone to tell me that I am not as bad as I think I am. If I am so depressed I go in there [the therapy session] and say I am going to kill myself, that I am bad, and the therapist says, 'Oh you're not.' That makes me realize that I am not that bad. But it only lasts for so long then I go back to the way I was. Some people think that I achieved a lot, but I could have achieved much more." Michael says that if he wrote his autobiography, he would call it *In Search of Me*.

Editor's Notes

The Shore family—Nancy, Charley, Rena, and Michael—have allowed us to enter their private lives and know their thoughts, feelings, and fantasies. They have displayed their weaknesses and their strengths, receiving nothing tangible for their efforts. They did it because I asked them and because they believed it would help others. They are good people who not only care about one another but also care about people they don't even know.

For all our theorizing in this book and in Volume 1 of *Paradigms of Clinical Social Work*, we could not have predicted the positive changes that they have made. They deserve to be proud, and we should be humbled in the face of their contribution. I have often wondered about the impact of this project on the Shore family. Nancy recalls that after reading Volume 1, she felt responsible for everything that was wrong in the family. She says, "I read it once, put it away and never picked it up again." Did the book make a difference in her life? "No," she says, "to be honest, I don't really remember the book any more. It was so long ago." Charley showed little interest in the first book. Rena and Michael, however, did ask their mother for permission to read it, but Nancy refused. Rena had hoped that the book would give her more objectivity about her family, reaffirming or negating some of her own positions. Michael was simply curious.

At the 10-year mark, the Shore children are adults and no longer subject to the discretion of their mother regarding whether or not they will read the accounts we have written. Rena and Michael have expressed their intent to read the complete works. Nancy worries that Michael's girlfriend will read the most recent Epilogue and use it to say bad things about her. Michael is still intensely curious about both volumes. Rena and Nancy are especially excited about an update that shows the family's positive changes.

What have we learned from this project? We are reminded of the power of "family," the ways in which members persist in their concern for each other. We also are reminded of the endurance of family issues over a decade and the impact of mental and physical illnesses on the family.

What is impressive is how the Shore family seeks its own solutions. They have tried nontraditional living arrangements, first with little success when Rena lived apart from the family at age 12 in the downstairs apartment and now with apparent success with Nancy and Charley living apart for most of the week. We are reminded also that the things that we think will make significant differences often do not. Rena was obsessed with locating her biological mother. When she did, the new relationship made little difference in her life.

Perhaps there will be a third volume and another update of the Shore family (a 15- or 20-year epilogue).[1] Then we shall know what has become of Michael, who is in the throes of his first love and an accentuated identity crisis. What will come of his deep sadness for his lost youth and his longing to revisit his childhood? I would like Michael to know that we are empathic to his suffering, his struggle with the women in his life, and his longing for a male role model. We are heartened that he was able to leave his "nest" successfully in socially sanctioned ways, first to college and later on his European jaunt. We hope he will find the courage, resources, and family blessings to do so again.

Exhibit 1. Excerpts from Rena's "Commitments to Myself"

Spirit, please provide me with the strength, courage and discipline I may need at times of weakness to keep the following commitments to myself:

1. I will not engage in any sexual activity with a man until I am confident that we have both shared enough with each other to have been "emotionally naked."
2. I will acknowledge & have consideration for Little Rena so that our issues may be dealt with & worked through.

---

[1] After the first interviews (for *Paradigms of Clinical Social Work*, Vol. 1) and the recent interviews for this book, I offered my services to clarify and explain the text and to counsel if needed.

3. I will retain my sense of self while involved with a man by deciding what will best serve myself and following through with that behavior.
4. I will identify my triggers of hurt and anger and withhold from reacting to them until I have given myself the opportunity to determine their issue of origin & work through it accordingly. I will then respond to each trigger in an appropriate and constructive way.
5. I will consistently journal and only discuss my issues with the people in my life who are safe.
6. I will allow myself to be vulnerable with the knowledge that only love, light and joy is intended for me.
7. I will permit myself to be imperfect. When I make a mistake I will take responsibility for my behavior, identify how I would have liked to have handled the situation and give myself the opportunity to correct that undesired behavior.
8. I will take advantage of opportunities to practice my new relationship behaviors. I will keep in mind that others may be on a different journey. I will not allow their behaviors to become my excuse for discouragement, negativity & destructive behavior.
9. I will pay attention to my inner voice and keep my eyes open for warning signals. I will trust my own judgment and address these warning signals by taking appropriate action.

Please let me learn my lessons quickly and gently. Thank you Spirit.

Exhibit 2. Excerpts from Michael's "Self-Description"
Written for His College Application

I would describe myself as a smart, likable, outgoing person who can be very talkative at times, especially about issues that concern me or that I am interested in like environmental problems, history, astronomy and religion. I am very motivated with a great deal of passion for life and learning.

In first grade I tested as learning disabled. My disability affected my fine and gross motor coordination and attention span. I was enrolled in special education classes. Now, I feel this was my greatest obstacle which my motivation has helped me overcome. In elementary and middle school, however, I felt trapped. Teachers only expected so much from me and didn't think I could handle more challenging courses usually not assigned to those classified as learning disabled.

Since childhood, I've had severe asthma which was extremely debilitating. I was heavily medicated and the combination of drugs caused behavior problems. Numerous hospitalizations due to asthma attacks disrupted my education as well as several personal relationships I tried to develop.

During this time my self-esteem was low. Eventually, the asthma medication was reduced causing the behavior problems to go away and my self-esteem to improve.

When it was time to enroll in high school, I wanted to start out fresh. A lot of things changed in tenth grade. I was enrolled in regular classes in a school where no one knew me. So many opportunities were available to me and I couldn't wait to be involved in everything.

In tenth and eleventh grade I had speaking parts in drama productions. In tenth grade I was a member of the local chapter of Amnesty International. I was a member of the debate team for three years. Also for three years I worked as an aide in the main [school] office. During twelfth grade I was an aide in the history department. I was also elected class representative in tenth and twelfth grade. In twelfth grade I ran for class president. In tenth grade I was on the swimming team and in twelfth grade I managed the field hockey team.

One thing which I am most proud and where I feel I have made a great contribution is my work in the environment. Our environment was in trouble and I wanted to do something about it. As a member of the [student council's] executive board in eleventh grade, I chaired the environmental committee. The committee worked to raise the conscience of all students and staff about environmental problems and we started a recycling program at the school which I continue to run.

When I was twelve I joined boy scouts. I am now a life scout. I need five more merit badges to become an eagle scout. I was elected a member of the Order of the Arrow, an honor camper organization within the scouts. I am presently at the second of three levels. In the Summer of 1989 I was Counselor in training at [scout camp]. This year I was elected senior patrol leader.

I made the honor roll for the first time in tenth grade, which I consider my most significant achievement. It was especially significant since I did it while enrolled in all regular courses. I really felt then that I had conquered my learning disability.

I am a member of the National Honor Society and have taken rapid and advanced placement history courses. History is one of my passions and I am seriously considering it as my major in College. I read a lot of other topics but when they begin to bore me I always return to historical reading. I am especially interested in American History.

I am proud that I have overcome many obstacles in my life. I have learned that through motivation and hard work, I can accomplish anything I put my mind to and I am rewarded by a great sense of achievement.

AUTHOR INDEX

365

SUBJECT INDEX